Lessons in elocution, or, A select and verse • William Scott

Publisher's Note

The book descriptions we ask booksellers to display prominently warn that the book may have numerous typos, missing text, images and indexes.

We scanned this book using character recognition software that includes an automated spell check. Our software is 99 percent accurate if the book is in good condition. However, we do understand that even one percent can be a very annoying number of typos! And sometimes all or part of a page is missing from our copy of a book. Or the paper may be so discolored from age that you can no longer read the type. Please accept our sincere apologies.

After we re-typeset and design a book, the page numbers change so the old index and table of contents no longer work. Therefore, we often remove them.

We would like to manually proof read and fix the typos and indexes, manually scan and add any illustrations, and track down another copy of the book to add any missing text. But our books sell so few copies, you would have to pay up to a thousand dollars for the book as a result.

Therefore, whenever possible, we let our customers download a free copy of the original typo-free scanned book. Simply enter the barcode number from the back cover of the paperback in the Free Book form at www.general-books. net. You may also qualify for a free trial membership in our book club to download up to four books for free. Simply enter the barcode number from the back cover onto the membership form on the same page. The book club entitles you to select from more than a million books at no additional charge. Simply enter the title or subject onto the search form to find the books.

If you have any questions, could you please be so kind as to consult our Frequently Asked Questions page at www. general-books.net/faqs.cfm? You are also welcome to contact us there.

General Books LLC®, Memphis, USA, 2012. ISBN: 9780217012997.

❧ ❧ ❧ ❧ ❧ ❧ ❧ ❧

ELEMENTS OF GESTURE. SECTION I. *On the Speaking of Speeches at Schools.*— Walkeh. ELOCUTION has, for some years past, been an object of attention in the most respectable schools in this country. A laudable ambition of instructing youth, in the pronunciation and delivery of their native language, has made English speeches a very conspicuous part of those exhibitions of oratory, which do our seminaries of learning so much credit.

This attention to English pronunciation, has induced several ingenious men to compile exercises in elocution, for the use of schools, which have answered very useful purposes; but none, so far as I have seen, have attempted to give us a regular system of gesture, suited to the wants and capacities of schoolboys. Mr. Burgh, in his Art of Speaking, has given us a system of the passions; and has shown us how they appear in the countenance, and operate on the body; but this system, however useful to people of riper years, is too delicate and complicated to be taught in schools. Indeed the exact adaptation of the action to the word, and the word to the action, as Shakespeare calls it, is the most difficult part of delivery, and, therefore, can never be taught perfectly to children; to say nothing of distracting their attention with two very difficult things, at the same time. But that boys should stand motionless, while they are pronouncing the most impassioned language, is extremely absurd and unnatural; and that they should sprawl into an awkward, unszain and desultory action, is still more offensive and disgusting— What then remains, but that such a general style of action be adopted, as shall be easily conceived, and easily execa ted; which, though not expressive of any particular pas sion, shall not be inconsistent with the expression of any passion; which shall always keep the body in a graceful position, and shall so vary its motions, at proper intervals, as to see the subject operating on the speaker, and not the speaker on the subject. This it will be confessed, is a great desideratum; and an attempt to this, is the principal object of the present publication.

The difficulty of describing action by words, will be allowed by every one; and if we were never to give any instructions, but such as should completely answer our wishes, this difficulty would be a good reason for not attempting to give any description of it. But there are many degrees between conveying a precise idea of a thing and no idea at all. Besides, in this part of delivery, instruction may be conveyed by the eye; and this organ is a much more rapid vehicle of knowledge than the ear. This vehicle is addressed on the present occasion; and plates, representing the attitudes which are described are annexed to the several descriptions, which it is not doubted, wiH greatly facilitate the reader's conception.

Plate I, represents the attitude in which a boy should always place himself when he begins to speak. He should rest the whole weight of his body on the right leg; the other, just touching the ground, at the distance at which it would naturally fall, if lifted up to show that the body does not bear upon it. The knees should be straight, and braced, and the body, though perfectly straight, not perpendicular, b'it inclining as far to the right as a firm position on the right leg will permit. The right arm must then be held out, with the palm open, the fingers stright and close, the thumb almost as distant from them as it will go; and the flat of the hand neither horizontal nor vertical, but exactly between both. The position of the arm, perhaps will be best described, by supposing an oblong hollow square formed by the measure of four arms as in plate I, where the arm, in its true position, forms the diagonal of such an imaginary figure. So that if lines were drawn at right angles from the shoulder, extending downwards, forwards and sideways, the aim will form an ftngle of forty-five degrees every way.._.

When the pupil has pronounced oue sentence, in the (position thus described, the hand, as if lifeless, must drop down to the side, the very moment the last accented word is pronounced; and the body, without altering the place of the feet, poise itself on the left leg, while the left hand raises itself, into.exactly the same position as the right was before, and continues in this position till the end of the next sentence, when it drops down on the side as if dead; and the body, poising itself 011 the right leg as before, continues with the right arm extended, tiil the end of the succeeding sentence; and so on, from right to left, and from left to right, alternately, till the speech is ended.

Great care must be taken, that the pupil end one sentence completely before he begin another. He must t the arm drop to the side, and continue, for a mometit, i.i that posture, in which he concluded, before he poises his body on the otlier leg, and raises the other arm into the diagonal position, before described; both which should be done, before he begins to pronounce the next sentence. Care must also be taken, in shifting the body from one leg to the other, that the feet do not alter their distance. In altering the position of the body, the feet will necessarily alter their position a little, but this change must be made, by turning the toes in a somewhat different direction without suffering them to shift their ground. The heels, in this transition, change their place, but not the toes. The toes may be considered as pivots, on which the body turns, from side to side.

If the pupil's knees are not well formed, or incline inwards, he must be taught to keep his legs at as great a distance as possible, and to incline his body so much to that side on which the arm is extended, as to oblige him to rest the opposite leg upon the toe; and this will, in a great measure, hide the defect of his make. Iu the same manner, if the arm be too long, or the elbow incline inwards, it will be proper to make him turn the palm of his hand downwards, so as to make it perfectly horizontal. This will infallibly incline the elbow outwards, and prevent the worst position the arm can p»ssibly fall into, which is that of inclining the elbow to the body. This position of the hand, so necessarily keeps the elbow out, that it would not be improper to make the pupil some. times practise it, though he may have Do defect in his make; as an occasional alteration of the former position to this, may often be necessary, both for the sake of justness and variety. These two last positions of the legs and arms are described in Plate II.

When the pupil has got the habit of holding his hand and arm properly, he may be taught to move it. In this motion he must be careful to keep the arm from the body. He must neither draw the elbow backwards, nor suffer it to approach to the side; but, while the hand and lower joint of the arm are curving towards the shoulder, the whole arm, with the elbow, forming nearly an angle of a. square, should move upwards from the shoulder, in the same position as when gracefully taking off the hat; that is, with the elbow extended from the side, and the upper joint of the arm nearly on a line with the shoulder, and forming an angle of a square with the body; (See Plate III) this motion of the arm will naturally bring the hand, with the palm downwards, into a horizontal position, and when it approaches to the head, the arm should, with a jerk, be suddenly straightened into its first position, at the very moment the emphatical word is pronounced. This coincidence of the hand and voice, will greatly enforce the pronunciation; and, if they keep time, they willbe in tune, as it were, to each other *y* and to force and energy, add harmony and variety.

As this motion of the arm is somewhat complicated, and may be found difficult to execute, it would be advisable to let the pupil at first speak without any motion of the arm at all. After some time, he will naturally fall into a small curviture of the elbow, to beat time, as it were, to the emphatic word; and if, doing'this, he is constantly urged to raise the elbow, and to keep it at a distance from the body, the action of the arm will naturally grow up into that we have just described. So the diagonal position of the arm, though the most graceful and easy when the body is at rest, may be too difficult for boys to fall into at first; and therefore it may be necessary, in order to avoid the worst extreme, for some time, to make them extend the arm as far from the body as they can, in a somewhat similar direction, but higher from the ground, and inclining more to the back. Great care must be tak en to keep the'hand open, and the thumb at some distance from the fingers; and particular attention must be paid, to keeping the hand in an exact line with the lower part of the arm, so as not to bend the wrist, either when it is held out, without motion, or when it gives the emphatic stroke. And, above all, the body must be kept in a straight line with the leg on which it bears and not suffered to bend to the opposite side.

At first, it may not be improper for the teacher, after placing the pupil in the position, (Plate I) to stand some distance, exactly opposite to him, in the same position, the right and left sides only reversed; and, while the pupil is speaking, to show him, by example, the action he is to make use of. In this case, the teacher's left hand will correspond to the pupil's right*;* by which means he will see, as in a lookingglass, how to regulate his gesture, and will soon catch the method of doing it by himself.

It is expected the master will be a little discouraged, at the awkward figure his pupil makes, in his first attempts to teach him. But this is no more than what happens in dancing, fencing, or any other exercise which depends on habit. By practice the pupil will soon begin to feel his position, and be easy in it. Those positions which were at first distressing to him, he will fall into naturally; and, if they are such as are really graceful and becoming (and such it is presumed are those which have been just described) they will be adopted, with more facility than any other that can be taught him.

SECTION II. *On the Acting of Plays at Schools.*—Walker. THOUGH the acting of plays, at schools, has been universally supposed a very useful practice, it has, of late years, been much laid aside. The advantages arising from it have not been judged equal to the inconveniences; and the speaking of single speeches, or the acting of single scenes, has been, generally, substituted in its stead. Indeed, when we consider the leading principle, and prevailing sentiments of most plays, we shall not wonder, that they are not always thought to be the most suitable employment for youth at school; nor, when we refifect on the long interruption to the common school exercises, which the preparation for a play must necessarily occasion, shall we think it consistent with general improvement. But, to wave every objection from prudence or morality, it may be confidently affirmed, that the acting of a play is not so conducive to improvement in elocution, as the speaking of single speeches.

In the first place, the acting of plays is of all kinds of delivery the most difficult; and therefore, cannot be the most suitable exercise for boys, at school. In the next place, a dramatic performance requires so mnch attention to the deportment of the body, so varied an expression of the passions, and so strict an adherence to character, that education is in danger of being neglected; besides, exact propriety of action, and a nice discrimination of the passions, however essential on the stage, are but of secondary importance in a school. It is plain, open, distinct and forcible pronunciation, which school boys should aim at j and not that quick transition from one passion to another, that archness of look, and that *jeu de theatre,* as it is called, so essential to a tolerable dramatic exhibition, and which actors themselves can scarcely attain. In short, it is speaking, rather than acting, which school boys should be taught; while the performance of plays is calculated to teach them acting, rather than speaking.

But there is a contrary extreme, into which many teachers are apt to run, and clrefly those who are incapable of speaking themselves; and that is, to condemn every thing, which is vehement and forcible, as *theatrical.* It is an odd trick, to depreciate what we cannot attain; and calling a spirited pronunciation *theatrical,* is but an artful method of hiding an utter inability of speaking, with force and energy. But, though school boys ought not to be taught those nice touches which form the greatest difficulties in the profession of an actor, they should not be too much restrained from the exertion of voice, so necessary to strengthening the organs of sound, because they may sometimes be too loud and vociferous. Perhaps nine out often, instead of too much confidence, and too violent a manner of speaking, which these teachers seem so much to dread, have, as Dr. Johnson calls it, a frigid equality, a stupid languor, and a torpid apathy. These roust be roused by something strong and excessive, or they will never rise even to mediocrity; while the few who have a tendency to rant, are very easily reclaimed, and ought to be treated, in pronunciation and action, as Quintillian advises us to do, in composition; that is, we should rather allow of an exuberance, than, by too much correctness, check the vigour and luxuriancy of nature.

Though school boys, therefore, ought not to be taught the finesses of acting, they should, as much as possible, be accustomed to speak such speeches, as require a full, open, animated pronunciation;. for which purpose they should be confined, chiefly, to orations, odes and such single speeches of plays, as are in the declamatory and vehement style. But as there are many scenes of plays, which are justly reckoned amongst the finest compositions in the language; some of these may be adopted among the upper class of boys, and those, more particularly, who have the best deportments; for action, in scenes, will be found much more difficult, than in single speeches. And here it will be necessary to give some additional instructions respecting action; as a speaker who delivers himself singly to an auditory, and one who addresses another speaker, in view of an auditory, arc under very different predicaments. The former has only one object to address j the Jatter has two. For if a speaker on the stage were to address the person he speaks to, without any regard to the point of view in which he stands, with respect to the audience, he would be apt to tarn his back on them, and to place himself in such positions as would be highly ungraceful and disgusting. When a scene, therefore, is represented, it is necessary that the two personages, who speak, should form a sort of picture, and place themselves in a position agreeable to the laws of perspective. In order to do this, it will be necessary that each of them should stand obliquely, and, chiefly make use of one band. That is, supposing the stage or platform where they stand to be quadrangle, each speaker should, respectively, face the corner of it next to the audience; and use that hand, and rest on that eg, which is eeKt to the person he speaks to, and which is farthest from the audience. This disposition is absolutely necessary, to form any thing like a picturesque grouping of objects, and without it, that is, if both speakers use the right hand, and stand exactly fronting each other, the impropriety will be palpable, and the spectacle disgusting.

Tt need scarcely be noted, that if the speaker in a scene, uses that hand which is next the audience, he ought likewise *to* poise his body upon the same leg: This is almost an invariable rule in action; the hand should act on that side only, on which the body bears. Good actors and speakers may sometimes depart from this rule, but such only, will know when to do it, with propriety.

Occasion may be taken in the course of the scene, to change sides. One speaker, at the end of an impassioned speech, may cross over to the place of the other, while the latter, at the same moment, crosses over to the place of the former. This, however, must be done with great oare, and so as to keep the back from being turned to the audience.

But if this transition be performed adroitly, it will have a very good effect, in varying the position of the speakers, and giving each an opportunity of using his right hand—the most favorable to grace and expression.—And, if, from so humble a scene as the school, we may be permitted to raise our observations to the senate, it might be hinted, that gentlemen on each side of the house, while addressing the chair, can, with grace and propriety only make use of one hand; namely, that which is next to the speaker; and it may be observed in passing, that to all the other advantages of speaking which are supposed to belong to one side-of the house—may be added—the graceful use of the right hand.

The better to cftnceive the position of two speakers in a scene, a Plate is given, representing their respective attitudes: And it must be carefully noted, that, when they are not speaking, the arms must hang in their natural place, by the sides: Unless what is spoken, by one, is of such importance, as to excite agitation and surprise in the other. But if we should be sparing of gesture at all times, we should be more particularly so, when we are not speaking.

From what has been laid down, it will evidently appear.

how much more difficult and complicated is the action of a scene, than that of a single speech; and, in teaching both to children, how necessary it is, to adopt as simple and easy a method as possible. The easiest method of conveying instruction, in this point, will be sufficiently difficult; and therefore, the avoiding of awkwardness and impropriety, should be more the object of instruction, than the conveying of beauties.

There are, indeed, some masters, who are against teaching boys any action at all, and are for leaving them in this point entirely to nature. It is happy, however, that they do not leave that action to nature, which is acquired by dancing; the deportment of their pupils, would soon convince them, they were imposed on by the sound of words. Improved and beautiful nature is the object of the painter's pencil, the poet's pen, and the rhetorician's action, and not tbat sordid and common nature, which is perfectly rude and uncultivated. Nature directs us to art, and art selects and polishes the beauties of nature: It is not sufficient for an orator, says Quintilian, that he is a man: He must be an improved and cultivated man; he must be a man, favoured by nature and fashioned by art.

But the necessity of adopting some method of teaching action, is too evident to need proof. Bqys will infallibly contract some action; to require them to stand stock still while they are speaking an impassioned speech, is not only exacting a very difficult task from them, but is in a great measure, checking their natural exertions. If they are left to tuemselves, they will, in all probability, fall into very wild and ungraceful action, which, when once formed into habit, can scarcely ever be corrected: Giving them therefore, a general outline of good action, must be of the utmost consequence to their progress and improvement, in pronunciation.

The great use, therefore, of a system of action like the present, is, that a boy will never be embarrassed, for want of knowing what to do with his legs and arms; nor will he bestow that attention on his action, which ought to be directed to his pronunciation: He will always be in a position which will not disgrace his figure, and when this, gesture is easy to him, it may serve as a groundwork to something more perfect: He may either by his oA g$nius or his master's instructions, build some other action upon it, which may, in time, give it additional force and variety.

Thus what seemed either unworthy the attention, or too. difficult for the execution, of others, the author of the present publication has ventured to attempt. A conviction of the necessity of teaching some system of action, and the abundant success of the present system, in one of the most respectable academies near London, has determined bim td publish it, for the use of such seminaries as make English pronunciation a part of their discipline.

It may not be useless to observe, that boys should be classed in this, as in every other kind of instruction, according to their abilities; that a class should not consist of more than ten; that about eight or ten lines of some speech should be read first by the teachers, then by the boy who reads best, aud then by the rest in order, all having a book of the same kind, and all reading the same portion. This portion they must be ordered to get by heart against the next lesson; and then the first boy must speak it, standing at some distance before the rest, in the manner directed in the Plates; the second boy must succeed him, and so on till they have all spoken. After 'which another portion must be read them, which ihey must read and speak in the same manner as before.— When they have gone through a speech in this manner by portions, the two or three first boys may be ordered, against the next lesson, to speak the whole speech; the next lesson, two or three more, and so on to the rest. This will excite emulation, and give the teacher an opportunity of ranking them according to their merit.

SECTION III. *Rules for expressing, with propriety, the principal Passions and Humors, which occur in Reading, or public Speaking,* EVERY part of the human frame contributes to express the passions and emotions of the mind, and to shew in general its present state. The head is sometimes e rected, sometimes hung down, sometimes drawn suddenly back with an air of disdain, sometimes shews by a nod a particular person, or object; gives assent, or denial, by different motions; threatens by one sort of movement, approves by another, and expresses suspicion by a third.

The arms are sometimes both thrown out, sometimes the right alone. Sometimes they are lifted up as high as the lace, to express wonder; sometimes held out before the breast, to shew fear; spread forth with the hands open, to express desire or affection; the hands clapped in surprise, and in sudden joy and grief; the right hand clenched, and the arms brandished, to threaten; the two arms set akimbo, to look big, and express contempt or courage. With the hands, we solicit, we refuse, we promise, we threaten, we dismiss, we invite, we in treat, we express aversion, fear, doubting, denial, asking, affirmation, negation, joy, grief,-confession, penitence. With the hands we describe, and point out all circumstances of time, place, and manner of what we relate; we excite the passions of others, and sooth them, we approve and disapprove, permit, or prohibit, admire or despise. The hands serve us instead of many sorts of words,-and where the language of the tongue is unknown, that of the hands is understood, being universal, and common to all nations.

The legs advance, or retreat to express desire, or aversion, love or hatred, courage or fear, and produce exultation, or leaping in sudden joy; and the stamping of the foot expresses earnestness, anger and threatening.

Especially the face, being furnished with a variety of muscles, does more in expressing the passions of the mind than the whole human frame besides. The change of colour (in white people) shews, by turns, anger by redness, and sometimes by paleness, fear, likewise by paleness, and shame by blushing. Every feature contributes its part. The mouth open, shews one state of mind, shut, another; the gnashing of the teeth, another. The forehead smooth, eyebrows arched and easy, shew tranquility or joy. Mirth opens the mouth towards the ears, crisps the nose, half shuts the eyes, and sometimes fills them with tears. The front wrinkled into frowns, and the eyebrows overhanging the eyes, like clouds, fraught with tempest, skew a mind agitated with fury. AbJve all, the eve shows the very spirit in a visible form. In every different state of the mind, it assumes a different appearance. Joy brightens and opens it. Grief half closes, and drowns it in tears. Hatred and anger, flash from it like lightning. Love, darts from it in glances, like the orient beam. Jealousy and squinting envy, dart their contagious blasts from the eye. And devotion raises it to the skies, as if the soul of the holy man were going to take its flight to heaven.

The force of attitude and looks alone appears in a woitdrously striking manner, in the works of the painter and statuary; who have the delicate art of making the flat canvass and rocky marble utter "every passion of the human mind, and touch the soul of the spectator, as if the picture, or statue, spoke the pathetic language of Shakespeare, ft is no wonder then, that masterly action, joined with powerful elocution, should be irresistible. And the variety of expression, by looks and gestures, is so great, that, as is well known, a whole play can be represented without a word spoken.

The following are, I believe, the principal passions, humours, sentiments and intentions which are to be expressed by speech and action. And I hope, it will be allowed by the reader, that it is nearly in the following manner, that riature expresses them.

Tranquility or apatliy, appears by the composure of the Countenance, and general repose of the body and limbs, without the exertion of any one muscle. The countenance open; the forehead smooth; the eyebrows arched; the moutlijust not shut; and the eyes passing with an easy motion from object to object but not dwelling long upon any one. *Cheerfulness,* adds a smile, opening the mouth a little more. *Mirth or laughter,* opens the mouth still more towards the ears; crisps the nose; lessens the aperture of the eyes, and sometimes fills them with tears; shakes and convulses the whole frame; giving considerable pain, which occasions holding the sides. *Raillery,* in sport, without real animosity, puts on the aspect of cheerfulness. The tone of voice is sprightly. With conlfctDpt, or disgust, it casts a look asquint, from tine to time, at the object; and quits the cheerful aspect for one mixed between an affected grin and sourness. The upper lip is drawn-up with an air of disdain. The arms are set akimbo on the hips; and the right hand now and then thrown out toward the object, as if one were going to strike another a slight back hand blow. The pitch of the voice rather loud, the tone arch and sneering, the sentences short; the expressions satirical, with mockpraise intermixed. There ate instances of raillery in scripture itself, as 1 Kings xviii, and Isaiah xliv. It is not, therefore, beneath the dignity of the pulpit orator, occasionally to use it in the cause of virtue by exhibiting vice in a ludicrous appearance. Nor should I think raillery unworthy the attention of the lawyer; as it may occasionally come in, not unusefully, in his pleadings, as well as any oilier stroke of ornament, or entertainment. *Buffoonery.* , assumes an arch, sly, leering-gravity. Must not quit its serious aspect, though all should laugh to burst ribs of steel. This command of face is somewhat difficult; though not so hard, I should think, as to restrain the contrary sympathy, I mean of weeping with those who weep. *Joy,* when sudden and violent, expresses itself by clapping of hands, and exultation or leaping. The eyes are opened wide; perhaps filled with tears; often raised to heaven-, especially by devout persons. The countenance is smiling not composedly, but with features aggravatedThe voice rises, from time to time, to very high notes. *Delight or Pleasure,* as when one is entertained, or ravished with music, painting, oratory, or any such elegancy, shews itself by the looks, gestures, and utterance of joy j but moderate. *Gravity or Seriousness,* the mind fixed upon some important subject, draws down the eyebrows a little, casts down, or shuts, or raises the eyes to heaven; shuts the mouth, and pinches the lips close. The posture of the body and limbs is composed, and without much motion. The speech, if any, slow and solemn; the tone unvarying. *Inquiry, into an Gjscurt subject,* fixes the body in one posture, the head stooping, and the eye poring, the eyebrows drawn down. *Attention,* to an esteemed, or superior character, has the same aspect; and requires silence; the eyes often cast down upon the ground; sometimes fixed on the speaker; but not loo pertly. *Modesty or submission,* bends the body forward levels the eyes to the breast, if not 10 the feet, of the superior character. The voice low; the tone submissive, and words few. *Perplexity, or anxiety,* which is always attended with some degree of fear and uneasiness, draws all the parts of the body together, gathers up the arms upon the breast, unless one hand covers the eyes, or rubs the forehead draws down the eyebrows;" hangs the head upon the breast; casts down the eyes, shuts and pinches the eyelids close; shuts the mouth, and pinches the lips close, or bites them. Suddenly the whole body is vehemently agitated. The person walks about busily, stops abruptly. Then he talks to himself, or makes grimaces. If he speak to another, his pauses are very long; the tone of his voice unvarying, and his sentences broken, expressing half, and keeping in half of what arises in his mind. *Vexation,* occasioned by some real or imaginary misfortune, agitates the whole frame; and besides expressing itself with the looks, gestures, restlessness, and tone of perplexity, it adds complaint, fretting and lamenting. *Pity,* a mixed passion of love and grief, looks down upon distress with lifted hands; eyebrows drawn down; mouth open; and features drawn together. Its expression, as to looks and gesture, is the same with those of suffering, *(see Svffering)* but more moderate, as the painful feelings are only sympathetic, and therefore one remove, as it were, more distant from the soul, than what one feels iu his own person. *Grief,* sudden and violent, expresses itself by beating the head; groveling on the ground, tearing of garments, hair and flesh; screaming aloud, weeping, stamping with the feet, lifting the eyes, from time to time, to heaven; hurrying to and fro, running distracted, or fainting away, sometimes without recovery. Sometimes violent grief produces a torpid silence, resembling total apathy. *Melancholy,* or fixed grief, is gloomy sedentary, motionless. The lower jstw falls j the lips pale, the *eyes* are cast down, half shut, eyelids swelled and red or livid, tears trickling silent and unwiped; with a total inattention to every thing that passes. Words, if any few, and those dragged out, rather than spoken; the accents weak, and interrupted, sighs breaking into the middle of sentences and words. *Despair,* as in a condemned criminal, or one, who has lost all hope of salvation, bends the eyebrows downward; clouds the forehead; rolls the eyes around frightfully; opens the mouth towards the ears; bites the lips; widens the nostrils; gnashes with the teeth, like a fierce wild beast. The heart is too much hardened to suffer tears to flow; yet the eyeballs will be red and inflamed like those of an animal in a rabid state. The head is hung down upon the breast. The arms are bended at the elbows, the fists are clenched hard; the veins and muscles swelled; the skin livid; and the whole body strained and violently agitated; groans, expressive of inward torture, more frequently uttered than words. If any words, they are few, and expressed with a sullen, eager, bitterness; the tone of voice often loud and furious. As it often drives people to distraction, and self murder, it can hardly be overacted by one, who would represent It. *Fear,* violent and sudden, opens very wide the eyes and mouth; shortens the nose; draws down the eyebrows; gives the countenance an air of wildness; covers it with a deadly paleness; draws back the elbows parallel with the sides; lifts up the open hands, the fingers together, to the height of the breast, so that the palms face the dreadful object, as shields opposed against it. One foot is drawn back behind the other-so that the body seems shrinking from the danger, and putting itself in a posture for flight. The heart beats violently; the breath is fetched quick and short; the whole body is thrown into a general tremour. The voice is weak and trembling; the sentences are short, and the meaning confused and incoherent. Imminent danger, real or fancied, produces in timorous persons, as women and children, violent shrieks without any articulate sound of words; and sometimes irrecoverably confounds the understanding; produces fainting, which is sometimes followed by death. *Shame,* or a sense of one's appearing to a disadvantage, before one's fellow creatures; turns away the face from the beholders; covers it with blushes; hangs the bead; casts down the eyes; draws down the eyebrows; either strikes the person dumb, or, if he attempts to say any thing in his own defence, causes his tongue to faulter and confounds his utterance; and puts him upon making a thousand gestures and grimaces, to keep himself in countenance; all of which only heighten the confusion of his appearance. *Remorse,* or a painful sense of guilt, casts down the countenance, and clouds it with anxiety; hangs down the head, draws the eyebrows down upon the eyes. The right hand beats the breast. The teeth gnash with anguish. The whole body is strained and violently agitated. If this strong remorse is succeeded by the more gracious disposition of penitence, or contrition; then the eyes are raised (but with great appearance of doubting and fear) to the throne of heavenly mercy; and immediately cast down again to the earth. Then floods of tears are seen to flow. The knees are bended; or the body prostrated on the ground. The arms are spread in a suppliant posture, and the voice of deprecation is uttered with sighs, groans, timidity, hesitation and trembling. *Courage,* steady and cool, opens the countenance, gives the whole form an erect and graceful air. The accents are strong, fullmouthed and articulate, the voice firm and even. *Boasting,* or affected courage, is loud, blustering, threatening. The eyes stare; the eyebrows drawn down; the face red and bloated; the mouth pouts out; the voice hollow and thundering; the arms set akimbo; the head often. nodding in a menacing manner; aik. the right fist, clenched, is brandished from time to lime, at the person threatened. The right foot is often stamped upon the ground, and the legs take such large strides, and the steps are so heavy, that the earth seems to tremble under them. *Pride,* assumes a lofty look, bordering upon the aspect and attitude of anger. The eyes open, but with the eye-' brows considerably drawn down; the mouth pouting out, mostly shut, and the lips pinched close. The words walk out astrut with a slow, stiff, bombastic affectation of im portance. The arms generally akimbo, and the legs at a distance from one another, taking large tragedy strides. *Obstinacy,* adds to the aspect of pride, a dogged sourness, like that of malice. See *Malice. Authority,* opens the countenance; but draws down the eyebrows a little, so far as to give the look of gravity. See *Gravity. Commanding,* requires an air a little more peremptory, with a look a little severe or stern. The hand is held out, and moved towardthe person, to whom the order is given, with the palm upwards, and the head nods toward him. *Forbidding,* on the contrary, draws the bead backwards and pushes the hand from one with the palm downward, as if going to lay it upon the person, to hold him down immoveable, that he may not do what is forbidden him. *Affirming,* especially with a judicial oath, is expressed by lifting the open right hand, and eyes, toward heaven; or, if conscience is appealed to, by laying the right hand upon the breast. *Denying,* is expressed by pushing the open right hand from one; and turning the face the contrary way. See *Aversion. Differing'* in sentiment, may be expressed as refusing. See *Refusing. Agreeing in opinion,* or *conviction,* as granting. See *Granting. Exhorting,* as by a general at the head of his army, requires a kind, complacent look; unless matter of offence has passed, as neglect of duty, or the like. *Judging,* demands a grave, steady look, with deep attention, the countenance altogether clear from any appearance of either disgust or favour. The accents slow, distinct, emphatical, accompanied with little action, and that very grave. *Reproving,* puts on a stern aspect, roughens the voice, and is accompanied with gestures not much different from those of *threatening,* but not so lively. *Acquitting,* is performed with a benevolent, tranquil countenance, and tone of voice; the right hand, if not both, open, waved gently toward the person acquitted, ex. pressing dismission. See *Dismissing. Condemning,* assumes a severe look, but mixed with pity. The sentence is to be expressed as with reluctance. *Teaching,* explaining, inculcating, or giving orders to an inferior, requires an air of superiority to be assumed.— The features are to be composed to an authoritative gravity. The eye steady, and open, the eyebrow a little drawn down over it; but not so much as to look surly or dogmatical. The tone of voice varying according as the emphasis requires, of which a good deal is necessary in expressing matter of this sort. The pitch of the voice to be strong and clear; the articulation distinct; the utterance slow, and the manner peremptory. This is the proper manner of pronouncing the commandments in the communion office. But (I am sorry to say it) they are too commonly spoken in the same manner as the prayers, than which nothing can be more unnatural. *Pardoning,* differs from acquitting, in that the latter means clearing a person after trial of guilt: whereas the former supposes guilt, and signifies merely delivering the guilty person from punishment. Pardoning requires some degree of severity of aspect and tone of voice, because the pardoned person is not an object of entire unmixed approbation, otherwise its expression is much the same as granting. See *Granting. Arguing,* requires a cool, sedate, attentive aspect, and a clear, slow, emphatical accent, with much demonstration by the hand. It diners from teaching (see *Teaching)* in that the look of authority is wanting in arguing. *Dismissing,* with approbation, is done with a kind aspect and tone of voice; the right hand open, gently waved toward the person; with displeasure, besides the look and tone of voice which suit displeasure, the hand is hastily thrown out toward the person dismissed, the back part toward him, the countenance at the same time turned away from him. *Refusing,* when accompanied with displeasure, is expressed nearly in the same way. Without displeasure, it is done with a visible reluctance, which occasions the bringing out ihe words slowly, with such a shake of the head, and shrug of the shoulders, as is natural upon hearing of somewhat, which gives us concern. *Granting,* when done with unreserved good will is accompanied with a benevolent aspect, and tone of voice; the right hand pressed to the left breast, to signify how heartily the favour is granted, and the benefactor's joy in conferring it. *Dependence.* See *Modesty. Feneration,* or worshipping, comprehends several articles, as ascription, confession, remorse, intercession, thanksgiving, deprecation, petition, &c. Ascription of honour and praise to the peerless supreme Majesty of heaven, and confession and deprecation, are to be uttered with all that humility of looks and gesture, which can exhibit the most profound selfabasement and annhilation, before One, whose superiority is infinite. The head is a little raised, but with the most apparent timidity, and dread; the eye is lifted; but immediately cast down again or closed for a moment; the eyebrows are drawn down in the most respectful manner; the features, and the whole body and limbs-, are all composed to the most profound gravity; one posture continuing, without considerable change, during the whole performance of the duty. The knees bended, or the whole body prostrate, or if the posture be standing, which scripture does not disallow, bending forward, as ready to prostrate itself. The arms spread out but modestly, as high as the breast; the hands open. The tone of the voice will be submissive, timid, equal, trembling, weak, suppliant. The words will be brought out with a visible anxiety and diffidence approaching to hesitation; few and slow; nothing of vain repetition, harranguing, flowers of rhetoric, or affected figures of speech; all simplicity, humility and lowliness, such as becomes a reptile of the dust, when presuming to address Him, whose greatness is tremendous beyond all created conceptionIn intercession for our fellow creatures which is prescnbec in the scriptures, and in thanksgiving, the countenance will naturally assume a small degree of cheerfulness, beyond what it was clothed with in confession of sin, and deprecation of punishment. But all affected ornament of speech or gesture in devotion, deserves the severest censure, as being somewhat much worse than absurd. *Respect,* for a *superiour,* puts on the looks and gesture of modesty. See *Modesty. Hope,* brightens the countenance; arches the eye-brows; gives the eyes an eager, wishful look; opens the mouth W half a smile: bends the body a little forward, the feet equal; spreads the arms, with the hands open, as to receive the object of its longings.

The tone of the voice is eager, and unevenly inclining to that of joy; but curbed by a degree of doubt and anxiety. Desire differs from hope as to expression, in this particular, that there is more appearance of doubt and anxiety in the former, than in the latter. For it is one thing to desire what is agreeable, and another to have a prospect of actuajly obtaining it. *Desire,* expresses itself by bending the body forward and stretching the arms toward the object as to grasp it. The countenance smiling, but eager and wishful; the eye wide open, *and* eyebrows raised; the mouth open; tone of voice suppliant, but lively and cheerful, unless there be distress as well as desire; the expression fluent and copious; if no words are used, sighs instead of them; but this is chiefly in distress. *Love,* (successful) lights up the countenance into smiles. The forehead is smoothed and enlarged; the eyebrows are arched; the mouth a little open, and smiling: the eyes languishing and half shut, doat upon the beloved object. The countenance assumes the eager and wishful look of desire; (see *Desire)* but mixed with an air of satisfaction and repose. The accents are soft and winning; the tone of voice persuasive, flattering, pathetic, various musical, rapturous as in joy. (See *Joy.)* the attitude much the same with that of desire. Sometimes both hands pressed eagerly to the bosom.' Love, unsuccessful, adds an air of anxiety and melancholy. See *Perplexity* and *Melancholy. Giving, inviting, soliciting,* and such like actions, which suppose some degree of affection, real or pretended, are accompanied with much the same looks and gestures as express love; but more moderate. *Wonder,* or amazement, (without any other *interesting* passion, as *love, esteem,* &c.) opens the eyes, and makes them appear very prominent; sometimes raises them to the skies; but oftener, and more expressively, fixes them on the object; if the cause of the passion be a present and Visible object, with the look, all except the wildness, of fear. (See *Fear.)* If the hands hold any thing, at the lime when the object of wonder appears, they immediately let it drop, unconscious; and the whole body fixes in the contracted, stooping posture of amazement; the mouth open; the hands held up open, nearly in the attitude of fear. (See *Fear.)* The first excess of this passion stops all utterance. But it makes amends afterwards by a copious flow of words and exclamations. *Admiration,* a mixed passion, consisting of wonder, with love or esteem, takes away the familiar gesture, and expression of simple love. (See *Love)* Keeps the respectful look and attitude. (See *Modesty* and *Veneration.)* The eyes are open wide, and now and then raised toward heaven. The mouth is opened. The hands are lifted up.— The tone of the voice rapturous. This passion expresses itself copiously, making great use of the figure hyperbole. *Gratitude,* puts on an aspect full of complacency. (See *hove.)* If the object of it is a character greatly superior, it expresses much submission, (See *Modesty.)* The right hand pressed upon the breast accompanies very properly, the expression of a sincere and hearty sensibility of obligation. *Curiosity,* as of a busy body, opens the eyes, and moutlt, lengthens the neck, bends the body forward, and fixes it in one posture, with the hands nearly in that of admiration. (See *Admiration.*—See also *Desire, Attention, Hope, Inquiry* and *Perplexity.)* *Persuasion,* puts on the looks of moderate love.. (See *Low.)* Its accents are soft, flattering, emphatical and articulate. *Tempting,* or *wheedling,* 'expresses itself much in the same way; o«ily carrying the fawning part to excess. *Promising* is expressed with benevolent looks, the nod of consent, and the open hands gently moved towards the person to whom the promise is made; the palms upwards. The sincerity of the prcmiser may be expressed by laying the right hand gently on the breast. *Affectation,* displays itself in a thousand different gestures, motions, airs and looks, according to the character which the person affects. Affectation of learning gives a stiff formality to the whole person. The words come stalking out with the pace of a funeral procession; and every sentence has the solemnity of an oracle. Affectation of piety turns up the goggling whites of the eyes to heaven, as if the person were in a trance, and fixes them in that posture so long that the brain of the beholder grows giddy. Then comes up deep grumbling, a holy groan from the lover parts of the thorax; but so tremendous in sound, and so long protracted, that you expect to see a goblin rise, like an exhalation thraugh the solid earth.— Then he begins to rock from side to side, or backward and forward, like an aged pine on the side of an hill, whew a brisk wind blows. The hands are clasped together, and often lifted, and the head often shaken with foolish vehemence. The tone of the voice is canting, or sing song lullaby, not much distant from an Irish howl; and the words godly dogered. Affectation of beauty, and killing, puts a fine woman by turns into all sorts of forms, appearances, and attitudes, but amiable ones. She undoes, by art, or rather by awkwardness, (for true art conceals itself) all that nature had done for her. Nature formed her almost an angel, and she, with infinite pains, makes herself a monkey. Therefore, this species of affectation is easily imitated, or taken off. Make as *many,* and as ugly grimaces, motions and gestures as can be made; and take eere that nature never peep out j and you represent coquelish affectation to the life. *Sloth,* appears by yawning, dozing, snoring, the head dangling sometimes to one side, sometimes to the other, the arms and legs stretched out, and every sinew of the body unstrung, the eyes heavy or closed; the words, if any, crawl out of the mouth, but half formed, scarce audible to any ear, and broken off in the middle by powerful sleep.

People who walk in their sleep, (of which our inimitable Shakespeare has, in his tragedy of Macbeth, drawn out a fine scene) are said to have their eyes open; though they are not the more for that, conscious of any thing, but the dream, which has got possession of their imagination. I never saw one of those persons; therefore cannot describe their manner from nature; but I suppose, their speech is pretty much like that of persons dreaming, inarticulate, incoherent, and very different, in its tone, from what it is when waking.

Intoxication, shews itself by the eyes half shut, sleepy, stupid, inflamed. An ideot smile, a ridiculous surliness, or affected bravado, disgraces the bloated countenance. The mouth open, tumbles out nonsense in heaps, without articulation enough for any ear to take it in, and unworthy of attention, it it could be taken in. The head seems too heavy for the neck. The arms dangle from the shoulders, as if they were almost cut away, and hung by shreds. The legs totter and bend at the knees, as ready to sink under the weight of the reeling body. And a general incapacity, corporeal and mental, exhibits human nature sunk below the brutal. *Anger,* (violent) or rage, expresses itself with rapidity, interruption, noise, harshness and trepidation. The neck stretched out; the head forward, often nodding and shaken in a menacing manner, against the object of the passion. The eyes red, inflamed, staring, rolling, and sparkling; the eyebrows drawn down over them; and the forehead wrinkled into clouds. The nostrils stretched wide; every vein swelled; every muscl e strained; the breast heaving and the breath fetched hard. The mouth open, and drawn on each side toward the ears, shewing the teeth, in a gnashing posture. The face bloated, pale, red, or sometimes almost black. The feet stamping; the right arm often thrown out, and menacing with a clenched fist shaken, and a general and violent agitation of the whole t›ody. *Peevishness,* or ill nature, is a lower degree of anger; and is therefore expressed in the above manner, only more moderate; with half sentences, and broken speeches, uttered hastily; the upper lip drawn up disdainfully; the eyes squint upon the object of displeasure. *Malice,* or spite, sets the jaws, or gnashes with the teeth; sends blasting flashes from the eyes; draws the mouth toward the ears; clenches both fists, and bends the elbows in a straining manner. The tone of voice and expression, are much the samt with that of anger; but the pitch not so loud. *Envy,* is a little more moderate in its gestures, than malice; but

much the same in kind. *Revenge,* expresses itself as malice. *Cruelty.* (See *Anger, Aversion, Malice,* and the oilier irascible passions.) *Complaining,* as when one is under violent bodily pain, distorts the features; almost closes the eyes; sometimes raises them wishfully; opens the mouth; gnashes with the teeth; draws up the upper lip; draws down the head upon the breast. and the whole body together. The arms are violently bent at the elbows, and the fists strongly clenched. The voice is uttered in groans, lamentations, and violent screams. Extreme torture produces fainting and death. *Fatigue,* from severe labour, gives a general langour to the whole body. The countenance is dejected. (See *Grief.*) The arms hang listless; the body, if sitting, or lying along, be not the posture, stoops, as in old age. (See *Dotage.*) The legs, if walking, are dragged heavily along, and seem at every step ready to bend under the weight of the body. The voice is weak, and the words hardly enough articulated, to be understood. *Aversion,* or hatred, expressed to, or of any person or thing, thatgs odious to the speaker, occasions his drawing back, as avoiding the approach of what he hates; the hands, at the same time, thrown out spread, as if to keep it off. The face turned away from that side toward which the hands are thrown out; the eyes looking angrily and asquint the same way the hands are directed; the eyebrows drawn downwards; the upper lip disdainfully drawn up; but the teeth set. The pitch of the voice loud; the tone chiding, and unequal, surly, vehement. The sentences short, and abrupt. *Commendation,* or approbation, from a superiour, puts on the aspect of love, (excluding *Desire* and *Respect)* and expresses itself in a mild tone of voice; the arms gently spread; the palms of the hands toward the person approved. Exhorting, or encouraging, as of an army by a general, is expressed with some part of the looks and actions of courage. *Jealousy,* would be likely to be well expressed by one who had often seen prisoners tortured in the dungeons of the inquisition, or who had seen what the

dungeons of the inquisition are the best earthly.emblem of; I mean bell. For next to being in the Pope's or in Satan's prison, is the torture of him who is possessed with the spirit of jealousy. Being a mixture of passions directly contrary to ODe another, the person, whose soul is the seat of such confusion and tumult, must be in as much greater misery than Prometheus, with the vulture tearing his liver, as the pains of the mind are greater than those of the body.— Jealousy is a ferment of *love, luttred, hope, fear, shame anxiety, suspicion, grief, pity, envy, pride, rage, cruelty, vengeance, madness,* ami if there be any other tormenting passion, which can agitate the human mind. Therefore, to express jealousy wel, requires that one know how to represent justly all nese passions by turns. (See *J.ove, Hatred,* &c.) And often, several of them together. Jealousy shews itself by restlessness, peevishness, thoughtfulness, anxiety, absence of mind. Sometimes it bursts out in piteous complaint, and weeping; then a gleam of hope, that all is yet well, lights up the countenance into a momentary smile. Immediately the face clouded with a general gloom, shews the mind overcast again with horrid suspicions and frightful imaginations. Then the arms are folded upon the breast; the fists violently clenched; the rolling bloody eyes dart fury. He hurries to and fro; he lias no more rest than a ship in a troubled sea, the sport of winds and waves. Again, he composes himself a little to reflect on the charms of the suspected person. She appears to his imagination like the sweetness of the rising dawn. Then his monster breeding fancy represents her as false as she is fair. Then he roars out as one on the rack, when the cruel engine rends every joint, and every sinew bursts. Then he throws himself on the ground. He beats his head against the pavement. Then he springs up, and with the look and action of a fury, bursting hot from the abyss, he snatches the instrument of death, and after ripping up the bosom of the loved, suspected, hated, lamented fair one, he stabs himself to the heart, and exhibits a striking proof, how terrible a creature a puny mortal is, when agitated by an infernal passion. *Dotage,* or infirm old age, shews itself by talkativeness, boasting of the past, hollowness of eyes and cheeks, dimness of sight, deafness, tremour of voice, the accents, through default of teeth, scarce intelligible; hams weak, knees tottering, head paralytic, hollow coughing, frequent expectoration, breathless wheezing, laborious groaning, the body stooping under the insupportable load of years which soon shall crush it into the dust, from whence it had its orig.n. *Folly,* that is of a natural idiot, gives the face an liabittual. ihought'e3S, brainless grin. The eyes dance from object to object, without ever fixing steadily upon any one. A thousand different and incoherent passions, looks, gestures, speeches and absurdities, are played off tvery moment. *Distraction,* opens the eyes to a frightful wideness; rolls them hastily and wildly from obj-- t to object; distorts-every feature; gnashes with the teeth; agitates all parts of the body; rolls in the dust; foams at the mouth; utters with hideous bellowings, execrations, blasphemies, and all that is fierce and outrageous; rushes furiously on all who approach; and if not restrained, tears its own flesh and destroys itself. _ *Sickness,* has infirmity and feebleness in every motion and utterance. The eyes dim and almost closed; cheeks pale and hollow; the jaw fallen; the head hung down, as if loo heavy to be supported by the neck. A general inertia prevails. The voice trembling; the utterance thro' the nose; every sentence accompanied with a groan; the hand shaking, and the knees tottering under the body; or the body stretched helpless on the bed. *Fainting,* produces a sudden relaxation of all that holds the human frame together, every sinew and ligament unstrung. The colour flies from the vermilion cheek; the sparkliug eye grows dim. Down the body drops, as helpleas and senseless as a mass of clay, to which, by its colour and appearance, it seems hastening to resolve itself. Which leads me to conclude with *Death,* the awful end of all flesh; which exhibits nothing in appearance different from what I have been just describing;

for fainting continued ends in death; a subject almost too serious to be made a matter of artificial imitation. *Lower* degrees of every passion are to be expressed by. more moderate exertions of voice and gesture, as every public speaker's discretion will suggest to him. *Mixed* passions, or emotions of the mind, require a mixed expression. *Pity,* for example, is composed of grief and love. It is therefore evident that a correct speaker must, by his looks and gestures, and hy the tone and pitch of his voice, express both grief and love, in expressing pity, and so of the rest.

It is to be remembered, that the action, in expressing the various humours and paisions, for which I have here given rules, is to be suited to the age, sex, condition and circumstances of the character. Violeut anger, or rage, for example, is to be expressed with great agitation, (see *Angtr)* but the rage of an infirm old man, of a woman, and of a youth, are all different from one another, and from that of a man in the flower of his age, as every speaker's discretion will suggest. A hero may shew fear or sensibility of pain; but not in the same manner as a girl would express those sensations. Grief may be expressed by a person reading a melancholy story, or a description in aroom. It may beaded upon the stage. Itmaybedwelt upon by the pleader at the bar; or it may have a place in a sermon. The passion is still grief. But the manner of expressing it will be different in each of the speakers, if they have judgment.

A correct speaker does not make a movement of limb, or feature for which he has not a reason. If he addresses heaven, he looks upward. If he speak of his fellowcreatures, he looks round upon them. The spirit of what he says, or is said to him, appears in his look. If he expresses amazement, or would excite it, he lifts up his hands and eyes. If he invites to virtue and happiness, he spreads his arms, and looks benevolent. If he threatens the vengeance of heaven against vice, he bends his eyebrows into wrath, and menaces with his arm and countenance. He does not needlessly saw the air with his arm, nor stab

himself with his finger. He does not clap his right hand upon his breast, unless he has occasion to speak of himself, or to introduce conscience, or somewhat sentimental. He does not start back, unless he wants to express horrour or aversion. He does not come forward, but when he has occasion to solicit. He does not raise' his voice, but to express somewhat peculiarly emphatical. He does not lower it, but to contrast the raising of it. His eyes, by turns, according to the humourof the matter he has to ex press, sparkle fury; brighten into joy; glance disdain; melt into grief; frown disgust and hatred; languish into love; or glare distraction.

RULES RESPECTING ELOCUTION,
Extracted from Walker's Speaker.

RULE I. *Let your* Articulation *be Distinct and Deliberate.* A GOOD articulation consists in giving a clear and full utterance to the several simple and complex sounds. The nature of these sounds, therefore, ought to be well understood; and much pains should be taken to discover and correct those faults in articulation, which though often ascribed to some defect in the organs of speech, are geuerally the consequence of inattention or bad example. Many of these respect the sounding of the consonants. Some cannot pronounce the letter *l,* and others the simple sounds *r, s, th, sh;* others generally omit the aspirate *k.* These faults may be corrected, by reading sentences, so contrived as often to repeat the faulty sounds, and by guarding against them in familiar conversation. Other defects in articulation regard the complex sounds, and consist iu a confused and cluttering pronunciation of words. The most effectual methods of conquering this habit, are, to read aloud passages chosen for the purpose (such for instance as abound with long and unusual words, or in which many short-syllables come together) and to read, at certain stated times, much slower than the sense and just speaking would require. Almost all persons, who have not studied the art of speaking, have a habit of utter ing their words so rapidly, that this latter exercise ought generally to be made use of for a considerable time at first; for where there is a uniformly rapid utterance, it is absolutely impossible that there should be strong emphasis, natural tones, or any just elocution.

Aim at nothing higher, till you can read distinctly and deliberately.

Learn to speak slow, all other graces, Will follow in their proper places.

RULE II.

Let your Pronunciation *he Bold and Forcible.* AN insipid flatness and languor is almost the universal fault in readmg, and even public speakers often suffer their words to drop from their lips with such *a.* faint and feeble utterance, that they appear neither to understand or feel what they say themselves, nor to have any desire that it should be understood or felt by their audience. This is a fundamental fault; a speaker without energy is a lifeless statue.

In order to acquire a forcible manner of pronouncing your wordj, inure yourself while reading, to draw in as much air as your lungs can contain with ease, and to expel it with vehemence, in uttering those sounds which require an emphatical pronunciation; read aloud in the open air, and with all the exertion you can command; preserve your body in an erect attitude while you are speaking; let all the consonant sounds be expressed with a full impulse or percussion of the breath, and a forcible action of the organs employed in forming them; and let all the Vowel sounds, have a full and bold utterance; Practice these rules with perseverance, till you have acquired strength and energy of speech.

Bt!t in observing this rule, beware of running into the extreme of vociferation. We find this fault chiefly among those, who, in contempt and despite of all rule and propropriety, are determined to command the attention of the vulgar. These are the speakers, who in Shakespeare's phrase, "offend the judicious hearer to the soul, by tearing a passion to rags, to very tatters, to split the ears of the groundlings." Cicero compares such speakers to cripples, who get on horseback because they oannot walk; they bellow, because they cannot speak.

RULE IIT. *Acquire a compass and variety in the Height of your voice.* THE monotony so much complained of in public speakers, is chiefly owing to the neglect of this rule. They generally content themselves with ene certain key which they employ on all occasions, and on every subject; or if they attempt variety, it is only in proportion to the number of their hearers, and the extent of the places in which, they speak; imagining that speaking in a high key, is the same thing as speaking loud; and not observing, that whether a speaker shall be heard or not, depends more upon the distinctness and force with which he utters his words, than upon the height, at which he pitches his voice.

But it is an essential qualification of a good speaker, to he able to alter the height, as well as the strength and the tone of his voice, as occasion requires. Different species of speaking require different heights of voice. Nature instructs us to relate a story, to support an argument, to command a servant, to utter exclamations of anger or rage, and to pour forth lamentations and sorrows, not only with different tones, but different elevations of voice.— Men at different ages of life, and in different situations, speak in very different keys. The vagrant, when he begs; the soldier, when he gives the word of command; the watchman, when he announces the hour of the night; the sovereign, when he issues his edict; the senator, when he harangues; the lover, when he whispers his tender tale, do not differ more in the tones which they use, than in the key in which they speak. Reading and speaking, therefore, in which all the variations of expression in real life are copied, must have continued variations in the height of the voice.

To acquire the power of changing the key on which you speak at pleasure, accustom yourself to pitch your voice in different key3, from the lowest to the highest notes you command. Many of those would neither be proper nor agreeable in speaking; but the exercise will give you such a command of voice as is scarcely to be acquired by any other method. Having repeated the experiment till you can speak with ease at several heights'of the voice; read, as exercises on this rule, such compositions as have a variety of speakers, or such as relate dialogues, observing the height of voice which is proper to each, and endeavouring to change them as nature directs.

In the same composition there may be frequent occasions to alter the height of the voice, in passing from one part to another, without any change of person. Shakespeare's "All the world's a stage," &c. and his description of the Queen of the Fairies, afford examples of this. Indeed every sentence which is read or spoken will admit of different elevations of the voice in different parts of it; and on this chiefly, perhaps entirely, depends the *melody* of pronunciation.

RULE IV.

Pronounce *your words with propriety and elegance.* IT is not easy indeed to fix upon your standard, by Yvhich the propriety of pronunciation is to be determined. Mere men of learning, in attempting to make the etymology of words the rule of pronunciation, often pronounce Words in a manner, which brings upon them the charge of affectation and.pedantry. Mere men of the world, notwithstanding all their politeness, often retain so much of their provincial dialect, or commit such errours both in speaking and writing, as to exclude them from the honour of being the standard of accurate pronunciation. We should perhaps look for this standard only among those-who unite these two characters, and with the correctness and precision of true learning combine the ease and elegance of genteel life. An attention to such models, and a free intercourse with the polite world, are the best guards against the peculiarities and vulgarisms of provincial dialects. Those which respect the pronunciation of words are innumerable. Some of the principal of them are—omitting the aspirate *h* where it ought to be used, and inserting it where there should be none: Confounding and interchanging the *v* and *w;* pronouncing the dipthong *ou* like *au* or like *oo,* and the vowel i like »*i* or «; and cluttering many consonants together without regarding the vowels. These faults, and all.others of the same nature, must be corrected.in the pronunciation of a gentleman, who is supposed to have seen too much of the world, to retain the peculiarities of the district in which he. was born.

RULE V. *Pronounce every word consisting of more than one syllable with its proper Accent.* THERE is a necessity for this direction, because many speakers have affected an unusal and pedantic mode of accenting words, laying it down as a rule, that the accent should be east as far backwards as possible; a rule which has no foundation in the construction of the English language, or in the laws of harmony. Iu accenting words, the general custom and a good ear are the best guides: Only it may be observed that accent should be regulated, not by any arbitrary rules of quantity, or by the false idea that there are only two lengths in syllables and that two short syllables are always equal to one long, but by the number and nature of the simple sounds. RULE VI. *In every Sentence, distinguish the more* Significant Words *by a natural, forcible and varied emphasis.* EMPHASIS points out the precise meaning of a sentence, shews in what manner one idea is connected with and rises out of another, marks the several clauses of a sentence, gives to every part its proper sound, and thus conveys to the mind of the reader the full import of the-whole. It is in the power of emphasis to make long and complex sentences appear intelligible and perspicuous. But for this purpose it is necessary that the reader should be perfectly acquainted with the exact construction and full meaning of every sentence which he recites. Without this it is impossible to give those inflections and variations to the voice, which nature requires; and it is for want of this previous study, more perhaps than from any other cause, that »e so often hear persons read with an improper emphasis, or with no emphasis at all, that is, with a stupid monotony. Much study and pains is necessary in acquiring the habit of just and forcible pronunciation; and it can only be the effect of close attention and

long practice, to be able with a mere glance of the eye, to read any.piece with *good emphasis and good discretion.* -Tt H another office of emphasis to express the opposition between the several parts of a sentence where the style is pointed and antithetical. Pope's Essay on Man, and his Moral Essays, and the Proverbs of Solomon, will furnish many proper exercises in this species of speaking. In some sentences the antithesis is double, and even treble? these must be expressed in reading, by a very distinct emphasis on each part of the opposition. The following instances are of this kind: Anger may glance into the breast of a wise man; but rests only in the bosom of fools.

An angry man who suppresses his passion, thinks worse than he speaks; and an angry man that will chide speaks worse than he thinks.

Better reign in hell, than serve in heaven.

He rais'd a mortal to the skies; She brought an angel down.

Emphasis likewise serves to express some particular meaning not immediately arising from the words, but depending upon the intention of the speaker, or some incidental circumstance. The following short'sentence may have three different meanings, according to the different places of the emphasis; Do *you* intend to go to *London this summer?*

In order to acquire a habit of speaking with a just aiid. forcible emphasis, nothing more is necessary than previously to study the construction, meaning and spirit of every sentence, and to adhere as nearly as possible to the manner in which we distinguish one word from another in conversation; for in familiar discourse we scarce ever fail to express ourselves emphatically, or place the emphasis improperly. With respect to artificial helps, such as distinguishing words or clauses of sentences by particular characters or marks; I believe it will always be found,. upon trial, that they mislead, instead of assist the reader, by not leaving him at full liberty to follow his own understanding and feelings.

The most common faults respecting emphasis are laying so strong an emphasis on one word as to leave no power of giving a particular force to other words, which, though not equally, are in a certain degree emphatical; and placing the greatest stress on conjunctive particles, and other words of secondary importance. These faults are strongly characterized in Churchill's censure of Mossop.

With studied improprieties of speech He soars beyond the hackney critic's refeth.

To epithets allots emphatic state, Whitst principles, ungrac'd like lacquies wait;

In ways first trodden by himself excells

And stands alone in undeclinabl's; Conjunction, preposition, adverb, join

To stamp new vigour on the nervous line.

In monosyllables his thunders roll He, Shis, It, And, We., Ye, They, fright the seut.

Emphasis is often destroyed by an injudicious attempt to read melodiously. Agreeable inflections and easy variations of the voice, as far as they arise from, or are consistent with just speaking, are worthy of attention. But to substitute one unmeaning tone, in the room of all the proprieties and graces of good elocution, and then to applaud this manner, under the appellation of *musical* speaking, can only be the effect of great ignorance and inattention, or of a depraved taste. If public speaking roust be musical, let the words be set to music in recitative, that these melodious speakers may no longer lie open to the sarcasm: *Do you read or sing? If you sing, you sing very ill.* Seriously, it is much to be wondered at that this kind of reading, which has so little merit considered as music, and none at all considered as speaking, should be so studiously practised by many speakers, and so much admired by many hearers. Can a method of reading, which is so entirely different from the usual manner of conversation, be natural and right.B Is it possible that all the varieties of sentiment which a public speaker has occasion to introduce, should be properly expressed by one melodious tone and cadence, employed alike on all occasions, and for all purposes?

RULE VIL *Acquire a just variety of* Pause *and* Cadence. ONE of the worst faults a speaker can have, is to make no other pauses, than what he finds barely necessary for breathing. I know of nothing that such a speaker can so. property be compared to, as an alarm bell, which, when once set a going, clatters on till the weight that moves it is run down. Without pauses, the sense must always appear confused and obscure, and often be misunderstood; and the spirit and energy of the piece must be wholly lost.

In executing this part of the office of a speaker, it will by no means be sufficient to attend to the points used in printing; for these are far from marking all the pauses-which ought to be made in speaking. A mechanical attention to these resting places has perhaps been one chief cause of monotony, by leading the reader (io an uniform cadence at every full peiiod. The use of points is to assist the reail er in discerning the grammatical construction, not to c'irect his pronunciation. In reading, it may often be pi t per to make a pause where the printer has made none. Nay, it is very allowable for the sake of pointing out the sense more strongly, preparing the audience for what is to follow, or enabling the speaker to alter the tone or height of the voice, sometimes to make a very considerable pause, where the grammatical construction requires none at.all. In doing this, however, it is necessary that in the word immediately preceding the pause, the voice be kept up in such a manner as to intimate to the hearer that the sense is not completed. Mr. Garrick, the first of speakers, often observed this rule with great success. This particular excellence Mr. Sterne has described in his usual sprightly manner. See the following work, Eook VI, Chapter III.

Before a full pause it has been customary in reading to drop the voice in an uniform manner; and this has been called the *cadence.* But surely nothing

can be more destructive of all propriety and energy than this habit. The tones and heights at the close of a sentence ought to be infinitely diversified, according to the general nature of the discourse, and the particular construction and meaning of the sentence. In plain narrative, and especially in argumentation, the least attention to the manner in wliich we relate a story, or support an argument in conversation, will shew, that it is more frequently proper to raise the voice, than to fall it at the end of a sentence. Interrogatives, where the speaker seems to expect an answer, should almost always be elevated at the close, with a particular tone, to indicate that a question is asked. Some sentences are so constructed, that the last words require a stronger emphasis than any of the preceding; while others admit of being closed with a soft and gentle sound.

Where there is nothing in the sense which requires the last sound to be elevated or emphalical, an easy fall sufficient to shew that the sense is finished, will be proper. And in pathetic pieces, especially those of the plaintive, tender or solemn kind, the tone of the passion will often require a still greater cadence of the voice. But before a speaker can be able to fall his voice with propriety and judgment at the close of a sentence, he must be able to keep it from falling, and raise it with all the variation-which the sense requires. The best method of correcting a uniform cadence is frequently to read select sentences, in which the style is pointed, and frequent *antitheses* are introduced, and argumentative pieces or such as abound with interrogatives.

Rule vnr.

Accompany the Emotions and Passiotis which your ward express, by correspondent Tones, Looks *and* Gestures. THERE is the language of emotions and passions as well as of ideas. To express the latter is the peculiar province of words; to express the former, nature teaches us to make use of tones, looks and gestures. When anger, fear, joy, grief, love, or any oilier active passion arises in our minds, we naturally discover it by the particular manner in which we utter our

words; by the features of the countenance, and by other well known signs. And even when we speak without any of the more violent emotions, some kind of feeling usually accompanies our words, and this, whatever it be, hath its proper external expression. Expression indeed hath been so little studied in public speaking, that we-seem almost to have forgotten the Ian. guage of nature, and are ready to consider every attempt to recover it, as the laboured and effected effort of art. But nature is always the same;-and every judicious imitation of it will always be pleasing. Nor can any one deserve the appellation of a good speaker, much less of a complete orator, till to distinct articulation, a good command of voice, and just emphasis, he is able to add the various expressions of emotion and passion.

To enumerate these expressions, and describe them in all their variations is impracticable. Attempts have been made with some success to analyze the language of ideas; but the language of sentiment and emotion has never yet been analyzed; and perhaps it is not within the reach of human ability, to write a philosophical grammar of the passions. Or if it were possible in any degree to execute this design, I cannot think, that from such a grammar it would be possible for any one to instruct himself in the use of the language. All endeavours therefore to make men orators by describing to them in words the manner in which their voice, countenance and hands are to be employed, in expressing the passions, must in my apprehension, be weak and ineffectual. And, perhaps, the only instruction which can be given with advantage on this head, is this general one: Observe in what manner the several emotions or passions are expressed in real life, or by those who have with great labour and taste acquired a power of imitating nature; and accustom yourself either to follow the great original itself, or the best copies you meet with, always however, "with this special observance, that you overstep not the modesty of nature. "

In the application of these rules to

practice, in order to acquire a just and graceful elocution, it will be necessary to go through a regular course of exercises; beginning with such as are most easy, and proceeding by slow steps to such as are most difficult. In the choice of these, the practitioner should pay a particular attention to his prevailing defects, whether they regard articulation, command of voice, emphasis or cadence: And he should content himself with reading and speaking with an immediate view to the correcting of his fundamental faults, before he aims at any thing higher. This-may be irksome and disagreeable; it may require much patience and resolution; but it is the only way to succeed. For if a man cannot read simple sentences, or plain narrative, or didactic pieces, with distinct articulation, just emphasis, and proper tones, how can he expect to do justice to the sublime descriptions of poetry, or the animated language of the passions?

In performing these exercises, the learner should daily read aloud by himself, and as often as he has an opportunity; under the direction of an instructor or friend. He should also frequently recite compositions *memorilcr.* This method has several advantages: It obliges the speaker to dwell upon the idea which he is to express, and hereby enables him to. discern their particular meaning and force, and gives him a previous knowledge of the several inflections, *emphasis* and tones which the words require. And by taking-his eyes from the book, it in part relieves him from the iufluence of the schoolboy habit of reading in a different key and tone from that of conversation; and gives him greater liberty to attempt the expression of the countenance and gesture.

It were much to be wished, that all public speakers would deliver their thoughts and sentiments, either from memory or immediate conception: For, besides that, there is an artificial uniformity which almost always distinguishes reading from speaking, the fixed posture, and the bending of the head, which reading requires, are inconsistent vy+th the freedom, ease and variety of just

elocution. But if this is too much to be expected, especially from preachers, who have so much to compose, and are so often called upon to speak in public; it is however extremely desirable, that they should make themselves so well acquainted with their discourse as to be able with a single glance of the eye, tq take ia several clauses, or the whole of a sentence.

PART I. LESSONS IN SECTION I. SELECT SENTENCES.

I.

MAN's chief good is an upright mind, which no earthly power can bestow, nor take from him.

We ought to distrust our passions, even when they appear-the most reasonable.

It is idle as well as absurd to impose our opinions upon others. The same ground of conviction operates differently on the same man in different circumstances, and on different men in the same circumstances, "Choose what is most fit; custom will make it the most agreeable.

A cheerful countenance betokens a good heart.

Hypocrisy is a' homage that vice pays to virtue.

Anxiety and constraint are the constant attendants of pride.

Men make themselves ridiculous, not so much by the qualities they have, as by the affectation of those they have not.

Nothing blunts the edge of ridicule so effectually as good humour.

To say little and perfonn much, is the chai acteristic of a great mind.

A man who gives his children a habit of industry, provides for them better than giving them a stock of money. II

OUR good or bad fortune depends greatly Oh the choice we make of our friends.

The young are slaves to novelty, the old to custom.

No preacher is so successful as time. It gives a turn of thought to the aged, which it was impossible to inspire while they were young.

Every man, however little, makes a figure in his own eyes

Self-partiality hides from us those

very faults in ourselves, which we see and blame in others.

The injuries we do, and those we suffer are seldom weighed in the same balance.

Men generally put a greater value upon the favours they bestow, than upon those they receive.

He who is puffed up with the first gale of prosperity, will bend beneath the first blast of adversity.

Adversity borrows its sharpest sting from our impatience..

Men commonly owe their virtue or their vice, to education as much as to nature.

There is no such fop as my young master, of his lady mother's making. She blows him up with self-conceit and there she stops. She makes a man of him at twelve, and a boy all his life after.

An infallible way to make your child miserable, is to satisfy all his demands. Passion swells by gratification; and the impossibility of satisfying every one of his desires will oblige you to stop short at last, after he has become headstrong.,

III.

WE esteem most things according to their intrinsic merit; it is strange, Man should be an exception. We prize a horse for his strength and courage, not for his furniture. We prize a man for his sumptuous palace, his great train, his vast revenue; yet these are his furniture, 'not his mind.

The true conveniences of life are common to the king with his meanest subject. The king's sleep is not sweeter, nor his appetite better.

The pomp which distinguishes the great man from the mob, defends him not from the fever, nor from grief. Give a prince all the names of majesty thaf are found in a folio dictionary, the first attack of the gout will make him forget his palace and his guards. If he be in choler, will his princedom prevent him from turning pale, and gnashing his teeth like afool? The smallest prick of a nail, the slightest passion *j(* the soul, is capable of rendering insipid the monarchy of the world.

Narrow minds think nothing right that is above their own capacity. '.

Those who are the most faulty, are the most prone to find fault in others..

The first and most important female quality is sweetness of temper. Heaven did not give to the female sex insinuation and persuasion, in order to be surly; it did not make them weak in order to be imperious; it did not give them a sweet voice in order to be employed in scolding; it did not provide them with delicate features in order to be disfigured with anger.

Let fame be regarded, but conscience much more. It is an empty joy to appear better than you are; but a great blessing to be what you ought to be.

Let your conduct be the result deliberation, never of impatience.

In the conduct of life, let it be one great aim to show that ever-thing you do proceeds from yourself, not from your. passions. Chrysippus rewards in joy, chastises in wrath, doth every thing in passion. No person stands in awe of Chrysippus, no person is grateful to him. Why? Because it is not Chrysippus who acts, but his passiops. We shun him in wrath, as we shun a wild beast; and this is all the authority he hath over us.

Indulge not desire, at the expence of the slightest article of virtue; pass once its limits, and you fall headlong into vice.

Examine well the counsel that favours your dpsires.

The gratification of desire *is* sometimes the worst thing that can befal us.

IV. TO be angry, is to punish myself for the fault of another.

A word dropped by chance from your friend, offends your delicacy. Avoid a hasty reply; and beware of opening your discontent t» the first person you meet When you are cool it will vanish, and leave no impression.

The most profitable revenge, the most rational, and the most pleasant, is to make it the interest of the injurious person, not to hurt you a second time.

It was a saying of Socrates, that we should eat and drink in order to live; instead of living,as many do, in order to eat and drink.

Be moderate in your pleasures, that your relish for them may continue.

Time is requisite to bring great projects to maturity.

Precipitation ruins the host contrived plan; patience ripens the most difficult.

When we sum up the miseries of life, the grief bestowed on trifles makes a great part of the account; trifles which, neglected, are nothing. How shameful such a weakness!

The pensionary de Witt being asked how he could transact such a variety of business without confusion, answered, that he never did hut one thing at a time.

Guard your weak side from being known. If it be attacked, the best way is to join in the attack.

Francis I, consulting with his generals how to lead his army over the Alps, into Italy, Amarel, his fool, sprung from a corner, and advised him to consult rather how to bring it back.

The best practical rule of morality is, never to do but what we are willing all the world should know.

Solicitude in hiding failings makes them appear the greater. It is a safer and easier course, frankly to acknowledge them. A man owns that he is ignorant; we admire his modesty. He says he is old; we scarce think him so. He declares himself poor; we do not believeit.

When you descant on the faults of others, consider whether you be not guilty of the same. To gain knowledge of ourselves, the best way is to convert the imperfections of others into a mirror, for discovering our own.

Apply yourself more toacquire knowledge than to show it. Men commonly take great pains to put off the little stock they have; but they take little pains to acquire more.

Never suffer your courage to be fierce, your resolution obstinate, your wisdom cunning, nor your patience sullen.

To measure all reason by our own, is a plain act oi injustice; it is an encroachment on the common rights of mankind.

If you would teach secrecy to others, begin with yourself. How can you expect another will keep your secret, when yourself cannot?

A man's fortune is more frequently made by his tongue than by his virtues;

and more frequently crushed by it than by his vices.

V.

EVEN self interest is a motive for benevolence. There are none so low, but may have it in their power to return a good office.

To deal with a man,' you must know his temper, by-which you can lead him; or his ends, by which you can persuade him; or his friends, by whom you can govern him.

The first ingredient in conversation is truth; the next good sense; the third good humor; the last, wit

The great errour in conversation is, to be fonder of speaking than of hearing. Few show more complaisance than to pretend to hearken, intent all the while upon what they themselves have to say, not considering, that to seek one's own pleasure, so passionately, is not the way to please others.

To bean Englishman in London, a Frenchman in Paris, a Spaniard in Madrid, is no easy matter, and yet it is necessary.

A man entirely without ceremony has need of great merit.

He who cannot bear a jest, ought never to make one.

In the deepest distress, virtue is more illustrious than vice in Its highest prosperity. - "

No man is so foolish but he may give good counsel at a time; no man so wise but he may err, if he take no counsel but his own.

He whose ruling passion is love of praise, is a slave to every one who has a tongue for detraction.

Always to indulge our appetites, is to extinguish them. Abstain, that you may enjojr.

To have your enemy in your power, and yet to do him good, is the greatest heroism.

Modesty, were it to be recommended for nothing else, leaves a man at ease, by pretending to little, whereas vain glory requires perpetual labour, to appear what one is not. If we have sense, modesty best sets it off; if not, best hides the want.

When, even in the heat of dispute, I

yield to. my antagonist, my victory over myself is more illustrious thart over him, had he yielded to me.

The refined luxuries of the table, besides enervating the body, poison that very-pleasure they are intended to promote; for, by soliciting the appetite, they exclude the greatest pleasure of taste, that which arises from the gratification of hunger.

VI.—*The Fox and the Goal.*—Dodsley's Fables. A FOX and a Goat travelling together, in a very sultry day, found themselves exceedingly thirsty; wjien looking round the country in order to discover a place where they might probably meet with water, they at length descried a clear spring, at the bottom of a well. They both eagerly descended; and having sufficiently allayed their thirst, began to consider how they should get out. Many expedients for that purpose, were mutually proposed and rejected. At last, the crafty Fox cried out with great joy—I have a thought just struck into my mind, which, I am confident, will extricate us out of our difficulty: Do you, said he to the Goat, only rear yourself up upon your hind legs, and test your fore feet against the side of the well. In this posture I will climb up to your head, from which I shall be able with a spring, to reach the top; and when I am once there, you are sensible it will be very easy for me to pull you out by the horns. The simple Goat liked the proposal well, and immediately placed himself as directed; by means of which, the Fox, without much difficulty gained the top. And now, said the Goat, give me the assistance you promised. Thou old fool, replied the Fox, hadst thou buthalf as much brains as beard, thou wouldst never have believed that I would hazard my own life to save thine. However, I will leave with tliee a piece of advice, which may be of service to thee hereafter, if thou shouldst have the good fortune to make thy escape: Never venture into a well again, before thou hast well considered how to get out of it. VIT *The Fox and the Stork—Its.* THE Fox, though, in general, more inclined to roguery than wit, had once a strong inclination to play the wag-with his

neighbour the Stork. He accordingly invited her to dinner in great form; but when it came upon the table, the Stork found it consisted entirely of different soups, served up in broad shallow dishes, so that-she could only dip in the end of her bill, but could not possibly satisfy her hunger. The Fox lapped it up very readily; and every now and then, addressing himself to bis guest, desired to know how she liked her entertainment; hope'd that every thing was seasoned to her mind; and protested he was very sorry to see her eat so sparingly. The Stork perceiving she was played upon, took no notice of it, but pretended to like every dish extremely; Snd, at parting, pressed the Fox so earnestly to return her visit, that he could not in civility refuse. The day arrived, and he repaired to his appointment; but to his great mortification, when dinner appeared, he found it composed of minced meat, served up in long narrow necked glasses; so that he was only tantalized with the sight of what it was impossible for him to taste. The Stork thrust in her loag bill and helped herself very plentifully; then, turning to Reynard, who was eagerly licking the outside of a jar, where some sauce had been spilled—I am very glad, said she, smiling, that you seem to have so good au appetite; I hope you will make as hearty a dinner at my table, as I did, the other day, at yours, Reynard hung down his head, and looked very much displeased. Nay, nay, said the Stork, don't pretend to be out of humour about the matter; they that cannot take a jest should never make one.

VIIL— *The Court of Death.—In.* DEATH, the l«ng of terrours, was determined to choose a prime minister; and his pale courtiers, the. ghastly train of diseases, were all summoned to attend; when eoch preferred his claim to the honour of this illustrious office. Fever urged the numbers he destroyed; cold Palsy set forth his pretensions, by shaking all his limbs; rmd Dropsy, by his swelled, unwieldly carcase. Gout hobbled up, and alledged his great power in racking every joint; and Asthma's inability to speak, was a strong though silent argument in favour of his claim.

Stone and Colic pleaded their violence; Plague his rapid progress in destruction; and Consumption, though slow, insisted that he was sure. In the midst of this contention, the court was disturbed with the noise of music, dancing, feasting and revelry; when immediately entered a lady, with a bold lascivious air, and a flushed and jovial countenance; she was attended on one hand by a troop of cooks and bacchanals; and on the other by a train of wanton youths and damsels, who danced, half naked, to the softest musical instruments; her name was Intemperance. She waved her hand, and thus addressed the crowd of diseases; give way ye sickly band of pretenders, nor dare to vie with my supeiiour merits in the service of this great monarch. Am I not your parent? the author of your beings? do ye not derive the power of shortening human life almost wholly from me? Who, then, so fit as myself for this important office? The grisly monarch grinned a smile of approbation, placed her at his right hand, and she immediately became his principal favourite and prune minister.

IX.—*The Partial Judge.—In.* A FARMER came to a neighbouring lawyer, expressing great concern for an accident which, he said, had just happened. One of your oxen, continued he, has been' gored by an unlucky bull of mine; and I should be glad to know how I am to make you reparation. Thou art a very honest fellow, replied the Lawyer, and wilt not think it unreasonable, that I expect one of thy oxen in return. It is no more than justice, quoth the Farmer, to be sure: But, what did I say?—I mistake. It is your bull that has killed one of my oxen. Indeed! says the Lawyer; that alters the case: I must inquire into the affair; and if— And Ip! said the Farmer—the business, I find, would have been concluded without an Ip, had you been as ready to do justice to others, as to exact it from them.

X.—*Tlie sick Lion, the Fox, and the Wolf.*—Ir. A LION, having surfeited himself with feasting too luxuriously on the carcase of a wild Boar, was seized with a violent and dangerous disorder. The beasts of the forest flocked, in great numbers, to pay their respects to him upon the occasion, and scarce one was absent except the Fox. The Wolf an ill-naturcd and malicious beast, seized this opportunity to accuse the Fox of pride, ingratitude and disaffection,.to his majesty. In the midst of this invective, the Fox entered; who, having heard part of the Wolf's accusation, and observed the Lion's countenance to be kindled into wrath, thus adroitly accused himself, and retorted upon his accuser: I see many here, who, with mere lip service, have pretended to show you fi;tir loyalty; but, for my part, from the moment I heard of your majesty's illness, neglecting useless compliments, I employed myself, day and night, to inquire, among the most learned physicians, an infallible remedy for your disease, and have, at length happily been informed of one. It is a plaster made of part of a Wolf's skin taken warm from his back, and laid to your majesty's stomach. This remedy was no sooner proposed than it was determined that the experiment should be tried; and whilst the operation was performing, the Fox, with a sarcastic smile, whispered this useful maxim in the Wolf's ear; if you would be safe from harm yourself, learn, for the future, not to meditate mischief against others.

XI.—*Dishonesty punislied.*—Kane's Hmts. AN usurer, having lost a hundred pounds in a bag, promised a reward of ten pounds to the person who should restore it. A man having brought it to him, demanded the reward. The usurer, loth-to give the reward, how that he had got the bag, alleged, after the bag was opened, that there was an hundred and ten pounds in it, when he lost it. The usurer, being called before the judge, unwarily acknowledged that the seal was broken open in his presence, and that there was no more at that time but a hundred pounds in the bag. "You say," says the judge, "that the bag you lost had a hundred and ten pounds in it." "Yes, my lord." "Then," replied the judge, " this cannot be your bag, as it contained but a hundred pounds j therefore the plaintiff must keep it till the true owner appears; and you must look for your bag where you can find it." XII. — *The Picture* In.'.

Sir William Lely, a famous painter in the reign of Charles I. agreed beforehand, for the price of a picture he was to draw for a rich London Alderman, who was not indebted to nature, either for shape or face. The picture being finished, the Alderman endeavoured to beat down the price, alleging, that if he did not purchase it, it would lie on the painter's hand. "That's your mistake," says Sir William; "for I can sell it at double the price I demand." "How can that be," says the Alderman, " foe 'iis l,ke nobody but myself?" "True," replied Sir William; "but I can draw a tail to it, and then it will be an excellent monkey." Mr. Alderman, to prevent being *exr* posed, paid down the money demanded, and carried off the picture.

XITI.—*The tioo Bees.*—Dodsley's Farles. ON a fine morning in May two Bees set forward in quest of honey; the one wise and temperate, the other careless and extravagant. They soon arrived at a garden enriched with aromatic herbs, the most fragrant flowers, and the most delicious fruits. They regaled themselves for a time, on the various dainties that were spread before iliem; the one loading his thigh, at intervals, with provisions for the hive, against the distant winter; the other reveling in sweets, without regard to any thing but his present gratification. At length they found a wide mouthed phial, that hung beneath the bough of a peach tree, Jilled with honey, ready tempered, and exposed to their faste, in the most alluring manner. The thoughtless epicure, in spite of all his friend's remonstrances, plunged headlong into the vessel, resolving to indulge himself in all the pleasures of sensuality. The philosopher, on the other hand, sipped a little with caution, but, being snspicious of danger, new off to fruits and flowers, where, by the moderation of his meals, he improved Lis relish for the true enjoyment of them. In the evening, however, he called upon bis friend, to inquire whether he would return to the hive; but lie found him surfeited in sweets, which he was as unable to leave

as to enjoy. Clogged in li'rs wings, enfeebled iu his feet, and his whole frame together enervated, he was but just able to bid his friend adieu, and to lament, with his latest breath, that, though a taste of pleasure might quicken the ielish of life, an unrestrained indulgence is inevitable destruction. XIV.—*Btauty and deformity.*—Percival's Tales. A YOUTH, who lived in the country, and who had not acquired, either by reading or conversation, any knowledge of the animals which inhabit foreign regions came to Manchester, to sec an exhibition of wild beasts. The size and figure of the Elephant struck him with awe; and he viewed the Rhinoceros with astonishment. But his attention was soon drawn from these animals, and directed to another, of the most elegant and beautiful form; and lie stood contemplating with silent admiration the glossy smoothness of his hair, the blackness and regularity of the 'Streaks with wliich he was marked, the symmetry of his limbs, and above all, the placid sweetness of his countenance. What is the name of this lovely animal, said he to the keeper, which you have placed near one of the ugliest beasts in your collection, as if you meant to contrast beauty with deformity? Beware, young man, replied the intelligent keeper, of being so easily captivated with external appearance. The animal which you admire is called a Tiger; and notwithstanding the meekness of his looks he is fierce and savage beyond description: I can neither terrifv him by correctionnor tame him by indulgence. But the other beast, which you despise, is in the highest degree docile, affectionate and useful. For the benefit of man, he traverses the sandy deserts of Arabia, where drink and pasture are seldom to be found; and will continue six or seven days without sustenance, yet stitl pa« tient of labour. His hair is manufactured into cloathing; his flesh is deemed wholesome nourishment and the milk of the female is much valued by the Arabs. The Camel, therefore, for such is the name given this animal, is more worthy of your admiration than the Tiger; notwithstanding the inelegance of make, and the two bunches upon his back. For mere external beauty is of little estimation; and deformity, when associated with amiable dispositions and useful qualities, does not preclude our respect and approbation. XV. —*Remarkable instance of Friendship.* —

Art Of Speaking. DAMON and Pythias, of the Pythagorean sect in philosophy, lived in the time of Dionysius, the tyrant of Sicily. Their mutual friendship was so strong that they were ready to die for one another. One of the two (for it is not known which) being condemned to death by the tyrant, obtained leave to go into his own country, to settle his affairs, on condition that the other should consent to be imprisoned in his stead, and put to death for hin, if he did not return before the day of execution. The attention of every one, and especially of the tyrant himself, was excited to the highest pitch, as every body was curious to see what would be the event of so strange an affair. When the time was almost elapsed, and he who was gone did not appear; the rashness of the other, whose sanguine friendship had put him upon running so seemingly desperate a hazard, was universally blamed. But he still declared, that he had not the least shadow of doubt in hi mind, of his friend's fidelity. The event showed how well he knew him. He came in due time, and surrendered himself to that fate, which he had no reason to think he should escape; and which he did not desire to escape, by leaving his friend to suffer in his place. Such fidelity softened even the savage heart of Dionysius himself. He pardoned the condemned; he gave the two friends to one another, and begged that they would take himself in for a third.

XVI.—*Dionysius and Damocles.*—*Ab.* 'DIONYS1US, the tyrant of Sicily, showed how far he was from being happy, even whilst he abounded in riches, and all the pleasures which riches can procure. Damocles, one of his flatterers, was complimenting him upon his power, his treasures, and the magnificence of his royal state, and affirming, that no monarch ever was greater Of happier than he. "Have you a mind Damocles," says the king, " to taste this happiness and know by experience, what my enjoyments are, of which you have so high an idea?" Damocles gladly accepted the offer. Upon which (lie king ordered that a royal banquet should be prepared, and a gilded couch placed for him, eovered with rich embroidery, and sideboards loaded with gold and silver plate of immense value. Pages of extraordinary beauty were ordered to wait on him at table, and to obey his commands with the greatest readiness, and the most profound submission. Neither ointments, chaplets of flowers, nor rich perfumes were wanting. The table was loaded with the most exquisite delicacies of every kind. Damocles fancied himself amongst the gods In the midst of all his happirfess, he sees let down from the roof, exactly over his neck, as lie lay indulging himself in state, a glittering sword, hung by a single hair. The sight of destruction, thus threatening him from on high, soon put a stop to his joy and revelling. The pomp of his attendance, and the glitter of the carved plate gave him no longer any pleasure. He dreads to stretch forth his hand to the table; he throws off the chaplet of roses; he hastens to remove from his dangerous situation; and at last, begs the king to restore him to his former humble condition, having no desire to enjoy any longer, such a dreadful kind of happiness. XVII.—*Cliaracter of CataHne.-SAi.LvsT.* LUCIUS CATALINE, by birth a Patrician, was, by nature, endowed with superiour advantages, both bodily and mental' but his dispositions were corrupt and wicked. From his youth, his supreme delight was in violence, slaughter, rapine and intestine confusions; and such works were the employment of his earliest years. His constitution qualified him for bearing hunger, cold and want of sleep, to a degree exceeding belief. His mind was daring, subtle, unsteady. There was no character which he could not assume, and put off at pleasure Rapacious of what belonged to others, prodigal of his own, violently bent on whatever became the object of his pursuit. He possessed a considerable share of eloquence, but little solid knowledge. His insatiable temper was ever pushing him to grasp at what was immoderate, romantic and out of his reach.

About the time of the disturbances raised by Sylla, Cataline was seized by a violent lust of power j nor did he at all hesitate about the means, so be could but attain bis purpose of raising himself to supreme dominion. His restless spirit was in a continual ferment, occasioned by the confusion of his own private affairs, and by the horrors of his guilty conscience; both which he had brought upon himself, by living the life above described. He was encouraged in his ambitious projects by the general corruption of manners, which then prevailed amongst a people infested with two vices, not less opposite to one another in their natures, than mischievous in their tendencies; I mean Luxury and Avarice.

XVIII.—*Avarice and Luxury.*—Spectator. THEHE were two very powerful tyrants engaged in a perpetual war against each other; the name of the first was Luxury, and of the second Avarice. The aim of each of them, was no less than universal monarchy over the hearts of mankind. Luxury had many generals under him, who did him great service; as Pleasure, Mirth, Pomp and Fashion. Avarice was likewise very strong in his officers, being faithfully served by Hunger, Industry, Care and Watchfulness; he had likewise a privy counsellor, who was always at his elbow, and whispering something or other in his ear; the name of this privy counsellor was Poverty. As Avarice conducted himself by the counsels of Poverty, his antagonist was entirely guided by the dictates and advice of Plenty, who was hisfi'St counsellor and minister of state, that concerted all his measures for him, and never departed out of his sight. While these two great rivals were thus contending for Empire, their conquests were very various. Luxury got possession of one heart, and Avarice of another. Tha father of the family would often range himself under the banners of Avarice, and the son under those of Luxury. The wife and husband would often declare themselves of the two different parties; nay, tiie same person would very often side with one in his youth, and revolt to the other in old age. Indeed, the wise men of the world stood neuter; but alas! their numbers were not considerable. At length, when these two potentates had wearied themselves with waging war. upon one another, they agreed upon an interview, at which neither of the counsellors was to he present It is said that Luxury began the parley; and after having represented the endless state of war in which they were engaged, told his enemy, with a frankness of heart which is natural to him, that he believed they two should be very good friends, were it not for the instigations of Poverty, that pernicious counsellor, who made an ill use of his ear, and filled him with groundless apprehensions and prejudices. To this Avarice replied that he looked upon Plenty, (the first minister *of* his antagonist) to be a much more destructive counsellor than Poverty: For that he was perpetually suggesting pleasures, banishing all the necessary cautions against want, and consequently undermining those principles on which the government df Avarice was founded. At last, in order to an accommodation, they agreed upon this preliminary; that each of thpm should immediately dismiss his privy counsellor. When things were thus far adjusted towards a peace, all other differences were s?5on accommodated;-insomuch, that for the future, they resolved to live as good friends and confederates, and to share between them whatever conquests were made on either side. For this reason we now find Luxury and Avarice taking possession of the same heart, and dividing the same person between them. To which I shall only add, that since the discarding of the counselors abovementioned, Avarice supplies Luxury, in the room of Plenty, as Luxury prompts Avarice, in the place of Poverty.

XfX.—*Hercuks's Choicer-TATThtr.*. WHEN Hercules was in that part of his youth, in which it was natural-for him to consider what course of life he ought to pursue, he one day retired into a desert, where the silence and solitude of the place very much favoured his meditations. As he was musing on his piesent condition, and very much perplexed in himself, on the state of life he shpuld choose, he saw two women of a larger stature than ordinary, approaching towards him. One of them had a very noble air and graceful deportment; her beauty was natural and easy, her person clean and unspotted, her eyes cast towards the ground, with an agreeable reserve, her motion-and behaviour full of modesty, and her raiment as white as snow. The other had a great deal of health and floridness in her countenance, which she had helped with an artificial white and red; and she endeavoured to appear more graceful than ordinary in her mien, by a mixture of affectation in all her gestures. She had a wonderful confidence and assurance in her looks, and all the variety of colours in her dress, that she thought were the most proper to show her complexion to advantage. She cast her eyes upon herself, then turned them on those that were present, to see how they liked her; and often looked on the figure she made in her own shadow. Upon her nearer approach to Hercules, she stepped before the other lady who came forward with a regular composed carriage; and running up to him, accosted him after the following manner: *"My* dear Hercules," says she, "I find you are very mud: divided in your thoughts, upon the way of life that you ought to choose; be my friend, and follow me; I will lead you into the possession of pleasure, and out of the reach of pain, and remove you from all the noise and disquietude of business. The affairs of either war or peace shall have no power to disturb you. Your whole employment shall be to make your life easy, and to entertain every sense with its proper gratifications. Sumptuous tables, beds of roses, clouds of perfumes, concerts of music, crowds of beauties, are all in readiness to receive you. Come along with ineinto this region of delights, this world of pleasure, and bid farewell forever, to care, to pain, to business."

Hercules, hearing the lady talk after this manner, desired to know her name; to which she answered, "my friends, and those who are well acquainted with me, call me Happiness; but my enemies, and those who would injure my reputation, have given me the name of Pleasure."

By this time the other lady was come up, who addressed herself to the young hero in avery different manner.

"Hercules," says she, "I offer myself to you, because I know you are descended from the gods, and give proofs of that descent by your love to virtue, and application to the studies proper for your age. This makes me hope you will gain, both for yourself and me, an immortal reputation. But, before I invite you into my society and friendship, T will be open and sincere with you, and must lay down (his, as an established truth, that there is nothing truly valuable which can be purchased without pains and labour. The gods have set a price upon every real noble pleasure. If you would gain the favour of the Deity, you must be at the pains of worshipping him; if the friendship of good men, you must study to oblige them; if you would be honoured by your country, you must take care to serve it: In short, if you would be eminent in war or peace, you must become master of all the qualifications that can make you so. These are the only terms and conditions upon which I can propose happiness." The goddess of Pleasure here broke in upon her discourse: "You see," said she, "Hercules, by her own confession, the way to her pleasure is long and difficult; whereas, that which I propose is short and easy." "Alas!" said the other lady, whose visage glowed with passion, made up of scorn and pity, "What are the pleasures you propose? To eat before you are hungry, drink before you are athirst, sleep before you are tired; to gratify your appetites before they are raised, and raise such appetites as nature never planted; You never heard the most delicious music, which is the praise of one's self; nor saw the most beautiful object, which is the work of one's own hands. Your votaries pass away their youth in a dream of mistaken pleasures, while they are hoarding up anguish, torment and remorse for old age." c

"*As* for me, I am the friend of gods and of good men, an agreeable companion to the artisan, an household guardian to the fathers of families, a patron and protector of servants, an associate in ail true and generous friendships. The banquets of my votaries are never costly but always delicious; for none eat and drink at them, who are not invited by hunger and thirst. Their slumbers are sound, ard their wakings cheerful. My young men have the pleasure of hearing themselves praised by those who are in years; and those who are in years of being honoured hy those who are young. In a word, my followers are favoured by the gods, beloved by their acquaintance, esteemed by their country, and after the close of their labours, honoured by posterity."

We know, by the life of this memorable hero, to which of these two ladies he gave up his heart,-and 1 believe every one who reads this, will do him the justice to approve his choice.

XX.—*Will HoneyannVs Spectator.*— Spectator. MY friend, Will Honeycomb, has told me, for above this half year, that he had a great mind to try his hand at a Spectator, and that he would fain have one of his writings in my works. This morning I received from him the following letter; which after having rectified some little orthographical mistakes, I shall make a present of to the public.

"Dear Spec—I was about two nights ago in company with very agreeable young people, of both sexes, where talking of some of your papers, which are written on con Jugal love, there arose a dispute among us, whether there were not more bad husbands in the world than bad wives. A gentleman, who was advocate for the ladies, took this occasion to tell us the story of a famous siege in Germany, which I have since found related in my historical dictionary; after the following manner. When the Emperor Conrad III, had besieged Guelphus, Duke of Bavaria, in the city of Hensberg, the women, finding that the town could not possibly hold out long, petitioned the Emperor that they might depart out of it, with so much as each of them could carry. The Emperor, knowing they could not convey away many of their effects, granted them their petition; when the women, to his great surprise, came out of the place with every one her husband upon her back. The Emperor was so moved at the sight, that he burst into tears; and after having very much extolled the women for their conjugal affection, gave the men to their wives, and received the Duke into his favour.

"The ladies did not a little triumph at this story; asking us, at the same time, whether, in our consciences, we believed, that the men in any town of Great-Britain would, upon the same offer, and at the same conjuncture, have loaded themselves with their wives? Or rather, whether they would not have been glad of such an opportunity to get rid of them? To this my very good friend, Tom Dapperwit, who took upon him to be the mouth of our sex, replied, that they would be very much to blame, if they would not do the same good office for the women, consiaering that their strength would be greater, and their burdens lighter. As we were amusing ourselves with discourses of this nature, in order to pass away the evening, which now began to grow tedious, we fell into that laudable and primitive diversion of questions and commands. I was no sooner vested with the regal authority, but I enjoined all the ladies, under pain of my displeasure, to tell the company ingenuously, in case they had been ki the siege abovementioned, and had tive same offers made them as the good women of that place, what every one of them would have brought off with her, and hav£ thought most worth the saving. There were several merry answers made to my question, which entertained us. until bedtime, This filled my mind with such a huddle of ideas, that upon my going to sleep, I fell into the following dream:

"I saw a tawn of this island, which shall ba nameless, invested on every side, aud the inhabitants of it so straitened as to cry for quarter? The general refused any other terms than those granted to the abovementioned town of Hensberg, namely, that the married women might come out, with what they could bring along with them. Immediately the city gates flew open, and a female procession appeared, multitudes of the sex following one another in a row, and staggering under their respective burdens. I took my stand upon an eminenoe, in the enemy's camp, which was appointed for the general rendezvous of these female carriers, being very desirous to look into their several ladings. The first of them had a huge sack upon her shoulders, which she set down with great care; upon the opening of it,-when I expected to have seen her husband shot out of it, T found it was filled with China ware. The next appeared in a more decent figure, carrying a handsome young fellow upon her back: I could not forbear commending the young woman for her conjugal affection, when, to my great surprise, I found that she had left the good man at home, and brought away her gallant. 1 saw a third at some distance, with a little withered face peeping over her shoulder, whom I could not suspect for any but her spouse, till, upon her setting him down, I heard lier call him her dear pug, and found him to be her favourite monkey. A fourth brought a huge bale of cards along with her j and the fifth a Bologna lapdog j for her husband, it seems, being a very bulky man, she thought it would be less trouble for her to being away little Cupid. The next was the wife of a rich usurer, loaded with a bag of gold; she told us that her spouse was very old, and by the course of nature, could not expect to live long; and that to show her tender regard for him, she had saved that which the poor man loved better than his life. The next came towards as with Iter son upon her back, who we were told, was the greatest rake in the place, but so much the mother's darling, that she left her husband behind, with a large family of "hopeful sons and daughters, for the sake of this graceless youth.

"It would be endless to mention the several persons, with their several loads, that appeared to me in this strange vision. All the place about me was covered with packs of ribbands, broaches, embroidery, and ten thousand other materials, sufficient to have furnished a whole street of toyshops. One of the women, having an husband who was none of the heaviest, was bringing him off upon her shoulders, at the same time that she carried a great bundle of Flanders lace under her arm; but finding herself so overloaden that she could not save both of them, she dropped the good man, and brought away the bundle. In short, I found but one husband among this great mountain of baggage, who was a lively cobler, that kicked and spurred all the while his wife was carrying him off, and, as it was said, had scarce passed a day in his life, without giving her the discipline of the strap.

"I cannot conclude my letter, dear Spec, without telling thee one very odd whim in this my dream. I saw, methought, a dozen women employed in bringing off one man: I could not guess who it should be, till, upon his nearer approach, I discovered thy shoit phiz. The women all declared it was for the sake of thy works, and not thy person, that they brought thee off, and that it was on condition that thou shouldst continue the Spectator. If thou thinkest this dream will make a tolerable one, it is at thy service, from, dear Spec, thine, sleeping and waking,

Will Honeycomr."

The ladies will see by this letter, what *J* have often told them, that Will is one of those old fashioned men of wit and pleasure of the town, who show their parts by railery on marriage, and one who has often tried his fortune iiv that way, without success. I cannot, however, dismiss this letter, without observing, that the true story on which it is buiit, does honour to the sex; and that, in order to abuse them, the writer is obliged to have recourse to dream and fiction.

XXI.—*On Good Breeding.*—Chesterfield. A FRIEND of yours and mine has very justly defined good breeding to be, " the result of much good sense, some good nature and a little selfdeniai, for

the sake of others, and with a view to obtain the same indulgence from them ' Taking this for granted (as I think it cannot be disputed) it is astonishing to me, that any body, who has good sense and good nature, can essentially fail in good breeding. As to the modes of it, indeed, they vary according to persons, places and circumstances, and are only to be acquired by observation and experience; but the substance of it is every where and eternally the same. Good manners are, to particular societies, what good morals arc to society in general—their cement and their security. And as laws are enacted to enforce good morals, or at least to prevent the ill effects of bad ones; so there are certain rules of civility, universally implied and received, to enforce good manners, and punish bad ones. And indeed, there seems to me to be less difference both between the crimes and punishments, than, at first, one would imagine. The immoral ruan, who invades another's property, is justly hanged for it; and the illbred man, who, by his ill manners, invades and disturbs the quiet and comforls of private life, is, by common consent, as justly banished society. Mutual complaisances, attentions, and sacrifices of little conveniences, are as natural an implied compact between civilized people, as protection and obedience are between kings and subjects; whoever, in cither, case, violates that compact, justly forfeits all advantages arising from it. For my own part, I really think that, next to the consciousness of doing a good action, that of doing a civil one is-one of the most pleasing; and the epithet which I should covet the most, next to that of Aristides, would be that of wellbred. Thus much for good breeding, ki general; I will now consider some of the various mode and. degrees of it.

Very few, scarely any, are wanting in the respect which they should show to those whom they acknowledge to be highly their superiors; such as crowned heads, princes, and piblic persons of distinguished and eminent posts. It is the manner of showing that respect which is different. The roan of fashion

and of the world, expresses it in its fullest extent; but naturally, easily and without concern: Whereas, a man who is not used to keep good Company, expresses it awkwardly; one sees that he is not used to it, and that it costs him a great deal; but I never saw the worst bred man living, guilty of lolling, whistling, scratching his head, and such like indecencies, in company that he respected. In such companies therefore, the only point to be attended to is, to show that respect, which every body means to show, in an easy, unembarrassed, and graceful manner. This is what observation and experience must teach you.

la mixed companies, whoever is admitted to make part of them, is for the time at least, supposed to be upon a footing of equality with the rest; and, consequently, as there is no one principal object of awe and respect, people are apt to take a.greater Iatitude in their behaviour, and to be less upon their guard; and so they may, provided it be within certain bounds, which are, upon no occasion, to be transgressed. But upon these occasions, though no one is entitled to distinguished marks of respect, every one claims, and very justly, every mark of civility and good breeding. Ease is allowed, but carelessness and negligence are strictly forbidden. If a man accosts you,and talks to you ever so dully or frivolously, it is worse than rudeness is brutality, to show him by a manifest inattention to what lie says, that you think him a fool, or a blockhead, and not worth hearing. It is much more so with regard to women, who, of whatever rank they are, are en tilled, in consideration of their sex, not only to an attentive, but an officious good breeding from men. Their little wants, likings,dislikes, preferences, antipathies and fancies, must be officiously attended to, and if possible, guessed at and anticipated, by a wellbred man. You must never usurp to yourself those conveniences and gratifications which are of conunon right, such as the best places, the best dishes, &c. but on the contrary, always decline them. yourself and offer them to others, who in their turns will offer them to you; so that upon the whole, you will in your turn, enjoy your share of the common right. It would be endless for me to enumerate all the particular circumstances, in which a welibred man shows his good breeding, in good company; and it would be injurious to you to suppose, that your own good sense will not point them out to you; and then your own good nature will recommend, and your self interest enforce the practice.

There is a third sort of good breeding, in which people are the most apt to fail, from a very mistaken notion, that they cannot fail at all. I mean with regard te one's most familiar friends and acquaintances, or those who really are our inferiors; and there, undoubtedly, a greater degree of ease is not only allowable, but proper, and contributes much to the comforts of a private social life. But ease and freedom have their bounds, which must by no means be violated. A certain degree of negligence and carelessness becomes injurious and insulting, from the real or supposed inferiority of the persons; and that delightful liberty of conversation, among a few friends, is soon destroyed, as liberty often has been, by being carried to licentiousness. But example explains things best; and I will put a pretty strong case. Suppose you and me alone together; 1 believe you will allow, that I have as good a right to unlimited freedom in your company, as either you or J can possibly have in an)' other; and I am apt to believe, too, that you would indulge me in that freedom as far as any body would. But notwithstanding this, do you imagine that I should think there were no "bounds to that freedom? 1 assure you I should not think so; and 1 take myself to be as much tied down, by a certain degree of good manners to you, as by other degrees of them to other people. The most familiar and intimate habitudes, connexions, and friendships, require a degree of good breeding, both to preserve and cement them. The best of us have our bad sides; and it is as imprudent as it is ill bred, to exhibit them. I shall not use ceremony with you; it would be misplaced between us;

but I shall eertainly observe that degree of good breeding with you, which is, in the first place, decent, and which, 1 am sure, is absolutely necessary, to make us like one another's company long.

XXII.—*Address to a young Student.*— Knox. YOUR parents have watched over your helpless infancy, and conducted you, with many a pang, to an age at which your mind is capable of manly improvement.— Their solicitude still continues, and no trouble nor expence is spared, in giving you all the instructions and accomplishments which may enable you to act your part in life, as a man of polished sense and confirmed virtue. You have, then, already contracted a great debt of gratitude tothem. You can pay it by no other method, but by using properly the advantages which their goodness has afforded you.

If your own endeavours are deficient, it is m vain that you have tutors, books, and all the external apparatus of literary pursuits. You roust love learning, if you would possess it. In order to love it, you must feel its delights; in order to feel its delights, you must apply to it, however irksome at first, closely, constantly, and for a considerable time. If you have resolution enough to do this, you cannot but love learning; for the mind always loves that to which it has been long, steadily, and voluntarily attached. Habits are formed, which render what was at first disagreeable, not only pleasant but necessary.

Pleasant, indeed, are all the paths which lead to polite and elegant literature. Yours then, is surely a lot particularly happy. Your education is of such a sort, that its principal scope is, to prepare you to receive a refined' pleasure during your life. Elegance, or delicacy of taste, is one of the first objects of classical discipline; and it is this fine quality, which opens a new world to the scholar's view. Elegance of taste has a connexion with many virtues, and all of them virtues of the most amiable kind. It tends to render you, at once good and agreeable. You must, therefore, be an enemy to your own enjoyment, if you enter on. the discipline which leads to the attainment of a classical and liberal

education, with reluctance. Val ue duly the opportunities you enjoy, and which are denied to thousands of your fellow creatures.

Without exemplary diligence you will make but a contemptible proficiency. You may, indeed, pass through the forms of schools and universities; but you will bring notliing away from them, ©f real value. The proper sort and degree of diligence, you cannot possess, but by the efforts of your own resolution. Your instructor may indeed confine you within the walls of a school, a certain number of hours. He may place books before you, and compel you to fix your eyes upon them; but no authority can chain down your mind Your thoughts will escape from every external restraint, and, amidst the most serious lectures, may be ranging in the wild pursuits of trifles and vice. Rules, restraints, commands and punishments, may, indeed, assist in strengthening your resolution; but, without your own voluntary choice, your diligence will not often conduce to your pleasure and advantage. Tho' this truth is obvious, yet it seems to be a secret to those parents, who expect to find their son's improvement increase, in proportion to the number of tutors, and external assistance which their opulence has enabled them te provide. These assistances, indeed, are sometimes afforded, chiefly, that the young heir to a title or estate may indulge himself in idleness and nominal pleasures. The lesson is construed to him, and the exercise written for him, by the private tutor, while the hapless youth is engaged in some ruinous pleasure, which, at the same time, prevents him from learning any thing desirable, and leads to the formation of destructive habits, which can seldom be removed.

But the principal obstacle to your improvement at school, especially if you are too plentifully supplied with money, is a perverse ambition of being distinguished as a boy of spirit, in mischievous pranks, in neglecting the tasks and lessons, and for every vice and irregularity which the puerile age can admit. You will have sense enough, I hope, to discover, beneath the mask of gaiety and good nature, that malignaut spirit of detraction, which endeavours to render the boy who applies to books, and to all the duties and proper business of the school, ridiculous. You will see, by the light of your reason, that the ridicule is misapplied. You will discover, that the boys who have recourse to ridicule, are, for the most part, stupid, unfeeling, ignorant and vicious. Their noisy folly, their bold confidence, their contempt of learning, and their defiance of authority, are for the most part, the genuine effects of hardened insensibility. Let not their i» suits and ill treatment dispirit you. If you yield to them, with a tame and abject submission, they will not fail to triumph over you with additional insolence. Display a fortitude in your pursuits, equal in degree to the obstinacy in which they persist in theirs. Your fortitude will soon overcome theirs, which is, indeed, seldom any thing more than the audacity of a bully. Indeed, you cannot go through a school with ease to yourself, and with success, without a considerable share of courage. I do not mean that sort of courage which leads to battles and contentions, but which enables you to have a will of your own and to pursue what is rigi,t, amidst all the persecutions of surrounding enviers, dunces, and detractors. Ridicule is the weapon made use of at school, as well as in the world, when the fortresses of virtue are to be assailed. You will effectually repel the attack'by a dauntless spirit and unyielding perseverance. Though numbers are against you, yet, with truth and rectitude on your side, you may, though alone, be equal to an army.

By laying in a store of useful knowledge,' adorning your mind with elegant literature, improving and establishing your conduct by virtuous principles, you cannot fail of being a comfort to those friends who have supported you, of being happy with yourself, and of being well received by mankind. Honour and success in life will probably attend you. Under all circumstances, you will have an internal source of consolation and entertainment, of which no sublu-

nary vicissitude can deprive you. Time will show how much wiser has been your choice, than that of your idle companions, who would gladly have drawn you into their association, or rather into their conspiracy, as it has been called, against good manners, and against all that is honourable and useful. While you appear in society as a respectable and valuable member of it, they will, perhaps, have sacrificed at the shrine of vatii ity, pride and extravagance, and false pleasure, their health and their sense, their fortune and their characters.

XXIII.—*Advantages of and Motives to Cheerfulness.*

Sprcvatob CHEERFULNESS is in the first place the best promoter of health. Repinings, and secret murmurs of the heart, give imperceptible strokes to those delicate fibres of which the vital parts are composed, and wear out the machine insensibly; not to mention those violent ferments which they stir up in the blood, and those irregular, disturbed motions which they raise in the animal spirits. I scarce remember, in my own observation, to have met-wilh many old men, or with such who, (to use our English phrase) *wear well* that had not at least a certain indolence in their humour, if not a more than ordinary gaiety and cheerfulness of heart. The truth of it is, health and cheerfulness mutually beget each other, with this difference, that we seldom meet with a great degree of health, which is not attended with a Certain cheerfulness, but very Often see cheerfulness. where there is no degree of health.

Cheerfulness bears the same friendly regard to the mind as to the body; it banishes all anxious care and discontent, soothes and composes the passions and keeps the soul in a perpetual calm.

If we consider the world in its subserviency to man, one would think it was made for our use; but if we consider it in its natural beauty and harmony, one would be apt to conclude, it was made for our pleasure. The sun, which is the great soul of the universe, and produces all the necessaries of life, has a particular influence in cheering the mind of man, and making the heart glad.

Those several living Creatures which are made for our service or sustenance, at the same time either fill the voods with their music, furnish us with game or raise pleasing ideas in us by the delightfuliiess of their appearance. Fountains, lakes and rivers are as refreshing to the imagination, as to the soil through which they pass.

There are writers Of great distinction, who have made it an argument for Providence, that the whole earth is covered with green, rather than with any other colour, as being-such a right mixture of light and shade, that it comforts and strengthens the eye, instead of weakening or grieving it. For this reason, several painters have a green cloth hanging hear them, to ease the eye upon, after too great an application to their colouring. A famous modern philosopher accounts for it in the following manner: All colours that are more luminous, overpower and. dissipate the animal spirits which are employed in sight; on the contrary, those that are more obscure, do not give the animal spirits a sufficient exercise; whereas, the rays that produce in us the idea of green, fall upon the eye rn such a due proportion, that they give the animal spirits their proper play, and by keeping up the struggle in a just balance, excite a very pleasing and agreeable sensation. Let the cause be what it will, the effect is certain; for which reason the poets ascribe to this particular colour, the epithet of cheerful.

To consider further this double end in the works of nature and how they are at the same time both useful and entertaining, we find that the most important parts in the vegetable world, are those which are the most beautiful. These are the seeds by which the several races of plants are propagated and continued, and which are always lodged in flowers or blossoms. Nature seems to hide her principal design, and to be industrious in making the earth gay and delightful, while she is carrying on her great work, and intent upon her own preservation. The husbandman, after the same manner, is employed in laying out the whole country into a kind of garden or landscape, and making every thing smile about him, whilst, in reality he thinks of nothing, but of the harvest and increase which is to arise from it.

We may further observe how Providence has taken care to keep up this cheerfulness in the mind of man, by having formed it after such a manner, as to make it capable of conceiving delight from several objects which seem to have very little use in them; as from the wildness of rocks and deserts, and the like grotesque parts of nature. Those who are versed in philosophy, may still carry this consideration higher, by observing, that if matter had appeared to us endowed only with those real qualities which it actually possesses, it would have made but a very joyless and uncomfortable figure 5 and why has Providence given it a power of producing in us such imaginary qualities, as tastes and colours, sounds and smells, heat and cold, but that man, while he is conversant in the lower stations of nature, might have his mind cheered and delighted with agreeable sensations? In short, the whole universe is a kind of theatre, rilled with objects that either raise in us pleasure, amusement or admiration.

The readers own (lioughts will suggest to him the vicis situdes of day and night, the change of seasons, with all that variety of scenes which diversify the face of nature, and fill the mind with a perpetual succession of beautiful and pleasing images.

I shall not here mention the several entertainments of art, with the pleasures of friendship, books, conversation and other accidental diversions of life, because I would only take notice of such incitements to a cheerful temper, as offer themselves to persons of all ranks and conditions, and which may sufficiently shew us that Providence did not design this world should be filled with murmurs and repinings, or that the heart of maJshould be involved in gloom and melancholy. "

I the more inculcate this cheerfulness of temper, as it is a virtue in which our countrymen are observed to be more deficient than any other nation. Melancholy is a kind of demon that haunts our island, and often conveys herself to us in an easterly wind. A celebrated French novelist, in opposition to those who begin their romances with the flowery seasons of the year, enters on his story thus: "In the gloomy month of November, when the people of England hang and drown themselves, a disconsolate lover walked out into the fields," &c.

Every one ought to fence against the temper of his climate or constitution, and frequently to indulge in himself those considerations which may give him a serenity of mind and enable him to bear up cheerfully, against those little evils and misfortunes, which are common to human nature, and which, by right improvement of them, will produce a satiety of joy, and uninterrupted happiness.

At the same time thatl would engage my reader to consider the world in its most agreeable lights, I must own there are many evils which naturally spring up, amidst the entertainments that are provided for us; but these, if rightly considered, should be far from overcasting the mind with sorrow, or destroying that cheerfulness of temper which I have been recommending. This in'terspersion of evil witli good, and pain with pleasure, in the works of nature, is very truly ascribed, by Mr. Locke, in his essay on human understanding, to a moral reason, in the following words:

"Beyond all this, we may find another reason why God hath scattered up and down several degrees of pleasure and pain, in all the things that environ and affect us, and blended them together in almost all that our thoughts and senses have to do with; that we, finding imperfection, riissatisfaction, and want of complete happiness in all the enjoyments which the creatures can afford us, might be led to seek it in the enjoyment of Him, with whom there is fullness of joy, and at whose right hand are pleasures fornvermore." i . y SECTION II.

I.—*The bad Reader.*—Percival's Tales. JULIUS had acquired great credit at Cambridge, by his compositions. They were elegant, animated and judicious; and several prizes, at different times, had been adjudged to him. An oration which he delivered the week before he left the university, had been hououred with particular applause; and on his return home he was impatient to gratify his vanity, and to extend his reputation, by having it read to a number of his father's literary friends.

A party was therefore collected; and after dinner the manuscript was produced. Julius declined the office of reader, because he had contracted a hoarseness on his journey; and a conceited young man, with great forwardness, offered his services. Whilst he was settling himself on his seat, licking his lips and adjusting his mouth, hawking, hemming and making other ridiculous preparations, for the performance which he had undertaken, a profound silence reigned through the company, the united effect of attention and expectation. The reader at length began; but his toue of voice was so shrill and dissonant, his utterance so vehement, his pronunciation so affected, his emphasis so injudicious, and his accents were so improperly placed, that good manners alone restrained the laughter of the audience. Julius was all this while upon the rack, and his arm was more than once extended to snatch his composition from the coxcomb who delivered it. But he proceeded with full confidence in his own elocution; uniformly overstepping, as Shakespeare expresses it, the modesty of nature.

When the oration was concluded, the gentlemen returned their thanks to the author; but the compliments which they paid him were more expressive of politeness and civility, than the conviction of his merit. Indeed, the beauties of his composition had been converted, by bad reading, into blemishes; and the sense of it rendered obscure, and even unintelligible. Julius and bis father could not conceal their vexation and disappointment j and the quests, perceiving they laid them under a painful restraint, withdrew, as soon as decency permitted, to their respective habitations.

If.—*Respect due to Old Age.*—Spectator. IT happened at Athens, during a public representation of some play exhibited in honour of the commonwealth, that an old gentleman came too late for a place suitable to his age and quality. Many of the young gentlemeH who observed the difficulty and confusion he was in, made signs to him that they would accommodate him, if he came where they sat. The good man bustled through the crowd accordingly; but when he came to the seat to which lie was invited, the jest was to sit close and expose him, as he stood out of countenance, to the whole audience.— The frolick went round all the Athenian benches. But on those occasions there were also particular places assigned for foreigners. When the good man skulked towards the boxes appointed for the Lacedemonians, that honest people, more virtuous than polite, rose up all to a man, and with the greatest respect, received him among them. The Athenians being suddenly touched with a sense of the Spartan virtue and their own degeneracy, gave a thunder of applause; aud the old man cried out, "the Athenians understand what is good, but the Lacedemonians practise it.'' III.—*Piety to God recommended to the Young.*— Blair. WHAT I shall first recommend, is piety to God. With this i begin, both as the foundation of good morals, and as a disposition particularly graceful and becoming in youth. To be void of it argues a cold heart, destitute of some of the best affections which belong to that age.

Youth is the season of warm and generous emotions. The heart should then spontaneously rise into the admiration of what is great; glow with the love of what is fair and excellent; and melt at the discovery of tenderness and goodness. Where can any object be found so proper to kindle these affections, as the Father of the universe, and the Author of all felicity? Unmoved by veneration, can you contemplate that grandeur and majesty which his works every where display? Untouched by gratitude, can you view that profusion of good, which, in this pleasing season of life, his beneficent hand pours around you? Happy in the love and affection of those with

whom you are connected, look up to the Supreme Being, as the inspirer of all the friendship which has ever been shewn you by dthers; himself your best and your first friend; formerly the supporter of your infancy and the guide of your childhood; now, the guardian of your youth, and the hope of your coming years. View religious homage as a natural expression of grdtitude to him for all his goodness. Consider it as the service of the God of your fathers; of Him to whom your parents devoted you; of Him, whom in former ages, your ancestors honoured; and by whom they are now rewarded and blessed in heaven. Connected with so many tender sensibilities of soul, let religion be with you, not the cold and barren offspring of speculation; but the warm and vigorous dictate of the heart. IV.—*Modesty and Docility.*—Ib. TO piety, join mojesty and docility, reverence to your parents, and submission to those who are your superiours in knowledge, in station and in years. Dependence and obedience belong to youth. Modesty is one of its chief ornaments; and has ever been esteemed a presage of rising merit.. When entering on the career of life it is your part not to assume the reins as yet, into your hands; but to commit yourself to the guidance of the more experienced, and to become wise by the wisdom of those who have gone before you. Of all the follies incident to youth, there are none which either deform its present appearance, or blast the prospect of its future prosperity, more than self conceit, presumption and obstinacy. By checking its natural progress in improvement, they fix it in long immaturity; and frequently produce mischiefs which can never be repaired.' Yet these are vices too commonly found among the yonng. Big with enterprise and elated by hope, they resolve to trust for success to none but themselves. Pull of their own abilities, they deride the admonitions-w!;ich nrep'veo t'im by t!i.:ir fi ieiittvy s» i»!vc!-:;».-4'.'X s'.ieerstas '-'-ng-.'.-Ivj wwe to L-.ri.-rvj KnJ impatient to deliberate, too forward to be restrained, they plunge with precipitant indiscretion, into the midst of all the dangers

with which life abounds.

V.—*Sincerity.*—Ir. IT is necessary to recommend to you sincerity and truth. These are the basis of every virtue. That darkness of character, where we can see no heart; those fold-ings of art, through which no native affection is allowed to penetrate, present an object unatniable in every season of life, but particularly odious in youth. If, at an age when the heart is warm, when the emotions are strong, and when nature is expected to show herself free and open, you can already smile and deceive, what are we to look for when you shall be longer hackneyed in the ways of men j when interest shall have completed the obduration of your heart, and experience shall have improved you iii all the arts of guile? Dissimulation in youth is the forerunner of perfidy in old age. Its first appearance is the fated omen of growing depravity and future shame.— It degrades parts and learning, obscures.the lustre of every accomplishment, and sinks you into contempt with. God and man. As you value, thereioie the approbation of heaven, or the esteem of the world, cultivate the love of truth. In all your proceedings, be direct and consistent. Ingenuity and candour possess the most powerful charm: They bespeak universal favour, and carry an apology for almost every failing. The path of truth is a plain and safe path; that of falsehood is a perplexing maze. After the first departure from sincerity, it is not in your power to stop. One artifice unavoidably leads on to another; till, as the intricacy of the labyrinth increases, you are left entangled in your own snare. Deceit discovers a little mind, which stops at temporary expedients, without rising to comprehensive views of conduct. It betrays, at the same time, a dastardly spirit. It is the resource of one who wants courage to avo-w his designs, or to test upon himseif. Whereas, openness of character displays that generous boldness which ought to distinguish youth-To set out in the world with no other principle than a erafty attention to interest, betokens one who is destined for creeping through tire inferior walks of life $ but to give an early preference to honour above gaiu, when they stand in competition; to despise every advantage which cannot be attained without dishonest arts; to brook no meanness, and to stoop to no dissimulation; are the indications of a great mind, the presages of future eminence and distinction in life. At the same time, this virtuous sincerity is perfectly consistent with the most prudent vigilance and caution. It is opposed to cunning, not to true-wisdom. It is not the simplicity of a weak and improvident, but the candour of an enlarged and noble mind; of one who scorns deceit, because he accounts it both base and unprofitable; and who seeks no disguise, because he needs none to hide him.

VI. *rBenevolence and Humanity.*—Ir. YOUTH is the proper season for cultivating the benevolent and humane affections. As a great part of your happiness is to depend on the connections which you form with others, it is of high importance that you acquire betimes, the temper and the manners which will render such connections comfortable. Let a sense of justice be the foundation of all your social qualities. In your most early intercourse with the world, and even in your youthful amusements, let no unfairness be found. Engrave on your mind that sacred rule of " doing in all things to others according to your wish that they should do unto you." For this end impress yourselves with a deep sense of the original and natural equality of men. Whatever advantage of birth or fortune you possess, never display them with an ostentatious superiority. Leave the subordinations of rank to regulate the intercourse of more advanced years. At present it becomes you to act among your companions as man with man. Remember how unknown to you are the vicissitudes of the world; and how often they, on whom ignorant and contemptuous young men once looked down with scorn, have risen to be their superiors in future years-. Compassion is an emotion of which you ought never to be ashamed. Graceful in youth is the tear of sympathy, and the heart that melts at the tale of woe. Let not ease and indulgence contract your affections, and wrap you up in selfish enjoyment. Accustom yourselves to think of the distress.es of human life; of the solitary cottage, the dying parent and the weeping orphan. Never sport with pain anJ distress in any of your amusements, nor treat even the meanest insect with wanton cruelty. VII.—*Industry and Application.*—le. DILIGENCE, industry, and proper improvement of time, are material duties of the young. To no purpose are they endowed with the best abilities, if they want activity for exerting them. Unavailing in this case, will be every direction that can be given them, either for their temporal or spiritual welfare. In youth the habits of industry are most easily acquired 3 in youth the incentives to it are strongest, from ambition and from duty, from emulation and hope, from all the prospects which the beginning of life affords. If dead to these calls, you already languish in slothful inaction, what will be able to quicken the more sluggish current of advancing years? Industry is not only the instrument of improvement, but the foundation of pleasure. Nothing is so opposite to true enjoyment of life, as the relaxed and feeble state of an indolent mind. He who is a stranger to industry may possess, but he cannot enjoy. For it is labour only which gives the relish to pleasure. It is the appointed vehicle of every good man. It is the indispensable condition of our possessing a soundmind in a sound body. Sloth is so inconsistent with both, that it is hard to detertime whether it be a greater foe to virtue, or to health and happiness. Inactive as it is in itself, its effects are fatally powerful. Though it appear a slowly flowing stream, yet it undermines all that is stable and flourishing. It not only saps the foundation of every virtue, but pours upon you a deluge of crimes and evils. It is like water, which first putrefies by stagnation, and then sends up noxious vapours, and fills the atmosphere with death. Fly therefore from idleness, as the certain parent both of guilt and ruin. And under idleness I include, not mere inaction only, but all that circle of triflingoccupations in which too many saunter away their youth; perpetually engaged in frivolous society or public amusements; in the labours of dress or the ostentation of their persons. Is this the foundation which you lay for future usefulness and esteem? By such accomplishments do you hope to rcconiaaeud yourselves to fie thmkhig put of the world, and to answer the expectations of your friends and your country? Amusements youth requires; it were vain, it were cruel to prohibit them. But though allowable as the relaxation, they are most culpable as the business of the young. For they then become the gulf of time, and the poison of the mind. They foment bad passions. They weaken the manly powers. They sink the native vigour of youth into contemptible effeminacy. VIII.—*Proper Employment of Time.*—Ir. REDEEMING your time from such dangerous waste, seek to fill it with employments which you may review with satisfaction. The acquisition ef knowledge is one of the most honourable occupations of youth. The desire of it discovers a liberal mind, and is connected with many accomplishments and many virtues. But though your train of life should not lead you to study, the course of education always furnishes proper employments to a well disposed mind. Whatever you pursue, be emulous to excel. Generous ambition, and sensibility to praise, are, especially at your age, among the marks of virtue. Think not that any affluence of fortune, or any elevation of rank, exempts you from the duties of application and industry. Industry is the law of our being; it is the demand of nature, of reason and of God. Remember, always that the years which now pass over your heads, leave permanent memorials behind them. From the thoughtless minds they may escape; but they remain in the remembrance of God. They form an important part of the register of your life. They will hereafter bear testimony, either for, or against you, at that day, when, for all your actions, but particularly for the employments of youth, you must give an account to God. Whether your future course is destined to be long or short, after this manner it should commence, and if It continue to be thus conducted, its conclusion, at what time soever it arrives, will not be inglorious or unhappy. IX.— *The true Patriot.*— Art Op Thmking. ANDREW DORIA, of Genoa, the greatest sea captain of the age he lived in, set his country free from the yoke of France. Beloved by his fellow citizens, and supported by the the Emperour Charles V. it was in his power to assume sovereignty, without the least struggle. But he preferred the virtuous satisfaction of giving liberty to his countrymen. He declared in public assembly, that the happiness of seeing them once more restored to liberty, was to him a full reward for all his services; that he claimed no pie-eminence above his equals, but remitted to them absolutely to settle a proper form of government. Doria's magnanimity put an end to factions, that had long vexed the state; and a form of government was established, with great unanimity, the same, that with very little alteration, subsists at present. Doria lived to a great age, beloved and honoured by hisxouutrymen; and without ever making a single step out of his rank, as a private citizen, he retained to his dying hour, great influence in the republic. Power, founded on lave and gratitude, was to him more pleasant than what is founded on sovereignty. His memory is reverenced by the Genoese; and, in their histories and public monuments, there is bestowed ou him the most honourable of all titles—Father of his COUNTRY, andRestorer of its LIBERTY,

X.—*On Contentment.*—Spectator. CONTENTMENT produces, in some measure, all those effects which the alchemist usually ascribes to what he calls the *philosopher's stone;* and if it does not bring riches, it does the same thing, by banishing the desire of them. If it cannot remove the disquietudes arising out of a man's mind, body or fortune, it makes him easy under them. It iias, indeed, a kindly influence on the soul of a man, in respect of every being to whom he stands related, It extinguishes all murmur, repining and ingratitude towards tha.t Being, who has allotted him his part to act in this world. It destroys all inordinate ambition, and every tendency to corruption, with regard to the community wherein he is placed. It gives sweetness to his conversation, and perpetual serenity to all his thoughts.

Among the many methods which might be made use of for acquiring this virtue, l shall only mention the two following. First of all, a man should always consider how much he has more than he wants; and, secondly, how much more unhappy he might be, than he really is,

First of all, a man should always consider how much he has more than he wants. T am wonderfully well pleased with the reply which Aristippus made to one who condoled him upon the loss of a farm: "Why," said he, "I have three farms still, and you have but one, so that I ought rather to be afflicted for you than you for me." On the contrary, foolish men are more apt to consider what they have lost, than what they possess; and to fix their eyes upon those who are richer than themselves, rather than on those who are under greater difficulties. AU the real pleasures and conveniences of life lie in a narrow compass; but it is the humour of mankind to be always looking forward, and straining after one who has got the start of them in wealth and honour. For this reason, as there are none can be properly called rich who have not more than they 'want; there are few rich men, in any of the politer nations, but among the middle sort of people, who keep their wishes within their fortunes, and have more wealth than they know how to enjoy. Persons of higher rank live in a kind of splendid poverty; and are perpetually wanting, because, instead of acquiescing in the solid pleasures of life, they endeavour to outvie one another in shadows and appearances. Men of sense have at all times beheld, with a great deal of mirth, this silly game that is playing over their heads; and by contracting their desires, enjoy all that secret satisfaction which others are always in quest of.

The truth is, this ridiculous chase after imaginary pleasure cannot be sufficiently exposed, as it is the great source of those evils which generally undo a nation. Let a man's estate be what it will, he is a poor man if he does not live within it, and naturally sets himself to sale to any one who can give him his price. When Pittacus, after the death of his brother, who had left him a good estate, was offered a great sum of money by the king of Lydia, he thanked him for his kindness, but told him he had already more by half than he knew what to do with In short, content is equivalent to wealth, and luxury to poverty; or, to give the thought a more agreeable turn, " Content is natural wealth," says Socrates; to which I shall add, Luxury is artificial poverty. I shall therefore recommend to the consideration of those who are always aiming after superfluous and imaginary enjoyments, and will not be at the trouble of contracting their desires, an excellent saying ©f Bion the philosopher, namely, "That no man has so much care as he who endeavours after the most happiness."

In the second place every one ought to reflect how much more unhappy he might be than he really is. The former consideration took in all those who are sufficiently provided with the means to make themselves easy; this regards such as actually lie under some pressure or misfortune. These may receive great alleviation from such a comparison as the unhappy person may make between himself and others, or between the misfortunes which he suffers, and greater misfortunes which might have befallen him.

I like the story of the honest Dutchman, who upon breaking his leg by a fall from the mainmast, told the standers by, it was a great mercy it was not his'neck. To which, since I am got into quotations, give me leave to add the saying of an old philosopher, who, after having invited some of his fi iends to dine with him, was ruffled by his wife, who came into the room in a passion, and threw down the table that stood before them: "Every one," says he, "has his calamity, and he is a happy man that has no greater than this." We find an instance to the same purpose in the life of doctor Hammond, written by bishop Fell. As this good man was troubled with a complication of distempers, when he had the gout upon him, he used to thank God that it was not the stone; and, when he had the stone, that he had not both these distempers on him at the same time.

I cannot conclude this essay without observing, that there was never any system, besides that of Christianity, which would effectually produce in the mind of man the virtue I have been hitherto speaking of. In order to make us contented with our condition, many of the present philosophers tell us that our discontent only hurts ourselves, without being able to make any alteration in our circumstances; others, that whatever evil befals us is derived to us by a fatal necessity, to which the gods themselves are subject; while others very gravely tell the man who is miserable, that it is necessary he should be so, to keep up the harmony of the universe, and that the scheme of Providence would be troubled and perverted were he oth erwise. These, and the like considerations, rather silence than satisfy a man. They may sliew him that his discontent is unreasonable, but are by no means sufficient to relieve it. They rather give despair than consolation. *In* a.word, a man might reply to one of these comforters, as Augustus did to his friend, who advised him not to grieve for the death of a person whom he loved, because his &rief could not fetch him again: "It is for that very reason," said the emperour, " that I grieve."

On the contrary, religion bears a more tender regard to human nature. It prescribes to every miserable man the means of bettering his condition: Nay, it shows him that the bearing of his afflictions as he ought to do, will naturally end in the removal of them. It makes him easy here, because it can make happy hereafter.

XI.—*Needlework recommended to the Ladies,—*Ir. ' I HAVE a couple of nieces under my direction, who so often ran gadding abroad, that I do not know where to to have them. Their dress, their tea, and their visits take up all their time, and they go to bed as tired with doing nothing, as 1 am after quilting a whole underpetticoat. The whole time they are not idle, is while they read your Spectators; which being dedicated to the interests of virtue, I desire you to recommend the long neglected art of needlework Those hours which, in this age, are thrown away in dress, play, visits, and the like, were employed in my time in writing out receipts, or working beds, chairs, and hangings for the family. For my part, I have plied my needle these fifty years, and by my good will would never have it out of my hand. It grieves my heart to see a couple of proud idle 'flirts sipping their tea, for a whole afternoon, in a great room hung round with the industry of their great grandmother, fray sir, take the laudable mystery of'embroidery into your serious consideration, and as you have a great deal of the virtue of the last age in you continue your endeavours to reform the present." *J am, #*e. IN obedience to the commands of my venerable correspondent, I have duly weighed this important subject, and promise mvself from the arguments here laid down, that all the fine ladies in England will be ready, as soon as their mourning is over, to appeal covered with the work of their own hands.

What a delightful entertainment must it be to the fair sex, whom their native modesty, and the tenderness of men towards them, exempts from public business, to pass their hours in imitating fruits and flowers, and transplanting all the beauties of nature into their own dress, or raising a new creation in their clothes and apartments. How pleasing is the amusement-of walking among the shades and groves planted by themselves, in surveying heroes slain by their needles, or little Cupids which they have brought into the world without pain.

This is, methinks, the most proper way wherein a lady can show a fine genius, and I cannot forbear wishing that several writers of that sex, had chosen rather to apply themselves to tapestry than rhyme. Your pastoral poetesses may vent their fancy in rural landscapes, and place despairing shepherds under silken willows, or drown them in a stream of mohair. The heroic writers msy work up battles as successfully, and inflame them with gold or stain them with crimson. Even those who have only a turn to a song, or an epigram, may put many valuable stitches into a purse, and crowd a thousand graces into a pair of garters. »

If I may without breach of good manners, imagine that any pretty creature is void of genius, and would perform her part herein but very awkwardly, I must nevertheless insist upon her working, if it be only to keep her out of harm's way.

Another argument for busying good women in works of fancy is, because it takes them off from scandal, the usual attendant of teatables, and all other inactive scenes of life. While they are forming their birds and beasts, their neighbours will be allowed to be the fathers of their own children; and Whig and Tory will be but seldom mentioned, where the great dispute is whether blue or red is the more proper colour. How much greater glory would Sophronia do the general, if she would choose rather to work the battle of Blenheim in tapestry, than signalise herself, with so much vehemence, against those who are Frenchmen in their hearts.

A third reason that I shall mention, is the profit that is brought to the family where these pretty arts are encouraged. It is manifest, that this way of life not only keeps fair ladies from running out into expences, but it is at the same time, an actual improvement. How memorable would that matron be, who shall have it inscribed upon her monument, "that she wrote out the whole Bible in tapestry, and died in a good old age, after having covered three hundred yards of wall in the mansion house-?"

These premises being considered, I humbly submit the following proposals to all mothers in Great-Britain.

I. That no young virgin whatsoever, be allowed to receive the addresses of her first lover but in a suit of her own embroidering, II. That before every fresh servant she be obliged to appear with a new stomacher at the least.

III. That no one be actually married until she hath tho childbed, pillows, &c.

ready stitched, as likewise the mantle for the boy quite finished.

These laws, if i mistake not, would effectually restore the decayed art of needlework, and make the virgins of Great-Britain, exceedingly nimble fingered in their business.

XII.—*On Pride.*—Guardian. IF there be any thing that makes human nature appear ridiculous to beings of superiour faculties, it must be pride. They know so well the vanity of those imaginary perfections that swell the heart of man, and of those little supernumerary advantages, whether in birth, fortune or title, which one man enjoys above another, that it must certainly very much astonish, if it does not very much divert them, when they see a mortal puffed up, and valuing him self above his neighbours, on any of these accounts, at the same time that he is obnoxious to all the common calamities of the species.

To set this thought in its true light, we will fancy, if you please, that yonder molehill is inhabited by reasonable creatures, and that every pismire (his shape and way of life only excepted) is endowed with human passions. How should we smile to hear one give us an account of the pedigrees, distinctions and titles that reign among them? Observe how the whole swarm divide, and make way (pv lh# pismire that passes through them; you must understand he is an emmet of quality, and has better blood in his veins than any pismire in the molehill. Don't you see how sensible he is of it, how slow he marches forward, how the whole rabble of ants keep their distance? Here you may observe one placed upon a little eminence, and looking down on a long row of labourers. He is the richest insect on this side the hillock, he has a walk of half a yard in length, and a quarter of an inch in breadth, he keeps an hundred menial servants, and has at least fifteen barley corns in his granary. He is now chiding and beslaving the emmet that stands before him, and who for all that we can discover, is as good an emmet as himself.

But here comes aa insect of figure! Don't you take notice of a little white straw he carries in his mouth? That straw, you must understand, he would not part with for the longest tract about the molehill: Did you but know what he has undergone to purchase it! See how the ants of all qualities and conditions swarm about him.—Should this straw drop out of his mouth, you would see all this numerous circle of attendants follow the next that took it up, and leave the discarded insect, or run over his back to come at its successor.

If now you have a mind to see all the ladies of the molehill, observe first the pismire that listens to the emmet on her left hand, at the same time that she seems to turn away her head from him. He tells this poor insect she is a goddess, that her eyes are brighter than the sun, that life and death are at her disposal. She believes him, and gives herself a thousand little airs upon it. Mark the vanity of the pismire on your left hand. She can scarce crawl with age, but you must know she values herself upon her birth; and if you mind, spurns at every one that comes within her reach. The little nimble coquette that is running along by the side of her is a wit. She has broke many a pismire's heart. Do but observe what a drove of lovers are running after her.

We will here finish this imaginary scene; but first of all to draw the parallel closer, will suppose, if you please, that death comes upon the molehill, in the shape of a cock sparrow, who picks up, without distinction, the pismire of quality and his flatterers, the pismire of substance and his day labourers, the whitestraw officer and his sycophants, with all the goddesses, wits, and beauties of the molehill.

May we not imagine, that beings of superiour natures and perfections regard all the instances of pride and vanity, among our own species in the same kind of view, when they take a survey of those who inhabit the earth, or in the language of an ingenious French poet, of those pismires that people this heap of dirt, which human vanity has divided into climates and regions.

XIII.—*Journal of the life of Alexander Severus.*—

Gibbon. ALEXANDER rose early. The first moments of the day were-consecrated to private devotion: But as he deemed the service of mankind the most acceptable worship of the gods, the greatest part of his morning hours-were employed in council *y* where he discussed public affairs, and determined private causes, with a patience and discretion above his years The dryness of business was enlivened by the charms of literature;. and a portion of time was always set apart for his favourite-studies of poetry, history, and' philosophy. The works of Virgil and Horace, the republics of Plato and Cicero, formed his taste, enlarged his understanding,- and gave him the noblest ideas of man and of government. The exercises of the body succeeded to those of the mind; and Alexander, who was tall, active, and robust, surpassed most of his equals in the gymnastic arts. Refreshed-by the use of his bath, and a slight dinner, lie resumed with new vigour, the business of the day:. And till the hour of supper, the principal meal of the Romans,.. he was attended by his secretaries, with whom lie read and answered the multitude of letters, memorials, and petitions that must have been addressed to the master of the greatest part of the world. His table was served with: the most frugal simplicity; and whenever he was at liberty to consult hisown inclination, the company consisted of a few select friends, men of learning and virtue.. His dress was plain and modest: his demeanor courteous and affable. Aft the proper hours, his palace was open to' all his subjects; but the voice of a crier was heard, as in the Eleusinlan mysteries, pronouncing the same sajutary admonition—

"Let none enter these holy walls, unless he is conscious of a pure and innocent mind." XIV.—*Character of Julius Cesar.*—Middleton. CESAR was endowed with every great and noble quality that could exalt human nature, and give a man Hie ascendant in society; formed to excel in peace as well as war, provident in council, fearless in action, and executing what he had resolved with an amazing celerity; generous beyond measure to his friends, placable to *his* enemies; for parts, learning and eloquence, scarce inferionr to any man. His orations were admired for two qualities, which are seldom found together, strength and elegance. Cicero ranks him among the greatest orators that Rome ever bred: And Quintilian says, that he spoke with the same force with which he fought; and, if he had devoted himself to the bar, would have been the only man capable of rivalling Cicero. Nor was he a master only of the politer arts, but conversant also with the most abstruse and critical parts of learning; and among other works which he published, addressed two books to Cicero, on the analogy of language, or the art of speaking and writing correctly. He was a most liberal patron of wit and learning, wheresoever they were found; and out of his love of these talents, would readily pardon those who had employed them against himself; rightly judging, that, by making such men his friends, he should draw praises from the same fountain from which he had been aspersed. His capital passions were ambition and love of pleasure; which he indulged in their turns, to the greatest excess: yet the first was always predominant; to which he could easily sacrifice all the charms of the second, and draw pleasure even from toils and dangers-, when they ministered to his glory. For he thought tyranny, as Cicero says, the greatest of goddesses; and had frequently in his mouth a verse of Euripides, which expressed the image of his souL That if right and justice were ever to be violated, they were to be violated for the sake of reigning. This was the chief end and purpose of his life; the scheme that he had formed from his early youth; so that, as Cato truly declared of him, he came with sobriety and meditation to the subversion of the re public. He used to say, that there were two things necessary to acquire and to support power—soldiers and money; which yet depended mutually on each other: With money, therefore, he provided soldiers, and with soldiers extorted money; and was, of all men, the most rapacious in plundering both friends and foes; spar-

ing neither prince nor state, nor temple, nor even private persons, who were known to possess any share of treasure. His great abilities would necessarily have made him one of the first citizens of Rome; but disdaining-the condition of a subject, he could never rest till he had made himself a monarch. In acting this last part, his usual prudence seemed to fail him; as if the height to which he was mounted had turned his head, and made him giddy: For by a vain ostentation of his power, he destroyed the stability of it; and as men shorten life by living too fast, so by an intemperance of reigning, he brought his reign to a violent end." XV——*On Misspent Time.* —Guardian. I WAS yesterday comparing the industry of man with that of-other creatures; in which I could not but observe, that notwithstanding we are obliged by duty to keep ourselves in constant employ, after the same manner as inferiour animals are prompted to it by instinct, we fall very short of them in this particular. We are here the more inexcusable, because there is a greater variety of business to which we may apply ourselves. Reason opens to us a large field of affairs, which other creatures are not capable of. Beasts of prey, and, I believe of all other kinds, in their natural state of being, divide their time between action and rest. They are always at work or asleep. la short, their waking hours are wholly taken up in seeking after their food, or consuming it. The human species only, to the great reproach of our natures, are filled with complaints, that "the day hangs heavy on them," that "they do not know what to do with themselves," that "they are at a loss how to pass away their time;" with many of the like shameful murmurs, which we often find in the mouths of those who are styled reasonable beings. How monstrous are such expressions, among creatures who have the labours of the mind, as well as those of the body, to furnish them with proper employments; who besides the business of their proper callings and professions, can apply themselves to the duties of religion, to meditation, to the reading of useful books, to discourse; in a word,

who may exercise themselves in the unbounded pursuits of knowledge and virtue, and, every hour of their lives, make themselves wiser or better than they were before.

After having been taken up for some time in this course of thought, I diverted myself with a book, according to my usual custom, in order to unbend my mind before I went to sleep. The book I made use of on this occasion was Lucian, where I amused my thoughts for about an hour, among the dialogues of the dead; which, in all probability, produced the following dream;

I was conveyed, methought, into the entrauce of the infernal regions, where *I* saw Rhadamanthus, one of the judges of the dead, seated on his tribunal. On his left hand stood the keeper of Erebus, on his right the keeper of Elysium. I was told he sat upon women that day, there being several of the sex lately arrived, who had not yet their mansions assigned them. I was surprised to hear him ask every one of them the same question, namely, what they had been doing? Upon this question being proposed to the whole assembly, they stared one upon another, as not knowing what to answer. He then interrogated each of them separately. Madam, says he, to the first of them, you have been upon the earth about fifty years t What have you been doing there all this while? Doing, says she; really, I do not know what I have been doing;I desire I may have time given me to recollect. After about half an hour's pause she told him that she had been playing at crimp; upon which, Rhadamauthus beckoned to the keeper on his left hand to take her into custody. And you, Madam, says the judge, that look with such a soft and languishing air; I think you set out.for this placein your nine and twentieth year, what have you been doing all this while? I had a great deal of business on my. hands, says she, being taken up-the first twelve years of pry life in dressing a jointed baby, and all the remaining part of it in reading plays and romances. Very well, says he, you have employed your time to good purpose. Away with her. The next wag a plain country woman?.

Well, mistress, says Rhadamanthus, and what have you been doing? An't please your worship, says she, I did not live quite forty years; and in that time brought my husband seven daughters, made him nine thousand cheeses, and left my youngest girl with him, to look after his house in my absence; and who, I may venture to say, is as pretty a housewife as any in the country. Rhadamanthus smiled at the simplicity of the good woman, and ordered the keeper of Elysium to take her into his tare. And you, fair lady, says he, what have you been doing these five and thirty years? I have been doing no hurt, I assuse you, sir, said she. That is well, said he: But what good have you been doing? The lady was in great confusion at this question: And not knowing what to answer, the two keepers leaped out to seize her at tli3 same time; the one took her by the hand *to* convey her to Elysium, the other caught hold of her, to carry her away to Erebus. But Rhadamanthus observing an ingenuous modesty in her countenance and behaviour, bid them both let her loose, and set her aside for re-examination when he was more at leisure. An old woman, of a proud and sour look, presented herself next at the bar; and being asked what she had been doing? Truly, said she, I lived three score and ten years in a very wicked world, and was so angry at the behaviour of a parcel of young flirts, that I passed most of my last years in condemning the follies of the times. I was every day blaming the silly conduct of the people about me, in order to deter those I conversed with from falling into the like errours and miscarriages. Very well, says Rhadamanthus, but did you keep the same watchful eye over your own actions? Why, truly, said she, I was so taken up with publishing the faults of others, that I had no time to consider my. own. Madam, says Rhadamanthus, be pleased to file off to the left, and make room for the venerable matron that stands behind you. Old gentlewoman, says he, I think you are forescore: You have heard the question—What have you been doing so

long in the world? Ah, sir, says she, I have been doing what I should not have done; but I had made a firm resolution to have changed my life, if I had not been snatched off by an untimely end. Madam, says he, you will please to follow your leader: And spying another of the same age, interrogated her in the same form. To which the matron replied, I have been the wife of a husband who was as dear to me in his old age as in his youth. T have been a mother, and very happy in my children, whom I endeavored to bring up in every thing that is good. My eldest son is blest by the poor, and beloved by every one that knows him. i lived within my own family, and left it much more wealthy than I foutod it. Rhadamanthus, who knew the value of the old lady, smiled upon her in such a manner, that the keeper of Elysium, who knew his office, reached out his hand to her. He no sooner touched her but her wrinkles vanished, her eyes-sparkled, her cheeks glowed with blushes, and she appeared in full bloom and beauty. A young woman, observing that this officer, who conducted the happy to Elysium, was so great a beautifier, longed to be in his hands; so that pressing through the crowd, she was the next that appeared at the bar: And being asked what she had been doing the five and twenty years that she had passed in the world? I have endeavoured, says she, ever since I came to years of discretion, to make myself lovely, and gain admirers. In order to it, *I* passed my time in bottling up Maydew, inventing whitewashes, mixing colours, cutting out patches, consulting my glass, suiting my complexion.Rhadamanthus without hearing her out, gave the sign to take her off. Upon Ihe approach of the keeper of Erebus, her colour faded, her face was puckered up with wrinkles and her whole person lost in deformity.-*i*

I was then surprised with a distant sound of a whole troop of females, that came forward, laughing, singing and dancing. I was very desirous to know the reception they would meet with, and, withall, was very apprehensive that Rhadamanthus would spoil their mirth;

but at their nearer approach, the noise grew so very great that it awakened me.

I lay some time, reflecting in myself on the oddness of this dream; and could not forbear asking my own heart, what I was doing? I answered myself, that I was writing *Guardians*. If my readers make as good a use of this-work as I design they should, I hope it will never be imputed to me, as a work that is vain and unprofitable.

I shall conclude this paper with recommending to them the same short self-examination. If every one of them frequently lays his hand upon his heart, and considers what he is doing, it will check him in all the idle, or what is worse, the vicious moments of his life; lift op his mind when it is running on in a series of indifferent actions, and encourage him when he is engaged in those which are virtuous and laudable. In a word, it will very much alleviate that guilt, which the best of men have reason to acknowledge in their daily confessions, of "leaving undone those things which they ought to have done, and of doing those things which they ought not to have done." XVI.—*Character of Francis I.*—Robertson. FRANCIS died atRamboulIet on the last day of March in the fifty third year of his age, and the thirty-third of his reign. During twentyeight years of that time an avowed rivalship subsisted between him and theemperour; which involved, not only their own dominions, but the greater part of Europe, in wars, prosecuted with the more violent animosity, and drawn out to a greater length than had been known in any former period. Many circumstances contributed to both. Their animosity was founded in opposition of interest, Iteightened by personal emulation, and exasperated, not only by mutual injuries, but by reciprocal insults. At the same time, whatever advantage one seemed to possess towards gaining the-ascendant, was wonderfully balanced by some favourable circumstances peculiar to the other. The emperour's dominions were of great extent; the French king's lay more compact; Francis governed his kingdom with absolute power; that of

Charles was limited, but he supplied the want of authority by address: The troops of the former were mora impetuous and enterprising; those of the latter better disciplined and more patient of fatigue.

The talents and abilities of the two monarchs were as different as the advantages which they possessed, and contributed no less to prolong the contest between them.— Francis took his resolutions suddenly; prosecuted them, at first with warmth; and pushed them into execution with rt most Adventurous courage; but, being destitute of the perseverance necessary to surmount difficulties, he often abandoned his designs, or relaxed the vigour of pursuit, from impatience, and sometimes from levity. Charles deliberated Jong, and determined with coolness: But having once fixed his plan, Tie adhered to it with inflexible obstinacy; and neither danger nor discouragement could turn him aside from the execution of it.

The success of their enterprises was as different as their characters, and was uniformly influenced by them. Francis, by his impetuous activity, often disconcerted the emperout's best laid schemes; Charles, by a more calm, but steady prosecution of his designs, checked the rapidity of his rival's career, and baffled or repulsed his most vigorous efforts. The former, at the opening of a war'or a campaign, broke in upon his enemy with the violence of a torrent, and carried all before him; the latter waiting until he saw the force of his rival begin to abate, recovered) in the end, not only all that he had lost, but made new acquisitions. Fyew of the French monarch's attempts towards conquest, whatever promising aspect they might wear at first, were conducted to an happy issue; many of the emperour's enterprises, even after they appeared desperate and impracticable, terminated in the most prosperous manner

The degree, however, of their comparative merit and reputation, has not been fixed, either by strict scrutiny into their abilities for government, or by an impartial consideration of the greatness and success of their undertakings; and Francis is one of those monarchs, who

occupy a higher rank in the temple of fame, than either their tal ents or performances entitle them to hold. This pre-eminence he owed to many different circumstances. The superiority which Charles acquired by the victory of Pavia, and which, from that period, he preserved through the remainder of his reign, was so manifest, that Francis struggle against his exorbitant and growing dominion, was viewed by most of the other powers not only with that partiality which naturally arises from those who gallantly 'maintain an unequal contest, but with the favour due to one who was resisting a common enemy, and endeavouring to set bounds to a monarch, equally formidable to them all. The characters of princes, too especially among their cotemporaries, depend, not only upon their talents for government, but upon their qualities as men. Francis, notwithstanding the many errours conspicuous in his foreign policy and domestic administration, was nevertheless, humane, beneficent, generous. He possessed dignity without pride, affability free from meanness, and courtesy exempt from deceit. All who had access to know him, and no man of merit was ever denied that privilege, respected and loved him. Captivated with his personal qualities, his subjects forgot his defects as a monarch; and admiring him, as the most accomplished and amiable gentleman in his dominions, they hardly murmured at acts of maladministration, which in a prince of less engaging disposition, would have been deemed unpardonable.

This admiration, however, must have been temporary only, and would have died away with the courtiers who bestowed it; the illusion arising from his private virtues must have ceased, and posterity would have judged of his public conduct with its usual impartiality: But another circumstance prevented this; and his name hath been transmitted to posterity with increasing reputation. Science and the arts had, at that time, made little progress in France. They were just beginning to advance beyond the limits of Italy, where they had revived, and which had hitherto been their

only seat. Francis took them immediately under his protection, and vied with Leo himself, in the zeal and munificence, with which he encouraged them. He invited learned men to his court, he conversed with them familiarly, he employed them in business, he raised them to offices of dignity, and honoured them with his confidence. That race of men, not more prone to complain when denied the respect to which they fancy themselves entitled, than apt to be pleased when treated with the distinction which they consider as their due, thought they could not exceed in gratitude to such a benefactor, and strained their invention, and employed all their ingenuity, in panegyric.

Succeeding authors, warmed with their descriptions of Francis' bounty, adopted their encomiums, and refined upon them. The appellation of *Father of Letters,* betowed upon Francis, had rendered his memory sacred among historians; and they seem to have regarded it as a sort of impiety, to uncover his infirmities, or to point out his defects. Thus Francis, notwithstanding his inferior abilities sind went of success, hath more than equalled the fame of Charles. The virtues which he possessed as a man, have entitled him to greater admiration and praise than have been bestowed upon the extensive genius, and fortunate arts, of a more capable, but less amiable rival.

XVII.—*The Supper and Grace.*—Sterne. A SHOE coming loose from the forefoot of the thillliorse, at the beginning of the ascent of mount Taurira, the postillion dismounted, twisted the shoe off and put it in his pocket: As the ascent was of five or six miles, and that horse our main dependence, I made a point of having the shoe fastened on again as well as we could; but the postillion had thrown away the nails, and the hammer in the chaise box being of no great use without them, I submitted to go on.

He had not mounted half a mile higher, when coming to a flinty piece of road, the poor devil lost a second shoe, and from off his other forefoot I then got out of the chaise in good earnestj and, seeing a house about a quarter of a mile to the left hand, with a great deal ado I prevailed upon the postillion to turn up to it. The look of the house, and every thing about it, as we drew nearer soon reconciled me to the disaster. It was a little farm house, surrounded with about twenty acres of vineyard, about as much corn; and close to the house, on one side, was a *potagerie* of an acre and a half, full of every thing-which could make plenty in a French peasant's house; and on the other side, was a little wood, which furnished-wherewithal to dress it. It was about eight in the evening when I got to the house; so I left the postillion to manage his point as be could; and, for mine, I walked directly into the house.

The family consisted of an old grey headed man and his wife, with five or six sons and sons in law, and their several wives, and a joyous genealogy out of them.

They wer.e all sitting down together to their lentil-soup: A large wheaten loaf was in the middle of the table; and a flaggon of wine at each end of it promised joy through the stages of the repast—it was a feast of love.

The old man rose up to meet me, and with a respectful coidiality would have me sit down at the table. My heart was sit down the moment I entered the room; so I sat down at once, like a son of the family; and, to invest myself in the character as speedily as I could, I instantly borrowed the old man's knife, and taking up the loaf, cut myself a hearty luncheon; and,'as I did it I saw a testimony in every eye, not only of an honest welcome, but of a welcome mixed with thanks, that I had not seemed to doubt it.

Was it this, or tell me, Nature, what else was it that made this morsel so sweet—and to what magic I owe it that the draught 1 took of their flaggon was so delicious with it, that it remains upon my palate to this hour?

If the supper was to my taste, the grace which followed was much more so.

When supper was over, the old man gave a knock upon the table with the haft of his knife, to bid them prepare for the dance. The moment the signal was given, the women and irls ran altogether into the back apartments to tie up their hair, and the young men to the door to wash their faces, and change their sabots, *(wooden shoes,)* and in three minutes every soul was ready, upon a little esplanade before the house to begin. The old man and his wife came out last, and, placing me betwixt them, sat down upon a sofa of turf by the door.

The old man had some fifty years ago, been no mean performer upon the vielle; and, at the age he was then of, touched it well enough for the purpose. His wife sung now and then a little to the tune, then intermitted, and joined her old man again, as their children and grand children danced before them.

It was not till the middle of the second dance, when for some pauses in the movement, wherein they all seemed to look up, I fancied I could distinguish an elevation of spirit, different from that which is the cause or the effect of simple jollity. In a word, I thought I beheld religion mixing in the dance; but, as I had never seen her so engaged, I should have looked upon it now as one of the illusions of an imagination which is eternally misleading me, had not the old man, as soon as the dance ended, said, that this was their constant way; and that all his life long, he made it a rule, after supper was over, to call out his family to dance and rejoice; believing, lie said.

that a cheerful and contented mind was the best sort of thanks to heaven that an illiterate peasant could pay.— Or a learned prelate either, said I. XVItL—*Rustic Felicity.-As.* MANY are the silent pleasures of the honest peasant, who rises cheerfully to his labour. Look into his dwelling —where the scene of every man's happiness chiefly lies; he has the same domestic endearments—as much joy and comfort in his children, and as flattering hopes of their doing well—to enliven his hours and gladden his heart, as you would conceive in the most affluent station. And I make no doubt, in general, but if the true account of his joys and sufferings were to be balanced with those of his betters—that the

upshot would prove to be little more than this; that the rich man had the more meat—but the poor man the beiter stomach; the one had more luxury—more able physicians to attend and set him to rights;—the other, more health and soundness in his bones, and less occasion for their help; that, after these two articles betwixt them were balanced—in all other things they stood upon a level—that the sun shines as warm—the air blows as fresh, and the earth breathes as fragrant upon the one as the oilier;—and they have an equal share in all the beauties and real benefits of nature. XIX.—*House of Mourning.*—Ir. LET us go into the house of mourning made so by such afflictions as have been brought in merely by the common cross accidents and disasters to which our condition is exposed—where, perhaps, the aged parents sit brokenhearted, pierced to their souls, with the folly and indiscretion pf a thankless child—the child of their prayers, in whom all their hopes and expectations centered:—Perhaps, a more affecting scene—a virtuous family lying pinched witli want, where the unfortunate support of it, having long struggled with a train of misfortunes, and bravely fought up against them, is now piteously borne down at the last— overwhelmed with a cruel blow, which no forecast or frugality could have prevented. O God! look upon his afflictions. Behold him distracted with many sorrows, surrounded with the tender pledges of his. love j aad the part-' ner of his cares—without bread to give them; unable from *the* remembrance of better days to dig;—to beg ashamed.. When we enter into the house or mourning, such as this—it is impossible to insult the unfortunate, even with an improper look. Under whatever levity and dissipation of heart such objects catch our eyes—they catch likewise our attentions, collect and call home our scattered thoughts. and exercise them with wisdom. A transient scene of distress, such as is here sketched, how soon does it furnisii materials to set the mind at work! How necessarily docs it engage it to the consideration of the miseries, and misfortunes, the dangers and calamities to which the life of man is subject! By holding up such a glass before it, it forces the mind tf-see and reflect upon the vanity—the perishing condition, and uncertain tenure of every thing in this world. From reflections of this sei ious cast, how insensibly do the thoughts carry us farther;—and, from considering what we are, what kind of world we live in,and what evils befal us in it, how naturally do they set us to look forward at what possibly we shall be;—for what kind of world we are intended—what; evils may befal us there—and what provisions we should make against them here, whilst we have time and opportunity! If these lessons are so inseparable from the house of mourning here supposed—we shall find it a still more instructive school of wisdom, when we take a view of the place in that affecting light in whichthe wise man seems to confine it in the text;—in which, bv-the house of-mourning, I believe he means that particular scene of sorrow, where there is lamentation and mourning for the dead. Turn in hither, I beseech you for a moment. Behold the dead man . ready to be carried out; the only son of his mother, and she a 'widow. Perhaps a still more affecting spectacle, a kind and indulgent father of a numerous family lies breathless —snatched away in the strength of his age—torn, and iu an evil hour, from his children, and the bosom of a disconsolate wife. Behold much people of the city gathered together to mix their tears, with settled sorrow in their looks, going heavily along to the ' house of mourning, to perform that last melancholy office, which when the debt of nature is paid we are called upon to pay to each other. If.this sad occasion, which leads him there, has not *dam 10J-'* it already, take notice to what a serious and devout frame of mind every man is reduced, the moment he enters *this* gats of affliction. The busy and fluttering spirits, which, in the house of mirth, were wont to transport him from one diverting object to another—see how they are fallen! how peacably they are laid! In this gloomy mansion, full of shades and uncomfortable damps to seize the soul—see the light and easy heart, which never knew what it was to think before, how pensive it is now, how soft, how susceptible, how full of religious impressions, how deep it is smitten with a sense, and with a love of virtue!—Could we, in this crisis, whilst this empire of reason and religion lasts, and the heart is thus exercised with wisdom, and busied with heavenly contemplations—Cmldwe see it naked as it is—stripped of its passions, unspotted by the world, and regardless of its pleasures—we might then safely rest our cause upon this single evidence, and appeal to the most sensual, whether Solomon has not made a just determination here in favour of the house of mournmg? Not for its own sake, but as it is fruitful in virtue, and becomes the occasion of so much good. Without this end, sorrow, 1 own, has no use but to shorten a man's days—nor can gravity, with all its studied solemnity of look and carriage, serve any end but to make one half of the world merry, and impose upon the oliier. SECTION III.

I.—*The Honour and Advantage of a constant adherence to Truth.*—Percival's Tales. PETRARCH, a celebrated Italian poet, who flourished about four hundred years ago, recommended himself to the confidence and affection of Cardinal Colonna, in whose family he resided, by his candour and strict regard to truth. A violent quarrel occurred in the household of this nobleman; which was carried so far, that recourse was had to arms. The Cardinal wished to know the foundation of this affair; and that he might be able to decide with justice, he assembled all his people, and obliged them to bind themselves, by a most solemn oath on the gospels, to declare the whole truth. Every one without exception, submrnitted to this determination; even pie Bishop of Luna, brother to the Cardinal, was not excused.— Petrarch, in his turn, presenting himself to take the oath, the Cardinal closed the book, and said, *As to you, I'etrach, your word is sufficient.* II.—*Impertinence in Discourse.*—Theothrastus..

THIS kind of impertinence is habit of talking much without thinking. '--'"'''

'.".'

A man who has this distemper in his tongue shall entertain you, though he never saw you before, with a long story in praise of his own wife; give you the particulars of last night's dream, or the description of a feast he has been at without letting a single dish escape him. / When he is thus entered into conversation, he grows very wise —descants upon the corruption of the times, and the degeneracy of the age we liveiujfrom which as his transitions ate somewhat sudden, he falls upon the price of corn, and the number of strangers that are in town. He-undertakes to prove, that it is better putting to sea in summer than in winter, and that rain is necessary to produce a good crop of corn; telling you in the sanie breath that he intends to plough up such a part of his estate next year, that the times are hard, and that a man has much ado to get through the world. His whole discourse is nothing but hurry and incoherence. He acquamts you that Demippus had the largest torch at the feast of Ceres; aks you if you remember how many pillars are in the music theatre; tells you that he took physic: yesterday; and desires to know what day of the month it is. If you have patience to hear him, he will inform you what festivals are kept in August, whet in October, and what in December.

When you see such a fellow as this coming towards you, run for *y* our life; A man had much better be visit' ed by a fever; so painful is it to be fastened upon by one of this make, who takes it for granted that you have nothing else to do, but to give him a hearing.

III.—*Character of Addison as a* JFWter. —Johnson; , AS a describer of life and manners, Mr. Addison must be allowed to stand perhaps the first in the first raitk. His humour is peculiar to himself; and, is so happily diffused, as to give the grace of novelty to domestic scenes and daily occurrences.-He never *o'ersteps the modeity of nature,* nor raises merriment or wonder by the violation of truth. His figures neither divert by distortion, nor amaze by aggravation. He copies life with so much fidelity, that he can hardly besaid Jo invent; yet his jexhibi-.tions have an air so much original, that it is difficult to suppose them not merely the product of imagination...--, As a teacher of wisdom he may be confidently followed. His religion has nothing in it enthusiastic or superstitious; he appears neither weakly credulous, nor wantonly sceptical; his morality is neither dangerously lax, nor implacably rigid AH the enchantments of fancy» and all the cogency of arguments, are employed, to rectorcmend to the reader his real interest,-the care of pleasing the Author of his bejng. Truth/ is. shown sometimes as the phantom of a vision, sometimes appears half veiled in an allegory, sometimes attracts regard in the robes of fancy, and sometimes steps forth in the confidence of rea son. She wears a thousand dresses, and in all is pleasing. His prose is the model of the middle style; on grave subjects not formal, on light occasions not groveling; pure without scrupulosity, a»4exsict; without apparent elabar ration; always equable, and always easy, without glowing words or pointed sentences. His page is always luminous, but never blazes in unexpected splendour. It seems to have been his principal endeavour to avoid all harshness and severity of diction; he is therefore sometimes verbose in his transitions and connexions, and sometimes descends too much to the language of conversation; yet, if his language had been less idiomatical, it might have lost somewhat of its genuine Anglicism. What he attempted he performed; he is never feeble, and he did not wish to be energetic; he is never rapid, and he never stagnates. His sentences have neither studied amplitude nor affected brevity; his periods, though not diligently rounded, are voluble and easy. Whoever wishes to attain an English style, familiar but not coarse, and elegant but not ostentatious, must give his days and nights to the volumes of Addison. IV.—*Pleasure and Pain.*—Spectator. THERE were two families, which, from the beginningof the world, were as opposite to each other as light and darkness. The one of them lived in heaven, and the other in hell. The youngest descendant of the first family was Pleasure, who was the daughter of Happiness, who was the child of Virtue, who was the offspring of the Gods. These, as I said before, had their habitation in heaven. The youngest of the opposite family was Pain, who was the son of Misery, who was the child of Vice, who was the offspring of the Furies. The habitation of this race of beings was in hell.

The middle station of nature between these two opposite extremes was the earth, which was inhabited by creatures of a middle kind; neither so virtuous as the one; nor so vicious as the other, but partaking of the good and bad qualities of those two opposite families. Jupiter, considering that this species, commonly called Man, was too virtuous to be miserable and too vicious to be happy, that he might make a distinction between the good and the bad, ordered the two youngest of the abovementioned families (Pleasure, who was the daughter of Happiness, and Pain, who was the son of Misery) to meet one another upon this part of nature which lay in the half way be tween them, having promised to settle it upon them both, provided they could agree upon the division of it, so as to share mankind between them.

Pleasure and Pain, were no sooner met in their new habitation, but they immediately agreed upon this point, that Pleasure should take possession of the virtuous, and Pain of the vicious part of that species which was given up to them. But upon examining to which Of them any individual they met with belonged, they found each of thein had a right to him; for that contrary to what they had seen in their old place of residence, there was no person so vicious who had not some good in him, nor any person so virtuous who had nottn him some evil.—The truth of it is, they generally found, upon search, that in the most vicious man Pleasure might lay claim to an hundredth part, and that in the most virtuous man Pain might come in for at least two thirds. This they saw would occasion endless disputes between them, unless they could come to some accommodation. To this end, there was a marriage proposed between them, and at length concluded. Hence it is that we find Pleasure and Pain are such constant yoke fellows, and that they either make their visits together, or are never far asunder. If Pain comes into an heart, he is quickly followed by Pleasure; and if Pleasure enters, you may be sure Pain is not far off.

But notwithstanding this marriage was very convenient for the two parlies, it did not seem to answer the intention, of Jupiter in sending them among mankind. To remedy, therefore, this inconvenience, it was stipulated between them by article, and confirmed by the consent of each family, that, notwithstanding they here possessed the species indifferently, upon the death of every single person, if he was found to have in him a certain proportion of evil, he should be dispatched into the infernal regions by a passport from Pain, there to dwell with Misery, Vice and the Furies; or, orf the contrary, if he had in him a certain proportion of good, he should be dispatched into heaven, by a passport from Pleasure, there to dwell with Happiness, Virtue and the Gods.

V.—*Sir Roger de Coverly's Family.* —Ib. HAVING often received an invitation from mv friend Sir Roger de CoverJy, to pass away a month with him in the country, I last week accompanied him thither, and am settled with him for some time at his country-house, where I intend to form several of my ensuing speculations. Sir Roger, who is very well acquainted with my humour, lets me rise and go to bed when I please, dine at his own table or in my chamber, as I think fit, sit still and say nothing, without bidding me be merry. When the gentlemen of the country come to see him, he only shows me at a distance. As I have been walking in the fields, I have observed them stealing a sight of me over an hedge, and have heard the knight desiring them not to let me see them, for that I hated to be stared at.

I am the more at ease in Sir Roger's family, because it consists of sober and staid persons; for as the knight is the best master in the world, he seldom changes his servants; and as he is beloved by all about him, his servants never care for leaving him; by thjs means his domestics are all in years and grown old with their master. You would take his valet de chambre for his brother; his butler is grey headed, his groom is one of the gravest men I have ever seen, and his coachman has the looks of a privy counsellor. You see the goodness of the master even in the old house dog, and in a gray pad that is kept in the stable with great care and tenderness, out of regard to his past services, though he has been nseless for several years.

I could not but observe, with a great deal of pleasure, the joy that appeared in the countenances of these ancient domestics, upon my friend's arrival at his country seat. Some of them could not refrain from tears at the sight of their old master; every one of them pressed forward to do something for him, and seemed discouraged if they were not employed. At the same time, the good old knight, with the mixture of the father and the master of the family, tempered the inquiries after his own affairs with several kind questions relating to themselves. This humanity and good nature engages every body to him; so that when he is pleasant upon any of them, all his family are in good humour, and none so much as the person whom he diverts himself with; on the contrary, if he coughs, or betrays any infirmity of old age, it is easy for a stander-by to observe a secret concern in the looks of ali ins servants.

My worthy friend has put me under the particular care of his butler, who is a very prudent man, and, as well as the rest of his fellow servants, wonderfully desirous of pleasing me, because they have often heard their master talk of me as his particular friend.

My chief companion when Sir Roger is diverting himself in the woods or in the fields, is a very venerable man who is ever with Sir Roger, and has lived at his house in the nature of a chaplain, above thirty years. This gentleman is a jierson of good sense and some learning, of a very regular life and obliging conversation; he heartily loves Sir Roger, and knows that he is very much in the old knight's esteem; so that he lives in the family rather as a relation than a dependant.

I have observed in several of my papers, that my friend Sir Roger, amidst all his good qualities, is something of an humourist; and that his virtues, as well as Imperfections, are, as it were, tinged by a certain extravagance, which makes them particularly his, and distinguishes them from those of other men.-This cast of mind, as it is generally very innocent in itself, so it renders his conversation highly agreeable, and more delightful than the same degree of sense and virtue would appear in their common and ordinary colours. As I was walking with him last night, he asked me how I liked the good man whom I have just now mentioned;—and, without staying for my answer, told me that he was afraid of being insulted with Latin and Greek at his own table; for which reason he desired a particular friend of his at the university, to find him out a clergyman rather of plain sense than much learning, of a good aspect, a clear voice, a sociable temper; and if possible, a man who understood a little back gammon. My friend, says Sir Roger, found me out this gentleman; who, besides the endowments required of him, is, they tell me a good scholar, though he does not show it. I have given him the parsonage of the parish 5 and because I know his value, have settled upon him a good annuity for life. If he outlives me, he shall find that he was higher in my esteem than perhaps he thinks he is. He has now been with me thirty years; and though he does not know I have taken notice of it, has never, in all that time, asked any thing of me for himself, though he is every day soliciting me for something in behalf of one or other of my tenants, his parishioners. There has not been a lawsuit in the parish since he has lived among them. If any dispute arises, they apply themselves to him for the decision; if they do not acquiesce in his judgment, which I think never happened above once or twice at most, they appeal to me.— At his first settling with me, I made him a present of all the good sermons which have been printed in English; and only begged of him that every Sunday. he would pronounce one of them in the pulpit. Accordingly he has digested them into such a series, that they follow one another naturally, and make a continued system of practical divinity.

As Sir Roger was going on in his story, the gentleman we were talking of came up to us; and, upon the knight's asking him who preached to-morrow (for it was Saturday night) told us the Bishop of St. Asaph, in the morning, and Dr. South in the afternoon. He then showed us his list of preachers for the whole year; where I saw with a great deal of pleasure, Archbishop Tillotson, Bishop Saunderson, Dr. Barrow, Dr. Calamy, with several living authors, who have published discourses of practical divinity. I no sooner saw this venerable man in the pulpit, but I very much approved of my friend's insisting upon the qualifications of a good aspect, and a clear voice; for I was so charmed with the gracefulness of his figure and delivery, as well as with the discourses he pronounced, that I think I never passed any time more to my satisfaction. A sermon repeated after this manner, is like the composition of a poet in the mouth of a graceful actor.

VI.—*The Folly of inconsistent Expectations.*—Aitkin. THIS world may be considered as a great mart of commerce, where fortune exposes to our view various commodities; riches, ease, tranquility, fame, integrity, knowledge. Every thing is marked at a settled price. Our time, our labour, our ingenuity, is so much ready money, which we are to lay out to the best advantage.—

Examine, compare, choose, reject; but stand to your own judgment; and do not, like children, when you have purchased one thing, repine that you do not possess another, which you did not purchase. Such is the force of well regulated industry, that a steady and vigorous exertion of our faculties, directed to one end, will generally insure success. Would-you, for instance, be rich? Do you think that single point worth the sacrificing every thing else to? You may then be rich. Thousands have become so from the loweit beginnings, by toil, and patient diligence, and attention to the minutest articles of expense and profit. But you must give up the pleasures of leisure, of a vacant mind, of a free unsuspicious temper. Tf you preserve your integrity, it must be a coarse spun and vulgar honesty. Those high andjofty notions of morals, which you brought with you from the schools must be considerably lowered, and mixed with the baser alloy of a jealous and worldly minded prudence. You must learn to do hard, if not unjust things; and for the nice embarrassments of a delicate and ingenuous spirit, it is necessary for you to get rid of them as fast as possible. You must shut your heart against the Muses, and be content to feed your understanding with plain household truths. In short you must not attempt to enlarge your ideas, or polish your taste, or refine your sentiments; but must keep on in one beaten track, without turning aside, either to the right hand or to the left.— " But 1 cannot submit to drudgery like this—I feel a spirit above it." It is well; be above it then; only do not repine that you are not rich. JIs knowledge the pearl of price? That, too, may be purchased—by steady application, and long solitary hours of study and reflection—Bestow these and you shall be learned. "But," sayslhe man of letters, "what a hardship it is, that many an illiterate fellow, who cannot construe the motto of the arms of his coach, shall raise a fortune and make a figure, while I have little more than the common conveniences of life!" Was it in order to raise a fortune, that you consumed the sprightly hours of youth in study and retirement? Was it to be rich, that you grew pale over the midnight lamp, and distilled the sweetness from the Greek and Roman spring? You have then mistaken your path, and ill employed your industry.— "What reward have I then for all ray labours?" What reward! a large comprehensive soul, well purged from vulgar fears, and perturbations, and prejudices, able to comprehend and interpret the works of man—of God. A rich, flourishing, cultivated mind, pregnant with inexhaustable stores of entertainment and reflection, A perpetual spring of fresh

ideas, and the conscious dignity of superiour intelligence. Gojd heaven! and what reward can you ask besides?

"But is it not some reproach upon the economy of Providence, that such a one, who is a mean dirty fellow, should have amassed wealth enough to buy half a nation?" Not in the least. He made himself a mean dirty fellow for that very end. He has paid his health, his conscience, his liberty, for it; and will you envy his bargain? Will you hang your head and blush in his presence, because he outshines you in equipage and show? Lft up your brow, with a noble confidence and say to yourself, "I have not these things, it is true; but it is because I have not sought, because I have not desired them; it is because I possess something better: I have chosen my lot; I am content and satisfied."

You are a modest man—you love quiet and independence, and have a delicacy and reserve in your temper, which renders it impossible for you to elbow your way in in the world, and be the herald of your own merits. Be content, then, with a modest retirement, with the esteem of your intimate friends, with the praises of a blameless heart, and a delicate ingenuous spirit; but resign the splendid distinctions of the world to those who can better scramble for them.

The man whose tender sensibility of conscience and strict regard to the rules of morality makes him scrupulous and fearful of offending, is often heard to complain of the disadvantages he lies under, in every path of honour and profit. "Could I but get over some nice points, and conform to the practice and opinion of those about me, I might stand as fair a chance as others for dignities and preferment." And why can you not? What hinders you from discarding this troublesome scrupulosity of yours which stands so grievously in your way? If it be a small thing to enjoy a healthful mind, sound at the very core, that does not shrink from the keenest inspection; inward freedom from remorse and peturbation, unsullied whiteness and simplicity of manners; a genuine integrity,

Pure in the last recesses of the mind;

if you think these advantages an inadequate recompence for what you resign, dismiss your scruples this instant, and be a slave merchant, a director—or what you please.

VII.—*Description of the Vale of Keswick, in Cumberland.*

Brown. THIS delightful vale is thus elegantly described by the late ingenious Dr. Brown, in a letter to a friend.

In my way to the north, from Hagley, I passed through Dovedale; and to say the truth, was disappointed in it. When I came to Buxton, I visited another or two of their romantic scenes; but these are inferiour to Dovedale.— They are all but poor miniatures of Keswick, which exr ceeds them more in grandeur than you can imagine; and mure, if possible, in beauty than in grandeur.

Instead of a narrow slip of valley, which is seen at Dovedale, you have at Keswick a vast amphitheatre, ia circumference above twenty miles. Instead of a-meagre rivulet, a noble living lake ten miles round, of an oblong form, adorned with a vaiiety of wooded islands. The rocks indeed of Dovedale are finely wild, pointed, and irregular; but the hills are both little and unanimated; and the margin of the brook is poorly edged with weeds, morass and brushwood. But at Keswick-you will on one side of the lake, *tee* a rich and beautiful landscape of cultivated fields, rising to the eye in fine inequalities, with noble groves of oak, happily dispersed, and climbing the adjacent hills, shade above shade, in the most various and picturesque forms. On the opposite shore, you will find rocks and cliffs of stupendous height hanging broken over the lake, in horrible grandeur, some of them a thousand feet high, the woods climbing up their steep and shaggy sides, where mortal foot never yet approached. On these dreadful heights the eagles build their nests; a variety of waterfalls are seen pouring from their summits, and tumbling in vast sheets from rock to rock, in rude and terrible magnificence; while, on all sides of this immense amphitheatre, the lofty mountains rise round, piercing the clouds, in shapes as spiry and fantastic as the very rocks of Dovedale. To this I must add the frequent and bold projections of the cliffs into the lake, forming noble bays and promontories: In other parts they finely retire from it, and often open in abrupt chasms or clefts, through which at hand, you see rich and uncultivated vales; and beyond these at various distance, mountain rising over mountain; among which, new prospects present themselves in mist, till the eye is lost in an agreeable perplexity;

Where active fancy travels beyond *sense,*
And pictures things unseen.—

Were I to analyse the.two places into their constituent principles, I should tell you, that the full perfection of Keswick consists in three circumstances; beauty, horror and immensity, united; the second of which alone is found in Dovedale. Of beauty it hath little, nature having left it almost a desert; neither its small extent nor the diminutive and lifeless form of the hills, admits magnificence; but to give you a complete idea of these three perfections, as they are joined in Keswick, would require the united powers of Claude, Salvator, and Poussin. The first should throw his delicate sunshine over the cultivated vales, the scatterd eots, the groves, the lake, and wooded islands. The second should dash out the horror of the rugged cliffs, the steeps, the hanging woods, and foaming waterfalls; while the grand pencil of Poussin should crown the whole, with the majesty of the impending mountains.

So much for what 1 would call the permanent beauty of this astonishing scene. Were I not afraid of being tiresome, I could now dwell as long upon its varying or accidental beauties. I would sail round the lake, anchor in every bay, and land you on every promontory and island. I would point out the perpetual change of prospect; the woods, rocks, cliffs and mountains, by turns vanishing or rising into view; now gaining on the sight, hanging over our heads in their full dimensions, beautifully dreadful, and now by a change of situation, assuming new romantic shapes; retiring and lessening on the eye, and insensibly losing themselves in an azure mist. I would remark the contrast of light and shade, produced by the morning and evening sun! Ihe one gilding the western, the other the eastern side of this immense amphitheatre; while the vast shadow, projected by the mountains, buries the opposite part in a deep and purple gloom, which the eye can hardly penetrate. The natural variety of colouring which the several objects produce, is no less wonderful and pleasing; the ruling tints in the valley being those of azure, green and gold; yet ever various, arising from an intermixture of the lake, the woods, the grass, and cornfields; these are finely contrasted by the gray rocks and diii's; and the whole heightened by the yellow streams of light, the purple hues, and misty azure of the mountains. Sometimes, a serene air and clear sky disclose the tops of the highest hills; at other times, you see the clouds involving their summits, resting on their sides, or descending to their base, and rolling among the valleys, as in a vast furnace. When the winds are high, they roar among the cliffs and caverns, like peals of thunder; then, too, the clouds are seen in vast bodies,'sweeping along the hills m gloomy greatness, while the lake joins the tumult, and tosses like a sea. But in calm weather, the whole scene becomes new; the lake is a perfect mirror, and the landscape in all its beauty; islands, fields, woods, rocks smcl mountains, are seen inverted, and floating on its surface. I will now carry you to the top of a cliff, where if you dare approach the ridge, a new scene of astonishment presents itself; where the valley, lake and islands, seem lying at your feet; where this expanse of water appears diminished to a little pool, amidst the vast and immeasurable objecls that surround it; Cor here the summits of more distant hills appear beyond those you have already seen; and, rising behind each other, in successive ranges, and azure groups Of craggy and broken steeps, form an immense and awful picture, which can only be expressed by the image of a tempestuous sea of mountains. Let me now conduct you down again to the valley and conclude with one circumstance more; which is that a walk by a still moonlight (at which time the distant water falls are heard in all their variety of sound) among these enchanting dales, open such scenes of delicate beauty, repose and solemnity, as exceed all description.

VIII.—*Pity, an Allegory.*—Aitkin. IN the happy period of the golden age, when all the celestial (inhabitants deseeded to the earth, and conversed familiarly with mortals, among the most cherished of the heavenly powers, were twins, the offspring of Jupiter, Love and Joy. Wherever they appeared, the flowers sprung up beneath their feet, the sun shone with a brighter radiance, and all nature seemed embellished by their presence.

They were inseparable companions; and their growing attachments, was favored by Jupiter, who had decreed, that a lasting union should be solemnized between them, so soon as they were arrived at maturer years.—But, in the meantime, the sons of men deviated from their native innocence; vice and ruin over ran the earth with giant strides; and Astrea, with her train *of* celestial visitants, forsook their polluted abodes. Love alone remained, having been stolen away by Hope, who was his nurse, and conveyed by her to the forests of Arcadia, where he was brought up among the shepherds. But Jupiter assigned him a different partner, and commanded him to espouse Sorrow, the daughter of Ate. He complied with reluctance; for her features were harsh and disagreeable, her eyes sunk, her forehead contracted into perpetual wrinkles, and her temples were covered: with a wreath of cypruss and wormwood.

-From this union sprang a virgin, in whom might be traced a strong resemblance to both her parents; but the sullen and unamiable features of her mother, were so mixed and blended with the sweetness of her father, that her countenance, though mournful, was highly pleasing.-The maids and shepherds of the neighbouring plains gathered round, and called her Pit. A red breast was observed to build in the cabin where she was born; and, while she was yet an infant, a dove, pursued by a hawk, flew into her bosom. The nymph had a dejected appearance; but so soft and gentle a mein, that she was beloved (o a degree of enthusiasm. Her voice was low and plaintive, but inexpressibly sweet, and she loved to lie, for hours together, on the banks of some wild and melancholy stream, singing to her lute. She taught men to weep, for she took a strange delight in tears; and often,, when the virgins of the hamlet were assembled at their evening sports, she would steal in among them and captivate their hearts by her tales, full of charming sadness. She wore on her head a garland, composed of her father's myrtles, twisted with her mother's cypruss.

One day, as she sat musing by the waters of Helicon, her tears by chance fell into the fountain, and ever since, the Muse's spring has retained a strong taste of the infusion. Pity was commanded by Jupiter, to follow the steps of her mother through the world, dropping balm into the wounds she made, and binding up the hearts she had broken. She follows with her hair loose, her bosom bare and throbbing, her garments torn by the briars, and her feet bleeding with the roughness of the path. The nymph is mortal, for her mother is so; and when she has fulfilled her destined course upon the earth, they shall both expire together, and Love be again united to Joy, his immortal and long betrothed bride.

IX.—*Advantages of Commerce.*—Spectator. THERE is no place in town which I so much love to frequent, as the Royal Exchange. It gives me a secret satisfaction, and in some measure gratifies my vanity, as I am an Englishman, to see so rich an assembly of my countrymen and foreigners consulting together upon the private.business of mankind, and making this metropolis a kind of emporium for the whole earth. I must confess I look upon High Change to be a grand council, in which all considerable nations have their representatives. Factors in the trading world, are what ambassadors are in the politic world. They negociate affairs, conclude treaties, and maintain a good correspondence between those wealthy societies of men, that are divided from one another by seas and oceans, or live on the different extremities of a continent. I have often been pleased to hear disputes adjusted between an inhabitant of Japan and an alderman of London; or to see a subject of the Great Mogul entering into a league with one of the Czar of Muscovy. I am infinitely delighted in mixing withthese several ministers of commerce, as they are distinguished by tlveir different walks and different languages. Sometimes I am jostled among a body of Armenians; sometimes I am lost in a crowd of Jews; and sometimes make one in a group of Dutchmen. I am a Dane, Swede, or Frenchman, at different times, or rather fancy myself like the old philosopher, who, upon being asked what countryman he was, replied, That he was a citizen of the world.

Nature seems to have taken a particular care to disseminate her blessings among the different regions of the world with an eye to this mutual intercourse and traffic among mankind, that the natives of the several parts of the globe might have a kind of dependance upon one another, and be united together by their common interests. Almost every degree produces something peculiar to it. The food often grows in one country, and the sauce in another.— The fruits of Portugal are corrected by the products of Barbadoes; the infusion of a China plant sweetened with the pith of an indian cane. The Philippine islands give a flavour to our European bowls. The single dress of a woman of quality is often the product of an hundred climates. The muff and the fan come together from the different ends of the earth. The scarf is sent from the torrid zone, and the tippet from beneath the pole. The brocade petticoat rises out of the mines of Peru, and the diamond necklace out of the bowels of Indostan.

If we consider our own country in its natural prospect, without any of the benefits and advantages of commerce, what a barren uncomfortable spot of the earth falls to our share! Natural historians tell us, that no fruit grows originally among us, besides hips and haws, acorns and pignuts, with other delicacies of the like nature; that our climate, of itself, and without the assistance of art, can make no further advances towards a plumb, than a sloe, and carries an apple to no greater perfection than a crab; that our melons, our peaches, our figs, our apricots and our cherries, are strangers among us, imported in different ages, and naturalized in our English gardens; and that they would all degenerate and fall away into the trash of our own country, if they were wholly neglected by the planter, and left to the mercy of jur sun and soil.

Nor has traffic more enriched our vegetable world, than it has improved the whole face of nature among us. Our ships are laden with the harvest of every climate; our tables are stored with spices, and oils, and wines; our rooms are filled with pyramids of China, and adorned with the workmanship of Japan; our morning's draught comes to u; from the remotest corners of the earth; we repair our bodies by the drugs of America, and repose ourselves under Indian canopies. My friend, Sir Andrew, calls the vineyards of France, our gardens; the spice Islands, our hot beds; the Persians, our silk weavers; and the Chinese, our potters. Nature, indeed, furnishes us with the bare necessaries of life; but traffic gives us a great variety of what is useful, and, at the same time, supplies us with every thing that is convenient and ornamental. Nor is it the least part of this our happiness, that, whilst we enjoy the remotest products of the north and south, we are free from those extremities of weather which give them birth; that our eyes are refreshed with the green fields of Britain, at the same time that our palates are feasted with fruits that rise between the tropics.

For these reasons, there are not more useful members in a commonwealth than merchants. They knit mankind together in a mutual intercourse of good offices, distribute the gifts of nature, find work for the poor, add wealth to the rich, and magnificence to the great. Our

English merchant converts the tin of his own country into gold, and exchanges his wool for rubies. The Mahometans are clothed in our British manufacture, and the inhabitants of the frozen zone warmed with the fleeces of our sheep,

X.— *On Public Speaking.*—»ir. MOST foreign writers who have given any character of the English nation, whatever ice they ascribe to it, allow, in general, that the people are naturally modest. It proceeds, perhaps, from this our national virtue, that our orators are observed to make use of less gesture or action than those of other countries. Our preachers stand stock still in the pulpit, and will not so much as move a finger to set off the best sermons in the world. We meet with the same speaking statues at our bars, and in all public places of debate. Our words flow from us in a smooth continued stream, without those strainings of the voice, motions of the body, and majesty of the hand which are go much celebrated in the orators of Greece and Rome. We can talk of life and death ia cold blood, and keep our temper in a discourse which turns upon every thing that is dear to us. Though our zeal breaks out in the finest tropes and figures, it is not able to stir a limb about us.

It is certain that proper gestures and exertions of the voice cannot be too much studied by a public orator.— They are a kind of comment to what he utters; and enforce every thing he says, with weak hearers, better than the strongest argument he can make use of. They keep the audience awake, and fix their attention to what is delivered to them; at the saine time that they show the speaker is in earnest, and affected himself with what he so passionately recommends to others.

We are told that the great Latin orator very much impaired his health, by the vehemence of action with which he used to deliver himself. The Greek orator was likewise so very famous for this particular in rhetoric, that one of his antagonists, whom he had banished from Athens, reading over the oration which had procured his banishment, and seeing his friends admire it, could not forbear asking them—If they were so much affected by the-bare reading it, how much more they would have been alarmed, had they heard him actually throwing out such a storm of eloquence.

How cold and dead a figure, in comparison of these two great men does an orator often make at the British bar, holding up his head with the most insipid serenity, and stroking the sides of a long wig that reaches down to his middle! Nothing can be more ridiculous than the gestures of most of our English speakers. You see some of them running their hands into their pockets as far as ever they can thrust them, and others looking with great attention on a piece of paper that has nothing written on it; yo may see many a smart rhetorician turning his hat in his hands, moulding it into several different cocks, examining sometimes the lining of it, and sometimes the button, during the whole course of his harangue. A deaf man would think that he was cheapening a beaver; when perhaps he was talking of the fate of the British nation, 1 remember when I was a young man and used to frequent Westminster hall, there was a counsellor who never pleaded without a piece of pack-thread in his hand, which he used to twist about a thumb or finger all the while he was speak ing; the wags of those days used to call it the thread of his discourse, for he was not able to utter a word without it-One of his clients who was more merry than wise, stole it from him one day, in the midst of his pleading; but he had better have let it alone, for he lost his cause by the jest.

XI.—*Advantages of History.*—Hume. THE advantages found in history seem to be of three kinds; as it amuses the fancy, as it improves the under Standing, and as it strengthens virtue.

In reality, what more agreeable entertainment to the mind, than to be transported into the remotest ages of the-world, and to observe human society, in its infancy, making the first faint essays towards the arts and sciences? To see the policy of government and the civility of conversation refining by degrees, and every thing that is ornamental to human life advancing towards its perfection? To mark the rise, progress, declension, and final extinction of the most flourishing empires; the virtues which contributed to their greatness, and the vices which drew on their ruin? In short, to see all the human race, from the beginning of time, pass as it were in review before us, appearing in their true colours, without any of those disguises, which, during their lifetime, so much perplexed the judgment of the beholders? What spectacle can be imagined so magnificent, so various, so interesting? What amusement, either of the senses or imagination, can be compared with it? Shall our trifling pastimes, which engross so much of our time, be preferred, as more satisfactory, and more fit to engage our attention? How perverse must that taste be, which is capable of so wrong a choice f pleasure?

But history is a most improving part of knowledge, as-well as an agreeable amusement; and, indeed, a great part of what we commonly call *erudition,* and value so highly, is nothing but art acquaintance with historical facts. An extensive knowledge of this kind belongs to men of letters; but I must think it an unpardonable ignorance in persons, of whatever sex or condition, not to be acquainted with the histories of their own country, along with the histories of ancient Greece and Rome.

I must add, that history is not only a valuable part of knowledge, but opens the door to many oilier parts of knowledge, and affords materials to most of the sciences. And, indeed, if we consider the shortness of human life, and our limited knowledge, even of what passes in our own time, we must be sensible that we should be forever children in understanding, were it not for this invention, which extends our experience to all past ages, and to most distant nations, making them contribute as much to our improvement in wisdom, as if they had actually lain under our observation. A man acquainted with history, may, in some respect, be said to have lived from the beginning of the world, and to have been making continualadditions in his stock of knowledge, in every country.

There is also an advantage in that knowledge which is acquired by history, above what is learned by the practice of the world, that it brings us acquainted with human affairs, without diminishing in the least from the most delicate sentiments of virtue. And, to tell the truth, I scarce know any study or occupation so unexceptionable as history, in this particular. Poets can paint virtue in the most charming colours; but, as they address themselves entirely to the passions, they often become advocates to vice. Even philosophers are apt to bewilder themselves in the sublilty of their speculations 5 and we have seen some go so far, as to deny the reality of all moral distinctions. But I think it a remark worthy the attention of the speculative reader, that the historians have been, almost without exception, the true friends of virtue-and have always represented it in its proper colours, however they may have erred in their judgments of particular persons. Nor is iliis combination of historians, in favour of virtue, at all difficult to be accounted for. When a man of business enters into life and action, he is more apt to consider the characters of men as they have relation to his interest, than as they stand in themselves, and has his judgment warped on every occasion, by the violence of his passion. When a philosopher contemplates character and manners, in his closet, the general abstract view of the objects leaves the mind so cold and unmoved, that the sentiments of nature have no room to play, and he scarce feels the difference betwixt vice and virtue. History keeps in a just medium betwixt these extremes and places the objects in their true point of view. The writers of history, as well as the readers, are sufficiently interested in the 'characters and events, to have a lively sentiment of blame or praise; and, at the same time, have no particular interest or concern to pervert their judgment.

XII.— *On the Immortality of the Soul.* —Spectator. AMONG other excellent arguments for the immortality of the soul, there is one drawn from the perpetual progress of the soul to its perfection, without a possibility of ever arriving at it; which is a-hint that I do not remember to have seen opened and improved by others who have written on this subject, though it seems to me to carry a great weight with it. How can it enter into the thoughts of man, that the soul, which is capable of such immense perfections, and of receiving new improvements to all eternity, shall fall away-into nothing, almost as soon as it is created? Are such abilities made for no purpose? A brute urrives at a point of perfection that he can never pass; in a few years he has all the endowments he is capable of; were he to live ten thousand more, he would be the same thing he is at present. Were a human soul thus at a stand in her accomplishments; were her faculties to be full blown, and incapable of further enlargements; I could imagine it might fall away insensibly, and drop at once into a state of annihilation. But, can we believe a thinking being, that is in a perpetual progress of improvements, and travelling on from perfection to perfection, after having just looked abroad into the works of its Creator, and made a few discoveries of his infinite goodness, wisdom and power, must perish at her first setting out, and in the very beginning of her inquiries?

Man, considered in his present state, does not seem born to enjoy life, but to deliver it down to others. This is not surprising, to-consider in animals, which are formed for eur use, and can finish their business in a short life. The silkworm after having spun her task, lays her eggs and dies. But in this life man can never take in his full "measure of knowledge; nor l,t he time to subdue his passions, establish his soul in virtue, and come up to the perfection of his nature, before he is hurried off the stage. Would an infinite wise Being make such glorious creatures, for so mean a purpose?Can lie delight in the production of such abortive intelligences, such short lived reasonable beings? Would he give us talents that are not to be exerted? Capacities that are never to be gratified? How can we find that wisdom which shines through all his works, in the formation of man, without looking on this world as only a nursery for the next; and believing that the several generations of rational creatures, which rise up and disappear in such quick successions, are only to ieceive their first rudiments of all existence here, and afterwards to be transplanted into a more friendly climate, where they may spread and flourish to all eternity?

There is not, in my opinion, a more pleasing and triumphant consideration in religion than this, of the perpetual progress which the soul makes towards the perfection of its nature, without ever arriving at a period in it. To. look upon the soul as going on from strength to strength j to consider that she is to shine, with new accessions of. glory, to all eternity; that she will be still adding virtue to virtue, and knowledge to knowledge; carriesin it something wonderfully agreeable to that ambition which isnatural to the mjnd of man.— Nay, it must be a prospect pleasing to God himself, to see his creation forever beau.tifying in his eyes, and drawing nearer to. him, by greater degrees of resemblance.

Methinks this single consideration, of.the progress of a finite spirit to perfection, will be sufficient to extinguish all envy in inferiour natures, and all contempt in superiour. That cherubim which now appears as a God to a human soul, knows very well that the period will come about in eternity, when the human soul shall be as perfect as he himself now is; nay, when she shall look down'upon that degree of perfection as much as she now falls short of it. It is true, the higher nature still advances, and by that means' preserves his distance and superiority in the scale of being;'but he knows, that how high soever the station is of which he stands possessed at present, the inferiour nature will at length mount up to it, and shine forth in the same degree of glory.

With what astonishment and veneration may we look into our souls, where there are such hidden stores of virtue and knowledge, such iuexhausted sources of perfection!.

We know not yet what we shall be, nor will it ever enter into the heart of man to conceive the glory that will be always in reserve for him. The soul, considered in relation "to its Creator, is like one of those mathematical lines, that may draw nearer to another for all eternity, without a possibility of touching it; and enn there be a thought so transporting, as to consider ourselves in these perpetual approaches of Him, who is not only the standard of perfection, but of happiness!

XIII. — *The Combat of the Horatii and the Curiatii.*—Lrvr. THE combat of the Horatii and Curiatii is painted in a very natural and animated manner by Livy. The cause was this. The inhabitants of Alba and Rome, roused by ambition and mutual complamts, took the field, and were on the eve of a bloody battlp. The Alban general, to prevent the effusion of blood, proposed to Hostilius, then king of Rome, to refer the destiny of both nations to three combatants of each side, and that empire should be the prize of the conquering party. The proposal was accepted. The Albans named the Curiatii, three brothers, for their champions. The three sons of Horatius were chosen for the Romans.

The treaty being concluded, the three brothers, on each side, arrayed themselves in armour, according to agreement. Each side exhorts its respective champions; representing to them, that their gods, their country, their parents, every individual in the city and army, now fixed their eyes on their arms and valour. The generous combatants, intrepid in themselves, and animated by such exhortations, march forth, and stood between the two armies. The armies placed themselves before the respective camps, and were less solicitous for any present danger, than for the consequence of this action. They therefore gave their whole attention to a sight, which could not but alarm them. The signal is given. The combatants engage with hostile weapons, and show themselves inspired with the intrepidity of two mighty armies. Both parties equally insensible of their own danger, had nothing in view but the slavery or liberty of their country, whose destiny depended upon their conduct. At the first onset, the clashing of their armour, and the terrific gleam of their swords, filled the spectators with such trepidation, fear and horror, that the faculty of speech and breath seemed totally suspended even while the hope of success inclined to neither side.— But when it came to a closer engagement, not only the motions of their bodies, and the furious agitation of their weapons, arrested the eyes of the spectators, but their opening wounds, and the streaming blood. Two of llieRomans fell, and expired at the feet of the Albans, who were all three wounded. Upon their fall, the Alban army shouted for joy, while the Roman legions remained without hope, but not without concern, being eagerly anxious for the surviving Roman, then surrounded by his three adversaries. Happily he was not wounded; but not being a match for three, though superiour to any of them singly, he had recourse to a stratagem for dividing them. Hebetook himself to flight; rightly supposing, thai they would follow him at unequal distance, as their strength, after so much loss of blood, would permit. Having fled a considerable way from the spot where they fought, he looked back, and saw the Curiatii pursuing, at a considerable distance from one another, and one of them very near him. He turned with all his fury upon the foremost; and, while the Alban army were crying out to his brothers to succour him, Horatius, having presently dispatched his first enemy, rushed forward to a second victory.' The Romans encourage their champion by such acclamations as generally proceed from unexpected success. He, on the other hand hastens to put an end to the second combat, and slew another, before the third, who was not far ofl, could come up to his assistance. There now remained only one combatant on each side: The Roman, who had still received no hurt, fired with gaining a double victory, advances with great confidence to his third combat. His antagonist, on the other hand, being. weakened by the loss of blood, and spent with running so far, could scarce drag his legs after him, and being already dispirited by the death of his brothers, presents his breast to'the victor, for it could not be called a contest. "Two (says the exulting Roman) two have I sacrificed to' the manes of my brothers—the third I will offer up to my country, that henceforth Rome may give laws to Alba." Upon which he transfixed him with his sword, and stripped him of his armour. The Ro mans received Horatius, the victor, into their camp, with an exultation, great as their former fear. After this, each army buried their respective dead, but with very different sentiments; the one reflecting on the sovereignty they had acquired, and the other on the subjection to slavery, to the power of the Romans.

This combat became still more remarkable: Horatius, returning to Rome, with the arms and spoils of his enemy, met his sister, who was to have been married to one of the Curiatii. Seeing her brother dressed in her lover's coat of armour, which she herself had wrought, she could not contain her grief.—She shed a flood of tears, she tore lier hair, and in the transports of her sorrow, uttered the most violent imprecations agamst her brother. Horatius, warm with his victory, and enraged at the grief which his sister expressed, with such unseasonable passion, in the midst of the public joy, in the heat of his anger, drove a poignard to her heart. "Begone to thy lover," says he, "and carry him that degenerate passion which makes thee prefer a dead enemy to the glory of thy country." Every body detested an action so cruel and inhuman. The murderer was immediately seized, and dragged befare the Duumviri, the proper judges of such crimes. Horatius was condemned to lose his life; and the very day of his triumph had been the day of his punishment, if he had not by the advice of Tullus Hostilius, appealed from that judgment to the assembly of the people. He appeared there with the same courage and resolution that he had shown in the combat with the Guriatii. —The people thought so great a service miht justly excuse them, if for once they moderated the rigour of the law; and, accordingly, he was acquitted, rather through admiration of his courage, than for the justice of his cause.

XIV.— *On the Power of Custom.*— Spectator. THERE is not a common saying which has a better turn of sense in it, than what we often hear in the mouths of the-vulgar, that custom is second nature.—It is, indeed, able to form the man anew, and give him inclinations and capacities altogether different from those he was born with. A person who is addicted to play or gaming, though he took but little delight in it at first, by degrees contracts so Strong an inclination towards it, and gives himself up so entirely to it, that it seems the only end of his being. The Jove of a retired or busy life will grow upon a man insensibly, as he is conversant in the one or the other, till he is utterly unqualified for relishing that to which he has been for some time disused. Nay, a roan may smoke, or drink-, or take snuff, till he is unable to pass away his time without it; not to mention how our delight in any particular study, art, or science, rises and improves, in proportion to the application which we bestow upon it. Thus, what was at first an exercise, becomes at length an entertainment.—Our employments are changed into diversions. — The mind grows fond of those actions it is accustomed to, and is drawn witli reluctancy from those paths in which it has been used to walk.

If we consider, attentively, this property of human nature, it must instruct us in very fine moralities. In the first place, I would have no man discouraged with that kind of life, or series of action, in which the choice of others, or his own necessities may have engaged him. It may, perhaps, be disagreeable to him at first; but use and application will certainly render it not only less painful, but pleasing and satisfactory.

In the second place, I would recommend to every one the admirable precept which Pythagoras is said to have given tcr his disciples, and which that philosopher must have drawn from the observation I have enlarged upon; "Pitch upon that course of life which is the most excellent, and custom will render it the most delightful." Men, whose circumstances will permit them to choose their own way of life are.nex-

cusable, if they do not pursue that which their judgement tells them is the most laudable. The voice of reason is more to be regarded than the bent of any present inclination, since, by the rule above-mentioned, inclination, will, at length, come over to reason, though we can never force reason to comply with inclination.

In the third place, this observation may teach the most sensual and irreligious man to. overlook those hardships and difficulties, which are apt to discourage him from the prosecution of a virtuous life. "The Gods" says Heisod, " have placed labour before virtue; the way to her is at first rough and difficult, but grows more.

smooth and easy the farther you advance in it." The man who proceeds in it with steadiness and resolution, will in a little time find that her "ways are ways of pleasantness, and that all her paths are peace"

To enforce this consideration, we may further observe that the practice of religion will not only be attended with that pleasure, which naturally accompanies those actions to which we are habituated j but with those supernumerary joys of heart, that rise from the consciousness of such a pleasure, from the satisfaction of acting up to the dictates of reason, and from the prospect of an happy immortality.

in the fourth place, we may learn from this observation, which we have made on the mind of man, to take particular care, when we are once settled in a regular course of life, how we too frequently indulge ourselves in any the most innocent diversions and entertainments % since the mind may insensibly fall off from the relish of virtuous actions, and, by degrees, exchange that pleasure which it takes in the performance of its duty, for delights of a much more inferiour and unprofitable nature.

The last use which I shall make of this remarkableproperty in human nature, of being delighted witlt. those actions to which it is accustomed, is, to show how absolutely necessary it is for us to gain habits of virtue in this life, if we would enjoy the pleasures of the next.— The

state of bliss we call Heaven, will not be capable of affecting those minds which are not thus qualified for it;; we must in this world gain a relish of truth and virtue, if we would be able to taste that knowledge and perfection which are to make us happy in the next.—The seeds of those spiritual joys and raptures, which are to rise up and flourish in the soul to all eternity, must be planted in it during this its preseut state of probation. —In short, heaven is not to be looked upon only as the reward, but asthe natural effect of a religious life.

XV.— *On Pedantry.*—Mirror. PEDANTRY, in the common sense of the word, means an absurd ostentation of learning, and stiffness of phraseology, proceeding from a misguided knowledge of booksand a total ignorance of men.

But I have often thought, that we might extend its signification a good deal farther; and in general, apply it to that failing, which disposes a person to obtrude upon others, subjects of conversation relating to his own business, studies or amusements.

In this sense of the phrase, we should find pedants in every character and condition of life. Instead of a black coat and a plain shirt, we should often see pedantry appear in an embroidered suit and Brussels lace; instead of being bedaubed with snuff, we should find it breathing perfumes; and, in place of a book worm, crawling through the gloomy cloisters of an university, we should mark it in the state of a gilded butterfly, buzzing through the gay region of the drawing room.

Robert Daisy, Esq. is a pedant of this last kind. When he tells you that his ruffles cost twenty guineas a pair; that his buttons were the first of the kind, made by one of the most eminent artists in Birmingham; that his buckles were procured by means of a friend at Paris, and are the exact pattern of those worn by theCompted'Artois; that the loop of his hat was of his own contrivance, and has set the fashion to half a dozen of the finest fellows in town: When he descants on all these particulars, with that smile of self complacency' which sits forever on his cheek, he is as much a pedant as his quandam tutor, who recites verses from Pindar, tells stories out of Herodotus, and talks for an hour on the energy of the Greek particles.

But Mr. Daisy is struck dumb by the approach of his brother, Sir Thomas, whose pedantry goes a pitch higher, and pours out all the intelligence of France and Italy, whence the young baronet is just returned, after a tour of fiftee n months over all the kingdoms of the continent. Talk of music, he cuts you short with the history of the first singer in Naples; of painting, he runs you down with the description of the gallery at Florence; of architecture, he overwhelms you with the dimensions of St. Peter's, or the great church at Antwerp, or, if you leave the province of art altogether, and introduce the name of a river or hill, he instantly deluges you with the Rhine, or makes you dizzy with the height of iEtna, or Mont Blanc.

Miss will have no difficulty of owning her great aunt to be a pedant, when she talks all the time of dinner, on the composition of the pudding, or the seasoning of the mince pies; or enters into a disquisition on the figure of the damask tablecloth, with a word or two on the thrift of making one's own linen; but the young lady will be surprised when I inform her, that her own history of last Thursday's assembly, with the episode of lady D's feather, and the digression to the qualities of Mr. Frizzle, the hairdresser, was also a piece of downright pedantry.

Mrs. Caudle is guilty of the same weakness, when she recounts the numberless witticisms of her daughter Emma, describes the droll figure her little Bill made yesterday at trying on his first pair of breeches, and informs us, that Bobby has got seven teeth, and is just cutting an eighth, though he will be but nine months old next Yvednesday, at six o'clock in the evening. Nor is her pedantry less disgusting, when she proceeds to enumerate the virtues and good qualities of her husband; though this last species is so uncommon, that it may, perhaps, be admitted into conversation, for the sake of novelty.

There is a pedantry in every disquisition, however masterly it may be, that stops the general' conversation of the company. When Silius delivers that sort of lecture he is apt to get into, though it is supported by the most extensive information aid the clearest discernment, it is still pedantry; and while I admire the talents of Silius, I cannot help being uneasy at his exhibition of them. Last night, after supper, Silius began upon Protestantism, proceeded to the Irish massacre, went through the Revolution, drew the character of King William, repeated anecdotes of Schomberg, and ended, at a quarter past twelve, by delineating the course of the Boyne, in half a bumper of port, upon my best table; which river, happening to overflow its banks, did infmite damage to my cousin Sophy's white satin petticoat.

In short, every thing, in this sense of the word, is pedantry, which tends to destroy that equality of coversation, which is necessary to the perfect case and good humour of the company. Every one would be struck with the unpoliteness of that person's behaviour, who should help himself to a whole plateful of peas or strawberrys, which some friend had sent him for a rarity, in the beginning of the season. Now conversation is one of those good things, which our friends or companions are equally entitled to share, as of any other constituent part of the entertainment; and it is as essential a want of politeness to engross the one, as to monopolize the other.

XVI.—*The Journey of a Day.—A Picture of Human Life.*

Ramrler. OBIDAH, the son of Abensiua, left the caravansera early in the morning, and pursued his journey through the plains of Indostan. He was fresh and vigorous with rest; he was animated with hope; he was incited by desire;'he walked swiftly forward over the valies, and saw the hills gradually rising before him. Ashe passed along, his ears were delighted with the morning song of the bird of paradise, he was fanned by the last flutters of the sinking breeze, and sprinkled with dew by groves of spices; lie sometimes contemplated the tower-

ing height of the oak, monarch of the hills; and sometimes caught the gentle fragrance of the primrose, eldest daughter of the spring; all his senses were gratified, and all care was banished from his heart.

Thus he went on till the sun approached his meridian, and the increasing heat preyed upon his strength; he then looked round about him for some more commodious path. He saw, on his right hand, a grove that seemed to wave its shades as-a sign of invitation-; he entered it, and found the coolness and verdure irresistibly pleasant. He did not, however, forget whither he was travelling, but found a narrow way, bordered with flowers, which appeared to have the same direction with the main road, and was pleased, that, by this happy experiment, he had found means to unite pleasure with business, and to gain the reward of diligence without suffering its fatigues. He, therefore, still continued to walk, for a time, without the least remission of his ardour, except that he was sometimes tempted to stop by the music of the birds, whom the heat had assembled in the shade, and sometimes amused himself with plucking the flowers that covered the banks on either side, or the fruits that hung upon the branches. At last, the green path began to decline from its first tendency, and to wind among hills and thickets, cooled with fountains, and murmuring with water falls. Here, Obidah paused for a time, and began to consider, whether it were longer safe to forsake the known and common track; but remembering that the heat was now in its greatest violence, and that the plain was dusty and uneven, he resolved to pursue the new path, which he supposed only to make a few meanders, in compliance with the varieties of the ground, and to end at last in the common road.

Having thus calmed his solicitude, he renewed his pace, though he suspected he was not gaining ground. This uneasiness of his mind inclined him to lay hold on every new object, aud give way to every sensation that might soothe or divert him. He listened to every echo, he mounted every hill for a fresh prospect, he turned aside to every cascade, and pleased himself with tracing the course of a gentle river, that rolled among the trees,' and-watered a large region, with innumerable circumvolutions. In these amusements, the hours passed away unaccounted, his deviations had perplexed his memory, and he knew not towards what point to travel. He stood pensive and confused, afraid to go forward, lest he should go wrong, yet conscious that the time of loitering was now past.— While he was thus tortured with uncertainty, the sky Was overspread with clouds, the day vanished from before him, and a sudden tempest gathered round his head. He was now roused by his danger, to a quick and painful remembrance of his folly; he now saw how happiness was lost when ease is consulted) he lamented the unmanly impatience that prompted him to seek shelter in the grove, and despised the petty curiosity that led him on from trifle to trifle. While he was thus reflecting, the air grew blacker, and a clap of thunder broke his meditation.

He now resolved to do what remained yet in his power, to tread back the ground which he had passed, and try to find some issue, where the wood mighfopen into the plain. He prostrated himself Upon the ground, and commended his life to the Lord of nature. He rose With confidence and tranquility, and pressed on with his sabre in his hand) for the beasts of the desert were in motion, and on every hand were heard the mingled howls of rage and fear, and ravage and expiration; all the horrours of darkness and solitude surrounded him;—the winds roared in the woods and the torrents tumbled from the hills.

Thus forlorn and distressed, he wandered through the wild) without knowing whither he was going, or whether he was every moment drawing nearer to safety or to destruction. At length, not fear but labour began to over come him; his breath grew short; and his knees trembled; and he Was on the point of lying down, in resignation to his fate, when he beheld, through the brambles, the glimmer of a taper. He advanced towards the light, and finding that it pro-

ceeded from a cottage of a hermit, he called humbly at the door, and obtained admission.— The old man set before him such provisions as he had collected for himself, on which Obidah fed with eagerness and gratitude.

When the repast was over, " Tell me said the hermit, by what ehance thou hast been brought hither; 1 have been now twenty years an inhabitant of the wilderness, in which I never Saw a man before." Obidah then related the occurrences of his journey, without any concealment or palliation.

"Son, said the hermit, let the errours and follies, the dangers and escapes of this day, sink deep into thy heart. Remember, my son, that human life is the journey of a day. We rise in the morning of youth, full of vigour, and full of expectation; we set forward with spirit and hope, with gaiety and With diligence, and travel on a While in the straight road of piety, towards the mansions of rest. In a short time we remit our fervour, and endeavour to find some mitigation of our duty, and some more easy means of obtaining the same end. We then relax our vigour, and resolve no longer tobe terrified With crimes at a distance, but rely upon our own constancy, and venture to approach what we resolve never to touch. We thus enter the bowers of ease, and repose in the shades of security. Here the heart softens, and vigilance subsides; we are then willing to inquire whether another advance cannot be made, and whether we may not, at least turn our eyes upon the gardens of pleasure. We approach them with scruple and hesitation; we enter them, bat enter timorous and trembling, and always hope to pass through them without losing the road of virtue, which we, for a while keep in our sight, and to which we propose to return. But temptation succeeds temptation, and one compliance prepares us for another; we in time lose the happiness of innocence, and solace our disquiet with sensual gratifications. By degrees, we let fall the remembrance of our original intention, and quit the only adequate object of rational desire. We entangle ourselves in business, immerge ourselves

in luxury, and rove through the labyrinths of inconstancy, till the dailsness of old age begins to invade us, and disease and anxiety obstruct our way. We then look back upon our lives with horrour, with sorrow, witli repentance; and wish but too often vainly wish, that we had not forsaken the ways of virtue. Happy are they, my son, who shall learn from thy example not to despair, hut shall remember, that though the day is past, and their strength is wasted, there yet remains one effort to be made; that reformation is never hopeless, nor sincere endeavours ever unassisted; that the wanderer may at length return, after all his errours; and that he who implores strength and courage from above, shall find danger and difficulty give way before him. Go now, my son, to thy repose, commt thyself to the care of Omnipotence; and when the morning calls again to toil, begin anew thy journey and thy life." SECTION IV.

I *Description of the Amphitlwalre of Titus.*—Gibbon. POSTERITY admires, and will long admire, the awful remains of the Amphitheatre of Titus, which so weH deserves the epithet of Colossal, It was a building of an eliptic figure, five hundred and sixty four feet in length, and four hundred and sixty seven in breadth;—founded on four score arches; and rising with four successive orders of architecture, to the height of one hundred and forty feet. The outside of the edifice was encrusted with marble, and decorated with statues. The slopes of the vast concave, which formed the inside, were filled and. surrounded with sixty or eighty rows of seats of marble, covered with cushions, and capable of receiving with ease, above four score thousand spectators. Sixty four vomitories (for by that name the doors were very aptly distinguished) poured forth the immense multitude; and the entrances, passages, and staircases, were contrived with such exquisite skill, that each person, whether of the senatorial, equestrian or the plebian order, arrived at his destined place, without trouble or confusion.

Nothing was omitted which, in any respect could be subservient to the convenience and pleasure of the spectators. They were protected from the sun and rain by an ample canopy, occasionally drawn over their heads. The air-was continually refreshed by the playing of fountains, and profusely impregnated by the grateful scent of aromatics. In the centre of the edifice, the arena, or stage, was strewed with the finest sand., and successively assumed the most different forms. At one moment, it seemed to rise out of the earth, like the garden of lire Hesperides j at another, it exhibited the rugged rocks and caverns of Thrace. The subterraneous pipes conveyed an inexhaustable supply of water; and what had just before appeared a level plain, might be suddenly converted into a wide lake, covered with armed vessels, and replenished with the monsters of the deep.

In the decorations of these scenes, the Roman Enape rotirs displayed their wealth and liberality; and we read, that on various occasions,the whole furniture oftbe amphitheatre consisted either of silver, or of gold, or of amber. The poet who describes the games of Carinas, in the character of a shepherd, attracted to the capital by the fame of tiieir magnificence, affirms that the nets, designed as a defence against the wild beasts, were of gold wire; that the porticos were gilded; and that the belt or circle, which divided the several ranks of spectators from each other, was studded with precious mosaic of beautiful Stones.. '---. _ II.—*Reflections en Westminster Abbey.*—Spectator. WHEN I am in a serious humour, I very often walk by myself in Westminster Abbey; where the gloominess of the place, and the use to which it is applied, with the solemnity of the building, and the condition of the people who lie in it, are apt to fill 4he mind with a kind of melancholy, or rather thoughtfulness-, that is not disagreeable. J yesterday passed a whole afternoon in the church yard, the cloisters and the church; amusing myself with the tomb stones and inscriptions, which I met with in those several regions of the dead. Most of them recorded nothing else of the buried person, but that he was born upon one day,

and died upon another; two circumstances that are common to all mankind. I could not but look upon those registers of existence,' whether of brass or marble, as a kind of satire upon the departed persons, whohad left no other memorial of themselves than that they were born, and that they died.

Upon my going into the church, I entertained myself with the digging of a grave; and saw in every shovelful of it that was thrown up. the fragment of a bone or skull, intermixed with a kind of fresh mouldering earth, that, some time or other had a place in the composition of a human body. Upon this 1 began to consider with myself, what innumerable multitudes of people lay confused together, under the pavement of that ancient cathedral; how men and women, friends and enemies, priests and soldiers, monks and prebendaries, were crumbled nmongst one another, and blended together in the same common mass; how beauty, strength and youth, with old *Age,* weakness and deformity, lay undistinguished, in the same promiscuous heap of matter.

After having thus surveyed this great magazine of mortality, as it were, in the lump, I examined it more particularly, by the accounts which I found on several of the monuments, which are raised in every quarter of that ancient fabric. Some of them are covered with-such extravagant epitaphs, that, if it were possible for the dead person to be acquainted with them, he would blush-at the praise which his friends have bestowed upon him. There" are others so excessively modest, that they deliver the character of the person departed in Greek or Hebrew; and by that means are not understood onee in a twelvemonth, lathe poetical quarter, I found there were poets who had no monuments, and monuments which had no poets. I observed, indeed, that the present war had filled the church with many of those uninhabited monuments, which had been erected to the memory of persons whose bodies were perhaps buried in the plains of Blenheim, or in the bosom of the ocean.-

I could not but be very much delight-

ed with. several modern epitaphs, which are written with great elegance ef expression and justness of thought, and which, therefore, da honour to the living as well as to the dead. As a foreigner is very apt to conceive an idea of the ignorance or politeness of a nation, from the turn of their public monuments and inscriptions, they should be submitted to the perusal of men of learning and genius before they are put into execution. Sir Cloudsly Shovel's monument has very often given me great offence. Instead of the brave rough English admiral, which was the distinguishing character of that plain gallant man, he is represented on his tomb, by the figure of a beau, dressed in a long periwig, and reposing himself upon velvet cushions, under a canopy of state. The inscription is answerable to the monument; for, instead of celebrating the many remarkable actions he had performed in the service of his country, it acquaints us only with the manner of his death, in which it was impossible for him to reap any honour.— The Dutch whom we are apt to despise for want of genius, show an infinitely greater taste in their buildings and works of tlats nature, than we meet with iu those of our country. Tile monuments of their admirals, which have been erected at the public expense, represent them like themselves, and are adorned with rostral crowus and naval ornaments. with beautiful festoons of seaweed, shells, and coral.

I know that entertainments of this nature are apt to raise dark and dismal thoughts in timorous minds and gloomy imaginations; but for my own part, though I am always serious, I do not know what it is to be melancholy; and can therefore, take a view of nature in her deep and solemn scenes, with the same pleasure as in her most gay and delightful ones. By this means I can. improve myself with objects which others consider with terrour. When I look upon the tombs of the great, every emotion of envy dies in me; when 1 read the epitaph of the beautiful, every inordinate desire goes out;" when I meet with the grief of parents upon a tombstone, my heart melts with compassion; when I see the tomb of the parents themselves, 1 consider the vanity of grieving for those whom we must quickly follow.— When I see kings lying by those who deposed them; when I consider rival wits placed side by side, or the holy men that divided the world with their contests and disputes; 1 reflect with sorrow and astonishment, on the Utile competitions, factions and debates of mankind. When I read the several dates of the tombs, of some that died yesterday, and some six hundred years ago, I consider that great day, when we shall all of us be contemporaries, and make our appearance together.

III.— *TJie Character of Mary, Queen of Scots.*—
Robertson. TO all the charms of beauty, and the utmost elegance of external form, Mary added those accomplishments which render their impression irresistable. Polite, affable, insinuating, sprightly, and capable of speaking and of writing with equal ease and dignity. Sudden, however, and violent in all her attachments, because her heart was warm and unsuspicious. Impatient of contradiction, because she had been accustomed, from her infancy, to be treated as a queen. No stranger, on some occasions, to dissimulation, wkicjb, ia that perfidious court, where she. received her education, was reckoned among the necessary arts of government. Not insensible to flattery, nor unconscious of that pleasure with which almost every womau.beholds theinflueuee of her own beauty. Formed with the qualities that we love, and not with the talents tliat we,admire, she was an agreeable woman, rather thaa an illustrious queen.
.....

The vivacity,of her spirit, not sufficiently tempered with sound judgment, and the warmth of her heart, which was not atall times under the restraint of discretion, betrayed her both into errours and into crimes. To say that she was always unfortunate, will,not account for that long and almost uninterrupted succession of calamities which befel her: we must likewise add, that she was often imprudent..Her passion for Darnly was.rash, youthful and. excessive. And

though the sudden transition to the opposite extreme, was the natural effect of her ill requited love, and of his ingratitude, insolence and brutality!—yet neither these, nw Both well's artful address and important services, can justify her attachment to that nobleman. Even the manners of the age, licentious as they were, are no apology for this unhappy passion; nor can they induce us to look on that tragical and infamous scene which followed upon it, with less abhorrence. Humanity will draw a veil over this" part of her character, which it cannot approve, and may, perhaps, prompt some to impute her actions to her situation, more than to her disposition; and to lament the unhappiuess of the former, rather than to accuse the perverseness of the latter. Mary's sufferings exceed, both in degree and in duration, those tragical distresses which fancy has feigned, to excite sorrow and commisseration; and while we survey them, we are apt altogether to forget her frailties; we think of her faults with 'ejs indignation, and approve of our tears, as if they were shed for a person who had attained much nearer to pure virtue.

With regard to the queen's person, a circumstance notl to be omitted in writing the history of a female reign, all' cotemporary authors agree in ascribing " to Mary the utmost beauty of countenance, and elegance of shape, of which the human form is.capable. Ilefhair was black, though according to the fashion of that age, she frequently wore,borrowed locks, and of. different colours. Her eyes.
were a dark gray, her complexion exquisitely fine, and her hands and arms remarkably delicate, both as to shape and colour. Her stature was of an height that rose to the majestick. She danced, she walked and rode with equal grace. Her taste for music was just; and she both song, and played upon the lute with uncommon skill. Towards the end of her life, she began to grow fat; and her long confinement, and the coldness of the houses in which she was imprisoned, brought on a rheumatism, which deprived her of the use of her limbs. No man, says Bran tome, ever beheld

her person without admiration and love, or wiH read her history without sorrow.
i *IV.-Character of Queen Elizabeth.*—Hume.' THERE are lew personages in history, who have been more exposed to the calumny of enemies, and the adulation of friends, than Queen Elizabeth; and yet there scarce is any, whose reputation has been more certainly determined, by the unanimous consent of posterity. The unusual length of her adminstration, and the strong features of her character, were able to overcome all prejudices, and, obliging her detractors to abate much of their invectives, and her admirers somewhat of their panegyric, have, at last, in spite of political factions, and what is more, of religious animosities, produced an uniform judgment with regard to her conduct. Her vigour, her constancy, her magnanimity, her penetration, vigilance and address, are allowed to merit the highest praises; and appear not to have been surpassed by any person, who ever filled a throne; a conduct less rigorous, less imperious, more sineere, more indulgent to her people, would have been requisite to form a perfect character. By the force of her mind, she controuled all her more active and stronger qualities; and prevented them from running into excess. Her heroism was exempted from all temerity,her frugality from avarice, her friendship from partiality, her enterprise from turbulency, and a vain ambition; she guarded not herself, with equal care or equal success, from lesser infirmities—the rivalship of beauty, the desire of admiration, the jealousy of love, and the sallies of anger. Her singular talents for government were founded equally ou her temper and on her capacity. Endowed with a great command over herself, she soon obtained an uncontrolled ascendant over the people; and, while she merited all their esteem by her real virtue, she also engaged their affection by her pretended ones. Few sovereigns of England succeeded to the throne in more difficult circumstances, and none ever conducted the government with such uniform success and felicity. Though unacquainted with the practice of toleration, the true

secret for managing religious factions, she preserved her people by her superiour prudence, from those confusions in which theological controversy had involved all the neighbouring nations; and though her enemies were the most powerful princes of Europe, the most active, the most enterprising, the least scrupulous, she was able, by her vigour, to make deep impressions on their state; her own greatness, meanwhile,remaining untouched and unimpaired.

The wise ministers and brave warriors who flourished during her reign, share the praise of her success; but, instead of lessening the applause due to her, they make great addition to it. They owed, all of them, their advancement to her choice; they were supported by her constancy; and, with all their ability, they were never able to acquire an undue ascendant over her. In her family, in. her court, in her kingdom, she remained equally mistress. The force of her tender passions was great over her, but the force of the mind was still superiour; and the combat which her victory visibly cost her, serves only to display the firmness of her resolution, and the loftiness of her ambitious sentiments.

The fame of this princess, though it has surmounted the prejudices both of faction and of bigotry, yet lies still exposed to another prejudice, which is more durable, because more natural; and which, according to the different views in which we survey her, is capable either of exalting beyond measure, or diminishing the lustre of her character. This prejudice is founded on the consideration of her sex. When we contemplate her as a woman, we are apt to be slmck with the highest admiration of her qualities, and extensive capacity; but we are also apt to require some more softness of disposition, some greater lenity of temper, some of those amiable weaknesses by which her sex is distinguished, But the true method of estimating her merit, is to lay aside all these considerations, and to consider her merely as a rational being, placed in authority, and trusted with the government of mankind. We may find it difficult to reconcile our fancy to her, as a wife or a mistress; but her qualities as a sovereign, though with some considerable exceptions, are the objects of indisputed applause and approbation.

V.—*Charles Vs Resignation of his Dominions.*—

Rorertson. CHARLES resolved to resign his dominions to his *son,* with a solemnity suitable to the importance of the transaction.; and to perform this last act of sovereignty with such formal pomp, as might leave an indelible impression on the minds, not only of his subjects, but of his successor. With this view, he called Philip out of England, where the peevish temper of his queen, which increased with the despair of having issue, rendered him extremely unhappy, and the jealousy of the English left him no hopes of obtaining the direction of their affairs-Having assembled the states of the Low Countries at Brussels, on the twentyfifth of October, one thousand five hundred and fiftyfive, Charles seated himself, for the last time, in the chair of state, on one side of which was placed his son, and on the other, his sister, the Queen of Hungary, regent of the Netherlands; with a splendid retinue, of the grandees of Spain, and princes of the empire, standing behind him. The president of the council of Flanders, by his command, explained, in a few words, his intention in calling this extraordinary meeting of the states. He then read the instrument of resignation, by which Charles surrendered to his son Philip all his territories, jurisdiction and authority in the Low Countries, absolving his subjects there, from their oath of allegiance to him, which he required them to transfer to Philip, his lawful heir; and to serve him, with the same loyalty and zeal which they had manifested, during so long a course of years, in support of his government.

Charles then rose from his seat, and leaning on the shoulder of the Prince of Orange, because he was unable to stand without support, he addressed the audience; and from a paper which he held in his hand, in order to assist his memory, he recounted witli dignity, but without ostentation, ail the great things which he had undertaken and performed, since the commencement of his administration. He observed, that from the seventeenth year of his age, he had dedicated all his thoughts and attention to public objects, reserving no portion of his time for the indulgence of his ease, and very little for the enjoyment of private pleasure; tiiat either in a pacific or hostile manner, he had visited Germany nine times, Spain six times, France four times, Italy seven times, the Low Countries ten times, England twice, Africa as often, and had made eleven voyages by sea % that, while his health permitted him to discharge his duly, and the vigour of his constitution was equal, in any degree, to the arduous office of governing such extensive dominions, he had never shunned labour, nor repined under fatigue; that now, when his health was broken, and his vigour exhausted, by the rage of an incurable distemper, his growing infirmities admonished him to retire j nor was he so fond of reigning, as to retain the sceptre in an impotent hand, which was no longer able to protect his subjects, or to render them happy; that, instead of a sovereign worn out with disease, and, scarcely half alive, he gave them one in the prime of life, accustomed already to govern, and who added to the vigour of youth, all the attention and sagacity of maturer years; that if, during the course of a long administration, he had committed any material errour.in government, or if, under the pressure of so many, and great affairs, and amidst the attention which he had been obliged to give tliemi he had either neglected or injured any of his subjects, he now implored their forgiveness; that, for his part, he should ever retain a grateful sense of their fidelity and attachment, and would carry the remembrance Of it along with him to the place of his retreat, as the sweetest consolation, as well as the best reward for all his services; and, in his last prayers to Almighty God would pour forth his ardent wishes for their welfare.

Then, turning towards'Philip, who fell upon his knees, and kissed his father's hand, "If," said he, "I had left you, by my death, this rich inheritance, to which I have made such large additions, some regard would have been justly due to my memory on that account; but now, when I voluntaHly resign to you what I might have still retained. I may well expect the warmest expressions of thanks on your part. With tliesef however, I dispense; and shall consider your concern for the welfare of your sub jects, and your love of them, as the best and most acceptable testimony of your gratitude to me. It is in your power,. by a wise and Virtuous administration", to-justify the extraordinary proof, which I this day give, of my paternal affection, and to demonstrate that you are worthy of the confidence which I repose in you. Preserve an inviolable regard for religion; maintain the. Catholic faitb in its purity; let the laws of your country be sacred to your eyes; encroach not on the rights and privileges of your people; and, if the time shall ever come, when you shall wish to enjoy the tranquility of a private life, may you have a son endowed with such qualities, that you can resign your sceptre to him, with as much satisfaction as I give up mine to you."

As soon as Charles had finished this long address to his subjects, and to their new sovereign, he sunk into the chair, exhausted and ready to faint with the fatigue of such an extraordinary effort. During this discourse, the whole audience melted into tears; some, from admiration of his magnanimity; others softened by the expressions of tenderness towards his son, and oflove to his people; and all were affected Willi the deepest sorrow, at losing a sovereign, who had distinguished the-Netherlands, his native country, with particular niarks of his regard and attachment.

A few weeks thereafter, Charles in an assembly no less splendid, and with a ceremonial equally as pompous, resigned to his son the crown of Spain, with all the territories depending on them, both in the old, and in the new world. Of all these vast possessions, he reserved nothing for himself, but an annual pension of an hundred thousand crowns, to defray the charges of his family, and td afford him a small sum for acts of beneficence and Charity.

The place he had chosen, for his retreat, was the monastary of St. Justus, in the province of Estremadura.— It was seated in a vale of no great extent, watered by a small brook,and surrounded by rising grounds, covered with tafty trees. From the nature of the soil, and, as well as the temperature of the climate, it was esteemed the most healthful and delicious situation in Spain. Some months before his resignation, he had sent an architect thither, to add a new apartment to the monastery, foi his accommodation; but he gave strict orders, that the style of the building should be such as suited his present situation, rather than his former dignity. It consisted only of six rooms; four of them in the form of friar's cells, with naked walls; the other two each twenty feet square, were hung with brown cloth, and furnished in the most simple manner. They were all on a level with the ground; with a door on one side into a garden, of which Charles himself had given the plan, and which he had filled with various plants, intending to.cultivate them with his own hands. On the other side, they communicated with the chapel of the monastery, in which he was to perform his devotions. Into this humble retreat, hardly sufficient for the comfortable accommodation of a private gentleman, did Charles enter, with twelve domestics only. He buried there, in solitude and silence, his grandeur, and his ambition, together with those vast projects, which during half a century, had alarmed and agitated Europe, filling every kingdom in it, by turns, with the terror of his arms, and the dread of being subjected to his power.

VI.—*Importance of Virtue*—Price. VIRTUE is of intrinsic value, and good desert, and of indispensable obligation; not the creature of will, but necessary and immutable; not local or temporary, but of equal extent and antiquity with the divine mind; not a mode of sensation, but everlasting truth; not dependent on power but the guide of all power/ Virtue is the foundation of honour and esteem, and the source of all beauty, order and happiness, in nature. It is what confers value on all the other endowments and qualities ofareasonable being, to which they ought to be obsolutely subservient; and without which, the more eminent they are, the more hideous deformities, and the greater cuvses they become.

The use of it is not confined to any one stage of our existence, or to any particular situation we can be,in, but reaches through all the periods and circumstances of our beings. Many of the endowments and talents we now possess, and of which we are too apt to be proud, will cease entirely with the present state; but this will be our ornament and dignity, in every future state, to which we may be removed. Beauty and wit will die, learning will vanish away, and all the arts of life be soon forgot; but virtue will remain forever. This unites us to the whole rational creation; and fits us for conversing with any or der of superiour natures, and for a place in any part of God's works. It procures us the approbation and love of all wise and good beings, and renders them our allies and friends. But what is of unspeakably greater consequence, is, that it mokes God our friend, assimilates and unites our minds to his, and engages his Almighty power in our defence. Superiour beings of all ranks are bound by it, no less than ourselves. It has the same authority in all worlds that it has in this. The further any being is advanced in excellence and perfection, the greater is his attachment to it, and the more he is under its influence. To say no more, it is the law of the whole universe, it stands first in the estimation of the Deity; its original is his nature, and it is the very object that makes him lovely.

Such is the importance of virtue.—Of what consequence, therefore, is it that we practice it? There is no argument or motive, in any respect fitted to influence a reasonable mind, which does not call us to this. One viituous disposition of soul, is preferable to the greatest natural accomplishments and abilities, and of more value than all the treasures of the world.lf you are wise then study virtue, and contemn every thing that can come in competition with it. Remember that nothing else deserves one anxious thought or wish. Remember that *this* alone is honour, glory, wealth and happiness. Secure this and you secure every thing. Lose this, and all is lost.

1.-Address to Art.—Harris.

O ART! Thou distinguishing attribute and honour of human kind Who art-not only able to imitate nature in her graces, but even to adorn her with graces of thine?

own! Possessed of thee, the meanest genius grows deserving, and has a just demand for a portion of our esteem; devoid of thee, the brightest of our kind lie lost and useless, and are but poorly distinguished from the most despicable and base. When we inhabited forests, in common witli brutes, not otherwise known from them than by the figure of our species, thou taughtest us to assert the sovereignty of our nature, and to assume that empire for-which Providence intended us. Thousands of utilities owe their birth to thee; thousands of elegancies, pleasures and joys, without which life itself would be but an insipid possession. *0*

Wide and extensive is the reach of thy dominion. No element is there either so violent or so subtle, soyielding or so sluggish, as by the powers of its nature to be superior to thy direction. Thoudreadest not the fierce impetuosity of fire, but compellest its violence to be both obedient and useful. By it thou softenest the stubborn tribe of minerals, so as to be formed and moulded into shapes innumerable. Hence weapons, armour, coin; and previous to these and thy other works and energies, hence all those various tools and instruments, which empower thee to proceed to farther ends more excellent. Nor is the subtile air less obedient to thy power, whether thou wiliest it to be a minister to our pleasure or utility. At thy command, it giveth birth to sounds, which charm the soul with all the powers of harmony. Under thy instruction it moves the ship over seas; while that yielding element, where otherwise we sink, even water itself, is by thee taught to bear us; the vast ocean, to promote

that intercourse of nations, which ignorance would imagine it was destined to intercept. To say how thy influence is seen on earth, would be to teach the meanest what he knows already. Suffice it but to mention, fields of arable and pasture; lawns,and groves, and gardens,and plantations; cottages, villages, castles, towns; palaces, temples, and spacious cities.

Nor does thy empire end in subjects thus inanimate. Its power also extends through the various race of animals, who either patiently submit to become thy slaves, or are sure to find thee an irresistible foe. The faithful dog, the patient ox, the generous horse, and the mighty elephant, are content all to receive their instructions from thee, and readily do lend their natural instincts or strength, to perform those offices which thy occasions call for. If there be found any species which are serviceable when dead, thou suggestest the means to investigate and take them; if any be so savage as to refuse being tamed, or of natures fierce enough to venture an attack, thou teachest us to scorn their btutal rage; to meet, repel; pursue and conquer.

Such, O Art, is thy amaaing influence, when thou art employed only on these inferiour subjects, on natures inanimate or at best irrational. But whenever thou choosest a subject more-hoble, and settest to the cultivation of mhid itself, then it is thou becomest truly amiable and divine—the overflowing source of those suWfmer beauties of which no subject but mind alone is capable. Then it is thou art enabled to exhibit to mankind the admired tribes of poets and orators; the sacred train of patriots and heroes; the godlike list of philosophers and legislators; the forms of virtuous and equal politics; where private welfare is made the same with public— where crowds themselves prove disinterested, and-virtue is made a national and popular characteristic.

Hail sacred source of all these wonders! Thyself, instruct me to praise thee worthily; through whom, whatever we do, is done with elegance and beauty; without whom, what we do is ever

graceless and deformed.—Venerable power! By what name shall I address thee? Shall I call thee ornament of the mind, or art thou more truly Mind itself? It is Mind thou art, most perfect Mind: Not rude, untaught; but fair and polished. In such thou dwellest;—of such thou art the form; nor is it a thing more possible to separate thee from such, than it would be to separate thee from thy own existence.

VIII.—*Flattery.*—Theophrastus. FLATTERY is a manner of conversation very shameful in itself, but beneficial to the flatterer.

If a flatterer is upon a public walk with you, "Do but mind," says he," how every one's eye is upon you.— Sure, there is not a man in Athens that is taken so much notice of. You had justice done you yesterday, in the portico. There were above thirty of us together; and, the question being started,-who was the most considerable person in the commonwealth—the whole company was of the same side. In short, Sir, every one made familiar with your name." He follows this whisper with a thousand other flatteries of the same nature.

Whenever the person to whom he would make his court begins to speak, the sycophant begs the company to be silent, most impudently praises him to his face, is in raptures all the while he talks, and as soon as he has. done, cries out," That is perfectly right *I"* When his patron aims at being witty upon any man, he is ready to burst at the smartness of his railery, and stops his mouth-with his handkerchief, that he may not laugh out. If he calls his children about him, the flatterer, has a pocketfull of apples for them, which he distributes among them with' a great deal of fondness; wonders to see so many fine boys; and turning to about to the father, tells him they. are all as like him as they can stare.

When he is invited to a feast, lie is the first man that calls for a glass of wine, and is wonderfully pleased with the deliciousness of the flavour; gets as near as possible to the man of the house, and tells him, with much concern, that he eats nothing himself. He singles out some particular dish and reccommends it to the rest of the company for a rarity. He desires the master of the feast to sit in a warmer pan of the room, begs him to take more care of his health, and advises him to put on a supernumerary garment in this cold weather. He is in a close whisper with hint during the whole entertainment, and has neither eyes nor ears for any one else in the company.

If a man shows him his house, he extols the architect, admires the gardens, and expatiates upon the furniture. If the owner is grossly flattered in a picture, he outflattersthe painter; andthough he discovers a great likeness in it, can by no means allow that it does justice to the original. In short, his whole business is to ingratiate himself with those who. hear him, and to. wheedle them out of their senses.

IX.—*The Absent Man*—Spectator. MENACLES comes down in the morning; opens hi» door to go out; but shuts it again, because he perceives. he has his nightcap on; and examining himself further, fmds that lie is but half shaved, that he has stuck his sword on his right side, that his stockings are about his heels, and that his shirt is over his breeches.

When he is dressed, he goes to court; comes into the drawing room; and, walking upright under a branch of candlesticks, his wig is caught up by one of them, and hangs dangling in the air. All the courtiers fall a laughing; but Menacles laughs louder than any of them, and looks about for the person that is the jest of the company. Coming down to the court gate, lis finds a coach; which taking for his own, he whips into it; and the coachman drives off", not doubting but he carries his master. As soon as he stops, Menacles throws himself out of thecoach, crosses the court, ascends the staircase, and runs through all the chambers with the greatest familiarity, reposes himself on a couch, and fancies himself at home. The master of the house at last comes in. Menacles rises to recieve him, and desires him to sit down. He talks, muses, and then talks again. The gentleman of the house is tired and

amazed. Menacles is no less so; but is every moment in hopes that his impertinent guest will at last end his tedious visit. Night comes on, when Menacles is hardly convinced.

When he is playing at backgammon, he calls for a full glass of wine and water. It is his turn to throw. He has the box in one hand, and his glass in the other; and, being extremely dry, and unwilling to lose time, he swallows down both the dice, and afthe same time throws his wine into the tables. He writes a letter, and flings the sand into the inkbottle. He whites a second, and mistakes the superscription. A nobleman receives one of them, and upon opening it, reads as follows:—" I would have you, honest Jack, immediately upon the receipt of this, take iu hay enough to serve the winter." His farmer receives the other and is amazed to see in it, " My Lord, I receive your Grace's commands."

If he is at an entertainment, you may see the pieces of bread continually multiplying round his plate; 'tis true, the company want it, as well as their knives and forks, which Menacles does not let them keep long. Sometimes, n a morning, he puts his whole family in a hurry, and at last goes out without being able to stay for his coach or breakfast; and for that day you may see him in every part of the town, except the very place where he had ap"pointed to be upsn business of importance.

You would often take him for every thing that he is not. For a fellow quite stupid, for he hears nothing: fora fool, for he talks to himself, and has a hundred grimaces and motions, with his head, which are altogether involuntary; for a proud man, for he looks full upon you, takes notice of your saluting him. The troth of it is, his eyes are open, but he makes no use of them, and neither sees you nor any man, nor any thing else. He came once from his country house, and his own footmen undertook to rob him and succeeded. They held a flambeau to his throat, and bid him deliver his purse. He did so; and coming home, told his friends he had been robbed. They desired to know the par-

ticulars.—" Ask my servants," said Menacles; " for they were with me."

X.—*The Monk*—Sterne.

A POOR Monk of the order of St. Francis, came into the room, to beg something for his convent. The moment I east my eyes upon him, I was determined not to give him a single sous; and accordingly I put my purse into my pocket—buttoned it up—set myself a little more upon my centre, and advanced up gravely to him; there was something, I fear forbidding m my look; I have his picture this moment before my eyes, and think there was that in it, which deserved better.

The Monk, as I judged from the break of his tonsure, a few scattered white hairs upon his temples being all that remained of it, might be about seventy—but from his! eyes and that sort of fire which was in them, which seemed more tempered by courtesy than years, could be no more than sixty.—Truth might lie between. He was certainly sixty five; and the general air of his countenance, notwithstanding something seemed to have been planting wrinkles in it before their timei agreed to the account.

It was one of those heads which Guido has often painted—mild, pa'.e, penetrating; free from all common place ideas of fat contented ignorance, looking downwards upon the earth. It looked forward; but looked as if it look ed at something beyond this world. How one of his order came by it, heaven above, who let it fall upon a Monk's shoulders, best knows; but it would have suited Bramin; and had I met it upon the plains of Indostan, I had reverenced it.

The rest of his outline may be given in a few strokes; one might put it into the hands of any one to design; for-it was neither elegant nor otherwise, but as character and expression made it so. It was a thin spare form, something above the common size, if it lost not the distinction by a bend forward in the figure—but it was the attitude of entreaty; and as at it now stands present to my imagination, it gained more than it lost by it.

When he had entered the room three paces, he stood still; and laying his left hand upon his breast (a slender white staff with which he journeyed being in his right) when I had got close up to him, he introduced himself with the little story of the wants of his convent and the poverty of his order—and did it with so simple a grace, and such an air of deprecation was there in the whole cast of his look and figure—*I* was bewitched not to have been Struck with it.

—— A better reason was, I had predetermined not to give him a single sous.

'Tis very true, said I, replying to a cast upwards with his eyes, with which he had concluded his address—it is very true—and heaven be their resources, who have no other but the charity of the world; the stock of which, I fear, is no way sufficient for the many great claims which are hourly made upon it.

As I pronounced the words *great claims,* he gave a slight glance with his eye downwards upon the sleeve of his tunic— I felt the full force of the appeal—*I* acknowledge it, said I— a coarse habit, and that but once in three years, with a meagre diet—are no great matters; but the true point of pity is, as they can be earned in the world with so little industry, that you order should wish to procure them by pressing Upon a fund, which is the property of the lame, the bkiid, the aged and the infirm; the captive, who lies down counting over and over again, in the days of his affliction, languishes also for his share of it; and had you been of the order of mercy, instead of the order of Si. Francis, poor as I am, continued I, pointing at nay portmanteau, full cheerfully should it have been opened to you for the ransom of the unfortunate.' The Monk made me a bow. But, resumed I, the unfortunate of our own country, surely have the first rights; and I have left thousands in distress upon the English shore. The Monk gave a cordial wave with his head—as much as to say, No doubt; there is misery enough in every corner of the world, as well as within our convent. But "we distinguish, said I, laying my hand upon the sleeve of his tunic, in return foi his appeal—we distinguish, my good father,

betwixt those who wish only to eat the bread of their own labour—and those who eat the bread of other peoples, and have no other plan in life, but to get through it in sloth and ignorance, *for the love of God.*

The poor Franciscan made no reply; a hectic of a moment passed across his cheek, but could not tarry.— Nature seemed to have done with her resentments in him. He showed none—but letting his staff fall within his arms, he pressed both his hands with resignation on his breast, and retired.

My heart smote me the moment he shut the door.— Pshaw! said I, with an air of carlessness, three several times. But it would not do; every ungracious syllable I had uttered, crowded back in my imagination. I reflected I had no right over the poor Franciscan, but to deny him; and that the punishment of that was enough to the disappointed, without the addition of unkind language— I considered his gray hairs, his courteous figure seemed to reenter, and gently ask me what injury he had done me, and why I could use him thus r— I would have given twenty livres for an advocate—1 have behaved very ill, said 1, within myself; but I have only just set out upon my travels, and shall learn better manners as I get along.

XI.—*On (he Headdress of the Ladies.* —Spectator. THERE is not so variable a thing in nature, as a lady's headdress; within my own memory, I have known it rise and fall above thirty degrees. About ten years ago, it shot up to a very great height, insomuch that the female part of our species were much taller than the men. The women were of such an enormous stature, that we appeared as grasshoppers before them." At present, the whole sex is in a manner dwarfed, and shrunk into a race of beauties, that seem almost another species. I remember several ladies who were once very near seven feet high, that at present want some inches of five: How they came to be thus curtailed, I cannot learn; whether the whole sex be at present under any pennance which we know nothing of, or whether they have cast their headdresses, in order to sur-

prize us with something in that kind which shall be entirely new; or whether some of the tallest of the sex, being too cunning for the rest, have contrived this method to make themselves appear sizeable, is still a secret; though I find most are of opinion, they are at present like trees new lopped and pruned, that will certainly sprout out, and flourish with greater heads than before. For my own part, as I do not love to be insulted by women who are taller than myself, I admire the sex much more in their present humiliation, which has reduced them to their natural dimensions, than when they had extended their persons, and lengthened themselves out into formidable and gigantic figures. I am not for adding to the beautiful edifices of nature, nor for raising any whimsical superstructure upon her plans: I must therefore repeat it, that I am highly pleased with the coiffure now in fashion, and think it shows the good sense which at present very much reigns among the valuable part of the sex. One may observe that women in all ages have taken more pains than men to adorn the outside of their heads; and indeed I very much admire that those architects who raise such powerful structures out of ribands, lace and wire, have not been recorded for their respective inventions. It is certain there have been as many orders in these kind of buildings, as in those which have been made of marble; sometimes they rise in the shape of a pyramid, sometimes like a tower, and sometimes like a steeple. In Juvenal's time, the building grew by several orders and stories, as he has very humourously described it:—
With curls on curls they build her head before,
And mount it with a formidable tower;
A giantess she seems; but look behind,
And then she dwindles to the pigmy kind.

But I do not remember, in any part of my reading, that the headdress aspired to so great an extravagance, as in the fourteenth century; when it was built up in a couple of cones or spires, which stood so excessively high on each side of the head, that a woman who was but a pigmy without her headdress, appeared like a colossus upon putting it on. Monsieur Paradin says, "That these old fashioned foiTtages rose an ell above the head, that they were pointed like steeples, and had long loose pieces of crape fastened *to* the tops of them, which were curiously fringed, and hung down their hacks like streamers."

The women might possibly have carried this Gothic building much higher, had oot a famous monk, Thomas Connecte by name, attacked it with great zeal and resolution. This holy man travelled from place to place, to preach down this monstrous commode; and succeeded so well in it, that-, as the magicians sacrifice their books to the flames, upon the preaching of an apostle, many of the women threw down their headdress in the middle of his sermon, and made a bonfire of them within sight of the pulpit. He was so renowned, as well for the sanctity of his life, as his manner of preaching, that he had often a congregation of twenty thousand people; the men placing themselves on the one side of his pulpit; and the women on the other—they appeared, to use the similitude of an ingenious writer, like a forest of cedars, with their heads reaching to the clouds. He so warmed and animated the people against this monstrous ornament, that it lay under a kind of persecution; and whenever it appeared in publie, was pelted down by the rabble, who flung stones at the person who Wore it. But, notwithstanding this prodigy vanished while the preacher was among them, it began to appear again some months after his departure, or to tell it in Monsieur Paradin's own words, "The women, that like snails in a fright, had drawn in their horns, shot them out again as soon as the danger was over.'' This extravagance of the women's headdresses in that age, is taken notice of by Monsieur d'Argentre, in the history of Bretagne, and by other historians, as well as the person *I* have here quoted.

It is usually observed, that a good reign is the only proper time for the making of laws against the exorbitance of power; in the same manner an excessive headdress may be attacked the most effectually when the fashion is against it. I do therefore recommend this paper to my female readers, by way of prevention.

I would desire the fair sex to consider how impossible it is for them to add any thing that can be ornamental,' to what is already the masterpiece of nature. The head has the most beautiful appearance, as well as the highest station in the human figure. Nature has laid out all her art in beautifying the face: She has touched it with Vermillion; planted in it a double row of ivory; made it the seat of smiles and blushes; lighted it up and enlivened it with the brightness of the eyes; huBg it on each side with curious organs of sense; given it airs and graces that cannot be described; and surrounded it with such a flowing shade of hair, as sets all its beauties in the most agreeable light; in short she seemed to have designed the head as the cupola to the most glorious of her works; and when we load it with such a pile of supernumerary ornaments, we destroy the symmetry of the human figure, and foolishly contrive to call off the eye from great and real beauties, to childish gewgaws, ribbands and bone lace.

XII.—*On the present and a future state.* —Ib. A LEWD 3oung fellow seeing an aged hermit go by him barefoot, " Father," says he, " you are in a very miserable condition, if there is not another world." "True, son," said the hermit; "but what is thy condition if there is?"— Man is a creature designed for two different states of being, or rather for two different lives. His first life is short and transient; his second permanent and lasting. The question we are all concerned in, is this—In which, of these two lives is it Our chief interest to make ourselves happy? Or, in other words— Whether we should endeavour to secure to ourselves the pleasures and gratifications of a life which is uncertain and precarious, and at its utmost length, of a very inconsiderable duration; or to secure to ourselves the pleasures of a life which is fixed and settled, and will never end? Every man, upon the first hearing of this question, knows very well which side of it he ought to close with. But however right we are in theory, it is plain, that in practice we adhere to the wrong side of the question. We make provision for this life as though it were never to have an end; and for the other life, as though it were never to have a beginning.

Should a spirit of superiour rank, who is a stranger to human nature, accidentally alight upon the earth, and take a survey of its inhabitants—What would his notions of us be? Would he not think that we are a species of beings made for quite different ends and purposes than what we really are? Must he not imagine thai we were placed in this world to get riches and honours? Would he not think that it was our duty to toil after wealth, and station, and titlfe? Nay, would he not believe we were forbidden poverty, by threats of eternal punishment, and enjoined to pursue our pleasures, under pain of damnation? He would certainly imagine that we were influenced by a scheme of duties quite opposite to those which are indeed prescribed to us. And, truly, according to such an imagination, he must conclude that we are a species of the most obedient creatures in the universe;—that we are constant to our duty;—and that we keep a steady eye on the end for which we were sent thither.

But how great would be his astonishment, when he learnt that we were beings not designed to exist in this world above three score and ten years; and that the greatest part of this busy species, fall shor even of that age! How would he be lost in horrour and admiration, when he should know that this set of creatures, who lay out all their endeavours for this life, which scarce deserves the name of existence, when, I say, he should know that this set of creatures are to exist to all eternity in another life, for which they make no preparations? Nothing can be a greater disgrace to reason, than that men, who are persuaded of these two different states of being, should be perpetually employed in providing for a life of threescore and ten years, and neglecting to make provision for that which, after many myriads of years, will be still new and still beginning; especially when we consider, that our endeavours for making ourselves great, or rich, or honourable, or whatever else we place our happiness in, may, after all, prove unsuccessful; whereas, if we constantly and sincerely endeavour to make ourselves happy in the other liffei we are sure that our endeavours will succeed, and that we shall not be disappointed of our hope.

The following question is started by one of our schoolrhen. Supposing the whole body of the earth were a great ball or mass of the finest sand, and that a single grain or particle of this sand should be annihilated every thousand years?—Supposing, then, that you had it in your choice to be happy all the while this prodigious mass of sand was Consuming, by this slow method, until there was not a grain left, on condition that you were to he miserable forever after? Or, supposing that you might be happy forever after, on condition you would be miserable until the whole mass of sand were thus annihilated, at the rate of one sand in a thousand years;—which of these two cases would you make your choice?

It must be confessed, In this tase, so many thousands of years are to the imagination as a kind of eternity, though, in reality, they do not bear so great a proportion to that duration which is to follow them, as an unit does to the greatest number which you can put together in figures, or as one of those sands to the supposed heap. Reason therefore tells us, without any manner of hesitation, which would be the better part in this choice. However, as I have before intimated, our reason might, in such a case, be so overset by imagination, as to dispose some persons to sink under the consideration of the great length of the first part of this duration, and of the great distance of that second duration which is to succeed itj—the mind, I say, might give itself up to that happiness which is at hand, considering, that it is so very near, and that it would last so very long. But when the choice we have actually before us is this—

Whether we will Choose to be happy for the space Of only three score and ten, nay, perhaps of only twenty or ten years, I might say for only a day or an hour, and miserable to all eternity; or on the contrary, miserable for this short term of years, and happy for a whole eternity——what words are sufficient to express that folly and want of consideration which, in such case, makes a wrong choice!

t here put the case even at the worst, by supposing what seldom happens, that a course of virtue makes us miserable in this life i But if we suppose, as it generally happens, that virtue would make us more happy, even in this life, than a contrary course of vice, how can we sufficiently admire the stupidity or madness ef those persons who are capable of making so absurd a choice?

Every wise man, therefore, will consider this life only as it may conduce to the happiness of the other, and cheerfully sacrifice the pleasures of a few years, to those of an eternity.

'X.IH,—Uncle Toby's Benevolence.—Sterne. MY uncle Toby was a man patient of injuries—not from want of courage. I have told you, in a former chapter, that he was a man of courage; and I will add here, that, where just occasions presented, or called it forth, I know no man under whose arm I would have sooner taken shelter. Nor did this arise from any insensibility or obtuseness of his intellectual parts, for he felt as feelingly as a man could do. But he was of a peaceful placid nature; no jarring element in him; all was mixed up so kindly within him, my uncle Toby had scarce a heart to retaliate upon a fly. Go—says he, one day at dinner, to an overgrown one which had buzzed about his nose, and tormented him cruelly all dinner time, and which, after infinite attempts, he had caught at last as it flew by him—I'll not hurt thee— says my uncle Toby, rising from his chair, and going across the room with the fly in his hand—I'll not hurt a hair of thy head: Go, says he, lifting up the sash, and opening his hand as he spoke, to let it escape—go, poor devil; get thee gone: Why should I hurt thee? This world is surely wide euough to hold both thee and me.

This lesson of universal good will, taught by my uncle Toby, may serve instead of a whole volume upon the subject." XIV.—Story of the Seige of Calais —Fool Of Quality. EDWARD III. after the battle of Cressy, laid seige to Calais. He had fortified his camp in so impregnable a manner, that all the efforts of France proved ineffectual to raise the seige, or throw succors into the city. The citizens, under count Vienne, their gallant governour, made an admirable defence. France had now put the sickle into her second harvest, since Edward, with his victorious army, sat down before the town. The eyes of all Europe were intent on the issue. At length famine did more for Edward than arms. After suffering unheard of calamities, they resolved to attempt the enemy's camp. They boldly sallied forth; the English joined battle; and, after a long and desperate engagement, count Vienne was taken prisoner, and the citizens who survived the slaughter, retired within their gates. The command devolving upon Eustace St. Pierre, a man of mean birth, hot of exalted virtue: He offered to capitulate with Edward, provided he permitted him to depart with life and liberty. Edward, to avoid the imputation of cruelty, consented to spare the bulk of the plebians, provided they delivered up to him six of their principal citizens, with halters about their necks, as victims of due atonement for that spirit of rebellion, with which they had inflamed the vulgar. When his messenger, Sir Walter Mauny, delivered the terms, consternation and pale dismay were impressed on every countenance.—To a long and dead silence, deep sighs and groans succeeded, till Eustace St. Pierre, getting up to a little eminence, thus addressed the assembly: "My friends, we are brought to great straits this day. We must either yield to the terms of our cruel and ensnaring conqueror, or give up our tender infants, our wives and daughters to the bloody and brutal lusts of the violating soldiers. Is there any expedient left, whereby we may avoid the guilt and infamy of delivering up those who have suffered every misery with you, on the one hand;—or the desolation and horrour of a sacked city, on the other? There is, my friends; there is one expedient left! a gracious, an excellent, a godlike expedient! Is there any here to whom virtue is dearer than life?—Let him offer himself an oblation for the safety of his people! He shall not fail of a blessed approbation from that Power, who offered up his only Son, for the salvation of mankind." He spoke—but an universal silence ensued. Each man looked around for the example of that virtue and magnanimity, which all wished to approve in themselves, though they wanted the resolution. At length St. Pierre resumed, " I doubt not but there are many here as ready, nay, more zealous of this martyrdom, than I can be; though the station to which I am raised, by the captivity of Lord Vienne, imparts a right to be the first in giving my life for your sakes. I give it freely;—I give it cheerfully. — Who comes next?" "Your son," exclaimed a youth, not yet come to maturity.—"Ah, my child," cried St. Pierre, "I am then twice sacrificed. —But no:— 1 have rather begotten thee a second time. Thy years are few, but full, my son. The victim of virtue has reached the utmost purpose and goal of mortality. Who next, my friends! This is the hour of heroes." "Your kinsman," cried John de Aire. "Your kinsman," cried James Wissant. "Your kinsman," cried Peter Wissant.—"Ah!" exclaimed Sit Walter Mauny, bursting into tears, "Why was not I a citizen of Calais!" The sixth victim was still wanting, but was quickly supplied by lot, from numbers who were now emulous of so ennobling an example. The keys of the city were then delivered to Sir Walter. He took the six prisoners into his custody; then ordered the gates to be opened, and gave charge to his attendants to conduct the remaining citizens, with their families, through the camp of the English. Before they departed, however, they desired permission to take their last adieu of their deliverers. What a parting! What a scene! They crowded, with their wives and children, about St. Pieire and

his fellow prisoners. They embraced they clung around they fell prostrate before them. They groaned—they wept aloud—and the joint clamour of their mourning passed the gates of the city, and was heard throughout the English camp. The English, by this time, were apprised of what passed within Calais. They heard the voice of lamentation, and their souls were touched with compassion. Each of the soldiers prepared a portion of his own victuals, to welcome and entertain-the half famished inhabitants; and they loaded them with as much as their present weakness was able to bear, in order to supply them with sustenance by the way. At length St. Pierre, and his fellow victims appeared under the conduct of Sir Walter and a guard. All the tents of the English were instantly emptied. The soldiers poured from all parts, and arranged themselves on each side, to behold, to contemplate, to admire this little band of patriots, as they passed. They bowed down to them oa all sides. They murmured their applause of that virtue, which they could not but revere, even in enemies; and they regarded those ropes which they had voluntarily assumed about their necks, as ensigns of greater dignity than that of the British garter. As soon as they had reached the presence, "Mauny," says the monarch, "are these the principal inhabitants of Calais?"—" They are," says Mauny: "They are not only the principal men of Calais—they are the principal men of France, my Lord, if virtue has any share in the act of ennobling." "Were ihey delivered peacably?" says Edward. "Was there no resistance, no commotion among the people?" "Not in the least, my Lord; the people would all have perished, rather than have delivered the least of these to your majesty. They are self delivered, self devoted; and come to offer up their inestimable heads, as an ample equivalent for the ransom of thousands." Edward was secretly piqued at this reply of Sir Walter: But he knew the privilege of a British subject, and suppressed his resentment. "Experience," says he, "has ever shown, that lenity only serves to invite people

to new crimes.—Severity, at limes, is indispensably necessary to compel subjects to submission, by punishment and example.— "Go," he cried to an officer, "lead these men to execution."

At this instant a sound of triumph was heard throughout the camp. The queen had just arrived with a powerful reinforcement of gallant troops. Sir Walter Mauny rlew to receive her majesty, and briefly informed her of the particulars respecting the six victims.

As soon as she had been welcomed by Edward and his court, she desired a private audience "My Lord," said she, " the question I am to enter upon, is not touching the lives of a few mechanicks—it respects the honour of the English nation; it respects the glory of my Edward, my husband, my king. You think you have sentenced six of your enemies to death. No, my Lord, they have sentenced themselves; and their execution would be the execution of their own orders, not the orders of Edward. The stage on which they would suffer, would be to them a stage of honour, but a stage of shame to Edward! a reproach on his conquests; an indeliable disgrace to his name. Let us rather disappoint these haughty burghers, who wish to invest themselves with glory at our expence. We cannot wholly deprive them of the merit of a sacrifice so nobly intended, but we may cut them short of their desires; in the place of that death by which their glory would be consummate, let us. bury them under gifts; let us put them to confusion with applauses. We shall thereby defeat them of that popular opinion, which never fails to attend those who suffer in the cause of virtue." "I am convinced; you have prevailed. Be it so,'.' replied Edward: "Prevent the execution; have them instantly before us." They came; when the queen, with an aspect and accent diffusing sweetness, thus bespoke them; "Natives of France, and inhabitants of Calais, you have put us to a vast expence of blood and treasure in the recovery of our just and natural inheritance; but you have acted up to the best of an erroneous judgment; and we admire and honour in you that valour and virtue, by which we are so long kept out of our rightful possessions. You noble burghers! You excellent citizens! Though you were tenfold the enemies of our person and our throne we can feel nothing on our part save respect and affection for you. You have been sufficiently tested. We loose your chains; we snatch you from the scaffold; and we thank you for that lesson of humiliation which you teach us, when you show us that excellence is not of blood, of title or station;—that virtue gives a dignity superiour to that of kings; and that those whom the Almighty informs, with sentiments like yours, are justly and eminently raised above all human distinctions. You are now free to depart to your kinsfolk, your countrymen, to all those whose lives and liberties you have so nobly redeemed, provided you refuse not the tokens of our esteem. Yet we would rather bind you to ourselves by every endearing obligation; and for this purpose, we offer to you your choice of the gifts and honours that Edward has to bestow. Rivals for fame, but always friends to virtue, we wish that England were entitled to call you her sons."— "Ah, my country!" exclaimed St. Pierre; "it is now that 1 tremble for you. Edward only wins our cities, but Phillippa conquers hearts." SECTION V.

I.— On *Grace in Writing.*— Fitzrorne's Lettehs.

I WILL not undertake to mark out, with any sort of precision, that idea which I would express by. the word *Grace;* and perhaps it can no more be clearly described, than justly defined. To give you, however, a general intimation of what I mean, when f apply that term to compositions of genius, I would resemble it to that easy air, which so remarkably distinguishes certain persons of a genteel and liberal cast. It consists not only in the particular beauty of single parts, but arises from the general symmetry and construction of the whole. An author may be just in his sentiments, lively in his figures, and clear in his expression; yet may have no claim to be admitted into the rank of finished writers. The several members must be so agreeably united, as mutu-

ally to reflect beauty upon each other; their arrangement must be so happily disposed, as not to admit of the least transposition without manifest prejudice to the entire piece. The thoughts, the metaphors, the allusions and the diction, should appear easy and natural, and seem to arise like so many spontaneous productions, rather than as the effects of ait or labour.

Whatever, therefore, is forced or affected in the sentiments;—whatever is pompous or pedantic in the expression, is the very reverse ef Grace. Her.mein is neither that of a prude nor a coquette; she is regular without formality, and sprightly without being fantastical. Grace, in short, is to good writing, what a proper light is to a fine picture: It not only shows all the figures in their several proportions and relations, but shows them in the most advantageous manner.

As gentility (to resume my former illustration) appears in the minutest action, and improves the most inconsiderable gesture; so grace is discovered in the placing even the single word, or the turn of a mere expletive. Neither is this inexpressible quality confined to one species of composition only, but extends to all the various kinds;— to the humble pastoral, as well as to the lofty epic;—from the slightest letter, to the most solemn discourse.

I know not whether Sir William Temple may not be considered as the first of our prose authors, who introduced a graceful manner into our language. At least that quality does not seem to have appeared early, or spread far amongst us. But wheresoever we may look for its origin, it is certainly to be found in its highest perfection, in the essays of a gentleman, whose writings will be distinguished so long as politeness and good sense have any admirers. That becoming air which Tully esteemed the criterion of fine composition, and which every reader, he says, imagines so easy to be imitated, yet will find so difficult to attain, is the prevailing characteristic of all that excellent author's most elegant performances. In a word one may justly apply to him what Plato, in his allegorical language, says of Aristo-

phanes, that the Graces, having searched all the world round for a temple, wherein they might forever dwell, settled at last in the breast of Mr. Addison.

II.— *On the Structure of Animals.*— Spectator. THOSE who were skilful in anatomy among the ancients, concluded from the outward and inward make of a human body, that it was the work of a being transcendantly wise and powerful. As the world grew more enlightened in this art, their discoveries gave them fresh opportunities of admiring the conduct of Providence, in the formation of a human body. Galen was converted by his dissections, and could not but own a Supreme Being, upon a survey of his handy work. There were, indeed, many parts of which the old anatomists did not know the certain use; but as they saw that most of those which they examined were adapted with admirable art, to their several functions, they did not question but those, whose uses they could-not determine were contrived with the same wisdom, for respective ends, and purposes. Since the circulation of the blood has been found out, and many other great discoveries have been made by our modern anatomists, we see new wonders in the human frame, and discern several important uses for those parts, which uses the ancients knew nothing of.— In short, the body of man is such a subject, as stands the utmost test of examination. Though it appears formed with the nicest wisdom, upon the most superficial survey of it, it still mends upon the search, and produces our surprise and amazement, in proportion as we pry into it. What I have here said of a human body, may be applied to the body of every animal which lias been the subject of anatomical observations.

The body of an animal is an object adequate to our senses. It is a particular system of Providence, that lies in a narrow compass. The eye is able to command it j and, by successive inquiries, can search into all its parts. Could the body of the whole earth, or indeed the whole universe, be thus submitted to the examination of our senses, were it not too big airfl disproportioned for our inquiries, too unwieldy for the management of the eye and hand, there is no question but it would appear to us, as curious and well contrived a frame as that of a human body. We should see the same concatenation and subserviency, the same necessity and usefulness, the same beauty and harmony, in all and every of its parts, as what we discover in the body of every single animal.

The more extended our reason is, and the more able to grapple with immense objects, the greater still are those discoveries which it makes, of wisdom and providence, in the works of creation. A Sir Isaac Newton, who stands up as the miracle of the present age, can look through a whole planetary system; consider it in its weight, number and measure; and draw from it as many demonstrations of infinite power and wisdom, as a more confmed understanding is able(to deduce from the system of a human body.

But to return to our speculations on anatomy, I shall here consider the fabric and texture of the bodies of animals in one particular view, which, in my opinion, shows the hand of a thinking and all wise Being in their formation, with the evidence of a thousand demonstrations. I think we may lay this down asanincontested principle, that chance never acts in a perpetual uniformity and consistence with itself. If one should always fling the same number with ten thousand dice, or see every throw just five times less, or five times more, in number, than the throw which immediately preceded it, who would not imagine there was some invisible power which directed the cast? This is the proceeding which we find in the operations of nature. Every kind of animal is diversified by different magnitudes, each of which gives rise to a different species. Let a man trace the dog or lion kind, and he will observe how many of the works of nature are published, if I may use the expression, in a variety of editions. If we look into the reptile world, or into those different kinds of animals that fill the element of water, we meet with the same repetitions among several species,

that differ very little from one another, but in size and bulk. You find the same creature that is drawn at large, copied out in several proportions, and ending in miniature. It would be tedious to produce instances of this regular conduct in Providence, as it would be superfluous to those who are versed in the natural history of animals. The magnificent harmony of the universe is such, that we may observe innumerable divisions running upon the same ground. I might also extend this speculation to the dead parts of nature, in which we may find matter disposed into many similar systems, as well in our survey of stars and planets, as of stones, vegetables, and other sublunary parts of the creation. In a word, Providence has shown the richness of its goodness and wisdom, not only in the production of many original species, but in the multiplicity of descants which it has made on every original species in particular.

But to pursue this thought still farther.—Every living creature, considered in itself, has many very many complicated parts, that are exact copies of some other parts, which it possesses, which are complicated in the same manner. One eye would have been sufficient for the subsistence and preservation of an animal; but in order to better his condition, we see another placed, with a mathematical exactness, in the same most advantgeous situation, and in every particular, of the same size and texture. It is impossible for chance to be thus delicate and uniform in her operations. Should a million of dice turn up twice together in the same number, the wonder would be nothing in comparison with this. But when we see this similitude and resemblance in the arm, the hand, the fingers; when we see one half of the body entirely correspond with the other, in all those minute strokes, without which a man might have very well subsisted; nay, when we often see a single part repeated an hundred times in the same body, notwithstanding it consists of the most intricate weaving of numberless fibres, and these parts differing still in magnitude, as the convenience of their particular situation

requires; sure a man must have a strange cast of understanding, who does not discover the finger of God. in so wonderful a work. These duplicates, in those parts of the body, without which a man might have very well subsisted, though not so well as with them, are a plain demonstration of an all wise Contriver; as those more numerous copyings, which are found among the vessels of the same body, are evident demonstrations that they could not be the work of chance. This argument receives additional strength, if we apply it to every animal and insect within our knowledge, as well as to those numberless living creatures, that are objects too minute for an human eye: And if we consider how the several species in this whole world of life resemble one another, in very many particulars, so far as is convenient for their respective states of existence, it is much more probable that an hundred million of dice should be casually thrown an hundred million of times in the same number, than that the body of any single animal should be produced by the the fortuitous concourse of matter. And that the like chance should arise in innumerable instances, requires a degree of credulity that is not under the direction of common sense.

III.— *On Natural and Fantastical Pleasures.*—Guardian. IT is of great use to consider the Pleasures which constitute human happiness, as they are distinguished into Natural and Fantastical. Natural Pleasures I call those which, not depending on the fashion and caprice of any particular age or nation, are suited to human nature in general, and were intended by Providence, as rewards for using our faculties agreeably to the ends for which they are given us. Fantastical Pleasures are those which, having no natural fitness to delight our minds, presuppose some particular whim or taste, accidentally prevailing in a set of people, to which it is owing that they please.

Now I take it, that the tranquility and cheerfulness 'with which 1 have passed my life, are the effects of having, ever since I came to years of discretion, continued my inclinations to the former sort of pleasures. But as my experience can he a rule only to my own actions, it may probably be a stronger motive to induce others to the same scheme of life, if they would consider that we are prompted to natural pleasures, by aninstict impressed on. our minds by the Author of our nature, who best understands our frames, and consequently best knows what those pleasures are, which will give us the least uneasiness in the pursuit, and the greatest satisfaction in the enjoyment of them. Hence it follows, that the object of our natural desires are cheap, and easy to be obtained; it being a maxim that liolds throughout the whole system. of created beings, "that nothing is made in vain," much less the instincts and appetites of animals, which the benevolence, as well as the wisdom of the Deity is concerned to provide for. Nor is the fruition of those objects less pleasing, than the acquisition is easy; and the pleasure is heightened by the sense of having answered som6 natural end, and the consciousness of acting in concert with the Supreme Governour of the universe.

Under natural pleasures I comprehend those which are universally suited, as well to the rational as the sensual part of our nature. And of the pleasures which affect our senses, those only are to be esteemed natural, that are contained within the rules of reason, which is allowed to be as necessary an ingredient of human nature, as sense. And indeed, excesses of any kind are hardly to be esteemed pleasures, much less natural pleasures.

It is evident that a desire terminated in money is fantastical; so is the desire of outward distinctions, which bring no delight of sense, nor recommend us as useful to mankind; and the desire of things, merely because they are new or foreign. Men who are indisposed to a due exertion of their higher parts, are driven to such pursuits as these, from the restlessness of the mind, and the sensitive appetites being easily satisfied. It is, in some sort, owing to the bounty of Providence, that, disdaining a cheap and vulgar happiness, they frame to themselves imaginary goods, in which there is nothing can raise desire, but the difficulty of obtaining them. Thus men become the contrivers of their own misery, as a punishment to themselves, for departing from the measures of nature. Having by an habitual reflection on these truths, made them familiar, the effect is, that I, among a number of persons who have debauched their natural taste, see things in a peculiar light, which I have arrived at, not by any uncommon force of genius, or acquired knowledge, but only by unlearning the false notions instilled by custom and education.

The various objects that compose the world, were, by nature, formed to delight our senses; and as it is this alone that makes them desirable to an uncorrupted taste, a man may be said naturally to possess them, when he possesses those enjoyments which they are fitted by nature to yield. Hence it is usual with me to consider myself as having a natural property in every object that administers pleasure to me. When 1 am in the country, all the fine seats near the place of my residence, and to which I have access, I regard as mine. The same I think of the groves and fields where I walk, and muse on the folly of the civil landlord in London, who has the fantastical pleasure of draining dry rent into his eoflers, but is a stranger to the fresh air and rural enjoyments. By these principles, I am possessed of half a dozen of the finest seats in England, which, in the eye of the law, belong to certain of my acquaintance, who, being men of business, choose to live near the court.

In some gieat families, where I choose to pass my time, a stranger would be apt to rank me with the other domestics; but, in my own thoughts and natural judgment, I am master of the house, and he who goes by that name is my steward, who eases me of the care of providing for myself the conveniences and pleasures of life.

When I walk the streets, I use the foregoing natural maxim, viz. That he is the true possessor of a thing, who enjoys it, and not he that owns it without the enjoyment of it, to convince myself that I have a property in the gay part, of all the gilt chariots that I meet, which 1 regard as amusements designed to delight my eyes, and the imagination of those kind of people who sit in them, gaily attired only to please me, I have a real, they only an imaginary pleasure, from their exterior embellishments. Upon the same principle, I have discovered that I am the natural proprietor of all the diamond necklaces, the crosses, stars, brocades and embroidered clothes, which I see at a play or birth night, as giving more natural delight to the spectator, than to those that wear them. And I look on the beaus and ladies as so many paroquets in an aviary, or tulips in a garden, designed purely for my diversion. A gallery of pictures, a cabinet or library, that I have free access to, I think my own. In a word, all that I desire is the use of things, let who will have the keeping of them; by which maxim I am grown one of the richest men in Great Britain; with this difference—that I am not a prey to my own cares, or the envy of others.

The same principles I find of great use in my private economy. As I cannot go to the price of history painting, I have purchased, at easy rates, several beautifully designed pieces of landskip and perspective, which are much more pleasing to a natural taste, than unknown faces or Dutch gambols, though done by the best masters; my couches, beds and window curtains are of Irish stuff, which those of that nation work very fine, and with a delightful mixture of colours. There is not a piece of china in my house; but I have glasses of all sorts, and some tinged with the finest colours; which are not the less pleasing because they are domestic, and cheaper than foreign toys. Every thing is neat, entire and clean, and fitted to the taste of one who would rather be happy, than be thought rich.

Every day numberless innocent and natural gratifications occur to me, while I behold my fellow creatures labouring in a toilsome and absurd pursuit of trifles; one, that he may be called by a particular appellation; another, that he may wear a particular ornament, which I regard as a piece of riband, that has an agreeable effect on my sight, but is so far from supplying tne place of merit, where it is not, that it serves only to make the want of it more conspicuous. Fair weather is the joy of my soul $ about noon, I behold a blue sky with rapture, and receive great consolation from the rosy dashes of light, which adorn the clouds both morning and evening. When I am lost among the green trees, I do not envy a great man, with a crowd at his levee. And I often lay aside thoughts of going to an opera, that I may enjoy the silent pleasures of walking by moonlight, or viewing the stars sparkle in their azure ground; which look upon as a part of my possessions, not without a secret indignation at the tastelessness of mortal men, who, in their race through life, overlook the real enjoyments of it.

But the pleasure which naturally affects a human mind with the most lively and transporting touches, I take to be the sense that we act in the eye of infinite wisdom, power and goodness, that will crown our virtuous endeavours here, with a happiness hereafter, large as our desires, and lasting as our immortal souls. This is a perpetual spring of gladness in the mind. This lessens our calamities, and doubles ourjoys. Without this, the highest state of life is insipid; and with it, the lowest is a paradise.

1Y.—*The Folly and Madness of Ambition illustrated.*

World. AMONG the variety of subjects with which you have entertained and instructed the public, I do not remember that you have any where touched upon the folly and madness of ambition; which, for the benefit of those who are dissatisfied with their present situations, I beg leave to illustrate, by giving the history of my own life.

I am the son of a younger brother, of a good family,-who, at his decease, left me a little fortune of a hundred pounds a year. I was put early to Eton school, where I learnt Latin and Greek; from which I went to the university, where I learnt——not totally to forget them. I came to my fortune while 1 was at college; and having no inclination to follow any profession, I removed myself to town, and lived for some time as most young gentlemen do, by spending four times my income. But it was my happiness, before it was too late, to fall in love, and to marry a very amiable joung creature, whose fortune was just sufficient to repair the breach made in my own. With this agreeable companion I retreated to the country, and endeavoured, as well as I was able, to square my wishes to my circumstances. In this endeavour I succeeded so well, that except a few private hankerings after a little more than I possessed, and now and then a sigh, when a coach and six, happened to drive by me in my walks, I was a very happy man.

I can truly assure you Mr.FitB Adam, that though our family economy was not much to be boasted of, and in consequence of it, we were frequently driven to great straits and difficulties, I experienced more real satisfaction in this humble situation, than I have ever done since, in more enviable circumstances. We were sometimes a little in debt, but when money came in, the pleasure of discharging what we owed, was more than equivalent for the pain it put us to; and though the narrowness of our circumstances subjected us to many cares and anxieties, it served to keep the body in action, as well as the mind; for, as our garden was somewhat large, and required more hands to keep it in order, than we could afford to hire, we laboured daily in it ourselves, and drew health from our necessities.

1 had a little boy who was the delight of my heart, and who probably might have been spoilt by nursing, if the attention of his parents had not been otherwise employed. His mother was naturally of a sickly constitution; but the affairs of her family, as they engrossed all her thoughts, gave her no time for complaint. Tire ordinary troubles of life, which, to those who have nothing else to think of are almost insupportable, were less terrible to us, than to persons in easier circumstances; for it is a certain truth, however your readers may please to receive it, that where the mind is divided between many cares, the anxiety is lighter than where there is only one to contend with. And even in the happiest situation, in the middle of ease, health and affluence, the mind is generally ingenious at tormenting itself; losing the immediate enjoyment of those invaluable blessings, by the painful suggestion that they are too great for continuance.

These are the reflections that I have had since; for I do not attempt to deny, that I sighed frequently for an addition to my fortune. The death of a distant relation, which happened ne years after our marriage, gave me this addition, and made me for a time the happiest mar living. My income was now increased to six hundred a year; and 1 hoped, with a little economy, to be able to make a figure with it. But the ill health of my wife, which in less easy circumstances had not touched me so nearly, was now constantly in my thoughts, and soured all my enjoyments. The consciousness, too, of having such an estate to leave my boy, made me so anxious to preserve him, that, instead of suffering him to run at pleasure, where he pleased, and grow hardy by exercise, I almost destroyed him by confinement. We now did nothing in our garden, because we were in circumstances to have it keep by others; but as air and exercise were necessary for our healths, we resolved to abridge ourselves in some unnecessary articles, and to set up au equipage. This, in time, brought with it a train of expenses, which we had neither prudence to foresee, nor courage to prevent. For as it enabled us to extend the circuit of our visits, it greatly increased our acquaintance, and subjected us to the necessity of making continual entertainments at home, in return for all those which we were invited to abroad. The charges that attended this new manner of living, were much too great for the income we possessed; insomuch that we found ourselves, in a very short time, more necessitous than ever. Pride would not suffer us to *lay* down our equipage; and to live in a manner unsuitable to it, was what he could not bear to think of. To pay the debts we had contracted, I was soon forced to mortgage, and at last to sell, the best part of my estate; and as it was utterly impossible to keep up the parade any longer, we thought it adviseable to remove on a sudden, to sell our coach in town, and to look out for a new situation, at a greater distance from our acquaintance.

But unfortunately for my peace, I carried the habit of expense along with me, and was very near being reduced to absolute want, when, by the unexpected death of an uncle and his two sons, who died within a few weeks of each other, I succeeded to an eslate of seven thousand pounds a year.

And now, Mr. Fitz Adam, both you and your readers will undoubtedly call me a very happy man; and so indeed I was. I set about the regulation of my family with the most pleasing satisfaction. The splendour of my equipages, the magnificence of my plate, the crowd of servants that attended me, the elegance of my house and furniture, the grandeur of my park and gardens, the luxury of my table, and the court that was every wheie paid me, gave me inexpressible delight, so long as they were novelties; but no sooner were they become habitual to me, than 1 lost all manner of relish for them; and I discovered, in a very little time, that, by having nothing te wish for, I had nothing to enjoy. My appetite grew palled by satiety, a perpetual crowd of visitors robbed me of all my domestic enjoyment, my servants plagued me, and my steward cheated me.

But the curse of greatness did not end here. Daily experience convinced me that 1 was compelled to live more for others than myself. My uncle had been a great party man, and a zealous opposer of all ministerial measures; and as his estate was the largest of any gentleman's in the country, he supported an interest in it, beyond any of his competitors. My father had been greatly obliged by the court party, which determined me in gratitude to declare myself on that side; but the difficulties 1 had to encounter, were too many and too great for me; insomuch that I have been baffled and defeated in almost every thing I have undertaken. To desert the cause

I have embarked in, would disgrace me, and to go greater lengths in it would undo *me*. I am engaged in a perpetual state of warfare with the principal gentry of the country, and am cursed by my tenants and dependents, for compelling them, at every election, to vote (as they are pleased to tell me) contrary to their conscience.

My wife and I had once pleased ourselves with the thought of being useful to the neighbourhood, by dealing out our charity to the poor and industrious; but the perpetual hurry in which we live, renders us incapable of looking out for objects ourselves; and the agents we intrust are either pocketing our bounty, or bestowing it on the undeserving. At night, when we retire to rest, we are venting our complaints on the miseries of the day, and praying heartily for the return of that peace, which was only the companion of our humblest situation.

This, sir, is my history; and if you give it a place in your paper, it may serve to inculcate this important truth — that where pain, sickness and absolute want are out of the question, no external change of circumstances can make a man more lastingly happy than he was before. It is to the ignorance of this truth, that the universal dissatisfaction of mankind is principally to be ascribed. Care is the lot of life; and he that aspires to greatness in hopes to get rid of it, is like one who thiows himself into a furnace to avoid the shivering of the ague.

The only satisfaction I can enjoy in my present situation is, that it has not pleased heaven in its wrath, to make me a king.

Y.—*Battle of Pharsalia, and death ofPnmpey.*—

Goldsmith. AS the armies approached, the two generals went from rank to rank encouraging their troops. Pompey represented to his men, that the glorious occasion which they had long besought him to grant, was now before them; "and indeed," cried he, "What advantages could you wish over an enemy, that you are not now possessed of? Your numbers, your vigour, a late victory, all ensure a speedy and an easy conquest over those harrassed and broken

troops, composed of men worn out with age, and impressed with the terrors of a recent defeat: But there is a still stronger bulwark for our protection, than the superiority of our strength—the justice of our cause. Yob are engaged in the defence of liberty, and of your country. You are supported by its laws, and foil wed by its magistrates. You have the world spectators of your conduct, and wishing you success.—On the contrary, he whom you oppose is a robber and oppressor of his country, and almost already sunk with the consciousness of his crimes, as well as the bad success of his arms. Show then, on this occasion, all that ardour and detestation of tyranny, that should animate Romans, and do justice to mankind." Cesar, on his side, went among his rnen with that steady serenity, for which he was so much admired in the midst of danger. He insisted on nothing so strongly, to his soldiers, as his frequent and unsuccessful endeavours for peace. He talked with terrour on the blood he was going to shed, and pleaded only the necessi tv that urged him to it. He deplored the many brave men that were to fall on both sides, and the wounds of his country, whoever should he victorious. His soldiers answered his speech with looks of ardour and impatience; which observing, lie gave the signal to begin. The word on Pompey's side, was *Hercules the invincible;* that on Cesar's, *Venus the victorious.* There was only so much space between both armies, as to give room for fighting; Wherefore, Pompey ordered his men to receive the first shock, without moving out of their places, expecting the enemy's ranks to be put into disorder by their motion.— Cesar's soldiers were now rushing on with their usual impetuosity, when, perceiving the enemy motionless, they all stopt short as if by general consent, and halted in the midst of their career. A terrible pause ensued, in which both armies continued to gaze upon each other with mutual terror. At length, Cesar's men, having taken breath, ran furiously upon the enemy, first discharging their javelins, and then drawing their swords. The same method "was observed by

Pompey's troops, who as vigorously opposed the attack. His cavalry, also, were ordered to charge at the very onset, which, with the multitude of archers and slingers, soon obliged Cesar's men to give ground; whereupon, Cesar immediately ordered the six cohorts, that were placed as a reinforcement, to advance, with orders to strike at the enemy's faces. This had its desired effect. The cavalry, that were but just now sure of victory, received an immediate check; the unusual method of fighting pursued by the cohorts, their aiming entirely at the visages of the assailants, and the horrible disfiguring wounds they made, all contributed to intimidate them so much, that, instead of defending their persons, their only endeavour was to save their faces.— A total rout ensued of their whole body, which fled in great disorder to the neighbouring mountains, while the archers and slingers, who were thus abandoned, were cut to pieces. Cesar now commanded the cohorts to pursue their success, and advanc ng, charged Pompey's troops upon the flank. This charge the enemy withstood for some time with great bravery, till he brought up his third line, which had not yet engaged. Pompey's infantry, being thus doubly attacked in front by fresh troops, and in rear by the victorious cohorts, could no longer resist, but fled to their camp. The right wing, however, still valiantly maintained their ground. But Cesar being now convinced that the victory was certain, with his usual clemency, cried out, to pursue the strangers, and to spare the Romans; upon which they all laid down their arms, and received quarter. The greatest slaughter was among the auxiliaries, who fled on all quarters, but principally went for safety to the camp. The battle had now lasted from the break of day till noon, although the weather was extremely hot; the conquerours, however, did not remit their ardour, being encouraged by the example of their general, who thought his victory not complete till he became master of the enemy's camp. Accordingly, marching on foot, at their head, he called upon them to follow, and

strike the decisive blow. The cohorts which were left to defend the camp, for some time made a formidable resistance, particularly a great number of Thracians, and other barbarians, who were appointed for its defence; but nothing could resist the ardour of Cesar's victorious army; they were at last driven from their trenches, and all fled to the mountains, not far off. Cesar seeing the field and camp strewed with his fallen countrymen, was strongly affected at so melancholy a prospect, and could not help crying out, to one that stood near him, " They would have it so." Upon entering the enemy's camp, every object presented fresh instances of the blind presumption and madness of his adversaries. On all sides were to be seen tents adorned with ivy, and branches of myrtles, couches covered with purple, and sideboards loaded with plate. Every thing gave proofs of the highest luxury, and seemed rather the preparatives for a banquet, the rejoicings for a victory, than the dispositions for a battle.

As for Pompey, who had formerly shown such instances of courage and conduct, when he saw his cavalry routed, on which he had placed his sole dependence, he absolutely lost his reason. Instead of thinking how to remedy this disorder, by rallying such troops as fled, or by opposing fresh troops to stop the progress of the conquerours, being totally amazed by this unexpected blow he returned to the camp, and, in his tent, waited the issue of an event, which it was his duty to direct not to follow. There he remained for some moments, without speaking; till, being told that the camp was attacked, "What," says he, " are we pursued to our very entrenchments?" And immediately quitting his armour, for a habit more suitable to his circumstances, he fled on horseback; giving way to all the agonizing reflections which his deplorable situation must naturally suggest—In this tnelahcnoly manner he passed along the vale of Tempe, and pursuing the course of the river Peneus, at last arrived at a fisherman's hut, in which he passed the night. From thence he went on board a little

bark, and keeping along the seashore, he descried a ship of some burden, which seemed preparing to sail, in which he embarked, the master of the vessel still paying him the homage which was due to his former station. From the mouth of the river Peneus he sailed to the Amphipolis; where, finding his affairs desperate, he steered to Lesbos, to take in his wife Cornelia, whom he had left there at a distance from the dangers and hurry of war. She, who had long flattered herself with the hopes of victory, felt the reverse of her fortune, in an agony of distress. She was desired by the messenger (whose tears more than words, proclaimed the greatness of her misfortunes) to hasten, if she expected to see Pompey, with but one ship, and even that not his own. Her grief, which before was violent, became now insupportable; she fainted away, and Jay a considerable time without any signs of life. At length, recovering herself, and reflecting that it was now no time for vain lamentations, she ran quite through the city to the seaside. Pompey embraced her without speaking a word, and for some time supported her in his arms, in silent despair.

Having taken in Cornelia, he now continued his course, steering to the southeast, and stopping no longer than was necessary to take in provisions, at the ports that occurred in his passage. He was at last prevailed upon to apply to Ptolemy, king of Egypt, to whose father Pompey had been a considerable benefactor. Ptolemy, who was as yet a minor, had not the government in his own hands, but he aud his kingdom were under the direction of Photinus, an eunuch, and Thcodotus, a master of the art of speaking. These advised, that Pompey should be invited on shore, and there slain; and accordingly, Achilles, the commander of the forces, and Septimius, by birth a Roman, and who had formerly been a centurion in Pompey's army, were appointed to carry their opinion into execution. Being attended by three or four more, they went into a little bark, and rowed off from land towards Pompey's ship, that lay about a mile from the shore. Pompey, after taking leave of Cornelia, who wept at his departure, and having repeated two verses of Sophocles, signifying, that he who trusts his freedom to a tyrant, from that moment becomes a slave, gave his hand to Achilles, and slept inlo the bark, with only two attendants of his own, They had now rowed from the ship a good way, and as, during that time, they all kept a profound silence, Pompey, willing to begin the discourse, accosted Septimius, whose face he recollected—" Methinks, friend," cried he, "you and I were once fellowsoldiers together." Septimius gave only a nod with his head, without uttering a word, or instancing the least civility. Pompey, therefore, took out a paper, on which he had minuted a speech he intended to make to the king, and began reading it. In this manner they approached the shore; and Cornelia, whose concern had never suffered her to lose sight of her husband, began to conceive hope, when she perceived the people on the strand, crowding down along the coast, as if willing to receive him; but her hopes were soon destroyed; for that instant, as Pompey rose, supporting himself upon his freedman's arm, Septimius stabbed him in the back, and was instantly seconded by Achilles. Pompey, perceiving his death inevitable, only disposed himself to meet it with decency—and covering his face with his robe, without speaking a word, with a sigh, resigned himself to his fate. At this horrid sight, Cornelia shrieked so loud as to be heard to the shore; but the danger she herself was in, did not allow the mariners time to look on; they immediately set sail, and, the wind proving favourable, fortunately they escaped the pursuit of the Egyptian galleys. In the mean time, Pompey's murderers having cut off his head, caused it to be embalmed, the belter to preserve its features, designing it for a present to Cesar The body was thrown naked on the strand, and exposed to the view of all those whose curiosity led them that way. However, his faithful freedman, Philip, still kept near it; and when the crowd was dispersed, he washed it in the sea; and looking round for materials to burn it with, he perceived the wreck of a fishingboat; of which he composed a pile. While he was thus piously employed, he was accosted by an old Roman soldier, who had served under Pompey in his youth. "Who art thou," said he,-" that art making these humble preparations for Pompey's funeral?" Philip having answered that he was one of his freedmen, "Alas!" replied the soldier, "permit me to share in this honour also; among all the miseries of my exile, it will be my last sad comfort, that I have been able to assist at the funeral of my old commander, and touch the body of the bravest general that ever Rome produced." After this they both joined in giving the corpse the last rites; and collecting his ashes, buried them under a little rising earth, scraped together with their hands; over which was afterwards placed the following inscription: "He whose merits deserve a temple, can scarce find a tomb." VI.—*Character of King Alfred.* —Hume. THE merit of this prince, both in private and public life,'may, with advantage, be set in opposition to that of any monarch or citizen, which the annals of any nation or any age can present to us. He seems, indeed, to be the complete model of that perfect character, which under the denomination of a sage or wise man, the philosophers have been fond of delineating, rather as a fiction of their imagination, than in hopes of ever seeing it reduced to practice; so happily we»-e all his virtues tempered together, so justly were they blended, and so powerfully did each prevent the other from exceeding its proper bounds! He knew how to conciliate the boldest enierprize wiin Uie coolest moderation; the most obstinate perseverance, with the easiest flexibility; the most severe justice with the greatest lenity; the most vigorous command with the greatest affability of deportment; the highest capacity and inclination for science, with the most shining talents for action. His civil and military virtues are almost equally the objects of our admiration; excepting, only, that the former being more rare among princes, as well as more useful, seem chiefly to challenge our applause. Nature, also, as if desirous that so bright a production of her skill should be set in the fairest light, had bestowed on him all bodily accomplishments; vigour of limbs, dignity of shape and air, and a pleasant, engaging and open countenance. Fortune alone, by throwing hrm into that barbarous age, deprived him of historians worthy to transmit his Tame to posterity; and we wish to see him delineated in more lively colours, and with more particular strokes, that we may at least perceive some of those small specks and blemishes, from which, as a man, it is impossible he could be entirely exempted.

VN.—*Awkwardness in Company.*—Chesterfield. WHEN an awkward fellow first comes into a room, he attempts to bow, and his sword, if he wears one, gets between his legs, and nearly throws him down. Confused and ashamed, he stumbles to the upper end of the room, and seats himself in the very place where he should not. He there begins playing with'his hat, which he presently drops; and recovering his hat, he lets fall his cane; and in picking up his cane, down goes his hat again. Thus, 'tis a considerable time before he is adjusted. When his tea or coffee is handed to him, he spreads his handkerchief upon his knees, scalds his mouth, drops either the cup or saucer, and spills the tea or coffee in his lap. At dinner, he seats himself upon the edge of the chair, at so great a distance froni the table that lie frequently drops the meat between his plate and his mouth; he holds his knife, fork and spoon differently from other people; eats with his knifeno the manifest danger of his mouth; and picks his teeth with his fork.

If he is to carve, he cannot hit the joint; but in labouring to cut through the bone, splashes the sauce over every body's clothes. He generally daubs himself all over; his elbows are in the next person's plate and he is up to the knuckles in strop and grease. If he drinks, 'tis with his mouth full, interrupting the whole company with—" To your good health, sir," and "My service to you:"' Perhaps coughs iti his glass and besprinkles the whole table.

He addresses the company by improper titles, as, *Sir,* for *My Lord;* mistakes one name for another; and tells you of Mr. Whatd'yecallhim, or You know who; Mrs. Thingum, What's her name, or Howd'ye call her. He begins a story; but not being able to finish it, breaks oft' in the middle, with—" I've forgpt the rest." VFII —*Virtue Man's highest Interest.*—Harris.

I FIND myself existing upon a little spot, surrounded every way by an immense unknown expansion Where am J? What sort of a place do I inhabit? Is-it exactly accommodated, in every instance, to my convenience? Is there no excess of cold, none of heat, to offend me? Am I never annoyed by animals, either of my own kind or a different? Is every thing subservient to me, as though I had ordered all myself? No, nothing like it—the farthest from it possible. The world appears not, then, originally made for the private convenience of me alone? It does not. But is it not possible so to accommodate it, by my own particular industry? If to accommodate man and beast, heaven and earth, if this be beyond me, it is not possible. What consequence, then, follows? Or can there be any other than this? If 1 seek an interest of my own, detached from that of others, I seek an interest which is chimerical, and can never have existence.

How then must I determine? Have I no interest at all? If I have not, I am a fool for staying here: 'Tis a smoaky house, and the sooner out of it the better. But why no interest? Can I be contented with none but one separate and detached? Is a social interest, joined with others such an absurdity as not to be admitted? The bee, the beaver, and the tribes of herding animals, are enow to convince me that the thing is, somewhere, at least, possible. How then, am I assured tljat 'tis not equally true of man? Admit it, and what follows? If so, then honour and justice are my interest; then the whole train of moral virtues are my interest; without some portion of which, not even thieves can maintain society.

But farther still—I stop not here-I pursue this social interest as far as I can trace my several relations. I pass from my own stock, my own neighborhood, my own na tion, to the whole race of mankind, as dispersed throughout the earth. Am I not related to them all, by the aw tual aids of commerce, by the general intercourse of arts and letters, by that common nature of which we all participate?

Again—I must have food and clothing. Without a proper genial warmth, I instantly perish. Am 1 not related, in this view, to the very earth itself? To the distant sun, from whose beams I derive vigour? To that stupendous course and order of the infinite host of heaven, by which the times and seasons ever uniformly pass on? Were this order once confounded, I could not probably survive a moment; so absolutely do I depend on this common, general welfare. What then have I to do but to enlarge virtue into piety! Not only honour and justice, and what I owe to man, are my interest: But gratitude also, acquiescence, resignation, adoration, and all I owe to this great polity, and its great Governour, our common Parent.

IX.—*On the Pleasure arising from Objects of Sight.*

Spectator. THOSE pleasures of the imagination which arise from the actual view and survey of outward objects, all proceed from the sight of what is *great, uncommon* or *beautiful.*

By *greatness,* I do not only mean the bulk of any single object, but the largeness of a whole view, considered as one entire piece. Such are the prospects of au open champaign country, a vast uncultivated desert, of huge heaps of mountains, high rocks and precipices, or a wide expanse of waters; where we are not struck with the novelty or beauty of the sight, but with that rude kind of magnificence, which appears in many of these stupendous works of nature. Our imagination loves to be filled with an object, or to grasp at any thing that is too big for its capacity. We are flung into a pleasing astonishment at such unbounded views, and feel a delightful stillness and amazement in the soul, at the apprehensions of them.— The mind of man naturally hates every thing that looks like restraint upon it, and is apt to fancy itself under a sort of confinement, when the sight is pent up in a narrow compass, and shortened, on every side, by the neighbourhood of walls and mountains. On the contrary, a spacious horizon is an image of liberty, where the eye)ms room to range abroad, to expatiate at large on the immensity of its views, and to lose itself amidst the variety of objecti that offer themselves to its observation. Sue! wide and undetermined prospects are pleasing to the fancy, as the speculations of eternity or infinitude are to the understanding. But if there be a beauty or uncoramonness joined with this grandeur, as in a troubled ocean, a heaven adorned with stars and meteors, or a spacious landscape cut out into rivers, woods, rocks and meadows, the pleasure still grows upon us, as it rises from more than a simple principle.

Every thing that is *new* or *uncommon* raises a pleasure in the imagination, because it fills the soul with an agreeable surprise, gratifies its curiosity, and gives it an idea of which it was not before possessed. We are, indeed, so often conversant with one set of objects, and tired out with so many repeated shows of the same things, that whatever is new or uncommon contributes a little to vary human life, and to divert our minds, for a while, witli the strangeness of its appearance; it serves us for a kind of refreshment, and takes off from that satiety we are apt to complain of, in our usual and ordinary entertainments. It is this that bestows charms on a monster, and makes even the imperfections of nature please us. It is this that recommends variety, where the mind is every instant called off to something new, and the attention not suffered to dwell too long, and waste itself on any particular object: It is this, likewise, that improves what is great or beautiful, and makes it afford the mind a double entertainment. Groves, fields and meadows are, at any season of the year, pleasant to look upon; but never so much as in the openmg of the spring, when they are all new and fresh, with their first gloss upon them, and not yet too much accustomed and familiar to the eye. For this reason, there is nothing that more enlivens a prospect, than rivers, jetteaus, or falls of water, where the scene is perpetually shifting, and entertaining the sight every moment, with something that is new. We are quickly tired with looking upon hills and vallies, where every thing continues fixed and settled in the same place and posture, but find our thoughts a little agitated and relieved, at the sight of such objects as are ever in motion, and sliding away from beneath the eye of the beholder.

But there is nothing that makes its way more directly to the soul, than *beauty,* which immediately diffuses a secret satisfaction and complacency through the imagination, and gives a finishing to any thing that is great or uncommon. The very first discovery of it strikes the mind with an inward joy. and spreads a cheerfulness and-delight through all its faculties. There is not, perhaps, any real beauty, or deformity more in one piece of matter than another; because we might have been made so, that whatsoever now appears loathsome to us, might have shown itself agreeable; but we find by experience, that there are several modifications of matter, which the mind, without auy previous consideration, pronounces at the first sight, beautiful or deformed. Thus we see that every different species of sensible creatures has its different notions of beauty, and that each of them is most affected with the beauties of its own kind. This is no where more remarkable than in birds of the same shape and proportion, where v.e often see the male determined in his courtship by the single grain or tincture of a feather, and never discovering any charms but in the colour of its species.

There is a second kind of beauty, that we find in the several products of art and nature, which does not work in the imagination with that warmth and violence, as the beauty that appears in our own proper species, but is apt however, to raise in us a secret delight, and a kind of fondness for the places, or objects, in which we discover it. This consists either in the gaiety or variety of colours,

in the symmetry and proportion of parts, in the arrangement and disposition of bodies, or in a just mixture and concurrence of all together. Among these several kinds of beauty, the eye takes most delight iu colours. We no where meet with a more glorious or pleasing show in nature, than what appears in the heavens at the rising and setting of the sun, which is wholly made up of those-different stains of light, that show themselves in tlouds of a different situation. For this reason we find the poets, who are always addressing themselves to the imagination, borrowing more of tiieir epithets from colours, than from any oilier topic.

As the fancy delights in every thing that is *great, ejj-tnge* or *beautiful,* and is still more pleased, the mure it finds of these perfections in the same object; so it is capable of receivng a new satisfaction, by the assistance of another sense. Thus any continued *sound,* as the music of birds, or a fall of water, awakens, every moment, the mind of the beholder, and makes him more attentive to the several beauties of the place that lie before him. Thus if there arise a fragrancy of *smells* or *perfumes,* they heighten the pleasures of the imagination, and make even the colours and verdure of the landscape appear more agreeable; for the ideas of both senses recommend each other, and are pleasanter together, than when they enter the mind separately; as the different colours of a picture, when they are well disposed, set off one another, and receive an additional beauty from the advantage of their situation.

X.—*Liberty and Slavery:*—Sterne. DISGUISE thyself as thou wilt, still, slavery! still thou art a bitter draught; and though thousands, in all ages, have been made to drink of thee, thou art no less bitter on that account. It is thou, liberty! thrice sweet and gracious Goddess, whom all, in public or in private worship; whose taste is grateful, and ever will be so till nature herself shall change. No tint of words can spot thy snowy mantle, or chy inic power turn thy sceptre into iron. With thee, to smile upon him as he eats his crust, the swain is happier than his monarch, from

whose court thou art exiled. Gracious heaven! Grant me but health, thou great beslower of it! And give me but this fair goddess as my companion; and shower down thy mitres, if it seem good unto thy Divine Providence, upon those heads which are aching for them.

Pursuing these ideas, I sat down close by my table; and leaning my head upon my hand, l began to figure to myself the miseries of confinement, i was in a right frame for it, and so I gave full scope to my imagination.

I was going to begin with the millions of my fellowcreatures, born to no inheritance but slavery; but finding, however affecting the picture was, that I could not bring it near me, and that the multitude of sad groups in it did but distract me, I took a single captive; and having first shut him up in his dungeon,! then looked through the twilight of his grated door to take bis picture

I beheld his body half wasted away, with long expectation and confinement; and felt what kind of sickness of the heart it is which arises from hope deferred. Upon looking nearer, I saw him pale and feverish.-In thirty years the western breeze had not once fanned his blood —he had seen no sun, no moon, in all that time—nor had the voice of friend or kinsman breathed through his lattice. His children—but here my heart began to bleed — and I was forced to go on with another part of the portrait.

He was silting upon the ground, upon a little straw, in the farthest corner of his dungeon, which was alternately his chair and bed. A little calender of small sticks was laid at the head, notched all over with the dismal days and nights he had passed there. He had one of these little sticks in his hand; and, with a rusty nail, he was etching another day of misery to add to the heap. As I darkened the little light he had, he lifted up a hopeless eye towards the door—then cast it down—shook his head— and went on with his work of affliction. I heard his chains upon his legs, as he turned his body to lay his little stick upon the bundle. He gave a deep sigh—I saw the iron enter into his soul. 1 burst into tears. I could not sustain the picture of confinement which my fancy had drawn.

XI.—*Cant of Criticism.*—Sterne. AND how did Garrick speak the soliloquy last night?—Oh, against all rule, my Lord; most ungrammatically! Betwixt the substantive and adjective (which should agree together, in number, case and gender) lie made a breach thus—stopping as if the point wanted settling. And after the nominative case (which your Lordship knows should govern the verb) he suspended his voice, in the epilogue, a dozen times, three seconds and three fifths, by a stop watch, my Lord, each time. Admirable grammarian! But, in suspending his voice, was the sense suspended likewise? Did no expression of attitude or countenance fill up the chasm? Was the eye silent? Did you narrowly look? I looked only at the stop watch, my Lord. Excellent observer!

And what of this new book the whole world makes such a rout about? Ob, 'tis out of all plumb, my Lord—quite an irregular thing; Not one of the angles at the four corners was a right angle. I had my rule and compasses, my Lord, in my pocket. Excellent critic.

And for the epic poem, your Lordship bade me look at —upon taking the length, breadth, height and depth of it, and trying them, at home, upon an exact scale of Bossu's, 'lis out, my Lord, in every one of its dimensions. Admirable connoisseur!

And did you step in, to take a look at the grand picture, in your way back r 'Tis a melancholy daub, my Lord; not one principle of the pyramid in any one group! And what a price! For there is nothing of the colouring of Titian—the expression of Rubens—the grace of Raphael—the purity of Dominichino—the corregiosity of Corregio—the learning of Pou»sin—the airs of Guido —the tase of the Carrachis—or the grand contour of Angelo!

Grant me patience! Of all the cants which are canted, in this canting world—though the cant of hypocrisy may be the worst—the cant of criticism is the most tormenting!-I would go fifty miles on foot, to kiss the hand of that man, whose generous heart will give up the reins of his imagination into his au-

thor's hands, be pleased, he knows not why, and cares not wherefore.

XII.—*Parallel between Pope and Dryden.*—Johnson. IN acquired knowledge, the superiority must be allowed to Dryden, whose education was more scholastic, and who, before he became an author, had been allowed more time for study, with better means of information. His mind has a larger range, and he collects his images and illustrations from a more extensive circumference of science. Dryden knew more of man, in his general nature; and Pope, in his local manuers. The notions of Dryden were formed by comprehensive speculation; those of Pope, by minute attention. There is more dignity in the knowledge of Dryden, and more certainty in that of Pope.

Poetry was not the sole praise of either; for both excelled likewise in prose; But Pope did not borrow his prose from his predecessor. The style of Dryden is capricious and varied; that of Pope is cautious and uniform: Dryden obeys the motions of his own mind; Pope constrains his mind to his own rules of composition.-Dryden is sometimes vehement and rapid; Pope is always smooth, uniform and gentle. Dryden's page is a natural field, rising into inequalities, and diversified by the varied exuberance of abundant vegitation; Pope's is a velvet lawn, shaven by the sythe, and levelled by the roller.

Of genius—that power that constitutes a poet; that quality, without which judgment is cold and knowledge is inert; that energy which collects, combines, amplifies and animates—the superiority must, with some hesitation, be allowed to Dryden. It is not to be inferred, that of this poetical vigour, Pope had only a little, because Dryden had more; for every other writer, since Milton, must give place to Pope; and even of Dryden it must be said, that if he has brighter paragraphs, he has not better poems. Dryden's performances were always hasty; either excited by some external occasion, or extorted by domestic necessity; he composed without consideration, and published without correction. What his mind could supply at call,

or gather in one excursion, was ail that he songht, and all that he gave. The dilatory caution of Pope enabled him to condense his sentiments, to multiply his images, and to accumulate all that study might produce or chance supply. If the flights of Dryden therefore are higher, Pope continues longer on the wing. If of Dryden's fire the blaze is brighter; of Pope's the heat is more regular and constant. Dryden often surpasses expectation, and Pope never falls below it. Dryden is read with frequent astonishment, and Pope with perpetual delight.

XIII.—*Story of Le Fever.*—Sterne. IT was sometime in the summer of that year in which Dendermond was taken by the allies, when my uncle Toby was one evening getting his supper, with Trim sitting behind him, at a small sideboard—I say sitting—for iu consideration of the coporal's lame knee (which sometimes gave him exquisite pain)—when my uncle Toby dined or supped alone, he would never suffer the corporal to stand: And the poor fellow's veneration for his master was such, that, with a proper artillery, my uncle Toby could have taken Dendermond itself, with less trouble than he was able to §-ain ihis point over hitn; for tnany a time when my uncle Toby supposed the corporal';? leg-was at rest, he would look back, and detect him standing behind him, with the most dutiful respect; this bred more little sqaubbles betwixt them, than all other causes, for five and twenty years together.

He was one evening sitting thus at his supper, when the landlord of a little inn in the village came into the parlor, with an empty phial in his hand, to beg a glass or two of sack: 'Tis for a poor gentleman—I think of the army, said the landlord, who has been taken ill at my house four days ago, and has never held up his head since, or had a desire to taste any thing till just now, that he has a fancy fora glass of sack, and a thin toast.— "I think," says he, taking his hand from his forehead—" It would comfort me."

—If I could neither beg, borrow, nor buy such a thing —added the landlord—I would almost steal it for the poor gentleman he is so ill.— I hope he will still mend, continued he—we are all of us concerned for him.

Thou art a good natured soul, I will answer for thee, cried my uncle Toby; and thou shalt drink the poor gentleman's health in a glass of sack thyself and take a couple of bottles with my sersice, and tell him he is heartily welcome to them. and to a dozen more, if they will do him good.

Though I am persuaded, said my uncle Toby, as the landlord shut the door, he is a very compassionate fellow, Trim—yet I cannot help entertaining a high opinion of his guest too; there must be something more than common in him, that in so short a time, fhould win so much upon the affections of his host—And of his whole family, added the corporal, for they are all concerned for him.— Step after him, said my uncle Toby—do Trim, and ask if he knows his name.

I have quite forgot it, truly, said the landlord, coming back into the parlour with the corporal—but I oan ask his son again—Has he a son with him, then? said my uncle Toby. A boy, replied the landlord, of about eleven or twelve years of age;—but the poor creature has tasied almost as little as his father; he does nothing but mourn and lament for him night and day. He has not stirred from the bed side these two days.

My uncle Toby laid down his knife and fork, and thrust his plate from before him, as the landlord gave him the account: And Trim, without being ordered, took them away, without saying one word, and in a few minutes after, brought him iiis pipe and tobacco.

Trim! said my uncle Toby, I have a project in my head, as it is a bad night, of wrapping myself up warm in my roquelaure, and paying a visit to this poor gentleman. Your honour's roquelaure, replied the corporal, has not once been had on since the night before your honour received your wound, when we mounted guard in the trenches before the gate of St. Nicholas;—and besides, it is so cold and rainy a night, that, what with the roquelaure, and what with the weather, it will be enough to give your honour your death. I fear so, replied my

uncle Toby; but I am not at rest in my mind, Trim, since the account the landlord has given me-I wish I had not known so much of this affair—added my uncle Toby—or that I had known more of it:—How shall we manage it? Leave it, an't please your honour to me, quoth the corporal;— I'll take my hat and stick, and go to the house, and reconoitre, and act accordingly; and I will bring your honour a full account in an hour. Thou shalt go, Trim, said my uncle Toby, and here's a shilling for thee to drink with his servant. I shall get it all out of him, said the corporal, shutting the door.

It was not till my uncle Toby had knocked the ashes out of his third pipe that corporal Trim returned from the inn, and gave him the following account:

I despaired at first, said the corporal, of being able to bring back your honour any kind of intelligence concerning the poor sick lieutenant—Is he of the army, then? said my uncle Toby.—He is said the corporal—-And in what regiment? said my uncle Toby— f'll tell your honour, replied the corporal, every thing straight forward, as I learnt it.—Then, Trim, I'll fill another pipe, said my uncle Toby, and not interrupt thee;—so sit down at thy ease, Trim, in the window seat, and begin thy story again. The corporal made his old bow, which generally spoke as plain as a bow could speak it," Your honour is good j" and having done that, he sat down as he was ordered— and began his story to my uncle Toby over again, in pretty near the same words.

I despaired at first, said the corporal, of being able to bring back any intelligence to your honour, about the lieutenant and his son; for when I asked where the servant was, from whom I made myself sure of knowing every thing that was proper to be asked That's a right distinction, Trim, said my uncle Toby— I was answered, an't please your honour, that he had no servant wilhhim. — That he had come to the inn with hired horses;—which upon finding himself unable to proceed (to join, I suppose, the regiment) he had dismissed the

morning after he came. If T get better, my dear, said he, as he gave his purse to his son to pay the man—we can hire horses from hence — But alas! The poor gentleman will never get from hence, said the landlady to me, for I heard the deathwatch all night long;—and when he dies, the youth, his son, will certainly die with him;for he is broken hearted already.

I was hearing this account, continued the corporal, when the youth came into the kitchen, to order the thin toast the landlord spoke of j but I will do it for my father myself, said "the youth. Pray let me save you the trouble, young gentleirfan, said I, taking up a fork for the purpose, and offering bim my chair to sit down upon by the fire, whilst I did it. I believe, Sir, said he, very modestly, I can please him best myself.—1 am sure, said I. his honour will not like the toast the worse for being toasted by an old soldier. The youth took hold of my hand, and instantly burst into tears. Poor youth! said my uncle Toby—he has been bred up from an infant in the army, and the name of a soldiei, Trim, sounded in his ears, like the name of a friend. 1 wish 1 had hrm here.

—I never, in the longest march, said the corporal, had so great a mind to my dinner, as I had to cry with him for company:—What could be the matter with me, an't please your honour? Nothing in the world, Trim, said rny uncle Tby, blowing his nose but that thou art a goodnatured fellow.

When I gave him the toast, continued the corporal—! thought it was proper to tell him I was captain Shandy's servant, and that your honour (though a stranger) was extremely concerned for his father; and that if there was any thing in your house or cellar (and thou mightest have added my purse too, said my uncle Toby) —he was heartily welcome to it: He made a very low bow (which was meant to your honour)—but no answer—for his heart was full—so he went up stairs with the toast; I warrant you, my dear, said I, as I opened the kitchen door, your father will be well again. Mr. Yorick's curate was smoking a pipe by the kitchen fire, but said not a word, good or bad, to comfort the youth. I thought it wrong, added the corporal—I think so too, said my uncle Toby.

When the Lieutenant had taken his glass of sack and toast, he felt himself a little revived, and sent down into the kitchen, to let me know, that in about ten minutes, he should be glad if I would step up stairs—I believe, said the landlord, he is going to say his prayers——for there was a book laid upon the chair, by his bed side, and as I shut the door, I saw his son take up a cushion.

I thought, said the curate, that you gentlemen of the army, Mr. Trim, never said your prayers at all. I heard the poor gentleman say his prayers last night, said the landlady, very devoutly, and with my own ears, or I could not have believed it. Are you sure of it? replied the corate. A soldier, an't please your reverence, said I, prays as often (of his own accord) as a parson;——and when he is fighting for his king, and for his own life, and for his honour too, he has the most reason to pray to God of any one in the whole world. 'Twas well said of thee, Trim, said my uncle Toby. But when a soldier, said I, an't please your reverence, has been standing for twelve hours together, in the trenches, up to his knees in cold water— or engaged, said I, for months together, in long and dangerous marches; harrassed, perhaps, in his rear to-day; harrassing others tomorrow;—detached here—countermanded there—resting this night out upon his arms— beat up in his shirt the next— benumbed in his joints —perhaps without straw in his tent to kneel on—he must say his prayers *how* and *when* he can. I believe, said I—for I was piqued, quoth the corporal, for the reputation of the army— I believe, an't please your reverence, said I, that when a soldier gets time to pray—he prays as heartily as a parson—though not with all his fuss and hypocrisy.— Thou shouldst not have said that, Trim, said my uncle Toby—for God only knows who is a hypocrite, and who is not. At the great and general review of us aH, corporal, at the day of judgment (and not till then)— it will be seen who have done

their duties in this world, and who have not; and we shall be advanced, Trim, accordingly. I hope we shall, said Trim— it is in the scripture, said my uncle Toby; and 1 will show it-thee, tomorrow:—In the mean time, we may depend upon it, Trim, for our comfort, said my uncle Toby, that God Almighty is so good and just a governour of the world, that if we have but done our duties in it—it will never be inquired into, whether we have done them in a red coat or a black one:—1 hope not, said the Corporal.—But go on, Trim, said my uncle Toby, with the story.

When I went up, continued the corporal, into the Lieutenant's room, which I did not do till theexpiration of the ten minutes, he was laying in his bed, with his head raised upon his hand, his elbows upon the pillow, and a clean-white cambric handkerchief beside it: The youth was just stooping down to take up the cushion upon which I supposed he had been kneeling—the book was laid upon the bed—and as he rose in taking up the cushion with one hand, he reached out his other to take the book away at the same time. Let it remain there, my dear, said the Lieutenant.

He did not offer to speak to me, till I had walked up close to his bedside: If you are Captain Shandy's scrvant, said he, you must present my thanks to your master, with my little boy's thanks along with them, for his courtesy to me;—if he was of Leven's——said the Lieutenant. I told him your honour was—then, said he, I served three campaigns with him in Flanders, and remember him; but 'tis most likely, as I had not the honour of any acquaintance with him, that he knows nothing of me. — You will tell him, however, that the person his good nature has laid under obligations to him, is Le Fever, a Lieutenant in Angus's but he knows rae not—said he a second time, musing;—possibly he may my story— added he—pray tell the Captain, I was the Ensign at Breda, whose wife was most unfortunately killed with a musket shot, as she lay in my arms in my tent. —I remember the story, an't please your honour, said I, very well. Do you

so? said he wiping his eyes with his handkerchief— then well may I. In saying this, he drew a little ring, out of liis boson, winch seemed tied with a black riband about his ne,ck, and kissed it twice—Here, Billy, sad he— the boy flew across the room to the bed side, and falling down upon his knee, took the ring in his hand, and kissed it too, then kissed his father, and sat dow upon the bed and wept.

I wish, said my uncle Toby with a deep sigh—I wish, Trim, I was asleep.

Your honour, replied the Corporal, is too much concerned; shall I pour your honour out a glass of sack to your pipe? Do, Trim, said my uncle Toby.

I remember, said my uncle Toby, sighing again, the story of the Ensign and his wife, and particularly well, that he as well as she, upon some account or other, (I forget what) was universally pitied by the whole regimentj but finish the story. 'Tis finished already, said the corporal, for 1 could stay no longer, so I wished his honour a good night j young Le Fever rose from off the bed, and saw me to the bottom of the stairs; and as we wept down together, told me they had come from Ireland, and were on their route to join the regiment in Flanders. — But alas! said the corporal, the Lieutenant's last day's march is over. Then what is to become of his poor boy? cried my uncle Toby. . '.

Thou has left this matter short, said my uncle Toby.to the Corporal as he was putting him to bed, and I will tell thee in what, Trim. In the first place, when thou mad'st an offer of my services to Le Fever, as sickness and travelling are both expensive, and thou knewest he was but a poor Lieutenant, with a son to subsist as well as himself out of his pay, that thou didst not make an oner to him of my purse; because, had he stood in need, thou knowes', Trim, he had been as welcome to it as myself.— Your honour knows, said the Corporal, 1 had no orders: True, quoth my uncle Toby, thou didst very right, Trim, as a *soldier,* buttertainly, very wrong as a *man.*

In the second place, for which, indeed, thou hast the same excuse, contmued my uncle Toby, when thou offeredst him whatever was *in* my house thou shouldst have offered him my *house too:* A sick brother officer should have the best quarters, Trim, and if we had him with us, we could tend and look to himj thou art au excellent rrtrse thyself, Trim; and what with thy care of him, and the old woman's, and his boy's, and mine together, we might recruit him again at once, and set him upon his legs.

In a fortnight or three weeks, added my uncle Toby, smiling, he might march. He will never march, an't please your honour, in this world, said the Corporal.. He will march, said my uncle Toby, rising up from the side of the bed, with one shoe 00". An't please your honour, said the Corporal, he will never march but to his grave. He shall march, cried my uncle Toby, marching the foot which had a shoe on, thouglr without advancing an inch, he shall march to his regiment. He cannot stand it, said the Corporal. He shall be supported, said my uncle Toby. He'll drop at last, said the Corporal, and what will become of his boy? He shall not drop said my uncle Toby, firmly. A well o'day, do what we can for hirrf, said Trim, maintaining his point, the poor soul will die. He shall not die, by H n, cried my uncle Toby.

—The Accusing Spirit, which flew up to Heaven's chancery with the oath, blushed as he gave it in: and the Recording Angel, as he wrote it down, dropped a tear upon the word, and blotted it out forever.

—My uncle Toby went to his bureau, and put his purse into his pocket, and having ordered the Corporal to go early in the morning for a physician, he went tobed and fell asleep.

The sun looked bright the morning after, to every eye in the village but Le Fever's and his afflicted son's; the hand of death pressed heavy upon his eyelids, and hardly could the wheel at the cistern turn round its circle, when my uncle Toby, who had got up an hour before his wonted time, entered the Lieutenant's room, and without preface or apology, sat himself down upon the chair upon the bed side, and independently of all modes aud customs, opened the curtain, in the manner an old friend and brother officer would have done it, and asked him how he did: —and how he had rested in the night—what was his com

Elaint—where was his pain-and what he-could do to elp him? And without giving him time to answer any one of these inquiries, went on and told him of the little' plan which he had heen concerting with the Corporal the. Bight before for him.

—You shall go home directly, Le Fever, said my uneie Toby, to my house—and we'll send for a doctor to see what's the matter—and we'll have an apothecary—and the corporal shall be your nurse—and I'll be your servant, Le Fever

There was a frankness in my uncle Toby—not the *effect* of familiarity, but the *cause* of it—which let you at once into his soul, and showed you the goodness of his nature; to this there was something in his looks, and voice, and manner, superadded, which eternally beckoned to the unfortunate to come and take shelter under him.; so that before my uncle Toby had half finished the kind offers he was making to the father, had the son insensibly pressed up close to his knees, and had taken hold of the breast of his coat, and was pulling it towards him. The blood and spirit of Le Fever, which were waxing cold and slow within him, and were retreating to their last citadel the heart, rallied back—the film forsook his eyes for a moment, he looked up wishfully in my uncle Toby's face —then cast a look upon his boy.

Nature instantly ebb'd again—the film returned to its place—the pulse fluttered, stopped—went on—throbbed —stopped again—moved—stopped— shall I go on?—No.

SECTION VI.

I.—*The Shepherd and the. Pphilospher.*
REMOTE from cities, liv'd a swain, Unvex'd with all the cires of gain. His head was silver'd o'er with age, And long experience made him sage; In summer's heat and winter's cold, He fed his flock and penn'd the fold: His hours in cheerful labour flew, Nor envy nor ambition knew j His wisdom and his honest fame, Through all the country rais'd his name.

A deep philosopher, (whose rules Of moral life were drawn from schools') The shepherd's homely cottage sought; And thus explor'd his reach of thought. Whence is thy learning? Hath thy toil O'er books consum'd the midnight oil? Hast thou old Greece and Rome survey'd, And the vast sense of Plato weigh'd? Hath Socrates thy soul refin'd? And hast thou fathom'd Tully's mind? Or, like the wise Ulysses thrown, By various fates on realms unknown? Hast thou through many cities stray'd, Their customs, laws and manners weigh'd?

The shepherd modestly reply'd, I ne'er the path of learning try'd; Nor have 1 roam'd in foreign parts, To read mankind, their laws and arts; For man is practis'd in disguise; He cheats the most discerning eyes; Who by that search shall wiser grow, When we ourselves can never know? The little knowledge I have gain'd, Was all from simple nature drain'd; Hence my life's maxims took their rise— Heuce grew my settled hate to vice.
The daily labours of the bee,
Awake my soul to industry.
Who can pbserve the careful ant,
And not provide for future want?
My dog, (the truest of his kind)
With gratitude inflames my mind;
I mark his true, his faithful way,
And in my service copy Tray.
In constancy and nuptial love,
I learn my duty from the dove.
The ben, who from the chilly air,
With pious wing protects her care,
And every fowl that flies at large,
Instructs me in a parent's charge,
From-Uure, too, I take my rule
To shun c._. tempt and ridicule.
I never with important air,
In conversation overbear:
Can grave and formal pass for wise,
When men the solemn owl despise;
My tongue within my lips I rein,
For who talks much must talk in vain:
We from the woody torrent fly:
Who listens to the chattering pie?
Nor would I with felonious flight,
By stealth invade my neighbour's right:

Rapacious animals we hate;
Kites, hawks, and wolves deserve their fate.
Do not we just abhorrence find
Against the toad and serpent kind?
But envy, calumny and spite,
Bear stronger venom in their bite;
Thus every object of creation
Can furnish hints for contemplation.
And, from the most minute and mean,
A virtuous mind can morals glean.
Thy fame is just the sage replies:
Thy virtue proves thee truly wise.
Pride often guides the author's pen j-
Books as affected are as men:
But he who studies nature's laws,
From certain truth his maxims draws;
And those, without our schools, suffice
To make men moral, good and wise.

II.—*Ode to Leven Water.* ON Leven's banks while free to rove And tune the rural pipe to love, 1 envied not the happiest swain That ever trod th' Arcadian plain. Pure stream! in whose transparent wave My youthful limbs I wont to lave; No torrents stain thy limped source; No rocks impede thy dimpling course, That sweetly warbles o'er its bed, With white, round polisb'd pebbles spread; While, lightly pois'd, the scaly brood, In myriads cleave thy chrystal flood; The springing trout, in speckl'd pride; The salmon monarch of the tide; The ruthless pike intent on war; The silver eel, and mottled par. Devolving from thy parent lake, A charming maze thy waters make, By bowers of birch and groves of pine, And hedges flower'd with eglantine.

Still on thy banks so gaily green, May num'rous herds and flocks be seen: And lasses, chanting o'er the pail; And shepherds, piping in the dale; And ancient faith, that knows no guile; And industry embrown'd with toil; And heart resolv'd and hands prepar'd, The blessings they enjoy to guard.

III.—*Ode from the* 19A *Psalm.* THE spacious Armament on high, With ail the blue etherial sky, And spangled heavens a shining frame, Their great original proclaim. Th' unwearied sun from day to day,. Does his Creator's power display; And publishes to ev'ry land, The work of an Almighty hand. Soon as the evening shades prevail,
The moon takes up the wond'rous tale,
And nightly, to the list'ning earth,
Repeats the story of her birth;
Whilst all the stars that round her burn,
And all the planets in their turn,
Confirm the tidings as ihey roll,
And spread the truth from pole to pole.-
What though, in solemn silence, all,
Move round the dark terrestrial ball?
What though no real voice nor sound
Amid these radiant orbs be found?
In reason's ear they all rejoice,
And utter forth a glorious voice,
Forever singing, as they shine,
"The hand that made us is divine."

IV.—*Rural Charms.*
SWEET Auburn J loveliest village of the plain!
Where health and plenty cheer'd the lab'ring swain;
Where smiling spring its earliest visits paid,
And parting summer's ling'ring blooms delay'd:
Dear lovely bowers of innocence and ease!
Seats of my youth, when ev'ry sport could please!
How often have I loiter'd o'er thy green,
Where humble happiness endear'd each scene!
How often have I paus'd on every charm!
The shelter'd cot the cultivated farm,
The never failing brook, the busy mill,
The decent church, that topp'd the neighb'ring hill;
The hawthorn bush with seats beneath the shade,
For talking age and whispering lovers made.
How often have I bless'd the coming day,
When toil, remitting, lent its turn to play,
And all the village train from labour free,
Led up their sports beneath the spreading tree f
While many a pastime cirled in the shade,
The young contending as the old survey'd: And many a gambol frolick'd o'er the ground,
And slights of art and feats of strength went round
And still, as each repeated pleasure tir'd,
Succeeding sports the mirthful band inspird:
The dancing pair that simply sought renown,
By holding out to tire eace other down;
The'swain, mistrustless of his smutted face,
"While secret laughter titter'd round the place;
The bashful virgin's sidelong looks of love,
The matron's glance, that would those looks reprove.
Sweet was the sound, when oft at evening's close,
Up yonder hill the village murmur rose.
There as I pass'd with careless sieps and slow,
The minglmg notes came soften'd from below;
The swain responsive as the milkmaid sung;
The sober herd that Jow'd to meet their young;
The noisy geese that gabbled o'er the pool;
The playful children just let loose from school;
The watch dog's voice, that bay'd the whisp'i ing wind J
And the loud laugh lhat spoke the vacant mind;
These all, in soft confusion sought the shade,
And fill'd each pause the nightingale had made.

V.—*The Painter who pleased Nobody and every Body.*
LEST men suspect your tale ui.true,
Keep probability in view,
The trav'ller, leaping o'er those bounds,
The credit of his book confounds,
Who with his tongue hath armies routed,
Make e'en his real courage doubted.
But flatt'ry never seems absurd;
The flatter'd always take your word;
Impossibilities seem just;

They take the strongest praise on trust;
Hyperboles, though e'er so great,
Will stili come short of self conceit.

So very like a painter-drew, That ev'ry eye the picture knew; « He hit complexion, feature, air,

So just that life itself was there;
No flatt'ry with his colours laid,
To bloom restoi'd the faded maid;
He gave each muscle all its strength;
The mouth, the chin, the *nose's* length,
His honest pencil touch'd with truth,
And mark'd the date of age and youth.
He lost his friends; his practice fail'd
Truth should not always be reveal'd j
In dusty piles his pictures lay,
For no one sent the second pay.
Two busto's, fraught with every trace)
A Venus' and Apolo's face,

He plac'd in view, resolv'd to please,
Whoever sat, he drew from these;
From these-corrected every feature,
And spirited each awkward creature.
All things were set; the hour was come,
His palette ready o'er his thumb;
My lord appear'd, and seated right,
In proper attitude and light,
The painter look'd, he sketch'd the piece:
ThAi dipt his pencil, lalk'd of Greece,
Of Titan's lints, of Ouido's air,
"Those eyes, my lord, the spirit there.
Might well a Raphael's hand require,
To give them all the native fire;
The features, fraught with sense and wit,
You'll grant, are very haTdto hit:
But yet, with patience, you shall view
As much as paint or art can do:
Observe the work."—My lord reply'd,
"Till now I thought my mouth was wide $
Besides, my nose is somewhat long;
Dear sir, for me 'tis far too young."
"O pardon me," the artist cry'd,
." In this, we painters must decide.
The piece e'en common eyes must strike j
I'll warrant it extremely like."
My lord examin'd it anew,
No lookingglass seem'd half so true.
A lady came. With borrow'd grace,
He from his Venus form'd her face,
Her lover prais'd the painter's art,
So like the picture in his heart!

To every age some charm he lent;
E'en beauties were almost content.
Through all the town his art they prais'd,
His custom grew, his price was rais'd.
Had he the real likeness shown,
Would any man the picture own?.
But when thus happily he wrought,
Each found the likeness in his thought.

VI.—*Diversity in the Human Character.*
VIRTUOUS and vicious every man must be, Few in tli' extreme, but all in the degree; The rogue and fool by fits are fair and wise, And e'en the best, by fits what they despise. 'Tis but by part we follow good or ill, Tor, Vice or Virtue, Self directs it still; Each individual seeks a sev'ral goal; , But Heaven's great view is one, and that the whole. That counterworks each folly and caprice; That disappoints th' effect of ev'ry vice; That happy frailties to all ranks apply'd— Shame to the virgin, to the matron pride, Fear to the statesman, rashness to the chief, To kings presumption, and to crowds belief.-That Virtue's end from vanity can raise, Which seeks no interest, no reward but praise; And build on wants, and on defects of mind, The joy, the peace, the glory of mankind.

Heaven, forming each on other to depend, A master, or a servant, or a friend, Bids each on other for assistance call, Till one man's weakness grows the strength of all. Wants, frailties, passions, closer still ally The common interest or endear the tie. To those we owe true friendship, love sincere, Each homefelt joy that life inherits here; Yet from the same, we learn, in its decline,-Those joys, those loves, those int'rests to resigns Taught, half by reason, half by mere decay, To welcome death, and calmly pass away.

Whate'er the passion, knowledge, fame or pelf, Not one would change his neighbour with himself. The learn'd is happy, nature to explore, The fool is happy that he knows no more; The rich is happy in the plenty given, The poor contents him with the care of heaven: 4

See the blind beggar dance, the cripple sing,
The sot a hero, lunatic a king;
The starving chymist in his golden

views
Supremely blest, the poet in his muse.
See some strange comfort ev'ry state attend,
And pride, bestow'd on all, a common friend;
See some fit passion ev'ry age supply,
Hope travels through, nor quits us when we die.

Behold the child by nature's kindly law, Pleas'd with a rattle, tickled with a straw; Some livelier plaything gives his youth delight, A little louder, but as empty quite; Scarfs, garters, gold, amuse his riper stage, And cards and counters are the toys of age: Pleas'd with this bauble still, as that before; Till tir'd he sleeps, and life's poor play is o er. Mean while opiuion gilds, with varying rays, Those painted clouds that beautify our days; Each want of happiness by hope supply'd And each vacuity of sense by pride. These build as fast as knowledge can destroy: la folly's cup still laughs the bubble, joy; One prospect lost, another still we gaini And not a vanity is given in vain: E'en mean selflove becomes, by force divine, The scale to measure other's wants by thine. See' and confess, one comfort still must rise; Tis this; Though man's a fool, yet God Is wise.

VIT.—*The Toilet.* AND now, unveil'd, the toilet stands display'd, Each silver vase in mystic order laid. First, rob'd in white, the nymph intent adores, With head uncovei'd, the cosmetic powers. A heavenly image in the glass appears; To that she bends, to that her eye she rears. Th' inferiour priestess, at the altar's side, Trembling, begins the sacred rites of pride. Unnumber'd treasures ope at once, and here The various offerings of the world appear; From each she nicely culls, with curious toil, And decks the goddess with the glittering spoil
This casket India's glowing gems unlocks,
And all Arabia breathes from yonder box.
The tortoise, here, and elephant unite,
Transfdrm'd to combs, thespeckled and the white;.
Here files of pins extend their shining

rows,

Puffs, powders, patches.-bibles, billet-doux.

Now awful beauty puts on alt its arms,

The fair, each moment, rises in her charms,

Repairs her smiles, awakens every grace,

And calls forth-all the wonders of her face.

VIII.—*The Hermit.* FAR in a wild, unknown to public view, From youth to age a rev'rend hermit grew. The moss his bed, the cave his humble cell, His food the fruit, his drink the cbrys-tal well r Remote from man, with God he pass'd the days,Prayer all his bus'ness, all hi pleasure praise.

A life so sacred, such serene repose, SeemM heaven itself, till one suggestion rose: That viee should triumph, virtue vice obey; Thus sprung some doubt of Providence's sway.. His hopes no more a certain prospect boast, And all the tenor of his soul is lost. So, when a smooth expanse receives, imprest Calm nature's image on its wat'ry breast,. Down bend the banks; the trees depending grow ,And skies beneath with answ'ring colours glow: But if a stone the gentle sea divide, Swift ruffling circles curl on ev'ry side: And glimm'ring fragments of a broken son, Banks, trees and skies in thick disorder run.

To clear this doubt; to know the world by sight i To find if books or swains report it right; (For yet by swains alone the world he knew, Whose feet came wand'ring o'er the nightly dew.) He quits his cell; the pilgrim's staff he bore, And fix'd the scallop in his hat before; Then, with the sun a rising journey went, Sedate to think, and watching each event.

The morn was wasted in the pathless grass, And long and loathsome was the wild to pass s

But when the southern sun had warm'd the day,

A youth came boasting o'er the crossing way;

His raiment decent, his complexion fair, And soft in graceful ringlets wav'd his hair.

Then near approaching, Father, hail! hecry'd;

And hail! my son, the rev'rend sire reply'd:

Words follow'd words; from question answer flow'd;

And talk of various kind deceiv'd the road;

Till, each with other pleas'd, and loth to part,

While in their age they differ, join'd in heart.

Thus stands an aged elm in ivy bound;

Thus youthful ivy clasps an elm around.

Now sunk the sun; the closing hour of day

Came onward, mantl'd o'er with sober gray;

Nature, in silence bid the world repose;

When near the road, a stately palace rose:

There, by the moon, through ranks of trees they pass,

Whose verdure crown'd their sloping sides of grass.

It chanc'd the noble master of the dome Still made his house the wand'ring stranger's home:

Yet stiJ, the kindness, from a thirst of praise,

Prov'd the vain flourish of expensive ease.

The pair arrive; the liv'ry'd servants wait,

The lord receives them at the pompous gate;

A table groans with costly piles of food;

And all is more than hospitably good.

Then led to rest the day's long toil they drown,

Deep sunk in sleep, and silk, and heaps of down.

At length 'tis morn; and at the dawn of day, Along the wide canals the zephyrs play; Fresh o'er the gay parterres, the breezes creep, And shake the neighb'ring wood, to banish sleep. Up rise the guests obedient to the call; An early banquet deck'd the splendid hall; Rich luscious wine a golden goblet grac'd, Which the kind master forc'd the guests to taste. Then, pleas'd and thankful from the porch they go; And, but the landlord, none had cause of woe; His cup was vanish'd; for in secret

guise, The younger guest purloin'd the glitt'ring prize.

As one who sees a serpent in his way, Glist'ning and basking in the summer ray,

Disordei'd stops, to shun the danger near,

Then walks with faintness on and looks with fear;

So seera'd the sire, when, far upon ihe road,

The shining spoil his wily partner show'd.

He stopt with silence, walk'd with trembling heart,

And much he wish'd, but durst not ask to part:

Murm'ring he-lifts his eyes, and thinks it hard,

That gen'rous actions meet a base reward.

While thus they pass, the sun his glory shrouds:

The changing skies hang out their sable clouds;

A sound in air presag'd approaching rain,

And beasts to covert scud across the plain.

Warn'd by the signs, the wand'ring pair retreat,

To seek for shelter in a neighboring seat.

'Twas built with turrets on a rising ground;

-And strong and large, and unimproved around;

Its owner's temper, tim'rous and severe, Unkind and griping, caus'd a desert there.

As near the miser's heavy doors they drew,

Fierce rising gusts with sudden fury blew;

The nimble lightning, mix'd with showers began,

And o'er their heads loud rolling thunder ran.

Here long they knock; but knock or call in vain,

Driven by the wind, and batter'd by the rain.

At length, some pity warm'd the master's breast:

('Twas then his threshold first received

a guest;)

Slow creaking turns the door, with jealous care,

And halt he welcomes in the shiv'iing pair.

One frugal faggot lights the naked walls,

And nature's fervour through their limbs recalls;

Bread of the coarsest sort, with meagre wine,

(Each hardly granted) serv'd them both to dine;.

And when the tempest fust apppar'd to cease,

A rendy warning bid them part In peace.

With still remark, the pond'nng hermit view'd,

In one so rich, a life so poor and rude:

And why should such (within himself he cry'd

Lock the lost wealth, a thousand want beside?

But, what new marks of wonder soon took place,

In every settling feature of his face,

When, from h;s vest, the young companion bore

Tiiat cup, the gen'rous landlord own'd before.

ly

And paid profusely with the precious bowl,

The stinted kindness of his churlish soul!

But, now the clouds in airy tumult fly:

The sun, emerging, opes an aaure sky;

A fresher green the smelling leaves display,

And glitt'ring as they tremble, cheer the day:

The weather courts them from the poor retreat;

And the glad master bolts the wary gate.

While hence they walk, the pilgrim's bosom wrought

With all the travail of uncertain thought.

His partner's acts without their cause appear—

'Twas there a vice, and seem'd a madness here.

Detesting that, and pitying this, he goes,

Lost and confounded with the various shows.

Now night's dim shades again involve the sky— *l* Again the wanderers want a place to lie—

Again they search, and find a lodging nigh— j

The soil improv'd around—the mansion neat—

And neither poorly low, nor idly great:

It seem'd to speak its master's turn of mind—

Content, and not for praise, but virtue, kind.

Hither the walkers turn with weary feet;

Then bless the mansion, and the master greet;

Their greeting fair, bestow'd with modest guise,

The courteous master hears, and thus replies.

Without a vain, without a grudging heart,

To bim who gives us all, l yield a part:

from him you come, from him accept it here—

A frank and sober, more than costly cheer.

He spoke; and bade the welcome table spread?

Then talk'd of virtue till the time of bed;

When the grave household round his hall repair,

Warn'd by the bell, and close the hours with prayer.

At length the world renew'd by calm repose,

Was srrong for toil; the dappled morn arose;

Before the pilgrims part, the younger crept

Near theclos'd cradle, where an infant slept,

And writh'd his neck; the landlord's little pride—

O strange return!—grew black, and gasp'd and died.

Horror of horrors! what! his only son!

How look'd our hermit when the deed was done!

Not hell, though hell's black jaws in sunder part,

And breath blue fire, could more assault his heart

Co.ifus'd and struck with silence at the deed,

He flies; but trembling, fails to fly with speed.

His steps the youth pursues. The country lay

Perplex'd with roads; a servant show'd the way.

A river cross'd the path. The passage 6'er

Was nice to find; the servant trod before;

Long arms of oak, an open bridge supply'd,

And the deep waves, beneath the bending. glide.

The youth who seem'd to watch a time to sin,

Approach'd the careless guide, and thrust him in:

Plunging, he falls; and rising, lifts his head;

Then flashing, turns, and sinks among the dead.

Wild sparkling rage inrl-imes the father's eyes;

He bursts the bands of fear, and madly cries,

Detested wretch!—But scarce his speech began,

When the strange partner seem'd no longer man;

His youthful face grew more serenely sweet,

His robe turn'd white, and flowd upon his feet;

Fair rounds of radiant points invest his hair,

Celestial odours breathe through purpled air;

And wings, whose colours glitter'd on the day.

Wide at his back, their gradual plumes display.

The form etherial bursts upon his sight,

And moves in all the majesty of light.

Though loud, at first, the pilgrim's passion grew,

Sudden he gaz'd, and wist not what to do;

Surprise, in secret chains, his word suspends,

And, in a calm, his settled temper ends.

But silence here, the beauteous angel broke:

The voice of music ravish'd as he spoke.

Thy prayer, thy praise, thy life, to vice unknown, In sweet memorial rise before the throne: These charms success in otir bright region find,. And force an angel down to calm thy mind. For this commission'd, I forsook the sky; Nay, cease to kneel, thy fellow servant I.

Then know the truth of government divine,

And let these scruples be no longer thine.

The Maker justly claims that world he made;

In this the right of Providence is laid;

Its sacred majesty, through all, depends On using second means to work his ends.

'Tis thus, withdrawn in state from human eye,

The Power exerts his attributes on high;

Your actions uses, nor controuls your will,

And bids the doubting sons of men be still.

What stiange events can strike with more surprise,

Than those which lately struck thy woud'ring eyes?

Yet taught by these, confess the Almighty just,

And where you can't unriddle, learn to trust.

The great, vain man, who far'd on costly food, Whose life was too luxurious to be good; Who made his *ivory* stand with goblets shine, And forc'd his guests to-morning draughts of wine; Has, with the cup, the graceless custom lost, And still he welcomes, but with less of cost.

The mean suspicious wretch, whose bolted door Ne'er mov'd in pity to the wand'ing poor; With him 1 left the cup, to teach his mind, That heaven can bless, if mortals v.ill be kind. Conscious of wanting worth, he views the bowl, And feels compaiion touch his grateful soul. Thus artist's melt the sullen ore of lead, With heaping coals of fire upon its head: In the kind warmth the metal learns to glow, And loose from dross, the silver runs below.

Long had our pious friend in virtue trod, But now the child half wean'd his heart from God;

(Child of his age) for him he liv'd in pain,

And measur'd bjck his steps to earth again..

To what excesses had his dotage run? But God, to save the father, took the son.

To all, but thee, in fits, he seem-d to go, And 'twas my ministry to deal the blow. The poor fond parent, humbled in the dust,

Now owns, in tears, the punishment was just

But how had all his fortune felt a wreck, Had that false sei vanl sped in safety back!

This night his treasur'd heaps he meant to steal,

And what a fund of charity would fail I

Thus heaven instructs thy mind. This trial o'er, Depart in peace, resign, and sin no more.

On sounding pinions here the youth withdrew, The sage stwd wQiid'ring as the seraph flew..

Thus look'd Elisha, when to mount on high,

His master took the chariot of the sky:

The fiery pomp, ascending, left the view;

The prophet j,az'd, and wish'd to follow too.

The bending hermit here a prayer begun:

"Lord, as in heaven on earth thy will be done."

Then, gladly turning, sought his ancient place,

And pass'd a life of piety and peace.

IX.—*On the Death of Mrs. Mason.*— Mason,

TAKE, holy earth! all that my soul holds dear:

Take that best gift, which heaven so lately gave; To Bristol's fount I bore, with trembling care,

Her faded form. She bow'd to taste the wave, And died. Does youth, does beauty read the line?

Does sympathetic fear their breast alarm? Speak, dead Maria! breathe a strain divine;

E'en from the grave thou shall have power to charm. Bid them be chaste, be innocent like thee;

Bid them in duty's sphere, as meekly move: And if as fair, from vanity as

free,

As firm in friendship, and as fond in love; Tell them, though 'tis an awful thing to die, ('Twas e'en to thee) yet the dread path once trod, Heaven lifts its everlasting portals high,

And bids the "pure in heart behold their God."

X.—*Extract from the Temple of Fame.*—Pope, AROUND these wonders as 1 cast a look, The trumpet sounded and the temple shook; And all the nations summon'd at the call, From different-quarters fill the spacious hall. Of various tongues the mingled sounds were heard; In various garbs promiscuous throngs appear'd: Millions of suppliant crowds the shrine attend, And all degrees before the goddess bend; The poor, the rich, the valiant and the sage, And boasting youth, and narrative old age.

First, at the shrine, the learned world appear, And to the goddess thus prefer their prayer: "Long have we sought t' instruct and please mankind, With studies pale, and midnight vigils blind: But thank'd by few, rewarded yet by none,

We here appeal to thy superiour throne;

On wit and learning the just prize bestow,

For fame is all we must expect below. "

The goddess heard, and bade the muses raise

The golden trumpet of eternal praise.

From pole to pole the winds diffuse the sound,

And fill the circuit of the world around:

Not all at once, as thunder breaks the cloud,

The notes at first were rather sweet than loud:

By just degress they every moment rise,

Spread round the earth, and gain upon the skies.

Next these, the good and just, an awful train, Thus, on their knees, address the sacred fane: "Since living virtue is with envy curs'd, And the best men are treated as the worst, Do thou, just goddess, call our merits forth, And give

each deed th exact intrinsic worth."
"Not with bare justice shall your acts be crown'd, (Said Fame) but high above desert renown'd, Let fuller notes th' applauding world amaze, And the loud clarion labour in your praise."

A troop came next, who crowns and armour wore, And proud defiance in their looks they bore. "For thee (they cry'd) amidst alarms and strife, We sail'd in tempests down the stream of life; For thee, whole nations fill'd with fire and blood, And swam to empire through the purple Hood. Those ills we dar'd, thy inspiration own; What virtue seem'd was done for thee alone." "Ambitious fools! (the queen reply'd and frown'd) Be all your deeds in dark oblivion drown'd; There sleep forgot, with mighty tyrants gone, Your statues moulder'd, and your names unknown." A sudden cloud straight snatch'd them from my sight, And each majestic phantom sunk in night.

Then came the smallest tribe 1 yet had seen; Plain was their dress, and modest was their mien: "Great idol of mankind, we never claim The praise of merit, nor aspire to fame; But, safe in deserts from the applause of men, Would die unheard of, as we liv'd unseen. 'Tis all we beg thee, to conceal from sight, Those acts of goodness which themselves requite.

O! let us still the sacred joy partake,
To follow virtue, e'en for virtue's sake.
"

And live there men who slight immortal fame?
Who, then, with iucense shall adore our nam?
But, mortals know, 'tis still our greatest pride,
To blaze those virtues which the good would hide.
Rise, muses, rise! add all your tuneful breath,
These must not sleep in darkness and in death."
She said. In air the trembling music floats,
And, on the winds triumphant swell the notes;
So soft, though high; so loud, and yet so clear,

E'en list'uing angels lean from heaven to hear;
To farthest shores the air.brosial spirit flies,
Sweet to the world, and grateful to the skies.

»

XI.—*Panegyric on Great Britain.*—Thompson,

HEAVENS! what a goodly prospect spreads around,
.Of hills and dales, and woods and lawns, and spires,
And glitt'ring towns, and gilded streams, till all
The stretching landscape into smoke decays!
Happy Britannia! where the Queen of Arts,
Inspiring vigor, Liberty, abroad
Walks unconfin'd, even to thy farthest cots,
And scatters plenty with unsparing hand,
Rich is the soil, and merciful thy clime;
Thy streams unfailing in the summer's drought,
Unmatch'd thy guardian oaks; thy vallies float
With golden waves; and on thy mountains flocks
Bleat numberless; while, roving round their sides,
Below the black'ning herds in lusty droves.
Beneath thy meadows glow, and rise unequall'd
Against the mewer's scythe. On every hand
Thy villas shine. Thy country teems with wealth,
And property assures it to the swain,
Pleas'd and unwearied in his guarded toil.
Full are thy cities with the sons of art—
And trade and joy, in every busy street,
Mingling are heard! even drudgery himself,
As at the car be sweats, or, dusty, hews
The palace stone, looks gay. The crowded ports,
Where rising masts, an endless prospect yield,
With labour burn, and echo to the shouts

Of hurried sailor, as he hearty waves
His last adieu, and loosening every sheet,
Resigns the spreading vessel to the wind.
Bold, firm and graceful are thy gen'rous youth,
By hardship sinew'd, and by danger fir'd,
Scattering the nations where they go; and first
Or on the listed plain, or stormy seas.
Mild are thy glories too, as o'er the plains
Of thriving peace thy thoughtful sires preside;
In genius and substantial learning, high;
For every virtue, every worth renowh'd!
Sincere, plain hearted, hospitable, kind;
Yet, like the mutt'ring thunder, when provok'd,
The dread of tyrants, and the sole resource I
Of those that under grim oppression groan.

Thy sons of Glory many! Alfred thine, I
In whom the splendour of heroic war,
And more heroic peace, when govern'd well
Combine! whose hallow'd name the virtues' saint,
And his own Muses love; the best of kings!
With him thy Edwards and thy Henrys ihine,
Names dear to fame; the first who deep impress'!
On haughty Gaul the terror of thy arms,
That awes her genius still. In statesmen thou,
A«d patriots fertile. Thine a steady More,"
Who, with a generous, though mistaken zeal,
Withstood a brutal tyrant's useful rage;
Like Cato firm, like Aristides just,
Like rigid Cincinnatus nobly poor,
A dauntless soul erect, who smil'd on death.
A Hampden too is thine, illustrious land!
Wise, strenuous, firm, of unsuhmitting soul;
Who slemm'd the torrent of a down-

ward age,
To slavery prone, and bade thee rise
again,
In all thy native pomp of freedom bold.
Thine is a Bacon; hapless in his choice;
Unfit to stand the civil storm of state,
And through the smooth barbarity of
courts,
With firm but pliant virtue, forward still
To urge his course; him for the studious
shade
Kind nature form'd, deep, comprehen-
sive, deaf,
Lxact and elegant; in one rich soul,
Plato, the Siagyrite, and Tully joiu'd.
Let Newton, p intelligence, whom God
   To mortals lent to trace his boundless
works
   From laws sublimely simple, speak
thy fame
   In all philosophy. For lofty sense,
   Creative fancy and inspection keen,
   Through the deep wmdings of the hu-
man heart
   Is not wild Shakespeare»thine and
nature's boast?
   Is not each great, each amiable Muse
   Of classic ages in thy Milton met?
   A genius universal as his theme:
   As (omening.as chaos, aflthe bloom
   Of kfewing-Fden fair, as heaven sub-
lime; Maroy song soften, as-thy Daugh-
ters I,
Britannia hail iToibcauiy is their own,
The feelmg heart, simplicity of life,
And elegauce, and taste; the faultless
form,
Shap'd by the hand of harmony; the
cheek,
Where the live crimson, through the na-
tive white,
Soft shooting, o'er the face diffuses
bloom,
And every nameless grace; the parted
lip,
Like the red tosebud moist with morn-
ing dew,
Breathing delight; and, under flowing
jet,
Or sunny ringlets, or of circling brown,
The neck slight shaded, and the
swelling breast;
The look resistless, piercing to the soul,
And by the soul inform'd, when dress'd
in love

She sits high smiling in the conscious
eye.
Island of bliss! amid the subject seas,
That thunder round thy rocky coasts set
up,
At once the wonder, terrour and delight
Of distant nations, whose remotest
shores
Can soon be shaken by thy naval arm;
Not to be shook thyself, but all assaults
Baffling, as thy hoar cliffs the loud sea
wave.
O thou *I* by whose Almighty nod, the
scale
Of empire rises, or alternate falls,
Send forth thy saving virtues round the
land,
In bright patrou!; white Peace, and so-
cial Love;
The tender looking Charity, intent
On gentle deeds, and shedding tears
through smiles J
Undaunted Truth and dignity ol mind;
Courage compos'd and keen—sound
Temperance,
Healthful in heart and look—clear
Chastitv,
   With blushes reddening as she moves
along,
Disoider'd at the deep regard she
draws—
Rough Industry—Activity until'd,
With copious life inform'd, and all
awake-
While in the radiant front, superiour
shines
That first paternal virtue, Public Zeal—
Who throws o'er all an equal wide sur-
vey,
And, ever musing on the common weal,
Still labours glorious with Sohw great
design.
XII.—*Ilymn to the Deity, on the Seasons
of the* F(i«%—Tb,
THESE, as they change, Almighty
Father, these
Are but the *varied God.* The rolingear
Is full of thee. Forth in the pleasing
Spring
Thy beauty walks, thy tenderness and
love.
Wide flush the fields—the softening air
is balm—
Echo the mountains round—the forest
smiles,

And every sense, and every heart is joy.
Then comes thy glory in the summer
months,
With light and heat refulgent. Then thy
son
Shoots full perfection through the
swelling year.
And oft thy voice in dreadful thunder
speaks;
And oft at dawn, deep noon or falling
eve.
By brooks and groves, and hollow whis-
pering gales,
Thy boMnty shines in Autumn uncon-
fin'd,
And spreads a common feast for all that
live.
In Winter awful thou! with clouds and
storms
Around thee thrown—tempest o'er tem-
pest roll'd-:
Majestic darkness! on the whirlwind's
wing
Riding sublime, thou bid'st the world
adore,
And humblest nature with thy northern
blast.
Mysterious round! what skill, what
force divine,,
Deep felt in these appear! a simple
tram—
Yet so delightful mix'd, with such kind
art, '.
   Such beauty and beneficence combin'd—
Shade, unperceiv'd, so softening in to
shade—
And all so forming. an harmonious
whole—
That, as they still succeed, they ravish
still.
But wandering oft with brute uncon-
cious gaze,
Man marks not thee, marks not the
mighty hand,
That, ever busy, wheels the silent
spheres—
Works in the secret deep—shoots,
streaming, thence
The fair profusion that o'erspreads the
spring—
   Flings from the sun direct the flaming
day:
Feeds every creature—hurls the tempest
forth:

And as on earth this grateful change re-
volves,
With transport touches all the springs of
life.
Nature, attend! join every living soul,
Beneath the spacious temple of the sky,
In adoration join—and ardent, raise
One general song! To him, ye vocal
gales,
Breathe soft, whose Spirit in your fresh-
ness breathes:
O talk of him in solitary gloom!
Where, o'er the rock, the scarcely wav-
ing pine
Fills the brown shade with a religious
awe.
And ye, whose bolder note is heard afar,
Who shake th' astonish'd world, lift
high to heaven
Th' impetuous song, and say from
whom you rage.
His praise, ye brooks attune, ye trem-
bling rills—
And let me catch it as I muse along.
Ye headlong torrents, rapid and pro-
found—
Ye softer floods, that lead the humid
maze
Along Ihe vale—and thou majestic
main,
A secret world of wonders in thyself—
Sound his stupendous praise, whose
greater voice
Or bids you roar, or bids your roarings
fall.
Soft roll your incense, herbs, and fruits,
and flowers.
In mingled clouds to him, whose sun
exalts,
Whose breath perfumes you, and whose
pencil paints,
Ye forests bend, ye harvests wave to
him—
Breathe your still song into the reaper's
heart,
As home he goes beneath the joyous
moon..
Ye that keep watch in heaven, as earth
asleep
Unconscious lies, effuse your mildest
beams
Ye constellations, while your angels
strike,
Amid the spangled sky, the silver lyre.
Great source of day! blest image here

below,
Of thy Creator, ever pouring wide,
From world to world, the vital ocean
round, i
On Nature write with every beam his
praise.
Ye thunders roll; be hush'd the pros-
trate world,
While cloud to cloud returns the solemn
hymn,
Bleat out afresh, ye hills; ye mossy
rocks
Retain the sound; the broad responsive
low,
Ye vallies raise , for the great Shepherd
reigns,
And hi? *unsuffering* kingdom yet will
come.
Ye woodlands all, awake; a bound-
less song
Burst from the groves; and when the
restless day,
Expiring, lays the warbling world
asleep,
Sweetest of birds, sweet Pnilomela,
charm
The listening shades, and teach the
night his praise.
Ye chief, for whom the whole cre-
ation smiles:
At once the heafl, the heart, the
tongue of all;
Crown the great hymn! In swarming
cities vast,
Assembled men to the deep organ
join
The long resounding voice, oft break-
ing clear,
At solemn pauses, through the
swelling base—
And, as each mingling flame increas-
es each,
In one united ardour rise to heaven—
Or if you rather choose the rural
shade,
And find a fane in every sacred
grove—
There let the shepherd's flute, the virgin's lay,
The prompting seraph, and the poet's
lyre,
Still sing the God of Seasons as they
roll.
For me, when I forget the darling
theme,

Whether the blossom blows, the summer ray
Russets the plain, inspiring Autumn
gleams,
Or winter rises in the blackening
east—
Be my tongue mute, my fancy paint
no more,
And, dead to joy, forget my heart to
beat!
Should fate command me to the farthest verge Of the green earth, to distant
barb'rous climes, Rivers unknown to
soeg; where first the sun Gildo Indian
mountains, or his setting beam Flames
on the Atlantic isles; 'tis nought to
me— Since God is ever present, ever
felt, In the void waste as in the city
full— And where He vital spreads,
there must be joy. When even at last the
solemn hour shall come, And wing my
mystic flight to future worlds, I cheerful will obey—there with new powers,
Will rising wonders sing—I cannot go,
Where Universal Love smiles not
around. Sustaining all yon orbs, and all
their suns— From *seeming evil* still
educing *good,* And *better* thence again,
and *better* still, In infinite progression—
but I lose Myself in Himj in Light In-
effable! Come then, expressive Silence,
muse His praise.

SECTION VIL I,—*The Camelion*—Mer-
rick.

OFT has it been ruy lot to mark
A proud, conceited, talking spark,
Returning from his finish'd tour,
Grown ten times percer than before j
Whatever word you chance to drop,
The travell'd fool your mouth will
stop—.
"Sir, if my judgment you'll allow—
I've seen—and sure I ought to know.
"—-
So begs you'd pay a due submission,
And acquiesce in his decision.
Two travellers of such a cast,
As o'er Arabia's wilds they pass'd;
And on their way in friendly chat,
Now talk'd of this and then of that—
Discours'd awhile 'mongst other mat-
ter,-
Of the Camelion's form and nature.
"A stranger animal," cries one,
"-Sure never liv'd beneath the sun:

A lizard's body, lean and long,
A fish's head, a serpent's tongue,
Its tooth with triple claw disjoin'd—
And what a length of tail behind!
How slow its pace! and then its hue—
Who ever saw so fine a blue?"
"Hold there," the other quick replies,
"'Tis green—I saw it with these eyes,
As late with open mouth it lay,
And warm'd it in the sunny ray:
Stretch'd at its ease the beast I view'd,
And saw it eat the air for food."
"Ive seen it, sir, as well as you,
And must again affi. in it blue.
At leisure I the beast survey'd,
Extended in tne cooling shade."
"'Tis green, 'tis green, sir, I nssure y.e,
« Green!" cries the other iu a fury—
"Why sir, d'ye th ink I've lost my
eyes?"
"'Twere no great loss," the friend
replies—
"For if they always serve you thus,
You'll find them of but little use."
So high at last the contest rose,
From words they almost came to
blows—
When luckily, came by a third;
To him the question they referr'd,
And begg'd he'd tell tbem if knew,
Whether the thing was green or blue.
'« Sirs," cries the umpire, " cease your
pother,
The creature's neither one nor t'other.
I caught the animal last night,
And view'd it o'er by candle light:
I mark'd it well—'twas black as jet—
You stare—but sirs I've got it yet,
And can produce it."—" Pray sir do:
I'll lay my life the thing is blue."
"And I'll be sworn that when you've
seen
The reptile, you'll pronounce it green."
« Well then, at once to end the doubt,"
Replies the man, " I'll turn him out:
And when before your eyes I've set
him,
If you don't find him black I'll eat him.
"
He said—then full before their sight
Produc'd the beast—aud low 'twas
white.
II.—*On the Order of Nature.*—Pope.
SEE, through this air, this ocean and this
earth, Al! matter quick, and bursting in-

to birth. Above, how high progressive
life may go, Around how wide! how
deep extend below! Vast chain of being,
which from God began: Natures etherial, human; angel, man; Beast, bird, fish,
insect, what no eye can see, No glass
can roach; from Infinite to theeFrom
thee to nothing. On superiour power-
sWere we to press, inferiour might on
ours; Or in the full creation leave a void,
Where, one step broken, the great
scale's destroyed; From Nature's chain
whatever link you strike, Tenth or ten
thousandth, breaks the chain alike.
What if the foot, ordain'd the dust to
tread,
Or hand, to toil, aspir'd to be the head?
What if the head, the eye, or ear repin'd
To serve mere engines to the ruling
mind?
Just as absurd for any part to claim
To be another, in this gen'ral frame.
Just as absurd to mourn the tasks or
pains,
The great directing Mind of All ordains.
Alt are but parts of one stupendous
whole,
Whose body Nature is, and God the
soul:
That, chang'd through all, and yet in all
the same,
Great in the earth, as in th etherial
frame,
Warms in the sun, refreshes in the
breeze,
Glows in the stars, and blossoms in the
trees,
Lives through all life, extends through
all extent,
Spreads undivided, operates unspent,
Breathes in our soul, informs our mortal
part,
As full, as perfect, in a hair as heart:
As full, as perfect, in vile man that
mourns,
As the rapt seraph that adores and
burns:
To him no high, no low, no great, no
small;
He fills, he bounds, connects and equals
all.
Cease, then, nor Order, imperfection
name:
Our proper bliss depends on what.we
blame.

Know thy own point; this kind, this due
degree
Of blindness, weakness, Heaven be-
stows on thee.
Submit.—In this, or any other sphere,
Secure to be as blest as thou canst bear;
Safe in the hand of one disposing Pow-
er,
Or in the natal, or the mortal hour.
All Nature is but Art unknown to thee;
All Chance, Direction which thou canst
not see;
All Discord, Harmony not understood;
All partial.Evil, universal Good;
And, spite of Pride, in erring Reason's
spite,
One truth is clear, "Whatever Is, Is
Right."
HI, *Description of a Country Alehouse.*
—Goldsmith. NEAR yonder thorn that
lifts its head on high, Where once the
signpost caught the passing eye 5 Low
lies that house, where nut brown
draughts inspir'd J Where gray beard
mirth, and smiling toil retir'd j
Where village statesmen talk'd with
looks profound,
And news, much older than their ale,
went round.
Imagination fondly stoops to trace
The parlour splendours of that festive
place;
The whitewash'd wall; the nicely sand-
ed floor;
The vamish'd clock, that cfick'd behind
the door;
The chest, coutriv'd a double debt to
pay,
A bed by night, a cliesi of drawers by
day;
The pictures pluc'd for ornament and
use,
The twelve good rules, the royal game
of goose j
The hearth, except when winter chill'd
the day,
With aspen boughs, and flowers, and
fennel gay;
While broken teacups, wisely kept for
show,
Rang'd o'er the chimney, glisten'd in a
row.
Vain transitory splendours! could not
all
Reprieve the tottering mansion from its

fall!

Obscure it sinks; nor shall it more impart

An hour's importance to the poor man's heart."

Thither no more the peasant shall repair,

To sweet oblivion of his daily care;

No more the farmer's news, the barber's tale,

No more the woodman's ballad shall prevail;

No more the smith his dusky brow shall clear,

Relax his pond'rous strength, and lean to hear.

The host himself no longer shall be found

Careful to see the mantling bliss go round;

Nor the coy maid, half willing to be press'd,

Shall kiss the cup, to pass it to the rest,

IV.— *Character of a Country School-master.*—Ib. BESIDE yon straggling fence that skirts the way). Wth blossom'd furze, unprofiiably gay, There, in his noisy mansion, skill'd to rule, The village master taught his little school. A man severe he was, and stern to view; I knew him well, and every truant knew. Well had the boding tremblers learn'd to trace The day's disasters in his morning face: Full well they laugh'd, and counterfeited glee, At all his jokes—for many a joke had he; Full well the busy whisper, circling round, ttonvey'd the dismal tidings when he frown'di

Yet he was kind; or, if severe in aught,

The love he bore to learning was in fault.

The village all declar'd how much he knew,'

'Twas certain he could write and cypher too;

Lands he could measure, times and tides presage;

And e'en the story ran that he could guage.

In arguing too the parson own'd his skill;

For, e'en though vanquish'd he could argue still;

While words of learned length and thund'ring sound,

Ainaz'd the gazing rustics, rang'd around;

And still they gaz'd—and still the wonder grew,

That ope small head could carry all he knew.

V.—*Story of Palemon and Lavinia.* —Thompson. The lovely young Lavinia once had friends,

And fortune smil'd deceitful, on her birth.

For, in her helpless years, depriv'd of all,

Of every stay, save innocence and Heaven,

She, with her widow'd mother, feeble, old

And poor, liv'd in a cottage, far retir'd

Among the windings of a woody vale;

By solitude and deep surrounding shades,

But more by bashful modesty conceal'd.

Together, thus they shun'd the cruel scorn.

Which virtue, sunk to poverty, would meet

From giddy passion and low minded pride;

Almost on nature's common bounty fed;

Like the gay birds that sung them to repose,

Content, and careless of tomorrow's fare.

Her form was fresher than the morning rose,

When the dew wets its leaves; unstain'd and pure,

As is the lilly, or the mountain snow.

The modest virtues mingled in her eyes,

Still on the ground dejected, darting all

Their humid beams into the blooming flowers;

Or, when the mournful tale her mother told,

Of what her faithless fortune promis'd once,

Thrill'd in her thought, they, like the dewy star

Of evening, shone in tears. A native grace

Sat, fair proportion'd, on her polish'd limbs,

Veil'd in a simple robe, their best attire,

Beyond the pomp of dress; for loveliness

Needs not the foreign aid of ornament,

But is, when unadorn'd, adorn'd the most.

Thoughtless of beauty, she was beauty's self,

Recluse, amid the close embowering woods.

As in the hollow breast of Appenine,

Beneath the shelter of encircling hills,

A myrtle rises, far from human eye,

And breathes its balmy fragrance o'er the wildj

So flourish'd blooming, and unseen by all,

The sweet Lavinia; till at length compell'd

By strong Necessity's supreme command,

With smiling patience in her looks, she went

To glean Palemon' fields.—The pride of swains

Palemon was; the generous and the rich;

Who led the rural life, in all its joy

And elegance, such as Arcadian snng

Transmits from ancient uncorrupted times,

When tyrant Custom had not shackled man,

But, free to follow nature, was the mode.

He then, his fancy with autumnal scenes

Amusing, chanc'd beside his reaper train

To walk, when poor Lavinia drew his eye,

Unconscious of her power, and turning quick.

With unaffected blushes, from his gaze:

He saw her charming; but he saw not half

The charms her downcast modesty conceal'd,

That very moment love and chaste desire

Sprung in his bosom, to himself unknown;

For still the world prevail'd, and its dread laugh

(Which scarce the firm philosopher can scorn)

Should his heart own a gleaner in the

field;

And thus in secret to his soul he sigh'cL

"What pity that so delicate a form, By beauty kindled, where enlivening sense, And more than vulgar goodness seems to dwell, Should be devoted to the rude embrace Of some indecent clown! She looks, me thinks, Of old Acasto's line; and to my mind Recalls that patron of my happy life, from whom my liberal fortune took its rise; Now to the dust gone down, his houses, lands, And once fair spreading family, dissolv'd.

Tis said that in some lone, obscure retreat,

Urg'd by remembrance sad, and decent pride,

Far from those scenes which knew their better days,

His aged widow and his daughter live,

Whom yet my fruitless search could never find;

Romantie wish! would this the daughter were."

When, strict inquiring, from herself he found She was the same, the daughter of his friend, Of bountiful Acasto— who can speak The mingled passions that surpriz'd his heart, And through his nerves, in shiv'ring transport ran! Then blaz'd his smother'd flame, avow'd, and bold! And as he view'd ber, ardent o'er and o'er, Love, gratitude and pity wept at once. Confus'd and frighteu'd at his sudden tears, Her rising beauties flush'd a higher bloom; As thus Palemon, passionate and just, Pour'd out the pious rapture of his soul.

"And art thou, then, Acasto's dear remains? She whom my restless gratitude has sought So long in vain? O yes.'' the very same, The soften'd image of my noble friend 5 Alive his every feature, every look, Mole elegantly touch'd. Sweeter than Spring! Thou sole surviving blossom from the root That nourish'd up my fortune! say, ah! where,-In what sequester'd desert hast thou drawn The kindest aspect of delighted heaven! Into such beauty spread and Mown so fair, Though poverty's cold wind and rushing rain, Beat keen and heavy on thy tender years. O let me now into a richer soil Transplant thee safe, where

vernal suns and showers Diffuse their warmest, largest influence; And of my garden be the pride and joy, III it befits thee, ch! it ill befits Acasto's daughter, his whose open stores, Though vast, were little to his ampler heart, The father of a country, thus to pick The very refuse of those harvest fields, Which from his bounteous friendship I enjoy. Then throw that shameful pittance from thy hand,

But ill applied to such a rugged task; The fields, the master, all, my fair, are thine;

If to the various blessings which thy house

Has on me lavished thou wilt add that bliss,

That dearest bliss, the power of blessing thee."

Here ceas'd the youth; yet still his speaking eye

Express'd the secret triumph of his soul, With conscious virtue, gratitude and love,

Above the vulgar joy divinely rais'd.

Nor waited he reply. Won by the charm Of goodness irresistible, and all

In sweet disorder lost—she blush'd consent.

The news immediate to her mother brought,

While pierc'd with anxious thought, she pin'd away

The lonely moments for Lavina's fate:

Amaz'd and scarce believing what she heard,

Joy seiz'd her wither'd veins, and one bright gleam

Of setting life shone on her evening hours:

Not less enraptur'd than the happy pair, Who flourish'd long in tender bliss, and reard

A numerous offspring, lovely like themselves,

And good the grace of all the country round.

VI —*Celadon and Amelia.*—!r. YOUNG Celadon

And his Amelia were a matchless pair, With equal virtue form'd, and equal grace,

The same, distinguish'd by their sex alone.

Hers, the mild lusture of the blooming mora,

And his the radiance of the risen day.

They lov'd. But such their guiltless passion was,

As in the dawn of time, inform'd the heart

Of innocence and utdissembling truth.

'Twas friendship, heighten'd by the mutual wish,

The enchanting ho)e and sympathetic glow

Beam'd from the mutual eye. Devoting all

To love, each was to each a dearer self; Supremely happy in th' awaken'd power

Of giving joy. Alone, amid the shades, Still, in harmonious intercourse, they livd

The rural day, and talk'd the flowing heart;

Or sigh'd and look'd—unutterable things.

So pass'd their life, a clear united stream, By care unruffled, till, in evil hour, The tempest caught them on the tender walk, Heedless how far and where ils mazes stray'd; While, with each other bless'd creative love Still bade eternal Eden smile around. Presaging instant fate, her bosom heaVd 'Unwonted siglrs; and stealing oft a look Tow'rds the big gloom, on Celadon her eye Fell tearful, wetting her disorder'd cheek. *litt* vain assuring love and confidence In heaven repress'd her fear; it grew, and shook Her frame near dissolution. He percerv'd Th' unequal conflict; and, as angels look On dying saints, his eyes compassion shed, With love illumin'd high. "Fear not," he said, Sweet innocence! thou stranger to offence And inward storm! He who yon skies involves In frowns of darkness, ever smiles on thee, With kind regard. O'er thee the secret shaft, That wastes at midnight, or th' undreaded hour Of noon, flies harmless; and that very voice Which thunders terrour through the guilty heart, With tongues of seraphs whispers peace to thine. 'Tis safety to be near thee, sure, and thus To clasp perfection-!" Fim his void embrace, (Mysterious Heaven!) that moment to the ground, A blacketr'd corse was struck the beauteous maicU But who can paint the lover as he stood, Pierc'd by severe amazement, hating life, Speechless, and fix'd in all the death of woe.

VII.—*Description of Mab, Queen of the Fairies.*—

Shakespeake. SHE is the fancy's mid-wife; and she comes

In shape no bigger than an agate stone,

On the forefinger of an Alderman;

Drawn by a team of little atomies,

Athwart men's noses as they lie asleep;

Her waggon spokes, made of long spin-ner's legs:

The cover, of the wings of grasshop-pers;

The traces, of the smallest spider's web;

The collars, of the moonshine's wat'ry beams i

Her whip, of cricket's bone; the lash, of film;

Her waggoner, a small gray coated gnat;

Her chariot is an empty hazle nut,

Made by the joiner Squirrel, or old Grub,

Time out of mind the fairies' coachmak-erS.

And in this state she gallops, night by night,

Through lovers' brains, and then they dream of love;

O'er lawyers' fingers, who straight dreem of fees;

O'er ladies' liis, who straight on kisses dream;

And sometimes comes she with the tithe pig's tail,

Tickling the parson as he lies asleep,

Then dreams he of another benefice.

Sometimes she driveth o'er a soldier's neck;

And then he dreams of cutting foreign throats,

Of breaches, ambuscadoes, Spanish blades;

Of healths five fathom deep; and then, anon,

Drums in his ears: at which he starts and wakes;

And being thus frighted, swears a prayer or two,

And sleeps again.

VHI.—*On the Existence of a Deity.*—

Young. RETIRE—The world shut out—thy tho'ts call homeImagination's airy wing repress. Lock up thy senses. Let no passion stir. Wake all to reason. Let her reign alone. Then, in thy soul's deep sr.ence, and the depth Of nature's silence midnight, thus inquire. What am I? and from whence? I nothing know But that I am; and since I am, conclude Something eternal. Had there e'er been nought, Nought still had been. Eternal there must be. But, what eternal? Why not human race, And Adam's ancestors, without an end *I* That's hard to be con-ceiv'd, since every link Of that long chain'd succession is so frail; Can every part depend, and not the whole*i* Yet, grant it true, new difficulties rise: I'm still quite out at sea, nor see the shore. Whence earth and these bright oibs? Eternal tool Grant matter was eternal; still these orbs Would want some other father. Much design

Is seen in all their motions, all their makes.

Design implies intelligence and art,

That can't be from themselves—or man; that art

Man scarce can comprehend, could man bestow:

And nothing greater yet allow'd than man.

Who, motion, foreign to the smallest grain,

Shot through vast masses of enor-mous weight?

sVho bid brute matter's restive lump as-sume

Such various forms, and gave it wings to fly?

Has matter innate motion? Then each atom,

Asserting its indisputable right

To dance, would form an universe of dust.

Has matter none?—Then whence these glorious forms,

And boundless flights, from shape-less and repos'd?

Has matter more than motion?-Has it thought,

Judgment and genius? Is it deeply learn'd

In mathematics? Has it frani'd such laws,

Which, but to guess, a Newton made immortal?

If art to form, and council to conduct,

And that with greater far than human skill,

Residei not in each block—a God-head reigns—

And if a God there is—that God how great!

IX.—*Evening in Paradise describzd. Adam and Eve'& Conversation and Evening Worship.*—Milton, NOW came still evening on, and twilight gray Had in her sober livery all things clad. Si-lence accompanied; for beast and bird, They to their grassy couch, these to their nest Were sunk, all but the wakeful nightingale; She all night long her amorous descant sung: Silence was pleas'd. Now glow'd the Armament With living sapphires: Hesperus, that led The starry host, rode brightest; till the moon, Rising in clouded majesty at length, Apparent queen, unveil'd her peerless light, And o'er the dark her sil-ver mantle threw.

When Adam thus to Eve. Fair consort th' hour Of night, and all things now retir'd to rest, Mind us of like repose; since God hath set Labour and rest, as day and night, to men, Successive; and the timely dew of sleep

Now falling, with soft slumb'rous weight inclines

Our eyelids. Other creatures all day long

Rove idle, unemployed, and less need rest:

Man hath his daily work of body or mind

Appointed, which declares his dignity,

And the regard of Heaven on all his ways:

While other animals inactive range,

And of their doings God takes no ac-count.

Tomorrow, ere fresh morning streak the east

With first approach of light, we must be risen,

And at our pleasant labour, to reform

Yon fl'ow'ry arbours, yonder alleys green,

Our walk at noon, with branches over-grown,

That mock our scant manuring, and require

More hands than ours to lop their wanton growth';

Those blossoms also, and those dropping gums,

That lie bestrown, unsightly and unsmooth,

Ask riddance, if we mean to tread with ease;

Meanwhile, as nature wills, night bids us rest.

To whom thus Eve, with perfect beauty adoru'd:

My author and disposer! what tbou bidd'st

Unargu'd I obey; so God ordains:

God is thy law, tbou mine, to know no more

Is woman's happiest knowledge, and her praise.

With thee conversing, I forget all time,

All seasons and their change: all please alike.

Sweet is the breath of mom, her rising sweet,

With charm of earliest birds: pleasant the sun,

When first on this delightful land he spreads

His orient beams, on herb, tree, fruit and flower,

Glist'ning with dew; fragrant the fertile earth

After soft showers; and sweet the coming on

Of grateful evening mild; then silent night,

With this her solemn bird, and this fair moon.

And these the gems of Heaven, her starry train:

But neither breath of morn, when she ascends

With charm of earliest birds; nor rising sun,

On this delightful land; nor herb, fruit, flower,

Glist'ning with dew; nor fragrance after showers;

Nor grateful evening mild; nor silent night,

With this her solemn bird; nor walk by moon,

Or glittering starlight, without thee is sweet.

Thus, at their shady lodge arriv'd, both stood, Both turn'd; and under open sky ador'd The God that made both sky, air, eartli and Heaven, Which they beheld; the moon's resplendent globe, And starry pole: Thou also mad'st the night, Maker omnipotent, and thou the day, Which we, in our appointed work employed, Have finished; happy in our mutual help And mutual love, the crown of all our bliss, Ordain'd by thee; and this delicious place, For us too large; where thy abundance wantsPartakers, and uncropt, falls to the ground: But tb'u hast promis'd from us two, a race To fill the earth, who shall with us extol Thy goodness infinite, both when we wake, And when we seek, as now, thy gift of sleep.

X.—*Elegy written in a Country Churchyard.*—Gray? THE curfew tolls the knell of parting day;

The lowing herds wind slowly o'er the lea;

The ploughman homeward plods his weary way,

And leaves the world to darkness and to me.

Now fades the glimm'ring landscape on the sight,.

And all the air a solemn stillness holds;

Save where the beetle wheels his droning flight,

And drowsy tinklings lull the distant folds.

Save that from yonder ivy mantled tower, The moping owl does to the moon complain Of such, as wand'ring near her secret bower, Molest her ancient solitary reign.

Beneath these rugged elms, that yewtrees shade,

Where heaves the turf in many a mouldeting heap,

Each in his narrow cell forever laid,

The rude forefathers of the hamlet sleep.

The breezy call of incense breathing morn,

The swallow, twitt'ring from the straw built shed,

The cock's shrill clarion or the echoing horn,

No,more shall rouse them from their lowly bed.

For them no more the blazing hearth shall burny

Or busy housewife ply her evening care;

No children run to lisp their sire's return,

Or climb his knees, the envied kiss to share.

Oft did the harvest to their sickle yield;

Their furrow oft the stubborn glebe has broke: How jocund did they drive their team afield! How bow'd the woods beneath their sturdy stroke!

Let not ambition mock their useful toil,

Their homely joys and destiny obscure:

Nor grandeur hear, with a disdainful smile,

The short and simple annals of the poor.

The boast of heraldry, the pomp of power,

And all that beauty, all that wealth e'er gave,

Await, alike the inevitable hour:

The paths of glory lead—but to the grave.

Nor you, ye proud, impute to these a fault,

If mem'ry o'er their tomb no trophies raise,

Where through the long drawn aisle and fretted vault,

The pealing anthem swells the note of praise.

Can story'd urn, or animated bust,

Back to its mansion call the fleeting breath?

Can bonoor's voice provoke the silent dust,

Or flatt'ry sooth the dull cold ear of death?

Perhaps, in this neglected spot is laid

Some heart, once pregnant with celestial fire:

Hands that the rod of empire might have sway'd,

Or wak'd to ecstacy the living lyre:

But knowledge to their eyes her ample page,

Rich with the spoils of time did ne'er enroll;

Chill penury repress'd their noble rage,

And froze the genial current of the soul.

Full many a gem of purest ray serene,

The dark, unfathom'd caves of ocean bear;

Full many a flower is born to blush unseen,

And waste its sweetness on the desert
air.

Some village Hampden, that, with
dauntless breast,

The little tyrant of his fields withstood;

Some mute, inglorious Milton here may
rest;

Some Cromwell, guiltless of his country's blood.

Th' applause of list'ning senates to
command,

The threats of pain and ruin to despise,.

To scatter plenty o'er a smiling land,

And read their hist'ry in a nation's eyes.

Their lot forbade; nor circumscrib'd
aJone,

Their growing virtues, but their crimes
oonfiu'd j

Forbade to wade through slaughter to a
throne,

And shut the gates of mercy on
mankind:

The struggling pangs of conscious truth
to hide,

To quench the blushes of ingenuous
shame;

Or heap the shrine of luxry and pride,

With incense kindled at the muse's
flame.

Far from the madd'ning crowd's ignoble strife,

Their sober wishes never learn'd to
stray—

Along the cool sequester'd vale of life,

They kept the noiseless tenor of their
way.

Yet e'en these bones from insult to protect,

Some frail memorial still erected nigh,

With uncouth rhymes and shapeless
sculpture deck'd,

Implores the passing tribute of a sigh.

Their name, their years, spelt by th'
unletter'd muse, The place of fame and
elegy supply; And many a holy text
around she strews, That teach the rustic
moralist to die.

For who, to dumb forgetfulness a
prey, This pleasing, anxious being e'er
resign'd, Left the warm precincts of the
cheerful day; Nor cast one longing,
ling'ring look behind?

On some fond breast the parting soul
relies; Some pious drops the closing eye
requires; E'en from the tomb the voice
of nature cries, E'en in our ashes live
their wonted sires.

For thee, who, mindful of the unbo-
nour'd dead,

Dost in these lines their artless tale relate,

If chance, by lonely:onteaiplation led,

Some kindred spirit shall inquire thy
fate.

Haply, some hoary headed swain may
say,

"Oft have we seen him at the peep of
dawn,.

Brushing, with hasty steps, the dews
away,

To meet the sun upon the upland lawn;

There at the foot of yonder nodding
beech,

That wreathes its old fantastic roots so
high,

His listless length at noontide would he
stretch,

And pore upon the brook that babbles
by.

Hard by yon wood, now smiling, as in
scorn,

Mutt'ring his wayward fancies he
would rove;

Now drooping, woeful wan, like one
forlorn,

Or cxaa'd with care, or cross'd in hopeless love.

One morn I miss'd Iiim on th' accustom'd hi!)

Along the heath, and near his fav'rite
tree,'

Another came, nor yet beside the lill

Nor up the lawn, nor at the wood was
he.

The next, with dirges due, in sad array,

Slow through the church way path we
saw him borne

Approach and read (for thou canst read)
the lay

'Grav'd on the stone beneath yon aged
thorn.

THE EPITAPH.

HERE rests his head upon the lap of earth
A youth to fortune and to fame unknown:'

Fair Science frown'd not on his humble
birth

And Melancholy mark'd him for her
own.

Large was his bounty, and his soul sin-
cere-

Heaven did a recompense as largely
send.

He gave to mis'ry all he had—a tear;

He gain'd from heaven ('twas all he
wish'd)— a friencL

No farther seek his merits to disclose, '

Or drsrw his frailties from their dread
abode

(There tliey, alike, in trembling hope repose)

The bosom of his Father and his Ood.

*XL—Scipio restoring the Captive Lady
to her Lover*

Tviipxt L Thompson. WHEN to his
glorious first essay in war, New
Carthage fell; there all the flower of
Spain Were kept in hostage; a full field
presenting For Scipio's generosity to
shine.—A noble virgin Conspicuous far
o'er all the captive dames, Was mark'd
the general's prize. She wept and
MmMk Young, fresh and blooming like
the morn. An eve As when the blue sky
trembles through a cloud Of purest
white. A secret charm combin'd Her
features, and in&s'd enchantment
through them, tter shape was harmony.
But eloquence Beneath her beauty fails
which seemed on purpose By nature
lavish'd on her, that mankind Might see
the virtue of a hero try'd Almost beyond
the stretch of human force. bof t as she
pass'd along, with downcast eyes,
Where gentle sorrow swell'd, aud now
and then, £roppd o'er her modest
cheeks a trickling tear, *Ihe* Roman leg.
ons Ianguish'd, and hard war

Felt more than pity; e'en their chief
himself,

As on his high tribunal rais'd he sat,

Turn'd from the dang'rous sight; and,
chiding, ask'd

His officers, if by this gift they meant

To cloud his glory in its very dawn.

She, question'd of her birth, in trembling accents,

With tears and blushes, broken told
her tale.

But when he found her royally descended;

Of her old captive parents the sole
joy;

And that a hapless Celtiberian prince,
Her lover and belov'd, forgot his chains,
His lost dominions, and for her alone
Wept out his tender soul: sudden the heart
Of this young, conquering, loving, godlike Roman,
Felt all the great divinity of virtue.
His wishing youth stood check'd, his tempting power,
Restrain'd by kind humanity.—At once,
He for her parents and her lover call'd.
The various scene imagine. How his troops
Look'd dubious on, and wonder'd what he meant;
While, stretch'd below, the trembling supplant lay
Rack'd by a thousand mingling passions—fear,
Hope, jealousy, disdain, submission, grief,
Anxiety and love, in every shape.
To these as different sentiments succeeded,
As roix'd emotions, when the man divine,
Thus the dread silence to the lover broke.
"We both are young—both charm'd. The right of war
Has put thy beauteous mistress in m' power;
With whom I could, in the most sacred ties,
Live out a happy life. But, know that Romans,
Their hearts, as well as enemies can conquer;
Then, take her to thy soul! and with her, take
Thy liberty and kingdom-In return,
I ask but this—when you behold these eyes,
These charms, with transport, be a friend to Rome."
Ecstatic wonder held the lovers mute;
While the loud camp, and all the clust'ring crowd
That huug around, rang with repeated shouts;
Fame took the alarm, and through re-sounding Spain,
Blew fast the fair report; which more than arms,
Admiring nations to the Romans gain'd.

XII.—*Popes humorous Complaint to Dr. Arbuthnot, of the Impertinence of Scribblers.*

SHUT, shut the door, good John!—fatigu'd, I said j
Tie up the knocker—say, I'm sick, I'm dead.
The dogscar rages! Nay, 'lis past a doubt,.
All Bedlam, or Parnassus, is let out.
Fire in each eye, and papers in each hand,
They rave, recite, and madden round the land.
What walls can guard me, or what shades can hide?
They pierce my thickets; through my grot they glide r
By land, by water, they renew the charge;
They stop the chariot, and they board the barge:
No place is sacred; not the church is free;
E'en Sunday shines no sabbathday to me.
Then, from the mint walks forth the man of rhyme—
"Happy to catch me just at dinnertime."
Friend to my life! (which did not you prolong,
The world had wanted many an idle song)
What drop or nostrum can this plague remove!
Or which must end me, a fool's wrath or love?
A dire dilemma!—either way I'm sped;
If foes, they write; if friends, they read me dead
Seiz'd and tir'd down to judge how wretched I!
Who can't be silent, and who will not lie.
To laugh were want of goodness and of grace;
And to be grave exceeds all power of face.
I sit, with sad civility; I read,
With serious anguish and an aching head:
Then drop at last, but in unwilling ears,
This saving courtsel—" Keep your piece nine years."
"Nine years!" (cries he, high in Drury-lane,
Lull'd by soft zephyrs through the broken pane,
Rhymes ere he wakes, and prinis before term ends,
Oblig'd by hunger, and request of friends;)
"The piece, you think is incorrect. Why, take it;
I'm all submission, what you'd have it, make it."
Three things another's modest wishes bound—
My friendship-and a prologue, and ten pound.
Pitholeou sends to me—" You know bis Grace:
I want a patron—ask him for a place."
"Pitholeon libell'd me."—" But here's a letter
Informs you, Sir, 'twas when he knew no better."
"Bless me! a packet!—'Tis a stranger sues
A virgin tragedy, an orphan muse."
'If I dislike it—"' Furies, deaili and rage,"
If I approve—" Commend it to the stage."
There, thank my stars, rry whole commission ends;
The players and I are luckily, no friends.
Fir'd that the house reject him—" 'Sdeath, I'll print it,
And shame tlie fools—Your interest, Sir, with Lintot." vJLintot (dull rogue) will think your price too much."
"" Not if you, Sir, revise it, and retouch. "
All my demurs but double his attacks;
At last he whispers—" Do, and we go snacks:"
Glad of a quarrel, straight I clap the door—
"Sir let me see you and your works no more."
There are, who to my person pay their court:
I cough like Horace, and though lean,

am short:
Ammon's great son one shoulder had too high;
Such Ovid's nose; and, " Sir you have an eye."
Go on, obliging creatures; make me see,
All that disgrae'd my betters met in me.
Say, for my comfort, languishing in bed,
Just so immortal Maro held his head;
And when I die, be sure you let me know,
    "Great Homer died—three thousand years ago.
XIII—*Hymn to Adversity.*—Gray.
DAUGHTER of Jove, relentless power,
Thou tamer of the human breast,
Whose iron scourge and torturing hour,
The bad affright, afflict the best!
Bound in thy adamantine chain,
The proud are taught to taste of pain;
And purple tyrants vainly groan,
With pangs unfelt before, unpitied and alone.
When first thy sire to send on earth
Virtue, his darling child, design'd,
To thee he eave the heavenly birth,
And bade thee form her infant mind.
Stern, rugged nurse! thy rigid lore
With pptience, many a year she bore;
What sorrow was, thou bad'st her know,
And from her own she learn'd to melt at other's woe.
Scar'd at thy frown, terrific, fly Self-pleasing folly's idle brood,
    Wild Laughter, Noise and thoughtless Joy,
    And leave us leisure to be good.
    Light they disperse, and with them go
The summer Friend, the flatt'ring Foe,
    By vain Prosperity receiv'd, To her they vow their troth, and are again believ'd. Wisdom, in sable garb array'd,
    Immers'd in rapturous thought profound, v
    And Melancholy, silent maid,
    With leaden eye, that loves the ground,
    Still on thy solemn steps attend:
    Warm Charity, the general friend;
With Justice, to herself severe;
And Pity, dropping soft th« sadly pleasing tear.
Oh! gently on thy suppliant's head,

Dread Goddess, lay thy chast'ning hand!
    Not in thy Gorgon terrors clad,
    Nor circled with the vengeful band.
(As by the impious thou art seen)
    With thund'ring voice and threatening mien,
    With screaming Horror's funeral cry,
Despair, and fell Disease, and ghastly Poverty, Thy form benign, Oh, Goddess! wear;
    Thy milder influence impart;
    Thy philosophic train be there,
    To soften, not to wound my heart.
    Thy gen'rous spark, extinct, revive;
    Teach me to love and to forgive: £
Exact my own defects to scan;
    What others are, to feel; and know myself a man.
XTV—*The Passions.—An Ode* —Collins. WHEN Music, heavenly Maid! was young,
While yet in early Greece she sung,
The Passions oft, to hear her shell,
Throng'd around her magie cell;
Exulting, tremb.ing, raging, fainting,
Possess'd beyond the Muse's painting.
By turns they felt the glowing mind
Disturb'd, delighted, rais'd, refin'd;'
Till once, 'tis said, when all were fir'd,
Fill'd with fury, rapt, inspir'd,
From the supporting myrtles round, .-
They snatcli'd her instruments of sound 5
And, as they oft had heard apart,
Sweet lessons of her forceful art,
Each (for madness rul'd the hour)
Would prove his own expressive power.
First, Fear, his hand, its skill to try,
Amid the chords bewilder'd-laid;
And back recoil'd, he knew not why,
    E'en at the sound himself had made.
    Next Anger rush'd, his eyes on fire,
In lightrings own'd his secret stings,
In one rude clash he struck the lyre,
And swept with hurried hand the strings.
With woful measures, wan Despair
Low sullen sounds his grief beguil'd;
A solemn, strange and mingled air:
'Twas sad by fits, by starts 'twas wHd.
But thou, O hope! with eyes so fair,
What was thy delighted measure!
Still it Whisper'd, promis'd pleasure,
And bade the lovely scenes at distance

hail!
Still would her touch the strain prolong;
And from the rocks, the woods, the vale,
She calPd on Echo still through all her song:
And where her sweetest theme she chose,
A soft responsive voice was heard at every close;
And Hope enchanted, smil'd, and wav'd her golden hair:
And longer had she sung, but with a frown,
Revenge impatient rose.
He threw his blood stain'd sword in thunder down;
And with a withering look,
The war denouncing trumpet took,
And blew a blast so loud and dread,
Were ne'er prophetic sounds so full of woe j
And ever and anon, he beat
The doubling drum with furious heat:
And though, sometimes, each dreary pause between,
Dejected Pity at his side,
Her soul subduing vohce applied,
Yet still he kept his wild unalter'd mien, head.
    While each strain'd ball of sight—seem'd bursting from his Thy numbers, Jealousy, to nought were fix'd; Sad proof of thy distressful state;
Of differing themes the veering song was mix'd:
And, now it courted Love; now, raving, call'd on Hate.
With eyes uprais'd, as one inspir'd
Pale Melancholy sat retir'd;
And, from her wild sequesler'd seat,
In notes, by distance made more sweet,
Pour'd through the mellow horn her pensive soul,
And dashing soft from rocks around,
Bubbling runnels join'd the sound;
Through glades and glooms, the mingled measure stole,
Or o'er some haunted streams with fond delay,
(Round an holy calm diffusing,
Love of peace, and lonely musing)
In follow murmurs died away.
But, O, how alter'd was its sprightlier tone?

When cheerfulness, a nymph of healthiest hue,
Her bow across her shoulder Hung,
Her buskins gemm'd with morning dew,
Blew an inspiring air, that dale and thicket rung,
The hunter's call, to Faun and Dryad known;
The oak crown'd sisters, and their chaste ey'd Queen)
Satyrs and sylvan Boys were seen,
Peeping from forth their alleys green;
Brown exercise rejoic'd to hear;
And Sport leap'd up and seiz'd his beechen spear.
Last came Joy's ecstatic trial,
He, with viny crown advancing,
First to the lively pipe his hand address'd—
But soon he saw the brisk awakening viol;
Whose sweet entrancing voice he lov'd the best.
They would have thought, who heard the strain,
They saw in Tempe's vale, her native maids,
Amidst the festal sounding shades,
To some unwearied minstrel dancing z
While as his flying fingers kiss'd the strings,
Love fram'd with Mirth a gay fantastic round,
(Loose were her tresses seen, her zone unbound)
And he, amidst his frolic play,
As if he would the charming air repay,
Shook thousand odours from his dewy wings.

SECTION VIII.

I.—*Milton's Lamentation for the Loss of his Sight.* HAIL, holy light! offspring of heaven firstborn! Or, of th' Eternal, coeternal beam! May I express thee unblam'd? Since God is light, And never, but in unapproached light Dwelt from eternity—dwelt then in thee, Bright effluence of bright essence increate. Or hear'st thou rather, pure etherial stream, Whose fountain who shall tell? Before the sun, Before the heavens thou wert, and at the voice Of God, as with a mantle did invest The rising world of waters dark and deep, Won from the void and formless infinite. Thee I revisit now with bolder wing, Escap'd the Stygian pool, though long detaln'd In that obscure sojourn 3 while In my flight, Through utter, and through middle darkness borne, With other notes, than, to the Orphean lyre, I sung of Chaos and eternal Night 5 Taught by the heavenly muse to venture down The dark descent, and up to reascend, Though hard and rare. Thee I revisit safe, And feel thy sovereign vital lamp—hut thou Revisitest not these eyes, that roll in vain To find thy piercing ray, and find no dawn 5 So thick a drop serene hath quench'd their orbs, Or dim suffusion veil'd. Yet not the more Cease I to wander where the Muses haunt, Clear spring, or shady grove, or sunny hill, Smit with the love of sacred song—but chief Thee, Zion, and the flowery brooks beneath, That wash thy hollow'd feet, and warbling flow, Nightly I visit—nor sometimes forget Those other two, equall'd with me in fate, So were I equall'd with them in renown, Blind Thamyiis, and blind JNhconides; And Tiresias, aud Pbjneus, prophets old 5

Then feed on thoughts, that voluntary move

Harmonious numbers—as the wakeful bird

Sings darkling, and in shadiest covert hid.

Tunes her nocturnal note. Thus with the year,

Seasons return—but not to me returns

Day, or the sweet approach of even or morn,

Or sight of vernal bloom, or summer's rose,

Or flocks or herds, or human face divine;

But cloud instead, and ever during dark

Surround me, from the cheerful ways of men

Cut off, and for the book of knowledge fair, ,

Presented with a universal blank

Of nature's works, to me expung'd and raz'd,

And wisdom, at one entrance, quite shut out.

So much the rather, thou, celestial light,

Shine inward, and the mind, through all her powers,

Irradiate; there plant eyes; all mist from thence,

Purge and disperse; that I may see and tell

Of things invisible to mortal sight.

II.—*VAllegro, or the Merry Man.*—Milton. HENCE, loathed Melancholy;
Of Cerberus and blackest midnight born,
In Stygian cave forlorn,
'Mongst horrid shapes, and shrieks, and sights unholy;
Find out some uncouth cell,
Wheie brooding darkness spreads his jealous wings,
And the night raven sings;
There under ebon shades, and low brow'd rocks,
As ragged as thy locks,
In dark Cimmerian desert ever dwell.
But come, thou goddess fair and free,
In heaven yclep'd Euphrosyne I
And by men, hearteasing Mirth,
Whom lovely Venus at a birth,
With two Sister Graces more,
To ivy crowned Bacchus bore.
Haste thee, nymph, and bring with thee
Jest and youthful jolity.
Quips aud cranks, and wanton wiles,
Nods and becks, and wreathed smiles
j
Such as hang on Hebe's cheek,
And love to live in dimple sleek;
Sport, that wrinkled Care deride?,
And Laughter, holding both his sides,
Come! and trip i t as you go
On the light fantastic toe;
And, in thy right hand lead with thee
The mountain nymph, sweet Liberty—
And, if Lgive thee honour due,
Mirth, admit me of thy crew,
To live with her and live with thee,
In unreproved pleasures free:.
To hear the lark begin his flight, *And,* singing, startle the dull Night,
From his watchtower in the skies,
Till the dappled dawn doth rise;
Then to eome in spite of sorrow
And at my window bid good morrow,

Through the sweetbriar or the vine,
Or the twisted eglantine;
While the cock, with lively din,
Scatters the rear of darkness thin,
And to the stack, or the barn door
Stoutly struts his dames before;
Oft list'ning how the hounds and horn,
Cheerly rouse the slumb'ring morn,
From the side of some hoar hill,
Through the high wood echoing shrill:
Sometime walking, not unseen, r
By hedge row elms, or hillocks green,
Right against the eastern gate,
Where the great sun begins his state,
Rob'd in flames and amber light,
The clouds in thousand liveries dight,
While the ploughman near at hand,
Whistles o'er the furrow'd land,
And the milkmaid singeth blithe,
And the mower whets his scythe,
And every shepherd tells his tale
Under the hawthorn in the dale;
Straight mine eye hath caught new pleasures Whilst the landskip round it measures j Russet lawns and fallows gray,.
Where the nibbling flocks do stray,
Mountains on whose barren breast
The lab'ring clouds do often rest,
Meadows trim, with dasies pied,
Shallow brooks, and rivers wide-
Towers and battlements it sees,
Bosom'd high in tufted trees,
Where, pherhaps, some beauty lies,
The Cynosure of neighbouring eyes.
Hard by a cottage chimney smokes,
From betwixt two aged oaks,
Where Corydon and Thyrsis met,
Are at their savoury dinner set,
Of herbs and other country messes,
Which the neathanded Phillis dresses;
And then in haste, her bower she leaves,
With Thestylis to bind the sheaves;
Or, if the earlier season lead,
To the tann'd haycock in the mead.
Towered cities please us then,
And the busy hum of men,
Where throngs of knights and barons bold,
In weeds of peace high triumph hold;
With slore of ladies, whose bright eyes-
Rain influence, and judge the prize
Of wit or arms, while both contend

To win her grace, whom all commend.
There let Hymen oft appear,
In saffron robe, with taper clear,
And pomp, and feast, and revelry,
With mask, and antique pageantry;
Such sights as youthful poets dream.
On summer eves, *by* haunted stream.
Then to the well trod stage anon,
If Johnson's learned sock be on,
Or sweetest Shakespeare, Fancy's child,
Warble his native wood notes wild.
And ever, against eating cares,
Lap me in soft Lydian airs,
Married to immortal verse,
Such as the meeting soql may pierce,
In notes with many a winding bout
Of linked sweetness long drawn out,
With wanton heed and giddy cunning,
The melting voice through mazes running;
Untwisting all the chains that tie
The hidden soul of Harmony:
That Orpheus' self may heave his head
From golden slumber, on a bed
Of heap'd Elysian flowers, and hear
Such strains, as would have won the ear
Of Pluto, to have quite set free,
His half regain'd Eurydice.
These delights, if thou canst give,
Mirth, with thee I mean to Jive.

III.—*On the Pursuits of Mankind.—*
Port:. HONOUR and shame from no conditioii rise;
Act well your part—there all the honour lies.
Fortune in men has some small difference made;
One flaunts in rags—one flutters in brocade;
The cobler apron'd, and the parson gown'd;
The friar hooded, and the monarch crown'd.
"What differ more," you cry, " than crown and cowl?"
I tell you friend—a wise man and a fool.
You'll find, if once the monarch acts the monk,
Or, cobler like, the parson will be drunk;
Worth makes the man, and want of it ihe fellow;

The rest is all but leather or prunella. _
Boast the pure blood of an illustrious race,
In quiet flow from Lucrece to Lucrece:
But by your father's worth if yours you rale,
Count me those only wbo were good and great.
Go! if your ancient, but ignoble blood
Has crept through scoundrels ever sense the flood:
Go! and pretend your family is young,
Nor own your fathers have been fool so long.
What can ennoble sots, or slaves, or cowards?
Alas! not all the blood of all the Howards.
Look next on greatness—say where greatness lies.
"Where, but among the heroes and the wise r"
Heroes are much the same, the point's agreed,
From Macedonia's madman to the Swede:
The whole strange purpose of their lnes, to find,
Or make an enemy of all mankind!
Not one looks backward; onward still he goes;
Yet ne'er looks forward, farther that his nose.
No less alike the politic and wise;
All fly slow things with circumspective eyes.
Men in their loose, unguarded hours they take.
Not that themselves are wise, but others weak.
But grant that those can conquer; these can cheat;
'Tis phrase absurd to call a villain great.
Who wickedly is wise, or madly brave,
Is but the more a fool, the more a knave
Who noble ends by noble means obtains,
Or, failing, smiles in ex'le or in chains;
Like good Aurelius let him reign, or bleed
Like Socrates—that man is great in-

deed.

What's fame? a fanci'd life in others' breath,

A thing beyond us, e'en before our death.

All fame is foreign, but of true desert,

Plays round the head but comes not to the heart;

One self approving hour whole years outweighs

Of stupid starers, and of loud huzzas:

And more true joy, Marcellus exil'd, feels,

Than Cesar, with a Senate at his heels-

In parts superiour what advantage lies?

Tell, (for you can) what is it to be wise?

'Tis but to know how little can be known;

To see all others' faults, and feel our own;

Condemn'd in business or in arts to drudge,

Without a second, or without a judge.

Truths would you teach, to save a sinking land;

All fear, none aid you, and few understand.

Painful preeminence! yourself to view

Above life's weakness, and its comforts too.

Bring then these blessings to a strict account;

Make fair deductions, see to what they 'mount:

How much, of other. each is sure to cost;

How each, for other, oft is wholly lost;

How inconsistent greater goods with these;

How sometimes life is risk'd, and always ease;

Think. And if still such things thy envy call,

Say, would'si thou be the man to whom-they fait?

To sigh for ribands, if thou. art. so silly,.

Mark how they grace Lord Umbra, or Sir Billy.

Is yellow dirt the passion of thy life?

Look but on Gripus, or on Gripus' wife.

If parts allure thee, think how Bacon shin'd j.

The wisest, brightest, meanest of mankind.

Or, ravish'd with the whistling of a name,

See Cromwell damn'd to everlasting fame.

If all, united, thy ambition call,

From ancient story, learn to scorn them all.

IV.—*Ailam and Eve's Morning Hymn.* —Milton. THESE are thy glorious works! Parent of good! Almighty! thine this universal frame, Thus wond'rous fair: Thyself how wond'rous, then, Unspeakable! who si tt'st above these heavens, To us invisible, or dimly seen In these thy lowest works; yet these declare Thy goodness beyond thought, and power divine. Speak ye who best can tell, ye sons of light, Angels! for ye behold him, and with songs And choral symphonies, day without night, Circle his throne, rejoicing. Ye in heaven! On earth, join, all ye creatures, to extol Him first, him last, him midst, and without endFairest of stars! last in train of night, If better thou belong not to the dawn, Sure pledge of day, that crown'st the smilingtmorn With the bright circlet, praise him in thy sphere, While day arises, that sweet hour of prime. Thou Sun! of this great world both eye and soul, Acknowledge him thy greater; sound-his praise i In thy eternal course, both when thou climb'st,

And when high noon hast gain'd, and when thou full's!.

Moon! that now meet'st the orient sun, now fly'st,

With the fix'd stars, fix'd in their orb that flies;

And ye five other wand'ring fires! that move

In mystic dance, not without song; resound

His praise, who out of darkness cail'd up light.

Air, and ye elements! the eldest birth Of nature's womb, that in quaternion run

Perpetual circle, multiform, and mix

Aud nourish all things, let your ceaseless change

Vary to our great Maker still new praise.

Ye mists and exhalations! that now rise

From hill or steaming lake, dusky or gray,

Till the sun paint your fleecy skirts with gold,

In honour to the world's great Author rise;

Whether to deck with clouds th' uncolour'd sky

Or wet the thirsty earth with falling showers,

Rising or falling, still advance his praise.

His praise, ye winds! that from four quarters blow,

Breathe soft or loud; and wave your tops, ye pines

With every plant, in sign of worship, wave.

Fountains! and ye that warble, as ye flow,

Melodious murmurs, warbling, tune his praise.

Join voices, all ye living souls. Ye birds,

That singing, up to heaven's gate ascend,

Bear on your wings, and in your notes his praise.

Ye that in waters glide, and ye that walk

The earth, and stately tread or lowly creep!

Witness if I be silent, morn or even,

To hill or valey, fountain or fresh shade,

Made vocal by my song, and taught his praise.—

Hail, universal Lord! be bounteous still,

To give us only good; and, if the night

Have gather'd aught of evil, or conceal'd—

Disperse it, as now light dispels the dark.

V—*Parting of Hector and Andromache* Homer. HECTOR now pass'd, with sad presaging heart,

To seek his spouse, his soul's far dearer part.

At home he sought her; but he sought in vain;

She, with one maid, of all her menial train,

Had thence retir'd; and with her second

joy,
The young Astyanax, the hope of Troy,
Pensive she stood on llion's towery height,
Beheld the war, and sicken'd at the sight:
There her sad eyes in vain her lord explore,
Or weep the wounds her bleeding country bore.
Hector, this heard, return'd without delay;
Swift through the town he took his former wav,
Through streets of palaces, and walks of slate,
And met the mourner at the Scan gate.
With haste to meet him sprung the joyful fair
His blameless wife, Acteon's wealthy heir.

The nurse stood near; in whose embraces press'd, His only hope hung, smiling at her breast; Whom each soft charm and early grace adorn, Fair as the newborn star that gilds the morn. Silent, the warriour smil'd; and pleas'd, resign'd To tender passions, all his mighty mind. His beaulious princess cast a mournful look, Hung on his hand, and then, dejected spoke. Her bosom labour'd with a boding sigh, And the big tear stood trembling in her eye.

"Too daring prince! ah! whither wilt thou run? Ah! too forgetful of thy wife and son! And think'st though not how wretched we shall be.? A widow I, an helpless orphan he! For sure, such courage length of life denies j And thou must fall, thy virtue's sacrifice. Greece in her single heroes strove in vain; Now hosts oppose thee—and thou must be slain. Oh, grant me» gods! ere Hector meets his doom, All I can ask of heaven—an early tomb! So shall my days in one sad tenor run, And end with sorrows, as they first begun. Thy wife, thy infant, in thy danger share; Oh! prove a husband's, and a parent's care. That quarter most the skilful Greeks annoy, Where yon wild figtree joins the wall of Troy: Thrice our bold foes the fierce attack have given; Or led by hopes, or dictated from heaven. Let others in the field their arms employ; But stay my

Hector here, and guard his Troy." The chief replied-" That post shall be my care;
Nor that alone, but all the Works of war.
How would the sons of Troy, in arms renown'd,
And Troy's proud dames, whose garments sweep the ground,
Attaint the lustre of my former name,
Should Hector basely quit the field of fame!
My early youth was bred to warlike pains;
My soul impels me to the martial plains.
Still foremost let rrie stand to guard the throne,
To save my father3 honours and my own.
Yet come it will! the day decreed by fates I
(How my heart trembles, while my tongue relates!)
The day when thou imperial Troy, must bend,
Must see thy warriours fall, thy glories end,
And yet, no dire presage so wounds my mind,
My mother's death, the ruin of my kind,
Not Priam's hoary hairs defil'd with gore,
Not'ai! m3' brother's gasping on the shore,
As thine, Andromache! Thy griefs I dread/ i see thee trembling, weeping, captive led,
In Argive looms our battles to design,
And woes, of which so large a part was thine.
There, while you groan beneath the load of life.
They cry—" Behold the mighty Hector's wife!
Some haughty Greek, who lives thy tears to see,
Embitters all thy woes by naming me.
The thoughts of glory past, and present shame,
A thousand griefs shall waken at the name!
May I lie cold before that dreadful day,
Press'd with a load of monumental

clay
Thy Hector wrapp'd in everlasting sleep,
Shall neither hear thee sigh, nor see thee weep."
Thus having spoke, th' illustrious chief of Troy Strelch'd his fond arms to clasp the lovely boy. The babe clung, crying, to the nurse's breast, Scar'd with the dazzling helm, and nodding crest. With secret pleasure, each fond parent smil'd, And Hector hasted to relieve his child: The glitt'ring terrors from his brows unbound, And plac'd the beaming helmet on the ground, Then kiss'd the child; and, lifting high in air, Thus to the gods preferr'd a parent's prayer.
"Oh thou, whose glory fills th' etherial throne! And ail ye deathless powers I protect my son! Grant him, like me, to purchase just renown, To guard the Trojans, to defend the crown $ Against his country's foes the war to wage, And rise the Hector of the future age. So when triumphant from successful toils, Of heroes slain he bears the reeking spoils, Whole hosts may hail him with deserv'd acclaim, And say, "This chief transcends his fathers fame;" While pleas'd amidst the general shouts of Troy, Hjs mother's conscious heart o'erflows with joy.' He spoke: and fondly gazing on her charms,
Restor'd the pleasing burden to her arms.
Soft on her fragrant breast the babe she laid,
Hush'd to repose, and with a smile survey'd:
The troubled pleasure, soon chastis'd with fear,
She mingled with a smile, a tender tear.
The soften'd chief with kind compassion view'd,
And dry'd the falling drops; and thus parsu'd—
"Andromache f my soul's far better part!
Why with untimely sorrow heaves thy heart?
No hostile hand can antedate my doom,
Till fate condemn me to the silent tomb:
Fix'd is the term of all the race of earth;
And such the hard condition of our birth.

No force can then resist, no flight can save;

AH sink alike, the fearful and the brave.

No more—but hasten to thy tasks at home;

There guide the spindle and direct the loom.,

Me, glory summons to the martial scene;

The field of combat is the sphere for men:

Where heroes war, the foremost place I claim,

The first in danger, as the first in fame."

Thug having said, th' undaunted chief resumes

His towery helmet, black with shading plumes.

His princess parts with a prophetic sigh,

Unwilling parts, and oft reverts her eye,

That streamed at every look'; then moving slow,

Sought her own palace, and indulg'd her woe.

There, while her tears deplor'd the god-like man,

Through all her train the soft infection ran:

The pious maids their mingled sorrows shed,

And mourn'd the living Hector as the dead.

VI.— *Facetious History of John GtiJpin.*—Cowper.

JOHN GILPIN was a citizen
Of credit and renown;
A train band captain eke was he,
  Of famous London town.

John Gilpin's spouse said to her dear—
  ' Though wedded we have been These twice ten tedious years, yet we
  No.holiday have seen.

Tomorrow is our wedding day,
And we shall then repair Unto the Bell at Edmonton, "All in a chaise and pair.

My sister and my sister's child, Myself and children three,
Will fill the chaise, so you must ride
  On horseback after we."

He soon replied—" I do admire Of woman kind but one;
And you are she, my dearest dear,
  Therefore it shall be done.

I am a linendraper bold, As all the world doth know;
And my good friend, Tom Callender,
  Will lend his horse to go."

Quoth Mrs. Gilpin—" That's well said; And, for that wine is dear,
We will be furnish'd with our own,
  Which is both brig!t and clear."

John Gilpin kiss'd his loving wife;
O'erjoy'd was he to find,
That, though on pleasure she was bent,
  She had a frugal mind.

The morning came, the chaise was brought, But yet was not allow'd
To drive up to the door, lest all
  Should say that she was proud.

So three doors off the chaise was stay'd, Where they did all get in;
Six precious souls; and all agog,
  To dash through thick and thin!

Smack went the whip, round went the wheels, Were never folk so glad;
The stoues did rattle underneath,
  As if Cheapside were mad.

John Gilpin at his horses side,
Seiz'd fast the flowing mane,
And up he got in haste to ride,
  But soon came down again:

For saddletree scarce reach'd had he,
His journey to begin,
When turning round his head, he saw,
  Three customers come in.

So down he came, for loss of time,
Although it griev'd him sore,
Yet loss of pence, full well he knew,
  Would trouble him much more.

'Twas long before the customers Were suited to their mind,
When Betty scream'd into his ears—
  "The wine is left behind."

"Good lack!" quoth he, "yet bring it me, My leathern belt likewise,
In which I wear my trusty sword,
  When I do exercise."

Now Mrs. Gilpin, careful soul,
  Had two stone bottles found, To hold the liqour that she lov'd,
  And keep it safe and sound.

Each bottle had a curling ear,
  Through which the belt he drew 5 He hung a bottle on each side,
  To make his balance true.

Then over all, that he might be
  Equipp'dfrom top to toe, His long red cloak, well brush'd and neat.

He manfully did throw.

Now see him mounted once again,
Upon his nimble steed;
Full slowly pacing o'er the stones,
  With caution and good heed. *vn*

But finding soon a smother road Beneath his wellshod feet,
The snorting beast began to trot,
  Which gall'd him in his seat.

So, "fair and softly," John he cried;
But John lie cried in vain;
The trot became a gallop soon;
  In spite of curb and rein.

So stooping down, as needs he must,
Who cannot sit upright;
He grasp'd the mane with both his hands,
  And eke with all his might.

Away went Gilpin, neck or nought;
Away went hat and wig;
He little dreamt, when he set out,'
  Of running such a rig.

His horse, who never had before Been handled in this kind,
Affrighted fled; and as he flew,
  Left all the world behind.

The wind did-blow, the cloak did fly,
Like streamer long and gay;
Till loop and button failing both,
  At last it flew away.

Then might all people well discern
The bottles he had slung:
A bottle swinging at each side,
  As hath been said or sung.

The dogs did bark, the children scream'd, Up flew the windows all;
And every soul cri'd out, "Well done!"
  As loud as they could bawl.

Away went Gilpin—who but he!
His fame soon spread around— "He carries weight! he rides a race! *jtf*
  'Tis for a thousand pound!"

And still, as fast as he drew near,
'Twas wonderful to view,
How in a trice the turnpike men
  Their gates wide open threw.

—V-And now as he went bowing down
His reeking head full low,
The bottles twain behind his back,
  Were shatter'd at a blow.

Down ran the wine into the road,
Most piteous to be seen,
Which made his horses flanks to smoke»

As they had basted been.
But still he seem'd to carry weight,
With leathern girdle brac'd; For all
might see the bottle necks
Still dangling at his waist.

Thus all through merry Islington,
These gambols he did play, And till
he came unto. the Wash
Of Edmonton so gay.

And there he threw the Wash about
On both sides of the way; Just like
unto a trundling mop,
Or a wild goose at play.

At Edmonton, his loving wifej From
the balcony, spied
Her tender husband, wond'ring much
To see how he did ride.

"Stop, stop, John Gilpin f here's the
house!
They all at once did cry;
The dinner waits, and we are tir'd!"
Said Gilpin—" So am 1 *l»*

But 3et his horse was not a whit In-
clin'd to tarry there j
For why?—His owner had a house
Full ten miles off, at Ware.

t(So like an arrow swift he flew,
Shot by an archer strong;
So did he fly—-which brings me to
The middle of my song.

Away went Gilpin, out of breath, And
sore against his will,
Till at his friend's Tom Callender's,.
His horse at last stood still.

Tool Calender, surpris'd to see His
friend in such a trim,
Laid down his pipe, flew to the gate,
And thus accosted him:—

"What news? What news? Your tid-
ings tell; Make haste and tell me all!
Say, Why bareheaded are you come?
Or, Why you come at all?"

Now Gilpin had a pleasant wit,
And lov'd a timely joke; And thus
unto Tom Callender,
In merry strains he spoke:—

' I came because your horse would
come; And if I well forebode,
My hat and wig will soon be here;
They are upon the road."

Tom Callender, right glad to find
His friend in merry pin, Return'd him
not a single word,
But to the house went in:

Whence straight he came with hat

and wig, A wig that flow'd behind,
A hat not much the worse for wear;
Each comely in its kind.

He held them up; and, in his turn,
Thus show'd his ready wit— "My
head is twice as big as yours,
They therefore needs must fit.

But let me scrape the dirt away
That hangs upon your face; And stop
and eat—for well you may
Be in a hungry case!

Said John—" It is my wedding day;
And folks would gape and stare, If
wife should dine at Edmonton,
And I should dine at Ware!"

So turning to his horse, he said, "I an
in baste to dine;
'Twas for your pleasure you came here,
You shall go back for mine."

Ah! luckless speech, and bootless
boast,
For which he paid full dear; For,
while he spake, a braying ass,
Did sing most loud and clear:

Whereat his horse did Snort, as if He
heard a lion roar;
And gallop'd off with all his might,
As he had done before.

Away went Gilpin, and away
Went Gilpin's hat and wig;
He lost them sooner than at first;
For why? They were too big.

Now Gilpin's wife, when she had
seen
Her husband posting down Into the
country, far away,
She pull'd out half a crown:

And thus unto the youth she said
That drove them to the Bell, "This
shall be yours, when you bring back
My husband safe and well."

The youth did ride, and soon they
met;
He tried to stop John's horse By seiz-
ing fast the flowing rein;
But only made things worse:

But not performing what he meant,
And gladly would have done, He
thereby frighted Gilpin's horse,
And made him faster run.

Away went Gilpin—and away Went
postboy at his heels;
The postboy's horse right glad to miss
The lumb'ring of the wheels.

Six gentlemen upon the road, Thus

seeing Gilpin fly,
With postboy scamp'iing in the rear,
They rais'd the hue and cry.

« Stop thief 1 stop thief! a highway-
man!" Not one of them was mute j
So they, and all that pass'd that wa,
Soon join'd in the pursuit.

And now the turnpikes gates again
Flew open in short space;
The tollmen thinking, as before,
That Gilpin rode a race:

And so he did, and won it too; For he
got first to town;
Nor stopp'd till where he had got up,
He did again get down.

Now let us sing—" Long live the
king; And Gilpin, long live he:
And when he next doth ride abroad,
May I be there to see!" VII.—*The
Creation of the World.*—Milton. MEAN-
WHILE the Son On his great expedition
now appear'd, Girt with omnipotence,
with radience crown'd Of majesty divine; sapience and love Immense, and
all his father in him shone. About his
chariot numberless were pour'd Cherub
and seraph, potentates and thrones, And
virtues; wing'd spirits and chariots
wing'd From the armoury of God;
where stand of old Myriads, between
two brazen mountains lodg'd Against a
solemn day, harness'd at hand. Celestial
equipage.' and now came forth Spontaneous, for within them spirit liv'd, Attendant on their Lord; heaven open'd
wide Her eyerduring gates, harmonious
sound! On golden hinges moving, to let
forth The King of Glory, in his powerful
Word And Spirit, coming to create new
worlds. On heavenly ground they stood,
and from the shore They view'd the vast
immeasurable abyss, Outrageous as a
sea; dark, wasteful, wild j Up from the
bottom turn'd by furious winds, And
surging waves, as mountains to assault
Heaven's height, and with the centre
mix the pole Silence, ye troubl'd waves!
and thou deep, peace *i*
Said then the omnific Word, your discord end:
Nor stay'd! but on the wings of cherubim
Uplifted, in paternal glory rode
Far into chaos, and the world unborn:
For chaos heard bis voice; him all his

train
Follow'd in bright procession to behold
Creation, and the wonders of his might.
Then stay'd the fervid wheels, and in his hand
He took the golden compasses, prepar'd
In God's eternal store, to circumscribe
This universe, and all created things.
One foot he ceuter'd, and the other turn'd
Round through the vast profundity obscure,
And said thus far extend, thus far thy bounds,
This be thy just circumference, 0 world!
Thus God the heaven created, thus the earth,
Matter unform'd and void! Darkness profound
Cover'd the abyss; but on the watery calm
His brooding wings the spirit of God outspread,
And vital virtue infus'd, and vital warmth
Throughout the fluid mass; but downward purg'd
The black, tartareous, cold, infernal dregs,
Adverse to life; then founded, then conglob'd
Like things to like, the rest to several place
Disparted; and between, spun out the air;
And earth self-balanc'd, on her centre hung.

VIII.—*Overthrow of the Rebel Angels.* —Ib.

So spake the Son, and into terror chang'd
His countenance, too severe to be beheld,
And full of wrath bent on his enemies.
At once the four spread out their starry wings,
With dreadful shape contiguous, and the orbs
Of his fierce chariot roll'd, as with the sound
Of torrent floods, or of a numerous host.
He on his impious foes, right onward drove,
Gloomy as night. Under his burning wheels
The stedfast empirean shook throughout,
All but the throne itself of God. Full soon
Among them he arriv'd; in his right hand
Grasping ten thousaud thunders, which he sent
Before him, such as in their souls infix'd
Plagues. They aslonish'd, all resistance lost,
All courage; down their idle weapons dropp'd:
O'er shields, and helms, and helmed heads he rode,
Of thrones, and mighty seraphim prostrate,
That wish'd the mountains, now, might be again
Thrown en them as a shelter from his ire.
Nor less on either side, tempestuous fell
His arrows, from the fourfold visag'd four
Distinct with eyes, and from the living wheels
Distinct alike with multitude of eyes:
One spirit in them rul'd; and every eye
Glar'd lightning, and shot forth pernicious fire
Among th' accurs'd, that wither'd all their strength,
And of their wonted vigour, left them drain'd,
Exhausted, spiritless, afflicted, fall'n.
Yet half his strength he put not forth; but check,d
His thunder in mid volley; for he meant
Not to destroy but to root them out of heaven.
The overthrown he rais'd; and as a herd
Of goats or timorous flock together throng'd
Drove them before him thunderstruck pursu'd
With terrors and with furies to the bounds
And chrystal wall of heaven; which opening wide
Roll'd inward, and a spacious gap disclos'd
Into the wasteful deep. The monstrous sight
Struck them with horrour backward; but far worse
Urg'd them behind. Headlong themselves they threw
Down from the verge of heaven; eternal wrath
Burnt after them to the bottomless pit.

IX.—*Alexander's Feast; or, the Power of Music.—An Ode for St. Cecilia's Day.*—Dryden.

'TWAS at the royal feast, for Persia won
By Philip's warlike son.—
Aloft in awful state
The godlike hero sat
On his imperial throne.
His valient peers were plac'd around,
Their brows with roses and with myrtles bound;
So should desert in arms be crown'd.
The lovely Thais by his side,
Sat like a blooming eastern bride,
    In flower of youth and beauty's pride.
—
    Happy, happy, happy pair!
    None but the brave, None but the brave,
None but the brave, deserve tbe fair.
Timotheous plac'd on high,
    Amid the tuneful choir, With flying fmgers touched the lyres
The trembling notes ascend the sky,
And heavenly joys inspire.
The Song began from Jove,
Who left his blissful seats above 5
(Such is the power of mighty love!)
A dragon's fiery form bely'd the god j
Sublime on radient spheres he rode,
    When he to fair G'ympia press'd, world.
    And Stamp'd an image of himself, a sovereign of ihe
The list'ning crowd admire the lofty sound;
A present deity, they shout around)
A present deity; the vaulted roofs rebound.
    With ravish'd ears the monarch hears,
    Assumes the god, affects to nod, And seems to shake the spheres. The praise of Bacchus, then the sweet musician

sung I Of Bacchus, ever fair and and
ever young.

The jolly god in triumph comes!
Sound the trumpet 5 beat the drums 5
Flush'd with a purple grace,
He shows his honest face: Now give
the hautboys breath—he comes! he
comes 1 Bacchus, ever fair and young,
Drinking joys did first ordain: Bacchus'
blessings are a treasure 5 Drinking is the
soldier's pleasure:
Rich the treasure
Sweet the pleasure; Sweet is plea-
sure, after pain.

Sooth'd with the sound, the king
grew vain J fought all his battles o'er
again; slain.
And thrice he routed all his foes, and
thrice he slew the The master saw the
madness rise;
His glowing cheeks, his ardent eyes;
And, while he heaven and earth defy'd,
Chpng'd his hand and check'd his pride.
He chose a mournful muse,
Soft pity to infuse:
He sung Darius, great and good,
By too severe ; fate,
Fall'n, fall'n, fall'n, fall'n,
Fall'n, from his high estate,
Anowelt'ring in his blood:
Deserted at his utmost need
By those his former bounty fed,
On the bare earth expos'd he lies,
With not a friend to close his eyes.

With downcast look the joyless victor
sat) Revolving, in his alter'd soul, The
various turns of fate below;
And now and then, a sigh he stole,
And tears began to flow.
The mighty master smil'd to see
That love was in the next degree;
'Twas but a kindred sound to move;
For pity melts the mind to love.

Softly sweet, in Lydian measures,
Soon he sooth'd his soul to pleasures,
War he sung, is toil and trouble;
Honour but an empty bubble!
Never ending, still beginning,
Fighting still, and still destroying.
If the world be worth thy winning,
Think, O think it worth enjoying;
Lovely Thais sits beside thee;
Take the good the gods provide thee,
The many reud the skies with loud ap-
plause,

So love was crown'd j but music won
the cause.
The prince, unable to conceal his pain,
Gaz'd on the fair,
Who caus'd his care;
And sigh'd and look'd, sigh'd and
look'd,
Sigh'd and look'd, and sigh'd again!
At length, with love and wine at once
oppress'df
The vanquish'd victor—sunk upori her
breast.

Now, strike the golden lyre again; A
louder yet, and yet a louder strain:
Break his bands of sleep asunder, And
rouse him like a rattling peal of thunder,
Hark! hark! the horrid sound Has rais'd
up his head, As awak'd from the dead;
And, amaz'd, he stares around. Revenge! revenge! Timotheus cries— See
the furies arise! See the snakes that they
rear, How they hiss in their hair, And
the sparkles that flush from their eyes!
Behold a ghastly band, Each a torch in
his hand! These are Grecian ghosts, that
in battle were slain, And, unbury'd, remain Inglorious en the plain. Give the
vengeance due to the valiant ;rew. Behold! how tbey toss their torches on
high, How they point to the Persian
abodes, And glittering temples of their
hostile gods! The princes applaud, with
a furious joy! And the king seiz'd a
flambeau, with zeal to destroy: Thais
led the way, To light hiro to his pray;
And, like another Helen—fir'd another
Troy. Thus long ago, Ere heaving bel-
lows learn'd to Mow,
While organs yet were mute;
Timotheus to his breathing flute
And sounding lyre,
Could swell the soul to rage, or kindle
soft desire.
At last divine Cecilia came,
Inventress of the vocal frame.
The sweet enthusiast, from her sacred
store,
Enlarg'd the former narrow bounds,
And added length to solemn sounds,
With nature's mother wit, and arts un-
known before,
Let old Timotheus yield the prize,
Or both divide the crown:
He rais'd a mortal to the skies;
She drew an angel down.

24
Part n.
LESSONS IN SPEAKING. SECTION I. ELO-
QUENCE OF THE PULPIT.
I.—On Truth and Integrity.—Tillotson.
TRUTH and integrity have all the advantages of appearance, and many more. If
the show of any thing be good for any
thing, I am sure the reality is better j for
why does any man dissemble, or seem
to be that which he is not, but because
he thinks it good to have the qualities he
pretends to? For, to counterfeit and dissemble, is to

Eut on the appearance of some real
excellency. Now, the est way for a man
to seem to be any thing, is really to be
what he would seem to be. Besides, it is
often as troublesome to support the pretence of a good quality, as to have it;
and if a man have it not, it is most likely he will be discovered to want it; and
then all his labour to seem to have it,
is lost. There a something unnatural in
painting, which a skilful eye will easily discern from native beauty and complexion.

Alt is hard to personate and act a part
long; for where truth is not at the bottom, nature will always be endeavouring to return, and will betray herself at
one time or other. Therefore, if any man
think it convenient to seem good, let
him be so indeed; and then his goodness
will ap-'pear to every one's satisfaction;
for truth is convincing, and carries its
own light and evidence along with it;
andwill not only commend us to every
man's conscience; but, which is much
more, to God, who searcheth our hearts:
so that, upon all accounts, sincerity is
true wisdom. Pat? ticularly as to the affairs of this world, integrity hath many
advantages over all the artificial modes
of dissimula tion and deceit. It is much
the plainer and easier, muchthe safer
and more secure way of dealing in the
world; it hath less of trouble and difficulty, of entanglement and perplexity,
of danger and hazard in it; it is the short-
est and nearest way to our end, carrying
us thither in a straight line; and will hold
out and last longest. The arts of deceit
and cunning continually grow weaker,
and less effectual and serviceable to

those that practise them; whereas, integrity gains strength by use; and the more and longer any man practiseth it the greater service it does him, by confirming his reputation, and encouraging those with whom he hath to do to repose the greatest confidence in him; which is an unspeakable advantage iu business and the affairs of life.

A dissembler must be always upon his guard, and watch himself carefully, that he do not contradict his own pretensions; for he acts an unnatural part, and therefore must put a continual force and restraint upon himself; whereas, he that acts sincerely, hath the easiest task in, the world; because he follows nature, and so is put to no trouble and care about his words and actions; he needs not invent any pretence beforehand, nor make excuses afterwards, for any thing he hath said or done.

But insincerity is very troublesome to manage. A hypocrite hath so many things to attend to, as make his life a very perplexed and intricate thing. A liar hath need of a good memory, lest he contradict at one time, what he said at another. But truth is always consistent with itself, and needs nothing to help it out; it is always near at hand, and sits upon our lips, and is ready to drop out before we are aware; whereas, a lie is troublesome, and one trick needs a great many more to make it good.

Add to all this, that sincerity is the most compendious wisdom, and an excellent instrument for the speedy dispatch of business. It creates confidence in those we have to deal with, saves the labour of many inquiries, and brings things to an issue in a few words. It is like travelling in a plain beaten road, which commonly brings a man sooner to his journey's end, than by ways in which men often lose themselves. In a word, whatever convenience may be thought to be in falsehood and dissimulation, it is soon over; but the inconvenience of it is perpetual, because it brings a man under an everlasting jealousy and suspicion, so that lie is not believed when he speaks the truth, nor trusted when perhaps he means honestly. When a man hath once forfeited the reputation of his integrity, nothing will then serve his turn, neither truth nor falsehood.

Indeed, if a man were only to deal in the world for a day, and should never have occasion to converse more with mankind, never more need their good opinion or good word, it were then no great matter (as far as respects the affairs of this world) if he spent his reputation all at once, and ventured it at one throw. But, if he be to continue in the world and would have the advantage of reputation whilst he is in it, let him make use of sincerity in all his words and actions; for nothing but this will hold out to the end. All other arts will fail; but truth and integrity will carry a man through and bear him out to the last.

II.—*On Doing as we would be Done unto.*— Atterbury. HUMAN raws are often so numerous as to escape our memories; so darkly, sometimes, and inconsistently worded, as to puzzle our understandings; and they are not unfrequently rendered still more obscure by the nice distinctions and subtile reasonings of those who profess to clear them: so that under these several disadvantages, they lose much of their force and influence; and in some cases raise more disputes than, perhaps, they determine. But here is a law, attended with none of these inconveniences; the grossest minds can scarce misapprehend it; the weakest memories are capable of retaining it; no perplexing comment can easily cloud it? the authority of no man's gloss upon earth can (if we are but sincerel sway ns to make a wrong construction of it. What is said of all the gospel precepts by the evangelical prophet, is more eminently true of this: "It is an high way; and the wayfaring man, though a fool, shall not err therein."

It is not enough that a rule, which is *Icrbc* of general use, is suited to all capacities, so that wherever it is represented to the mind, it is presently agreed to; it must also be apt to offer itself to our thoughts, and lie ready for present use, upon all exigencies and occasions. And such, remarkably such, is that which our Lord here recommends to us. We can scarce be so far surprised by any immediate necessity of acting, as not to have time for a short recourse to it, room for a sudden glance as it were upon it, in our minds; where it rests and sparkles always, like the Urim and Thummim, on the breast of Aaron. There is no occasion for us to go in search of it to the oracles of law, dead or living; to the code or pandects; to the volumes of divines or moralists. We need look no farther than ourselves for it; for (to use the apposite expression of Moses) "This commandment which I command thee this day is not hidden from thee, neither is it far oft'. It is not in heaven, that thou shouldst say, Who shall go up for us to heaven, and bring it unto us, that we may hear it, and do it? Neither is it beyond the sea, that thou shouldst say, Who shall go over the sea for us, and bring it unto us, that we may hear it and do it?But the word is very nigh unto thee, in thy mouth, and in thy heart, that thou mayest do it?"

It is moreover, a precept particularly fitted for practice, as it involves in the very notion of it a motive stirring us; up to do what it enjoins. Other moral maxims propose naked truths to the understandings, which-operate often but faintly and slowly, on the will aud passions, the two active principles of the mind of man; but it is the peculiar character of this, that it addresseth itself equally to all these powers; impaits both light and heat to us; and at the same time that it informs us certainly and clearly what we are to do, excites us also, in the most tender and moving manner, to the performance of it. We can often see our neighbor's misfortune without a sensible degree of concern; which yet we cannot forbear expressing, when we have once made his condition our own, and' determin ed the measure of our obligation towards him, by what we' ourselves should, in such a case, expect from him; our duty grows immediately our interest and pleasure, by means of this powerful principle; the seat of which is, ia truth, not more in the brain than in the heart of man; it appeals to our very senses;-and exerts its secret force inso prevailing a way, that it is even felt, as well as understood by us.

The last recommendation of this rule I shall mention ia its vast and comprehensive influence; for it extenJs to» all ranks and conditions of men, and to all kinds of action and intercourse between them; to matters of charity, generosity and civility, as well as justice; to negative no less than positive duties. The ruler and the ruled are alike subject to it: public communities can no more exempt themselves from its obligation than private persons: "All persons must fall down before it, all nations must do it service." And, with respect to this extent of it, it is that our blessed Lord pronounces it in the text to be, "the law and the prophets." His meaning is, that whatever rules of the second table are delivered in the law of Moses, or in the larger comments and explanations of that law made by the other writers of the Old Testament (here and elsewhere styled the Prophets) they are all virtually comprised in this one short significant saying, "Whatsoever ye would that men should do unto you, do ye even so unto them."

Ill—*On Benevolence and Charity*—Seed. FORM as amiable sentiments as you can, of nations, communities of men, and individuals. If they are true, you do them only justice; if false, though your opinion does not alter their nature and make them lovely, you yourself are more lovely for entertaining such sentiments. When you feel the bright warmth of a temper thoroughly good in your own breast, you will see something good in every one about you. It is a mark of littleness of spirit to confine yourself to some minute part of a man's character; a man of generous, open, extended views, will grasp the whole of it; without which he cannot pass a right judgement on any part. He will not arraign a man's general conduct for two or three particular actions as knowing that man is a changeable creature, and will not cease to be so, till he is united to that Being, who is "the same yesterday, today and forever." He strives to outdo his friends in good offices, and overcomes his enemies by

thetn. He thinks he then receives the greatest injury, when he returns and revenges one; for then he is " overcome of evil." Is the person young who has injured him? He will reflect, that inexperience of the world and a warmth of constitution, may betray his unpractised years into several inadvertencies,which a more advanced age, his own good sense, and the advice of a judicious friend, will correct aud rectify. Is he old? The infirmities of age and want of health may have set an edge upon his spirits, and made him "speak unadvisedly with his lips." Is he weak and ignorant? He considers that it is a duty incumbent upon the wise to bear with those that are not so: "You suffer fools gladly," says St. Paul, "seeing you yourselves are wise" In short, he judges of himself, as far as he can, with the strict rigor of justice; but of others with the softenings of humanity.

From charitable and benevolent thoughts, the transition is unavoidable to charitable actions. For wherever there is an inexhaustable fund of goodness at the heart, it will under all the disadvantages of circumstances, exert itself in acts of substantial kindness. He that is substantially good, will be doing good. The man that has a hearty determinate will to be charitable, will seldom put men off with the mere will for the deed. For a sincere desire to do good, implies some uneasiness till the thing be done; and uneasiness sets the mind at work, and puts it upon the stretch to find out a thousand ways and means of obliging, which will ever escape the unconcerned, the indifferent, aud the unfeeling.

The most proper objects of your bounty are the neces. sitous. Give the same sum of money, which you bestow on a person in tolerable circumstances, to one in extremepoverty j and observe what a wide disproportion of happiness is produced. In the latter case, it is like giving a cordial to a fainting person; in the former, it is like giving wine to him who has already quenched his thirst. "Mercy is seasonable in time of affliction, like clouds of rain in time of drought."

And among the variety of necessitous objects, none have a better title to our compassion, than those, who, after having tasted-the sweets of plenty, are, by some undeserved calamity, obliged, without some charitable relief, to drag out the remainder of life in misery and woe; who little thought they should ask their daily bread of any but of God; who, after a life led in affluence, "cannot dig, and are ashamed to beg." And they are to be relieved in such an endearing manner, with such a beauty of holiness, that at the same time that their wants are supplied, their confusion of face may be prevented.

There is not an instance of this kind in history so affecting as that beautiful one of Boaz to Ruth. He knew her family, and ho she was reduced to the lowest ebb; when, therefore, she begged leave to glean in his fields, he ordered his reapers to let fall several handfuls, with a seeming carelessness, but really with a set design, that she might gather them up without being ashamed.—Thus did he form an artful scheme, that he might give without the vanity and ostentation of giving; and she receive, without the shame and confusion of making acknowledgments. Take the history in the words of scripture, as it is recorded in the book of Ruth. "And when she was risen up to glean, Boaz commanded his young men, saying, let her glean even among the sheaves, and rebuke her not; and let fall also some of the handfuls on purpose, and leave them that she may glean them, and reproach her not." This was not only doing a good action; it was doing it likewise with a good grace,

It is not enough we do no harm, that we be negatively good! we must do good, positive good, if we would "enter into life." When it would have been as good for theworld if such a man had never lived; it would perhaps have been better for him, if " he had never been born."'

A scanty fortune may limit your beneficene,. and confine it chiefly to the circle of your domestics, relations. and neighbours; but let your benevolence extend as far as thought can travel, to the utmost bounds of the world J. just as it may be only in-your power to beautify the spot of ground that lies near and close to you; but you could wish that as far as your eye can reach, the whole prospect before you were cheerful, everything disagreeable wereremoved, and. every thing beautiful made more so.

IV.—*On Happiness.*—Stearnk. THE great pursuit of man is after happiness;—it isthe first and strongest desire of his nature;—in every stage of his life he searches for it as for hid treasure; courts it under a thousand different shapes; and, thoughperpetually disappointed—still persists—runs after and inquires for it afresh—asks every passenger who comes io. .his way, "Who will show him any good;"—who will assist him in the attainment of it or direct him to the discovery of this great end of all his wishes?

He is told by one, to search for it among the more gay and youthful pleasures of life; in scenes of mirth and sprightliness, where happiness ever presides, and is ever to be known by the joy and laughter which he will see at once painted in her looks.

A second, with a graver aspect, points out to him the costly dwellings which pride and extravagance have erected; tells the inquirer that the object he is in search of inhabits there; that happiness lives only in company with the great, in the midst of much pomp and outward state. That be will easily find her out by the coat of many colours she has on, and the great luxury and expense of equipage and furniture with which she always sits surrounded.

The miser wonders how any one would mislead and wilfully put him upon so wrong a scent—convinces him that happiness and extravagance never inhabited under the same roof;—that, if he would not be disappointed inhis search, he must look into the plain and thrifty dwelling of the prudent mall, who knows and understands the worth of money, and cautiously lays it up against an evil hour. That it is not the prostitution of wealth upon the passions, or the parting with it at all that constitutes happiness—but that it is the

keeping it together, and the *having* and *holding* it fast to him and his heirs forever, which are the chief attributes that form this great idol of human worship, to which so much incense is offered up every day.

The epicure, though he easily rectifies so gross a mistake, yet, at the same time, he plunges him, if possible, into a greater; for hearing the object of his pursuit to be happiness, and knowing of no other happiness than what is seated immediately in his senses—he sends the inquirer there; tells him it is in vain to search elsewhere for it, than where nature herself has placed it—in the indulgence and gratification of the appetites, which are given us for that end: and in a word—if he will not take his opinion in the matter—he may trust the word of a much wiser man, who has assured us—that theie is nothing better in this world, than that a man should eat and drink, and rejoice in his works, and make his soul enjoy good in his labor—— for that is his poition.

To rescue him from this brutal experiment—ambition takes him by the baud and carries him into the world— Shows him all the kingdoms of the earth, and the glory of them—points out the many ways of advancing his fortune, and raising himself to honor—lays before his eyes all the charms and bewitching temptations of power, and asks if there be any happiness in. this world like that of being carressed, courted, flattered, and followed.

To close all, the philosopher meets him bustling in the full career of this pursuit—stops him—tells him, if he is in search of happiness, he has gone far out of his way:——. That this deity has long been banished from noise and tumults, where there was no rest found for her, and was fled into solitude, far from all commerce of the world; and, in a word, if he would find her, he must leave this busy and intriguing scene, and go back to that peaceful scene of retirement and books, from which he first set out.

In this circle, too often does a man run, tries all experiments, and generally siU down wearied and dissatisfied with

them all at last—in utter despair of ever accomplishing what he wants—not knowing what to trust to after so many disappointments—or where to lay the fault, whether in the incapacity of his own nature, or the insufficiency of the enjoyments themselves.

In this uncertain and perplexed state—without kaowledge which way turn, or where to betake ourselves for refuge—so often abused and deceived by the many who pretend thus to show us any good—Lord! says the Psalmist, lift up the light of thy countenance upon us. Send us some rays of thy grace and heavenly wisdom, in this benighted search after happiness, to direct us safely to it. O God! let us not wander forever without a guide, in this dark region, in endless pursuit of our mistaken good; but enlighten-our eyes that we sleep not in death —open to them the comforts of thy holy word and religion—lift up the light of thy countenance upon us— and make us know the joy and satisfaction of living in the true faith and fear of Thee, which only can carry us to this haven of rest, where we would be— that sure haven where true joys are to be found, which wiil at length not only answer all our expectations—but satisfy the most unbounded of our wishes, forever and ever.

There is hardly any subject mose exhausted, or which, at one time or other, has afforded more matter for argument and declamation, than this one, of the insufficiency of our enjoy merits. Scarce a reformed sensualist, from Solomon down to our own days, who has not, in some fits of repentance or disappointment, uttered some sharp reflection upon the emptiness of human pleasure, and of the vanity of vanities which discovers itself in all the pursuits of mortal man. But the mischief has been, that, though so many good things have been said, they have generally bad the fate to be considered, either as the overflowings of disgust from sated appetites, which could no longer relish the pleasures of life, or as the declamatory opinions of recluse and splenetic men who had never tasted them at all, and consequently were thought no judges of the matter. So that it is no great wonder, if the greatest part of such reflections however just in themselves, and founded on truth and a knowledge of the world, are found to have little impression where the imagination was already heated with great expectations of future happiness; and that the best lectures that have been read upon the vanity of the world, so seldom stop a man in the pursuit of the objects of his desire, or give him half the conviction that the possession of it will, and what the experience of his own life, or a careful observation upon the life of others, does at length generally confirm to us all.

I would not be understood as if I were denying the reality of pleasures, or disputing the being of them, any more than any one would the reality of pain; yet I must observe, that there is a plain distinction.;to be made betwixt pleasure and happiness. For though there can be no happiness without pleasure—yet the reverse of the proposition will not hold true. We are so made, that from the common gratifications of our appetites, and the impressions of a thousand objects, we snatch the one like a transient gleam, without being suffered to taste the other, and enjoy the perpetual sunshine and fair weather, which constantly attend it. This, I contend, is only to be found in religion—in the consciousness of virtue—and the sure and certain hopes of a better life, which brightens all our prospects, and leaves no room to dread disappointments—because the expectation of it is built upon a rock, whose foundations are as deep as those of heaven or hell.

And though in our pilgrimage through this world—some of us may be so fortunate as to meet with some clear fountains by the way, that may cool for a few moments the heat of this great (hirst of happiness—yet our Savior, who knew the world, though he enjoyed but Utile of it, tells us, that whosoever drinketh of this water will thirst again; and we all find by experience it is so, and by reason that it always must be so.

I conclude with a short observation upon Solomon's evidence in this case.

Never did the busy brain of a lean and hectic chymist search for the philosopher's stone, with more pains and ardour than this great man did after happiness. He was ©ne of the wisest inquirers into nature—had tried all her powers and capacities; and after a thousand vain speculations and idle experiments, he affirmed at length it lay hid in no one thing he had tried; like the chymist's projections, all had ended in smoke, or, what was worse, in vanity and vexation of spirit. The conclusion of the whole matter was this—that he advises every man who would be happy, to fear God and keep his commandments.

V.—*On the Death of Christ.*—Blaik.

THE redemption of man is one of the most gloriotis works of the Almighty, If the hour of the creation of the world was great aud illustrious; that hour, when, from the dark and formless mass, this fair system of nature across at the Divipe command; when "the morning stars sang together, and all the sons of God shouted for joy;"— no less illustrious is the hour of the restoration of the world; the hour when, from condemnation and misery, it emerged into happiness and peace. With less external majestj' it was attended, but is, on that account, the more wonderful, that, under an appearance so simple, such great events were covered.

In the hour of Christ's death, the long series of prophecies, visions, types and figures, was accomplished. This was the centre in which they all met; this, the point towards which they had tended and verged, throughout the course of so many generations. You behold the Law and the Prophets standing, if we may so speak, at the foot of the cross, and doing homage. You behold Moses and Aaron bearing the ark of the covenant: David and Elijah presenting the oracle of testimony. You behold all the priests and sacrifices, all the rites and ordinances, all the types and symbols, assembled together to receive their consummation. Without the death of Christ, the worship and ceremonies of the law would have remained a pompous but unmeaning institution. In the hour when he was crucified, "the book with the seven seals" was opened. Every rite assumed its significancy; every prediction met its event; every symbol displayed its correspondence.

This was the hour of the abolition of the Law, and the introduction of the Gospel; the hour of terminating the old, and of beginning the new dispensation of religious knowledge and worship throughout the earth. Viewed in this light, it forms the most august era which is to be found in the history of mankind. When Christ was suffering, on the cross, we are informed by one of the Evangelists, that he said, "I thirst;" and that they filled a sponge with vinegar, and put it to his mouth. "After he had tased the vinegar knowing that all things were now accomplished, and the scripture fulfilled, he said, It is finished," that s, This offered draught of vinegar was the last circumstance, predicted by an ancient prophet, that remained to be fulfilled. The vision and the prophecy are now sealed; the Mosaic dispensation is closed. "And he bowed his head and gave up the ghost."—Significantly was the veil of the temple tent in this hour; for the glory then departed from between the cherubims. The legal high priest delivered up his Urim and Thummim, his breastplate, his robes, and his incense; and Christ stood forth as the great High Priest of all succeeding generations. By that one sacrifice which he now offered, he abolished saciifices forever. Altars on which the fire had blazed for ages, were now to smoke no more. Victims were no more to bleed. "Not with the blood of bulls and goats, but with his own blood, he now entered into the holy place, there to appear in the presence of God for us."

This was the hour of association and union to all the worshippers of God. When Christ said, "It is finished," he threw down the wall or partition, which had so long divided the Gentile from the Jew. He gathered into one, all the faithful, out of every kindred and people. He proclaimed the hour to be come, when the knowledge of the true God should be no longer confined to one nation, nor his worship to one temple; but over all the earth, the worshippers of the Father should "serve him in spirit and in truth.

" From that hour, they who dwelt in the "uttermost ends of the earth, strangers to the covenant of promise,'' began to be " brought nigh." In that hour, the light of the gospel dawned from afar on the British Islands. This was the hour of Christ's triumph over all the powers of darkness; the hour in which he over-threw dominions and thrones, "led captivity captive, and gave gifts unto men." The contest which the kingdom of darkness had long maintained against the kingdom of light, was now brought to its crisis. The period was come, when "the seed of the woman should bruise the head of the serpent." For many ages the most gross superstition had filled the earth. "The glory of the incorruptible God, was," every where,except in the land of Judea, "changed into images made like to corruptible man, and to birds, and beasts, and creeping things. " The world, which the Almighty created for himself, seemed to have become a temple of idols. Even to vices and passions, altars were raised; and what was entitled religion, was, in effect, a discipline of impurity. In the midst of this universal darkness, Satan had erected his throne; and the learned and polished, as well as the savage nations, bQwed dowu before him. But at the hour when Christ appeared on the cross the signal of his defeat was given. His kingdom suddenly departed from him; the reign of idolatry passedaway; he was " beheld to fall like lightning from heaven." In that hour, the foundation of every Pagan temple shook; the statue of every false god tottered on its base; the priest fled from his falling shrine j and the heathen oracles became dumb forever.

Death also, the last foe to man, was the victim of this hour. The formidable appearance of the spectre remained, but his dart was taken away; for, in the hour when. Christ expiated guilt, he disarmed death, by securing the resurrection of the just. When he said to his penitent fellow-sufferer. " Today thou shalt be with me in paradise," he announced to all his followers, the certainty of heavenly bliss. He declared " the cherubims" to be dismissed, and the flaming sword" to be sheathed, which had been appointed at the fall, to keep from man the way of the tree of life." Faint, before this period, had been the hope, indistinct the prospect, which even good men enjoyed of the heavenly kingdom. "Life and immortality were now brought to light." From the hill of Calvary, the first clear and certain view was given to the world, of the everlasting mansions. Since that hour, they have been the perpetual consolation of believers in Christ. Under trouble, they sooth their minds; amidst temptations, they support their virtue; and, in. their dying moments, enable them to say, " O death! Where is thy sting? O grave! Where is thy victory?" SECTION II.

ELOQUENCE OF THE SENATE. *I.—Speech of the Earl of Chesterfield, in the House of Lords, February* 22, 1740, *on t/ie Pension Bill.* My Lords, IT is now so late, and so much lias been said in favour of the motion for tlie second reading of the Pension Bill, by Lords much abler than I am, that I shall detain you but a very short while with what I have to say upon the subject It has been said, by a noble Duke, that this bill can be looked on only as a bill for preventing a grievance that is foreseen, and not as a bill for remedying a grievance that is already felt; because it is not asserted, nor so much as insinuated, in the preamble of the bill, that any corrupt practices are now made use of, for gaining an undue influence over the other House. My Lords, this was the very reason for bringing in the bill. They could not assert, that any such practices are now made use of, without a proof; and the means for coming at this proof is what they want, and what they propose to get by this bill. They suspect there are such practices, but they cannot prove it. The crime is of such a secret nature, that it can very seldom be proved by witnesses; and therefore they want to put it to the trial, at least, of being proved by the oath of one of the parties; which is a method often taken, in cases that can admit of no other proof. This is, therefore, no argument of the grievance not being felt; for a man may, very sensibly, feel a grievance, and yet may not be able to prove it.

That there is a suspicion of some suoh practices being now made use of, or that they will soon be made use of, the many remonstrances from all part's of the united kingdoms are a sufficient proof. That this suspicion has crept into the other House, their having so frequently sent up this bill, is a manifest demonstration, and a' strong argument for its being necessary to have some such bill passed into a law. The other House must be allowed to be better judges of what passes, or must pass, within' their own walls, than we can pretend to be. It is evident, they suspect that corrupt practices have been, or soon may be, made use of, for gaining an undue influence over some of their measures; and they have calculated this bill for curing the evil, if it is felt, for preventing it, if it is only foreseen. That any such practices have been actually made use of, or are now made use of, is what I shall not pretend to affirm; but I am sure I shall not affirm the contrary. If any such are made use of I will, with confidence, vindicate his Majesty. I am sure he knows nothing of them. I am sure he will disdain to suffer them; but I cannot pass such a compliment upon his ministers, nor upon any set of ministers that ever was, or ever will *be,* in this nation; rind therefore, 1 think I cannot more faithfully, more effectually, serve his present Majesty, as well as his successors, than by putting it out of the power of ministers to gain any corrupt influence over either House of Parliament. Such an attempt may be necessary for the security of the minister; but never can be necessary for, must always be inconsistent with, the security of his master; and the more necessary it is for the minister's security, the more inconsistent it will always be with the king's, and the more dangerous to the liberties of the nation.

To pretend, my Lords, that this bill diminishes, or any way encroaches upon the prerogative, is something very strange. What prerogative, my Lords? Has the crown a prerogative to bribe, to infringe the law, by sending its pensioners into the other House? To say so, is destroying the credit, the authority of the crown, under the pretence of supporting its prerogative. If his Majesty knew that any man received a pension from him, or any thing like a pension, and yet kept his seat in the other house, he would himself declare it, or withdraw his pension, because he knows it is against the law. This bill, therefore. no way diminishes or encroaches upon the prerogative of the crown, which can never be exercised but for the public good. It diminishes only the prerogative usurped by ministers, which is never exercised but for its destruction. The crown may still reward merit in the proper way, that is, openly. The bill is intended, and can operate only against clandestine rewards, or gratuities given by ministers. These ate scandalous, and never were, nor will be, given but for scandalous services.

It is very remarkable, my Lords, it is even diverting, to see such a squeamisliness about peijury upon this occasion, amongst those, who, upon other occasions, have invented and enacted multitudes of oaths, to be taken by men, who are under great temptations, from their private interests, to be guilty of perjury. Is not this the case of almost every oath that relates to the collection of the public revenue, or to the exercise of any office? Is not this perjury one of the chief objections made by the Dissenters against the Test and Corporation Act? And shall we show a less concern for the preservation of our constitution than for the preservation of our church? The reverend bench should be cautious of making use of this argument; for, if they will not allow us an oath for the preservation of the former, it will induce many people to think, they ought not to be allowed an oath for the preservation of the latter.

By this time, I hope, my Lords, all the inconveniences pretended to arise from this' bill, have vanished; and therefore, I shall consider some of the arguments brought to show that it is not necessary. Here I must observe, that most of the arguments made use of for this purpose, are equally strong for a repeal of the laws we have already in being against admitting pensioners to sit and vote in the other House. If it be impossible to suppose, that a gentleman of great estate and ancient family, can, by a pension, be influenced to do what he ought not to do; and if we must suppose, that none but such gentlemen can ever get into the other House, I am sure the laws for preventing pensioners from having seats in that House are quite unnecessary, and ought to be repealed. Therefore, if these arguments prevail with your lordships to put a negative upon the present question,1 shall expect to see that negative followed by a motion for the repeal of those laws; nay, in a few sessions, I shall expect to see a bill brought in, for preventing any man's being a member of the other House, but such as have some place or pension under the crown. As an argument for such a bill, it might be said, that his Majestv's most faithful subjects ought to be-chosen Members af Parliament, and that those gentlemen will always be most faithful to the King, that receive the King's money'. I shall grant, my Lords, that such gentlemen will be always the most faithful, and the most obedient to the minister; but for this very reason I should be for excluding them from Parliament. The King's real interest, however much he may be made by his ministers to mistake it, must always be the same with the people's; but the minister's interest is generally distinct from, and often contrary to both: therefore, I shall always be for excluding, a much as possible, from Parliament, every man who is under the least iuducement to prefer the interest of the minister, to that of both king and people; and this I take to be the case of every gentleman, let his estate and family be what they will, that holds a pension.at the will of the minister.

Those who say, they depend so much upon the honour, integrity and impartiality of men of family and fortune, seem to think our constitution can never be dissolved, as long as we have a shadow of a Parliament. My opinion my lords, is so very different, that if ever our constitution be dissolved, if ever an absolute monarchy be established in this kingkom, I am convinced it will be under that shadow. Our constitution consists in the Houses of Parliament being a check upon the crown, as well as upon one another. If that check should ever be removed, if the crown should, by corrupt means, by places, pensions and bribes, get the absolute direction of our two Houses of Parliament, our constitution will from that moment be destroyed. There would be no occasion for the ciown to proceed any farther. It would be ridiculous to lay aside the forms of Parliament; for, under that shadow, our king would be more absolute, and might govern more absolutely, than he could do without it. A gentleman of family and fortune, would not, perhaps, for the sake of a pension, agree to lay aside the forms of government; because, by his venal service there, be earns his infamous pension, and could not expect the comiuuence of it, if those forms were laid aside; but a gentleman of family and fortune may, for the sake of a pension, whilst he is in Parliament, approve of the most blundering measures, consent to the most excessive and useless grants, enact the most oppressive laws, pass the most villanous ac couuts, acquit the most Iienious criminals, and condemn the most innocent persons, at the desire of that minister who pays him his pension. And if a majority of such House of Parliament consisted of such men, would it not be ridiculous in us to talk of our constitution, or to say we had any liberty left. —This misfortune, this terrible condition we may be reduced to by corruption; as brave, as l'iee people as we; the Romans, were reduced to it by the same means; and to prevent such a horrid catastruphe, is the design of this bill.

If people would at all think, if they would consider the consequences of corruption, there would be no occasion, my Lords, for making laws against it. It would appear so horrible, that no man would allow it to approach him.— The corrupted ought to consider, that they do not sell their vote, or their country only; these, perhaps, they may disregard; but they sell likewise themselves; they become the bond slaves of the corrupter, who corrupts them, not for their sakes, but for his own.-No man ever corrupted another, for the sake of doing him a service;. And therefore, if people would but consider, they would always reject the offer with disdain. But this is not to be expected. The histories of all countries, the history even of our own country, shows it is not to be depended on.:— The proffered bribe, people think, will satisfy the immediate craving of some infamous appetite; and this makes them swallow the alluring bait, though the liberties of their country, the happiness of their posterity, and even their own liberty, evidently depend upon their refusing it.— This makes it necessary, in every free state, t contrive if possible, effectual laws against corruption; and as the laws we now have for excluding pensioners from the otlw er house, are allowed to be ineffectual, we ought to make a trial, at least, of the remedy now proposed; for, though it should prove ineffectual, it will be attended with this advantage, that it will put us upon contriving some other remedy that may be effectual; and the sooner such a remedy is contrived and applied, the less danger we shall be exposed to of falling into that fatal distemper, from which no free state, where it has once become general, lias ever yet recovered.

II.—*Lord Mansfield's Speech in the House of Lords,* 1770, *on the Bill for the further preventing the Delays of Justice, by reason of Privilege of Parliament.*
My Lords, WHEN I consider the importance of this bill to your Lordships, I am not surprised it lias taken up so much of your consideration. It is a bill, indeed, of no common magnitude; it is no less than to take away from two thirds of the legislative body of this great kingdom, certain privileges and immunities, of which they have longbeen possessed. Perhaps therefs no situation the human mind can be placed in, that is so difficult and so trying, as when it is made a judge in its own cause. There is something implanted in the breast of man, so attached to self, so tenacious of privileges once obtained, that, in such a situation, either to discuss with impartiality or decide with justice, has ever been held as the summit of all hu« man virtue. The

bill now in question, puts your Lordships in this very predicament; and I doubt not but the wisdom of your decision will convince the world, that-where selfinterest and justice are in opposite scales, the latter will ever preponderate with your Lordships.
Privileges have been granted to legislators, in all ages and in all countries. The practice is founded in wisdom; and indeed, it is peculiarly essential to the constitution of this country, that the members of both Houses should be free in their persons, incases of civil suits; for there may come a time, when Die safety and welfare of this whole empire, may depend upon their attendance in Parliament. God forbid that I should advise any measure that would in future endanger the state—but the bill before your Lordships, has, I am confident, no such tendency; for it expressly secures the persons of/ members of either House, in all civil suits. This being'the case, I confess, when I see many noble Lords, for 4hose judgment I have a very great respect, standing up to oppose a bill, which is calculated merely to facilitate the recovery of just and legal debts, I am astonished and amazed. They, I doubt not, oppose the bill upon public principles. I would not wish to insinuate, that vprivate interest had the least weight in their determination.

This bill has been frequently proposed, and as frequently miscarried; but it was always lost in the Lower House. Little did I think, when it had passed the Commons, that it possibly could have met with such opposition here. Shall it be said that you, my Lords, the grand council of the nation, tire highest judicial and legislative body of the realm, endeavour to evade, by privilege, those very laws which you enforce on your fellow subjects? Forbid it, justice!—I am sure were the noble Lords as well acquainted as I am, with but half the difficulties and delays occasioned in the courts of justice, under pretence of privilege, they would not, nay, they could not, oppose this bill.

I have waited with patience, to hear what arguments might be urged against the bill, but I have waited in vain; the

truth is, there is no argument that can weigh against it. The justice and expediency of the bill are such as render it self-evident. It is a proposition of that nature, that can neither be weakened by argument, nor entangled with sophistry. Much, indeed, has been said by some noble Lords, on the wisdom of our ancestors, and how differently they thought from us. They not only decreed, that privilege should prevent all civil suits from proceeding, during the sitting of Parliament, but likewise granted protection to the very servants of members. I shall say nothing on the wisdom of our ancestors: it might, perhaps appear invidious; that is not necessary in the present case. I shall only say, that the noble Lords who natter themselves with the weight of that reflection, should remember, that as circumstances alter, things themselves should alter. Formerly) it was not so fashionable, either for masters or servants to run in debt, as it is at present. Formerly, we were not that great commercial nation we are at present; nor,, formely, were merchants and manufacturers members of Parliament, as at present. The case now is very different; both merchants and manufacturers are, with great propriety, elected members of the Lower House. Commerce having thus got into the legislative body of the kingdom, privilege must be done away. We all know that the very soul and essence of trade, are regular payments; and sad experience teaches us that there are men, who will not make their regular payments, without the compulsive power of the laws. —The law then, ought to be equally open to all; any exemption of particular men, or particular ranks of men, is, in a free and commercial country, a solecism of the grossest nature

But I will not trouble your Lordships with arguments for that which" is sufficiently evident without any. I shall only say a few words to some noble Lords, who foresee much inconveniency from the persons of their servants being liable to be arrested. One noble Lord observes,. that the coachman of a Peer may be arrested while he is.driving his master to the house, and consequently lie will not be able to attend bis duty in Parliament. If this were actually to happen, there are so many methods by which the member might still get to the House, that I can hardly think the noble Lord is serious in his objection. Another noble Peer said, That by this bill one might lose. their most valuable and honest servants. This I hold to be a contradiction in terms; for he can neither be a valuable servant, nor an honest man, who gets into debt, which he is neither able nor" willing to pay, till compelled by law. If my servant, by unforseen accidents, has got in debt, and I still wish to retain. him, I certainly would pay the debt. But upon no principal of liberal legislation whatever, can my servant have a title to set his creditors at defiance, while, for forty shillings only, the hoiiest tradesman may be torn from his family, and locked up in a gaol. It is monstrous injustice! 1 flatter-myself, however, t!.e determination of this day will entirely put an end to all such partial proceedings for the future, by passing into a law, the bill now under your Lordships' consideration.

I come now to speak upon what, indeed, I would have gladly avoided, had I not been particularly pointed at, for the part I have taken in this bill. It has been said, by a noble Lord on my left hand, that I likewise am running the race of popularity. If the noble Lord means by popularity, that applause bestowed by after ages, on good and virtuous actions, I have long been struggling ifttliat race; to what purpose, all trying time can alone determine; but if the noble Lord means that mushroom popularity, that is raised without merit, and lost without a crime, he is much mistaken in his opinion. I defy the noble Lord to point out a single action of my life, where the popularity of the times ever had the smallest influence on my determinations. I thank God, I have a more permanent and steady rule for my conduct, the dictates of my own breast. Those that have foregone that pleasing adviser, and given up the mind to be the slave of every popular impulse, I sincerely pity: 1 pily them still more, if their vanily leads them to mistake ihe shouts of a mob, for

the trumpst of fame. Experience might inform them, that many who have been saluted with the huzzas of a crowd one day, have received their execrations the next; and many, who, by the popularity of their times, have been held up as spotless patriots, have nevertheless appealed upon the historian's page-when truth has triumphed over delusion, the assassins of liberty. Why then, the noble Lord can think I am ambitious of present popularity, that echo of folly, and shadow of renown, lam at a loss to determine. Besides, 1 do not know that the bill now before your Lordships will be popular; it depends much upon the captice of the day. It may not be popular to compel people to pay their debts; and, in that case, the present must be a very unpopular bill. It may not be popular, neither, to take away any of the privileges of Parliament: for I very well remember, and many of your Lordships may remember, that not long ago, the popular cry was for the extension of privilege; and so far did they carry it at that time, that it was said that the privilege protected members even in criminal actions; nay, such was the power of popular prejudices over weak minds, that the very deceissions of some of the courts were tinctured with that doctrine. It was, undoubtedly, an abominable doctrine; I thought so then, and think so still: but nevertheless, it was a popular doctrine, and came immediately from those who were called the friends of liberty; how desoedly, time will show. True liberty, in my opinion, can only exist when justice is equally administered to all; to the king, and to the beggar. Where is the justice, then, or where is the law, that protects a member of Parlament, more than any other min, from the punishment due to his crimes? The laws of his country allow of no place,nor anyemploymenr, to be a sanctuary for crimes; and where I have the honor to sit as judge, neither royal favour, nor popular applause, shall ever protect the guilty. I have now only to beg pardon for having employed so much of your Lordship's time; and I am sorry a bill, fraught with so many good consequences, has not met with

an abler advocate; but I doubt not your lordship's determination will convince the world, that a bill calculated to contribute so much to the equal distribution of justice as the preseot,requires, withyour Lordships, but very little support.

SECTION III. ELOQUENCE OF THE BAR.

I.— *Cicero against Verres.* THE time is come, Fathers, when that which has Jong been wished for, towards allaying the envy your order has been subject to, and removing the imputations against trials, is effectually put in your power. An opinion lias long prevailed, not only here at home, but likewise in foreign countries, both dangerous to you, and pernicious to the stfhe, that, in prosecutions, men of wealth are always safe, however clearly convicted. There is now to be brought upon this trial before vou, to the confusion, I hope, of the propagators of this slanderous imputation, one, whose life and actions condemn him, in the opinion of all impartial persons; but *who/* according to his own reckoning and declared dependence upon his riches, is already acquitted: T mean Caius Verres. I demand justice of you, Fathers, upon the robber of the public treasury, the oppressor of Asia Minor and Pamphylia, the invader of the rights and privileges of Romans, the scourge and curse of Sicily. If that sentence is passed upon him which his crimes deserve, your authority, Fathers, will he venerable and sacred in the eyes of the public; but if his great riches should bias you in his favour, I shall still gain one point—to make it apparent to all the world, that what was wanting in this case, was not a criminal, nor a prosecutor, but justice and adequate punishment.

To pass over the shameful irregularities of his youth, What does his quaestorsliip, the first public employment he held, what does it exhibit, but one continued scene of villanies? Cneius Carbo plundered of the public money, by his own treasurer, a consul stripped and betrayed, an army deserted and reduced to want, a province robbed, the civil and religious rights.of a people violated. The employment he held in Asia Mmor and Pamphylia, What did it produce but the ruin of those countries?—in which houses, cities and temples were robbed by him. What was his conduct in his prsetorship here at home? Let the plundered temples, and public works, neglected (that he might embezzle the money intended for carrying them on) bear witness. How did he discharge the office of a judge? Let those who suffered by his injustice answer. But his proctorship in Sicily crowns all his works of wickedness, and finishes a lasting monument'to his infamy. The mischief done by him in that unhappy country, during the three years of his iniquitous administration, are such, that many years, under the wisest and best of praetors, will not be sufficient to restore things to the condition in which he found them; for, it is notorious, that during the time of his tyranny, the Sicilians neither enjoyed the protection of their own original laws, of the regulations made for their benefit by the Roman Senate, upon their coming under the protection of the commonwealth, nor of the natural and unalienable rights of men. His nod has decided all causes in Sicily for these three years: and his decisions have broke all law, all precedent, all right. The sums he has, by arbitrary taxes and unheard of impositions, extorted from the industrious poor, are not to be computed. The most faithful allies of the commonwealth have been treated as enemies. Roman citizens have, like slaves, been put to death with tortures. The most atrocious criminals, for money, have been exempted from the deserved punishments; and men of the most unexceptionable characters, condemned and banished unheard. The hai hours, though sufficiently fortified, and the gates of strong towns opened to pirates and ravagers.. The soldiery and sailors, belonging to a province under the protection of the commonwealth, starved to death. Whole fleets, to the great detriment of the province, suffered to perish. The ancient monuments of either Sicilian or Roman greatness, the statues of heroes and princes carried off; and the t; mples stripped of their images. Having, by his iniquitous sentences, filled the prisons with the most

industrious and deserving of the people, he then proceeded to order numbers of Roman citizens to be strangled in the gaols; so that the exclamation, "1 am a citizen of Rome.'"which has often, in the most distant regions, and among the most barbarous people, been a protection, was of no service to them; but on the contrary, brought a speedier and more severe punishment upon them.

1 ask now, Verres, what you have to advance against this charge? Will you pretend to deny it? Will you pretend that any thing false, that even any thing aggravated, is ailedged against you? Had any prince, or any. state, committed the same outrage against the privilege of Roman citizens, should we not think we had sufficient ground for declaring immediate war against them? What punishment ought then to be inflicted upon a tyrannical and vncked praetor, who dared, at no greater distance than Sicily, within sight of the Italian coast, to put to the infamous death of crucifixion, that unfortunate and innocent citizen, Publius Gavious Cosanus, only for his having asserted his privilege of citizenship, and declared his intention of appealing to the justice of his country, against a Cruel oppressor, who had unjustly confined him in prison, at Syracusa, whence he had just made his escape? The unhappy man, arrested as he was going to embark for his native country, is brought before the wicked praetor. With eyes darting fury, and a countenance distorted with cruelty, he orders the helpless victim of his rage to be stripped, and rods to be brought; accusing him, but without the least shadow of evidence, or even of suspicion, of having come to Sicily as a spy. It was in vain that the unhappy man cried out, "I am a Roman citizen: I have served under Lucius Pretius, who is now at Panormous, and will attest my innocence." The blood thirsty prastor, deaf to all he could urge in his own defence, ordered the infamous punishment to be inflicted. Thus, Fathers, was an innocent Roman citizen publicly mangled with scourging; whilst the only words he uttered amidst his cruel sufferings, were, "I am a Roman citizen!" With

these he hoped to defend himself from violence and infamy. But of so little service was this privilege to him, that while he was thus asserting his citizenship, the order was given foi his execution—for his execution upon the cross! O liberty!—O sound once delightful to every Roman ear!—O sacred privilege of Roman citizenship!—once sacred!—now trampled upon!—but what then!—Is it come to this? Shall an inferiour magistrate, a governour, who holds his whole power of (lie Roman people in a Roman province, within sight of Italy, bind, scourge, torture with fire, and red hot plates of iron, and at last put to the infamous death of the cross, a Roman citizen? Shall neither the cries of innocence, expiring in agony, nor the tears of pitying spectators, nor the majesty of the Roman commonwealth, nor the fear of the justice of his country, restrain the licentious and wanton cruelty of a monster, who, in confidence of his riches, strikes at the root of liberty, and sets mankind at defiance?

I conclude with expressing my hopes, that your wisdom and justice, fathers, will not, by suffering the attrocious arid unexampled insolence of Caius Verres to escape the due punishment, leave room to apprehend the danger of a total subversion of authority, and introduction of general anarchy and confusion.

II.—*Cicero for Milo.* My Lords, THAT you may be able the more easily to determine upon this point before you, I shall beg the favour of an attentive hearing, while, in a few words, I lay open the whole affair.— Clodius being determined, when created praetor, to harrass his country with every species of oppression, and finding the comitia had been dslayed so long the year before, that he could not hold this office many months, all on a sudden threw up his own year, and reserved himself to the next; not from any religious scruple, but that he might have, as he said himself, a full, entire year for exercising his praetorship; that is, for overturning the commonwealth. Being sensible he must be controuled and cramped in the exercise of his pisetoriao authority under Milo, who, he plainly saw, would be chosen consul, by the unanimous consent of the Roman people; he joined the candidates that opposed Milo, but in such a manner that he overruled them in every thing, bad the sole management of the election, and, as he often used to boast, bore all the comitia upon his own shoulders. He assembled the tribes; he thrust himself into their councils; and formed a new tribe-of the most abandoned of the citizens. The more confusion and disturbance he made, the more Milo prevailed. When this wretch, who was bent upon all manner of wickedness, saw that so brave a man, and his most inveterate enemy, would certainly be consul; when he perceived this, not only by the discourses, buf by the votes of the Roman people, he began to throw off all disguise, and to declare openly that Milo must be killed. He often intimated this in the Senate, and declared it expressly before the people; insomuch that when Favonious, that brave man, asked him what prospect he could have of carrying on his furious designs, while Milo was alive—lie replied, that in three or four days at most he should he taken out of the way; which reply Favoniug immediately communicated to Cato.

In the mean time, as soon as Clodius knew (nor indeed-was there any difficulty to come to the intelligence) ihat Milo was obliged by the 18th of January to be at Lanuvium, where he was dictator, in order to nominate a priest, a duty which the laws rendered necessary to be performed every year; he went suddenly from Rome the day before, in order, as appears by the events, to waylay Milo on his own grounds; and this at a time when he was obliged to leave a tumultuous assembly which he had summoned that very day, where his presence was necessary t8 carry on his mad designs; a thing he never would have done, if he bad not been desirous to take the advantage of that particular lime and place, for perpetrating his villany. But Milo, after having staid in the Senate that day till the house was broke up,-went home, changed his clothes, waited a while,-as usual, till his wife had got ready to at-tend him, and then set for-

ward, about the time that Clodius, if he had proposed to come back to Rome that day, might have returned. He meets Clodius near his own estate, a-little before sunset, and is immediately attacked by a body of men, who throw their darts at him from an eminence, and kill his coachman. Upon which he threw off his cloak, leaped from his chariot, and defended himself with great bravery. In the mean time Clodius' attendants drawing their swords, some of them ran back tothe chariot, in order to attack Milo in the rear; whilst others thinking that he was already killed, fell upon his servants who. were behind; these being resolute and faithful to their master, were some of them slain-; whilst the. lest, seeing a warm engagement near the chariot, being prevented from going to. their master's assistance, hearW besides from Clodius himself, that Milo was killed, and believing it to be a fact, acted upon this occasion (I mention it not with a view to elude the accusation, but because it was the true slate of the case) without the orders, without the knowledge, without the presence of their master, as every man would wish Mis own servants should act in the like circumstances.

This, my Lords, is a faithful account of the matter of fact: the person who lay in wait was himself overcome, and force subdued by force, or rather audaciousness chastised by true valour. I say nothing of the advantage-which accrues to the state in general, to yourselves in particular, and to all good men; I am content to wave the argument I might draw from hence in favour of my client, whose destiny was so peculiar, that he could not secure his own safety, without securing yours, and that of the republic at the same time. If he could not do it lawfully, there is no room for attempting his defence. But if reason teaches the learned, necessity the barbarian, common custom all nations in general, and even nature itself instructs the brutes to defend their bodies, limbs and lives wheu attacked, by all possible methods, you cannot pronounce this action criminal, without determining, at the same time, that whoever falls into

the hands of a highwayman, must of necessity perish either of the sword or your decisions. Had Milo been of this opinion, he would certainly have chosen to have fallen by the hands of Clodius, who had more than once before this, made an attempt upon his life, rather than be executed by jour order, because he had not tamely yielded himself a victim to his rage. But if none of you are of this opinion, the proper question is, not whether Clodius was killed; for that we grant: But whether justly or unjustly. If it appears that Milo was the aggressor, we ask no favour; but if Clodius, you will then acquit him of the crime that has been laid to his charge.

What method, then, can we take to prove that Clodius lay in wait for Milo? It is sufficient, considering what an audacious abandoned wretch he was, to show that he lay under a strong temptation to it, that he formed great hopes and proposed to himself great advantages, from Milo's death. By Milo's death, Clodius would not only have gained his point of being praetor, without that restraint which his adversary's power as consul, would have laid upon his "wicked designs, but likewise that of being prsetor under those consuls, by whose connivance, at least, if not assistance, he hoped he should be able to betray the state into the mad schemes he had been fovming; persuading himself, that, as they thought themselves under so great an obligation to him, they would have no inclination to oppose any of his attempts, even if they should have it in their power; and that if they were inclined to do it, they would, perhaps, be scarce able to controul the most profligate of all men, who had been confirmed and hardened in his audaciousness, by a long series of villanies.

Milo is so far fiom receiving any benefit from Clodius' death, that he is reafly a sufferer by it. But it may be said, that hatred prevailed, that anger and resentment urged him on, that he avenged his own wrongs and redressed his own grievances. Now if all these particular's may be applied, not merely with greater propriety to Clodius than to Milo, but with the utmost propriety to the one, and not the least to the other; what more can you desire? For why should Milo bear any other hatred to Clo tlius, who furnished him with such a rich harvest of glory, but that which every patriot must bear to all bad men? As. to Clodius, he had motives enough for bearing ill will to Milo; first, as my protector and guardian: then, as the opposer of his mad schemes, and the controuler of his armed force; and, lastly, as his accuser.

Every circumstance, my lords, concurs to prove, that it was for Milo's interest, Clodius should live; that, on the contrary, Milo's death was a most desirable event for answering the purposes of Clodius; that on the one side, there was a most implacable hatred; on the other, not the least; that the one had been continually employing himself in acts of violence, the other only in opposing them; that the life of Milo was threatened, and his death publicly foretold by Clodius; whereas nothing of that kind was ever heard from Milo; that the day fixed for Milo's journey, was well known by his adversary; while Milo knew not when Clodius was to return; that Milo's journey was necessary, but that of Clodius rather the Contrary; that the one openly declared his intention of leaving Rome that day, while the other concealed his intention of return ing; that Milo made no alteration in his measures, but that Clodius feigned an excuse foe. altering his; that if Milo had designed to waylay Clodius, he would have waited for him near the theity, till it was dark; but that Clodius, even, if lie had been under no apprehensions from Milo, ought to have been afraid of coming to town so late at night.

Let us how consider, whether the place where they encountered, was most favorable to Milo, or to Clodius. But can there, my Lords, be any room for doubt, or deliberation upon that? It was near the estate of Clodius, where at least a thousand able-bodied men were employed in his mad schemes of building. Did Milo think he should have an advantage by attacking him from an eminence, and did he, for this reason, pitch upon that spot, for the engagement; or,

was he not rather expected in that place by his adversary, who hoped the situation would favour his assault? The thing, my Lords, speaks for itself, which must be allowed to be of the greatest importance in determining the question. Were the affair to be represented only by painting, instead of being expressed by words, it would even then clearly appear which was the traitor, and whieh was free from all mischievous designs; when the one was sitting in his chariot! muffled up in his cloak, and his wife along with him. Which of these circumstances was not a very great incumbrance?—the dress, the chariot, or the companion? How could he be worse equipped for an engagement, when he was wrapped up in a cloak, embarrassed with a chariot, and almost fettered by his wife? Observe the other, now, in the first place, salying out on a sudden from his seat: for what reason? In the evening, what urged him?—Late, to what purpose, espe cially at that season? He calls at Pompey's seat; With what view; To-see Pompey? He knew he was at Alsiura: To see his house? He had been at it a thousand times. What, then, could be the reason of his loitering and shifting about? He wanted to be upon the spot when Milo came up.

But if, my Lords, you are not yet convinced, though the thing shines out with such strong and full evidence, that Milo returned to Rome with an innocent mind, unstained with guilt, undisturbed with fear, and free from the accusations of conscience; call to mind, 1 beseech you, by the immortal gods, the expedition with which he came back, his entrance into the forum while the senate house was in flames, the greatness of soul he discovered, the look he assumed, the speech he made on the occasion. He delivered himself up, not only to the people, but even to the senate: nor to the senate alone, but even to guards appointed for the public security; nor merely to them, but even to the authority of him whom the senate had entrusted with the care of the whole republic; to whom he never would have delivered himself, if lie had not been confident of the goodness of his cause.

What now remains, but to beseech and adjure you, my Lords, to extend that compassion to a brave man, which he disdains to implore, but which I, even against his consent, implore and earnestly entreat. Though you have not seen him shed a single tear, while all were weeping around him, though he has preserved the same steady countenance, the same firmness of voice and language, donot on this account withhold it from him.

On you, on you I call, ye heroes, who have lost somuch blood in the service of your country! To you, ye centurions, ye soldiers, i appeal, in this hour of danger to the best of men, and bravest of citizens! While you are looking on, while you stand here with arms in your hands, and guard this tribunal, shall virtue like this be expelled, exterminated, cast out with dishonour? By the immortal gods, I wish (pardon me, O my country! for I fear, what I shall say, out of a pious regard for Milo, may be deemed impiety against thee) that Clodius not only lived, but were praetor, consul, dictator, rather than be witness' to such a scene as this. Shall this man, then who was born to save his country, die any where but in his country? Shall he not, at least, die in the service of his country? Will you retain the memorials of his gallant soul, and deny his body a grave in Italy? Will any person give his voice for banishing a man from this city, whom every city on earth would be proud to receive within its walls? Happy the country that shall receive him! Ungrateful this, if it shall banish him! Wretched if it should loose him! But I must conclude—my tears will not allow me to proceed, and Milo forbids tears to be employed in his defence. Yoti, my Lords, I beseech and adjure, that, in your decision, you would dare to act as you think. Trust me, your fortitude, your justice, your fidelity, will more especially be approved of by him *(Pompey)* who, in his choice of judges, has raised to the bench, the bravest, the wisest, and the best of men.

SECTION IV. SPEECHES ON VARIOUS SUBJECTS.

I.—*Romulun to the people of Rome, after building the City.* IF all the strength of cities lay in the height of their ramparts, or the depth of their ditches, we should have great reason to be in fear for that which we have now built. But are there in reality any walls too high to be scaled by a valiant enemy? And of what use are ramparts in intestine divisions? They may serve for a defence against sudden incursions from abroad; but it is by courage and prudence, chiefly, that the invasions of foreign enemies are repelled; and by unanimity, sobriety and justice, that domestic seditions are prevented. Cities fortified by the strongest bulwarks have been often seen to yield to force from without, or to tumults from within. An exact military discipline, and a steady observance of civil polity, are the surest barriers against these evils.

But there is still another point of great importance to be considered. The prosperity of some rising colonies and the speedy ruin of others, have, in a great measure, been owing to their form of government. Were there but one manner of ruling states and cities, that could make them happy, the choice would not be difficult. But I have learnt, that of the various forms of government among the Greeks and barbarians, there are three which are highly extolled by those who have experienced them; and yet, that no one of these is in all respects perfect, but each oi' them has some innate and incurable defect. Choose you, then, in what manner this city shall be governed. Shall it be by one man? Shall it be by a select number of the wisest among us? Or shall the legislative power be in the people? As for me, 1 shall submit to whatever form of administration, you shall please to establish. As I think myself not unworthy to command, so neither am I unwilling to obey. Your having chosen me to be trie leader of this colony, and your calling the city after my name, are honours sufficient to content me; honours of which, living or dead, I can never be deprived, II.—*Hannibal to Scipio Afrlcanus, at their Interview preceding the Battle of Zama.* SINCE fate lias so ordained it, that I, who began the war, and who have been so often on the point of ending it by a complete conquest, should now come of my own motion, to ask a peace—I am glad that il is of you, Scipio, I have the foriane to ask it. Nor will this be among the least of your glories, that Hannibal, victorious over so many Homan geoerais, submitted at last to you.

I could wish, that our fathers and we had confined our ambition within the limits v-hich nature seems to have prescribed to it; the shores of Africa, and the shores of Italy. The gods did not give us that mind. On both sides we have been so eager after foreign possessions, as to put our own to the hazard of war. Rome and Carthage have had, each in her turn, the enemy at her gates. But since errours past may be more easily blamed than corrected, let it now be the work of you and me, to put an end, if possible, to the obstinate contention.— For my own part, my years, and the experience I have had of the instability of fortune, incline me to leave nothing to her determination which reason can decide. But much, I fear, Scipio, that your youth, your want of the like experience, your uninterrupted success, may render you averse from the thoughts of peace. He, whom fortuue has never failed, rarely reflects upon her inconstancy. Yet without recurring to former examples, my own may perhaps suffice to teach you moderation. I am the same Hannibal, who after my victory at Cannae, became master of the greatest part of your country, and deliberated with myself what fate I should decree to Italy and Rome. And now—see the charge! Here, in Africa, I am come to treat with a Roman, for my own preservation and my country's. Such are the sports of fortune-Is she then to be trusted because she smiles? An advantageous peace is preferable to the hope of victory. The one is in your own power, the other at the pleasure of the gods. Should you prove victorious, it would add little to your own glory, or the glory of your country; if vanquished, you lose in one hour, all the honour and reputation you have been so many years acquiring. But what is my aim in all this? That you should content yourself with ourcession of Spain, Sicily, Sardinia, and all the Islands between Italy and Africa. A peace on these conditions, will, in my opinion, not only secure the future tranquility of Carthage, but be sufficiently glorious for you, and for the Roman name. And do not tell me, that some of our citizens dealt fraudulently with you fa the late treaty.—It is I, Hannibal, that now ask a peace:— I ask it, because I think it expedient for my country; and thinking it expedient, I will inviolably maintain it. HI.—*Scipio's Reply.*

I KNEW very well, Hannibal, that it was the hope of your return, which emboldened ihe Carthagenians to break the truce with us, and lay aside all thoughts of peace, when it was just upon the point of being concluded; and your present proposal is a proof of it. You retrench from their concessions, every thing but what we are and have been, long possessed of. But as it is your care, that your fellow citizens should have the obligation to you, of being eased from a great part of their burden, so it ought to be mine, that they draw no advantage from their perfidiousness. Nobody is more sensible than I am of the weakness of man, and the power of fortune, and that whatever we enterprise, is subject to a thousand chances. If before the Romans passed into Africa, you had, of your own accord, quitted Italy, and made the offers you now make, I believe they would not have been rejected. But, as you have been forced out of Italy, and we are masters here of the open country, the situation of things is much altered. And what is chiefly to be considered, the Carthagenians, by the late treaty, which we entered into at their request, were, over and above what you offer, to have restored to us our prisoners without ransom, delivered up their ships of war, paid us five thousand talents, and to have given hostages for the performance of all. The senate accepted these conditions, but Carthage failed on her part: Carthage deceived us. What then is to be done? Are the Carthagenians to be released from the most important articles of the treaty, as a teward for their breach of faith? No, certainly. If to the conditions before agreed upon, you had lidded some new articles, to our advantage, there would have been matter of reference to the Roman people; but when, instead of adding, you retrench, there is no room for deliberation. The Carthagenians, therefore, must submit to us at discretion, or must vanquish us in battle.

IV.—*Calisthenes' Reproof of Clean's Flattery to Alexander, on whom he had proposed to confer Divinity by vote.* IF the king were present, Cleon, (here would be no need-of my answering to what you have just proposed. He would himself reprove you, for endeavouring to draw him into an imitation of foreign absurdities, and for bringing envy upon him by such unmanly flattery. As he is absent, I take upon me to tell you, in his name, that no praise is lasting, but what is rational; and-that you do what you can to lessen his glory, instead of adding to it. Heroes have never, among us, been deified, till after their death; and, whatever may be your way of thinking, Cleon, for my part, I wish the king may not, for many years to come, obtain that honour. '.-

You have mentioned, as precedents of what you propose, Hercules and Bacchus. Do you imagine, Cleon, that they were deified over a cup of wine? And are you and I qualified to make gods? Is the king, our sovereign, to receive his divinity from you and me, who are his subjects? First try your power, whether you can make a king. It is surely easier to make a king than a god; to give an earthly dominion, than a throne in heaven. I only wish that the gods may have heard, without offence, the arrogant proposal you have made, of adding one to their number,-and that they may still be so propitious to us, as to grant the continuance of that success to our affairs, with which they have hitherto favoured us. For my part, lam not ashamed of my country, nor do I approve of our adopting the rites of foreign nations, or learning from them how we ought to reverence our kings. To receive laws or rules of conduct from them, What is it but to confess ourselves inferiour to them?

V.—*Caius Marins to the Romans; shewing the absurdity of their hesitating*

to confer on him the Rank of General, merely on account of his Extraction. IT is but too common, my countrymen, to observe a material difference between the behaviour of those who stand candidates for places of power and trust, before and af ter their obtaining them. They solicit them In one manner, and execute them in another. They set out with a great appearance of activity, humility and moderation, and they publicly fall into sloth, pride and avarice.— It is, undoubtedly no easy matter to discharge, to the general satisfaction, the duty of a supreme commander, in troublesome times. To carry on with effect, an expensive war, and yet be frugal of public money; to oblige those to serve, whom it may be delicate to offend; to conduct, at the same time, a complicated variety of operations; to concert measures at home, answerable to the state of things abroad; and to gain eveiy valuable end, in spite of opposition from the envious, the factious, and the disaffected—to do all this, my countrymen, is more difficult than is generally thought.

But, besides thedisadvantages which are common to me, with all others in eminent stations, my case, is in this respect, peculiarly hard—that whereas a commander of Patrician rank, if he is guilty of neglect or breach of duty, has his great connexions, the antiquity of his family, the important services of his ancestors, and the multitudes he has by power, engaged in his interest, to screen him from condign punishment—my whole safety depends upon myself; which renders it the more indispensably necessary for me to take care, that my conduct be clear and unexceptionable. Besides, I am well aware, my countrymen, that the eye of the public is upon me; and t. at though the impartial, who prefer the real advantage of the commonwealth to all other considerations, favour my pretensions, the Patricians, want nothing so much, as an occasion against me. It is, therefore, my fixed resolution, to use my best endeavours, that you be not disappointed in me, and that their indirect designs against me may be defeated.

I have from my youth, been familiar with toils and with danger. I was faithful to your interest, my countrymen, when I served you for no reward but that of honour. It is not my design to betray you, now that you have conferred upon me a place of profit. You have committed to my conduct, the war against Jugurtha.—The Patricians are offended at this. But where would be the wisdom of giving such a command to one of their honourable body? A person of illustrious birth, of ancient family, of innumerable statues—but of no experience! What service would this long line of dead ancestors, or his multitude of motionless statues, do his country in the day of battle? What could such a general do, but in his trepidation and inexperience, have recourse to some inferiour commander for direction, in difficulties to which he was not himself equal? Thus, your Patrician general would, in fact, have a general over him; so that the acting commander would still be a Plebian. So true is this, my countrymen, that I liave, myself, known those that have been chosen consuls, begin then to read the history of their own country, of-which, till that time, they were totally ignorant; that it, they first obtained the employment, and then bethought themselves of the qualifications necessary for the proper discharge of it.

I submit to your judgment, Romans, on which side the advantage lies, when a comparison is made between Patrician haughtiness, and Plebian experience. The very actions which they have only read, I have partly seen, and partly myself achieved. What they know by reading, I know by action. They are pleased to slight-my mean birth: I despise their mean characters. Want of birth and fortune is the objection against me; want of personal worth against them. But are not all men of the same species? What can make a difference between one man and another, but the endowments of the mind? For my part, I shall always look upon the bravest man, as the noblest man. Suppose it were required of the fathers of such Patricians as Albinos and Bestia, whether if they had their choice, they would desire sons of their character, or of mine: What would they answer, but that they would wish the worthiest to be their sons? If the Patricians have reason to despise me, let them likewise despise their ancestors, whose nobility was the fruit of their virtue. Do they envy the honours bestowed upon me? Let them envy, likewise, my labours, my abstinence, and the dangers I have undergone for my country, by which I have acquired them. But those worthless men lead such a life of inactivity, as if they despised any honours you can bestow; whilst they aspire to honours as if they had deserved them by the most industrious virtue. They lay claim to the rewards of actity, for their having enjoyed the pleasures of luxury.

Yet none can be more lavish than they are, in praise of their ancestors. And they imagine they honour themselves by celebrating their forefathers; whereas they do the very contrary; for, as much as their ancestors were distinguished for their virtues, so much are they disgraced by their vices. The glory of ancestors cast a light indeed, upon their posterity; but it only serves to shew what the decendants are. It alike exhibits to public view, their degeneracy and their worth. I own I cannot boast of the deeds of my forefathers; but I hope I may answer the cavils of the Patricians, by standing up in defence of what I have myself done. Observe now, iny countrymen, the injustice of the Patricians. They arrogate to themselves honours, on account of the exploits done by their forefathers, whilst they will not allow me the due praise, for peforming the very same sort of actions iu my own person. He has no statues, they cry, of his family. He can trace no venerable line of ancestors. What then? Is it matter of more praise to disgrace one's illustrious ancestors, than to become illustrious by one's own good behaviour? What if I can show no statues of my family? I can show the standards, the armour, and the trappings, which I have myself taken from the vanquished: I can show the scars of those wounds which I have received by facing the enemies of my country. These are my statues.—These are the honours I boast of.

Not left me by inheritance, as theirs; but earned by toil, by abstinence, by valour; amidst clouds of dust and seas of blood; scenes of action, where those effeminate Patricians, who endeavour, by indirect means to deprecate me in your esteem, have never dared to show their faces.

VI.—*Speech of Publius Scipio to the Roman Army, before the Battle of Ticin.*

WERE you, soldiers, the same army which I had with me in Gaul, 1 might well forbear saying any thing to you at this time; for what occasion could there be to use exhortations to a cavalry, that had so signally vanquished the squadrons of the enemy upon the Rhone, or to legions, by whom that same enemy, flying be/ore them, to avoid a battle, did, in effect, confess themselves conquered? But as these troops, having been enrolled for Spain, are there with my brothel Cneius, making war under my auspices, (as was the will of tlie senate and People of Rome) I, that you might.have a consul for your captain against Hannibal and the Carthagenians, have freely offered myself for this war." You, then, have a new general, and I a new army. On this account a few words from me to you, will; be neither improper nor unseasonable. That you may not be unapprised of what sort of enemies you are going to encounter, or what is to be feared from them, they are the very same, whom in a former war, you vanquished both by land and sea; the same from whom you took Sicily and Sardinia, and who have been these twenty years your tributaries. You-will not,. I presume,inarch against these men with only that courage with which you are wont to face other enemies: but with a certain anger and indignation, such as you would feel if you saw your slaves on a sudden rise up in arms against you. Conquered and enslaved, it is not boldness, but necessity that urges them to battle; uuless you could believe, that those who avoided fighting when their army was entire, have acquired better hope, by the loss of two thirds of their horse and foot in the passage of the Alps..

But you have heard, perhaps, that though they are few in number, they are men of stout hearts and robust bodies; heroes of such strength and vigour, as nothing is able to resist. Mere effigies! Nay, shadows of men;—wretches emaciated with hunger, and benumbed with cold! bruised and battered to pieces among the rocks and craggy cliffs! their weapons broken, and their horses weak and foundered! Such are the cavalry, and such the infantry, with which you are.going to contend; not enemies, but the fragments of enemies. There is nothing which I more apprehend, than (hat it will be thought Hannibal was vanquished *by.* the Alps, before we had any conflict with him. But perhaps, it was fitting it should be so; and that, with a people and a leader who had violated leagues and covenants,-the gods themselves, without man's help, should begin the war, and bring it to a near conclusion; and that we, who, next to the gods, have been injured and. offended should happily finish what they have begun.

I need not be in any fear, that you should suspect me af saving these things merely to encourage you, while.in? wardly I have a different sentiment. What hindered me from going into Spain? That was my province, where I should have had the less dreaded Asdrubal, not Hannibal, to deal with. But hearing, as I passed along the coast of Gaul, of this enemy's inarch, I landed my troops, sent my horse forward,' and pitched my camp upon the Rhone. A part of my cavalry encountered and defeated that of the enemy. My infantry not being able to overtake theirs, which fled before us, I returned to my fleet; and with all the expedition 1 could use, in so long a voyage by sea and land, am come to meet them at tlie foot of the Alps. Was it then my inclination to avoid a contest with this tremendous Hannibal? And have I met with him only by accident and unawares? Oram I come on purpose to challenge him to the combat? I would gladly try, whether the earth, within these twenty years has brought forth a new kind of Carthagenians; or whether they be the same sort of men who fought at the iEgates, 'and whom,.at Eryx, you suffered to redeem themselves at eighteen denarii pec head; whether this Hannibal, for labours and journies, be, as he would be thought, the rival of Hercules; or whether he be, what his father left him, a tributary, a vassal, a slave to the Roman people. Did not the consciousness of his wicked deed at Saguntum, torment him and make him desperate, he would have some regard, if not to his conquered country, yet surely to his own family, to his father's memory, to the treaty written with Amilcar's own hand. We might have starved him in Eryx; we might have passed into Africa with our victorious fleet, and in a few days, have destroyed Carthage. At their humble supplication, we pardoned them; we released them when they were closely shut up without a possibility of escaping; we made peace with them when they were conquered. When the were distressed by the African war, we considered them, we treated them as a people under our protection. And what is the return they make for all these favours? Under the conduct of a hairbrained young man, they come hither to overturn our state, and lay waste our country. 1 could wish indeed, that it were not so; and ihat the war we are now engaged in, concerned only our own glory, and not our preservation. But the contest, at present, is not for the possession of Sicily and Sardi nia, but of Italy itself; nor is there behind us another army, which, if we should net prove the conquerors, may make head against our victorious enemies. There are no more Alps for them to pass, which might give us leisure to raise new forces. No, soldiers; here you must make your stand, as if you were just now before the walls of Rome. Let every one reflect, that he has now to defend, not only his own person, but his wife, his children, his helpless infants. Yet let not private considerations alone possess our minds; let us remember that the eyes of the senate and people of Rome are upon us; and that as our force and courage shall now prove, such will be the fortune of that city, and of the Roman empire.

VII.—-*Speech of Hannibal to the Carthagenian Army, on the same Occasion.*

I KNOW not, soldiers, whether you or your prisoners 'be encompassed by fortune, with the stricter bonds and necessities. Two seas inclose you on the right and left; not a ship to fly too for escaping. Before you is the Po, a river broader and more rapid than the Rhone; behind you are the Alps, over which, even when your numbers were undiminished, you were hardly able to force a passage. Here, then, soldiers, you must either conquer or die, the very first hour you meet the enemy.

But the same fortune, which has thus laid you under the necessity of fighting, has set before your eyes the most glorious reward of victory. Should we by our valour, recover only Sicily and Sardinia, which were ravished from our fathers, those would be no inconsiderable prizes. Yet what are those? The wealth of Rome; whatever riches she has heaped together in the spoils of nations; all these with the masters of them, will be yonrs. The time is now come to reap the full recompense of your toilsome marches over so many mountains and rivers, and through so many nations, all of them in arms. This, the place which fortune has appointed to be the limits of your labour; it is here that you will finish your glorious warfare, and receive an ample recompense of your completed service. For I would not have you imagine, that victory will be as difficult as the name of a Roman war is great and sounding. It has ofteu happened, that a despised enemy has given a bloody battle; and the most renowned kings and nations, have by a small force been overthrown. And if you but take away the glitter of the Roman name, what is there wherein they may stand in competition with you? For (to say nothing of your service in war, for twenty years together, with so much valour and success) from the very pillars of Hercules, from theocean, from the utmost bounds of the earth, through so many warlike nations of Spain and Gaul, are you not come hither victorious? and with whom are you now to fight? With raw soldiers, an undisciplined army, beaten, vanquished, besieged by the Gauls, the very last summer; an army unknown to their Leader, and unacquainted with him.

Or shall I who was born, I might almost say, but certainly brought up, in the tent of my father, that most excellent general; shall I, the conqueror of Spain and Gaul, and not only of the Alpine nations, but which is still greater, of the Alps themselves—shall I compare myself with' this halfyear's captain? A captain, before whom should one place the two armies without their ensigns, I am persuaded he would not know to which of them he is consul. 1 esteem it no small advantage, soldiers, that there is not one among you who has not often been an eye witness of my exploits in war; not one of whose valour I myself have not been a spectator, so as to be able to name the times and places of his noble achievements; that with soldiers, whom I have a thousand times praised and rewarded, and whose pupil I was before I became their general., I shall march against an army of men, strangers to one another.

On what side soever I turn my eyes, I behold all full of courage and strength. A veteran infantry; a most gallant cavalry; you, my allies, most faithful and valiant; you, Carthagenians, whom not only your country's cause but the justest anger impels to battle. The hope, the courage of assailants is always greater than of those who act upon the defensive. With hostile banners displayed you are come down upon Italy: You bring the war. Grief injuries, indignities, fire your minds and spur you forward' to revenge. First, they demand me, that I, your general, should be delivered up to them; next, all of you who had faught at the siege of Saguntum; and we were to be put to death by the extremest tortures. Proud and cruel mv tion! Everything mugt be yours, and at your disposal!

You are to prescribe to us with whom we shall make war, with whom we shall make peace! You are to set us bounds; to shut us up within hills and rivers; but you, you are not to observe the limits which yourselves have fixed!" Pass not the Iberus." What next?" Touch not the Saguntines: Saguntum is upon the Iberus; move not a step towards that city." Is it a small matter, then, that you have deprived us of our ancient possessions) Sicily and.Sardinia? you would have Spain too. Well; we shall yield Spain, and then—you will pass into Africa. Will pass, did I say?—This very year they ordered one of their consuls into Africa—the other into Spain. No, soldiers, there is nothing left for us, but what we can vindicate with our swords. Come on, then. Be men. The Romans may, with more safety, be cowards; they have their own country behind them, have places of refuge to fly to, and are secure from danger in the roads thither; but for you, there is no middle fortune between death and victory. Let this be but well fixed in your minds; and once again, I say you are conquerors.

VIII.—*Speech of Adherlal to the Roman Senate, imploring their Assistance against Jugurtha.* Fathers! IT h known to you, that king Micipsa, my father, on his death bed, left in charge to Jugurtha, his adopted son, conjunctly with my unfortunate brother Hiempsal and myself, the children of his own body, the administration of the kingdom of Numidia, directing us to consider the senate and people of Rome, as proprietors of it. He charged us to use our best endeavours to be serviceable to the Roman commonwealth, in peace and war; assuring us, that your protection would prove to us a defence against all enemies, and would be instead of armies, fortifications and treasures.

While my brother and I were thinking of nothing but how to regulate ourselves according to the directions of our deceased father—Jugurtha—the most infamous of mankind!—breaking through all ties of gratitude, and of common humanity, and trampling on the authority of the Roman commonwealth, procured the murder of my unfortunate brother, and has driven me from my throne and native country, though he knows I inherit from my grandfather Massiuissa, and my father Micipsa, the friendship and alliance of (he Romans.

For a Prince to be reduced by villany, to my distressful circumstances, is calamity enough; but my misfortunes are heightened by the consideration—that I find myself obliged to solicit your assistance, Fathers, for the services done you by my ancestors, not for any I have been able to render you in my own person. Jugurtha has put it out of my power to deserve any thing at your hands; and has forced me to be burthensome, before I could be useful to you. And yet, if I had no plea but my undeserved misery—a once powerful prince, the descendant of a race of illustrious monarchs, noV, without any fault of my own, destitute of everj'support, and reduced to the necessity of begging foreign assistance against an enemy who has seized my throne and my kingdom—if my unequalled distresses were all I had to plead—it would become the greatness of the Roman commonwealth, the arbitress of the world, to protect the injured, and to check the triumph of daring wickedness over helpless innocence.—But to provoke your vengeance to the utmost, Jugurtha has driven me from. the very dominions, which the senate and the people of Rome gave to' my ancestors; and from which, my grandfather and my father, under your umbrage, expelled Syphax and the Carthagenians. Thus, Fathers, your kindness to our family is defeated; and Jugurtha, in injuring me, throws contempt on you.

O wretched prince.' O cruel reverse of fortune! O father Micipsa! Is thrs the consequence of your generosity; that he whom your goodness raised to an equality.with your own children, should be the murderer of your children? Must then, the royal house of Numidia always be a scene of havoc and blood? While Carthage remained, we suffered, as was to be expected, all sorts of hardships from their hostile attacks; our enemy near; our only powerful ally, the Rom.in commonwealth, at a distance. While we were so circumstanced, we were always in rms and in action. When that scourge of Africa was no more, we congratulated ourselves on the prospect of established peace. But instead of peace behold the kingdom of Numidia drenched

with royal blood j and the only surviving son of its late ting, flying from an adopted murderer, and seeking that safety in foreign parts, which he cannot command in his own kingdom..

Whither—Oh! Whither shall I fly J If 1 return to the royal palace of my ancestors, toy father's throne is seized by the murderer of my brother. What can I there expect, but that Jugurtha should hasten to imbrue, in my blood, those hands which are now reeking with my brother's! If I were to fly for refuge or assitance to any other court— from what prince can I hope for protection, if the Roman commonwealth give me up? From my own family or friends, I have no expectations. My royal father is no more. He is beyond the reach of violence, and out of hearing of the complaints of his unhappy son. Were my brother alive, our mutual sympathy would be some alleviation. But he is hurried out of life, in his early youth, by the very hand, which should have been the last to injure any of the royal family of Niimidia. The bloody Jugurtha has butchered all whom he suspected to be in my interest. Some have been destroyed by the lingering torment of the cross. Others have been given a prey to wild beasts, and their anguish made the sport of men, mote cruel than wild beasts. If there be any yet alive, they are shut up in dungeons, there to drag cut a life, more intolerable than death itself.

Look down illustrious senators of Rome! from that height of power to which you are raised, on the unexampled distress of a prince, who is, by the cruelty of a wick.ed intruder, become an outcast from all mankind. Let not the crafty insinuations of him who returns murder for adoption, prejudice your judgment. Do not listen to the wretch who has butchered the son and relations of a king, who gave him power to sit on the same throne with his own sons. I have been informed that he labours, by his emissaries, to prevent your determining any thing against him in his absence: pretending that I magnify my distress, and might for him have staid in peace in my own kingdom. But if ever the time comes when due vengeance from above shall overtake him, he will then dissemble as I do. Then he who now hardened in wickedness, triumphs over those whom his violence has laid low, will, in his turn, feel distress, and suffer for his impious ingratitude to my father, and his blood thirsty cruelty to my brother.

Oh murdered,.butchered brother! Oh, dearest to my heart—now gone forever from my sight! but why should I lament his death? He is, indeed, deprived.of the blessed light of heaven, of life and kingdom, at once, by the very person who ought to have been the first to hazard his own life in defence of any one of Alicipsa's family! But as things are, my brother is not so much deprived of these comforts, as delivered from terrour, from flight, from exile, and the endless train of miseries, which render life *to* me a burden. He lies full low, gored with wounds, and festering in his own blood. But he lies in peace. He feels none of the miseries which rend my soul with agony and distraction, while I am set up a spectacle to all mankind, of the uncertainty of human affairs. So far from having it in my power to revenge his death, 1 am not master of the means of securing my own life. So far from being in a condition to defend my kingdom from the violence of the usurper, I am obliged to apply for foreign protection for my own person.

Fathers! Senators of Rome!—The arbiters of the world! To you I fly for refuge from the murderous fury of Jugurtha. By your affection for your children, by your love for your country, by your own virtues, by the majesty of the Roman commonwealth, by all that is sacred, and all that is dear to you, deliver a wretched prince from undeserved, unprovoked injury; and save the kingdom of Numidia, which is your own property,' from being the prey of violence, usurpation and cruelty.

IX.—*Speech of Canuleius to the Consuls; in which he demands tluxt the Plebeians my be admitted into the Consulship, and that the Laws prohibiting Patricians and Plebeians from intermarrying, may be repealed.* WHAT an insult upon us is this? If we are not so rich

as the Patricians, Are we not citizens of Rome as well as they? Inhabitants of the same country?—Members of the same community? The nalious bordering upon Rome, and even strangers more remote, are admitted, not only to marriage with us, but to what is of much greater importance—the freedom of the city. Are we, because we are commoners, to be worse treated than strangers? And when we demand that the people may be free to bestow their offices and dignities on whom tliey please, Do we ask any thing unreasonable or new? Do we claim more than their original inherent right? What occasion then, for all this uproar, as if the universe were falling to ruin? They were just going to lay violent hands upon me in the senate Uouse. What! Must this empire, then, be unavoidably overturned! Must Rome of necessity sink at once, if a Plebeian worthy of the office, should be raised to the consulship? The Patricians, 1 am persuaded, if they could, would deprive you of the common light. It certainly offends them that you breathe, that you speak, that you have the shapes of men. Nay, but to make a commoner a consul, would be, say they, a most enormous thing-.—Numa Pompilius, however, without being so much as a Roman citizen, was made king of Rome. The elder Tarquin, by birth not even an Italian, was nevertheless placed upon the throne. Servius Tullius, the son of a captive woman, (no body knows who his father was) obtained the kingdom, as the reward of his wisdom and virtue. In those days, no man in whom virtue shone conspicuous, was rejected or despised on account of his race and descent. And did the state prosper the less for that? Were not these strangers the very best of all our kings? And supposing, now, that a Plebeian should have their talents and merit, Would he be suffered to govern us?

But, " we find, that, upon the abolition of the regal power, no commoner was chosen to the consulate."—And, what of that? Before Numa's time, there were no pontiff's in Rome. Before Servius Tellius's days, there was no census, no division of the people into

classes and centuries. Who ever heard of consuls before the expulsion of Tarquin the proud? Dictators, we all know, are of modern invention; and so are the officers of tribunes, sedilles, quaestors. Within these ten years we have made decemvirs, and we have unmade them. Is nothing to be done but what has been done before? That very law, forbidding marriages of Patricians with Plebeians, Is not that a new thing? Was there any such law before the decemvirs enacted it? And a most shameful one it is in a free state. Such marriages, it seems, will taint the pure blood of the nobility! Why, if they think so, let them take care to match their sisters and daughters with men of their own sort. No Plebeian will do violence to the daughter of a Patrician. Those are exploits for our prime nobles. There is no need to fear that we shall force any body into a contract of marriage. But, to make an express law to prohibit marriages of Patricians with Plebeians, What is this but to show the utmost contempt of us, and to declare one part of the community 10 be impure and unclean?

They talk to us of the confusion there would be in families, if this statute should be repealed. I wonder they don't make a law against a commoner's living near a noble man, going the same road that he is going or being present at the same feast, or appearing in the same market place. They might as well pretend that these things make confusion in families, as that intermarriages will do it. Does not every one know that the children will be ranked according to the quality of their father, let him be a Patrician or a Plebeian? In short, it is manifest enough that we have nothing in view, but to be treated as men and citizens; nor can they who oppose our demand have any motive to it, but the love of domineering. I would fain know of you, consuls and Patricians, Is the sovereign power in the people of Rome, or in you? I hope you will allow, that the people can, at their pleasure, either make a law or repeal one. And will you, then, as soon as any law is proposed to them, pretend to list them immediately for the war, and hinder them from giving their suffrages, by leading them into the field?

Hear nie consuls. Whether the news of the war you talk of be true, or whether it be only a false rumour, spread abroad for nothing but a colour to send the people out of the city: I declare, as a tribune, that this people, wtio have already so often spilt their blood in our country's cause, are again ready to arm for its defence and its glory, if they may be restored to their natural rights, and you will no longer treat us like strangers in our own conntry; but if you account us unworthy of your alliance, by intermarriages; if you will not suffer the entrance to the chief offices in the state to be open to all persons of merit, indifferently, but will confine your choice of magistrates to the Senate alone—talk of wars as much as ever you please—paint in your ordinary discourses, the league and power of our enemies, ten times more dreadful than you do now—1 declare, that this people, whom you so much despise, and to whom, you are nevertheless indebted for all your victories, shall never more enlist themselves—not a man of them shall take arms—not a man of them shall expose his life for imperious lords, with whom he can neither share the dignities of the state, nor in private life, have any alliance by marriage.

X.—*Speech of Junius Brutus, over the dead Body of Lucretia.* YES, noble lady, Tswear by this blood, which was once so pure, and which nothing but royal villany could have polluted, that I will pursue Lucius Tarquinius the proud, his wicked wife and their children, with fire and sword; nor will I ever suffer any of that family, or of any other whatsoever, to be king in Rome: Ye gods, 1 call you to witness this my oath!—There, Romans, turn your eyes to that sad spectacle—the daughter of Lucretia, Catalinus' wife—she died by her own hand. See there a noble lady, whom the lust of a Tarquin reduced to the necessity of being her own executioner, to attest her innocence. Hospitably entertained by her, as a kinsman of her husband's, Sextus, the perfidious guest, became her brutal ravish-

er. The chaste, the generous Lucretia, could not survive the insult. Glorious woman! But once only treated as a slave, she thought life no longer to be endured. Lucretia, as a woman, disdained a life that depended on a tyrant's will; and shall we—shall men, with such an example before our eyes, and after five and twenty years of ignominious servitude, shall we, through a fear of dying, defer one single instant to assert our liberty? No, Romans, now is the time;—the favourable moment we have so long waited for, is come. Tarquin is not at Rome. The Patricians are at the head of the enterprise, The city is abundantly provided with men, arms, and all things necessary.—There is nothing wanting to secure the success, if our own courage does not fail us. And shall those warriors who have ever been so brave when foreign enemies were to be subdued, or when conquests were to be made to gratify the ambition and avarice of a Tarquin, be then only cowards, when they are to deliver themselves from slavery?—Some of you are perhaps intimidated by the army which Tarquin now commands. The soldiers, you imagine, will take the part of their general. Banish so groundless a fear. The love of liberty is natural to ail men. Your fellow citizens in the camp feel the weight of oppression, with as quick a sense as you that are in Rome; they will as eagerly seiee the occasion of throwing off the yoke. But let us grant that there are some among them, who, through baseness of spirit, or a bad education, will be disposed to favour the tyrant. The number of these can be but small, and we have means sufficient in our hands to reduce them to reason. They have left us hostages, more dear to them than life.—Their wives, their children, their fathers, their mothers, are here in the city. Courage, Romans, the gods are for us;—those gods, whose temples and altars the impious Tarquin has profaned, by sacrifices and libations, made with polluted hands, polluted with blood, and with numberless unexpiated crimes committed agaiust his subjects,— Ye gods, who protected out forefathers—ye genii, who watch for

the preservation and glory of Rome, do you inspire us with courage and unanimity in this glorious cause, and we will, to our last breath, defend your worship from all profanation f XI.—*Demosthenes to the-Athenians, exciting them to prosecute the War against Philip.* WHEN I compare, Athenians, the speeches of some amongst us, with their actions, I am at a loss to reconcile-what 1 see with what I hear. Their protestations are full of zeal against the public enemy; but their measures are so inconsistent, that all their professions become suspected. By confounding you with a variety of projects, they perplex your resolutions; and lead you from executing what is in your power, by engaging you in schemes not reducible to practice.

'Tis true, there was a time, when we were powerful enough, not only to defend our own borders, and protect our allies, but even to invade Philip in his own dominions. Yes, Athenians, there was such a juncture; I remember it well. But, by neglect of proper opportunities, we are no longer in a situation to be invaders; it will be well for us, if we can provide for our own defence, and our allies.

Never did any conjuncture require so much prudence as this. However, I should not despair of seasonable remedies, had I the art to prevail with you. to be unanimous in right measures. The opportunities which have so often escaped us, have not been lost through ignorance or want of judgment, hut through negligence or treachery. If I assume at this time, more than ordinary liberty of speech, I conjure you to suffer patiently those truths, which have no other end but your own good. You have too many reasons to be sensible how much you have suffered by hearkening to sycophants. I shall therefore, be plain, in laying before you the grounds of past miscarriages, in order to correct you in your future conduct.

You may remember it is not above three or four years since we had the news of Philip's laying siege to. the fortress of Juno, in Thrace.' It was, as I think, in October we received this intelligence.. We voted an immediate supply of threescore talents; forty men of war were ordered to sea; and so zealous were we, that preferring the necessities of the state to our very laws, our citizens above the age of five and forty years, were commanded toserve. What followed?. A whole year was spent idly, without any thing done, and it was but in the third month,of the following year, a little after the celebration of the feast of Ceres, that Charademus set sail, furnished with no more than five talents, and ten galleys, not half manned.. A rutrior was spread that Philip was sick. That rumour was followed by another— that Philip was dead. And then, as if all danger died, with him, you dropped your preparations; whereas then, then was your time to push and be active; then was your time to secure yourselves and confound him at once. Had your resolutions, taken with so much heat, been as warmly seconded by action,, you bad then been as terrible to Philip, as Philip, recovered, is now to you. "To what purpose, at this time, these reflections? What is done cannot be undone. " But by your leave, Athenians, though past moments are not to be. recalled, past errors may be repeated. Have we not, now,. a fresh provocation to war? Let the memory of oversights, by which.you-have suffered so much,, instruct you: to be more vigilant in the present danger. If the Olynr tliians are not instantly succoured, and. with your utmost aa, efforts, you become assistants to Philip, and serve him more effectually than he can help himself.

It is not, surely, necessary to warn you, that votes alone can be of no consequence. Had your resolutions, of themselves, the virtue to compass what you intend, we should not see them multiply every day, as they do, and upon every occasion, with so little effect; nor would Philip be in a condition to brave and affront us in this manner.— Proceed then, Athenians, to support your deliberations with vigor. You have heads capable of advising what is best; you have judgment and experience to discern what is right 5 and you have power and opportunity to execute what you determine.

What time so proper for action? What occasion so happy? And when can vou hope for such another if this be neglected? Has not lJhilip, contrary to all treaties, insulted you in Thrace? Does he not, at this instant, straiten and invade your confederates, whom you have solemnly sworn to protect? Is he not an implacable enemy? A faithless ally? The usurper of provinces, to which he has no title nor pretence? A stranger, a barbarian, a tyrant? And, indeed, what is he not?

Observe, I beseech you, men of Athens, how different your conduct appears, from the practices of your ancestors. They were friends to truth and plain dealing, and detested flattery and servile compliance. By unanimous consent, they continued arbiters of all Greece, for the space of forty-live years,-without interruption; a public fund of no less than ten thousand talents was ready for any emergency; they exercised over the kings of Macedon, that authority which is due to barbarians; obtained both by sea and land, in their own persons, frequent and signal victories; and, by their noble exploits, transmitted to posterity an immortal memory of their virtue, superiour to the reach of malice and detraction. It is to them we owe that great number of public edifices, by which the city of Athens exceeds all the rest of the world in beauty and magnificence. It is to them we owe so many stalely temples, so richly embellished, but above all, adorned with the spoils of vanquished enemies. But visit their own private habitations; visit the houses of Aristides, Miltiades, or any other of those patriots of antiquity; you will find nothing, not the least mark or ornament, to distinguish them from their neighbours. They took part in the government, not to enrich themselves, but the public; they had no scheme or ambition but tor the public; nor knew any interest, but for the public. It was by a close and steady application to the general good of their country, by an exemplary piety towards the immortal gods, by a strict faith and religious honesty betwixt man and man, and a moderation always uniform, and of a peace,

they established that reputation, which remanins to this day, and will last to utmost posterity.

Such, O men of Athens, were your ancestors; so glorious in the eye of the world; so bountiful and munificent to their country; so sparing, so modest, so self-denying to themselves. What resemblance can we find in the present generation, of these great men? At a time when your ancient competitors have left you a clear stage; 'when the Lacedemonians are disabled; the Thebans employed in troubles of their own; when no other state whatever is in a condition to rival or molest you; in short, when you are at full liberty; when you have the opportunity and the power to become once more the sole arbiters of Greece; you permit, patiently, whole provinces to be wrested from you; you lavish the public money in scandalous and obscure uses; you suffer your allies to perish in time of peace, whom you preserved in time of war: and to sum up all, you yourselves, by your mercenary court, and servile resignation to the will and pleasure of designing insidious leaders, abet, encourage and strengthen the most dangerous and formidable of your enemies. Yes, Athenians, I repeat it, you yourselves are the contrivers of your own ruin. Lives there a man who has confidence enough to deny it?—Let him arise and assign, if he can, any other cause of the success and prosperity of Philip. "But," you reply, "what Athens may have lost in reputation abroad, she has gained in splendor at home. Was there ever a greater appearance of prosperity? A greater face of plenty? Is not the city enlarged? Are not the streets better paved, houses repaired and beautified?" Away with such trifles; shall I be paid with counters? An old square new vamped up! A fountain! An Aqueduct! Are these acquisitions to brag of? Cast your eye upon the magistrate, under whose ministry you boast these precious improvements. Behold the despicable creature, raised, all at once, from dirt to oppulence; from the lowest obscurity to the highest honours. Have not some of these upstarts built private houses and seats, vieing with tbe most sumptuous of our public palaces? And how have their fortunes and their power increased, but as the commonwealth has been ruined and impoverished?

To what are we to impute these disorders? And to what cause assign the decay of a state, so powerful and flourishing in past times? The reasou is plain.—The servant is now become the master. The magistrate-was then subservient to the people; punishments and rewards were properties of the people; all honours, dignities and preferments, were disposed by the voice and favour of the people; but the magistrate now has usurped the right of the people, and exercises an arbitrary authority over his ancient and natural lord. You, miserable people! (the meanwhile without money, without friends) from being the ruler, are become the servant; from being the master, the dependent; happy that these governours, into whose hands you have thus resigned your own power, are so good and so gracious as to continue your poor allowance to see plays.

Believe me, Athenians, if recovering from this lethargy, you would assume the ancient freedom and spirit of your fathers; if you would be your own soldiers and your own commanders, confiding no longer your affairs in foreign or mercenary hands; if you would charge yourselves with your own defence, employing abroad, for the public, what you waste in unprofitable pleasures at home; the world might, once more, behold you making a figure worthy of Athenians. "You would have us then (you say) do service in our armies, in our own persons; and for so doing, you would have the pensions-we receive, in time of peace, accepted as pay in time of war. Is it thus we are to understand you?"—Yes, Athenians, 'tis my plain meaning,I would make it a standing rule, that no person, great or little, should be the better for the public money, who should grudge to employ it for the public service. Arewe in peace? The public is charged witkyour subsistence. Are we in war, or under a necessity at this time, to enter into a war? Let your gratitude oblige you. to accept, as jay, in

defence of your benefactors, what you receive, Ut peace, as mere bounty.—Thus, without ajay innovation; without altering or abolishing any thing, but pernicious novelties, introduced for the encouragement of sloth and idleness; by converting only, for the future, the same funds, for the use of the serviceable, which are spent, at present, upon the unprofitable; you may be well served in your armies; your troops regularly paid; justice duly administered; the public revenues reformed and increased; and every member of the commonwealth rendered useful to his country, according to his age and ability, without any further burthen to the state.

This, O men of Athens, is what my duty prompted me to represent to you upon this occasion. May the Gods inspire you, to determine upon such measures, as may be expedient for the particular and general good of oar country!

XII—*Jupiter to the inferiour Deities, forbidding them to take any part in the Contention between the Greeks and Trojans.*—Homer. AURORA, now, fair daughter of the dawn,
Sprinkled with rosy light the dewy lawn;
When Jove conven'd the senate of the skies,
Where high Olympus' cloudy tops arise.
The sire of gods his awful silence broke;
The heavens, attentive, trembled as he spoke:—
"Celestial states! Immortal gods! Give ear:
Hear our decree; and rev'rence what ye hear:
The fix'd decree, which not all heaven can move:
Thou fate fulfil it: and ye powers, approve.
What god shall enter yon forbidden field,
Who yields assistance or but wills to yield;
Back to the skies, with shame he shall be driven,
Gash'd with dishonest wounds, the scorn of heaven:
Or, from our sacred hill, with fury thrown,

Deep in the dark Tartarean gulf shall groan;
With burning chains fix'd to the brazen floors,
And lock'd by hell's inexorable doors:
As far beneath th' infernal centre hurl'd,
As from that centre to th' etherial world.
Let each, submissive, dread those dire abodes,
Nor tempt the vengeance of the god of gods.
League all your forces, then, ye powers above,
7
Your strength unite against the might of Jove-
Let down our golden everlasting chain,
Whose strong embrace holds heaven, and earth & main,
Strive all of mortal and immortal birth,
To drag, by this, the thund'rer down to earth.
Ye strive in vain. If I but stretch this hand,
I heave the gods, the ocean and the land.
I fix the chain to great Olympus' height,
And the vast world hangs trembling in my sight.
For such I reign unbounded and above:
And such are men, and gods, compar'd to Jove."

XIII.—*Mneas to Queen Dido, giving an Account of tht Sack of Troy.*—Virgil.

ALL were attentive to the godlike man,
When, from his lofty couch, he thus began:—
Great Queen! What you command me to relate
Renews the sad remembrance of our fate;
An empire from its old foundations rent,
And every woe the Trojans underwent;
A pop'lous city made a desert place;
All that I saw and part of which I was,
Not e'en the hardest of our foes could hear,
Nor stern Ulysses tell without a tear.
'Twas now the dead of night, when sleep repairs
Our bodies worn with toils, our mind with cares,
When Hector's ghost before my sight appears:
Shrouded in blood he stood, and bath'd

in tears:

Such as when, by the fierce Pelides slain,

Thessalian coursers dragg'd him o'er the plain.

Swoln were his feet, as when the thongs were thrust

Through the pierc'd limbs; his body black with dust.

Unlike that Hector, who, return'd from toils

Of war, triumphant, in yEacian spoils;

Or, him who made the fainting Greeks retire,

Hurling amidst their fleets the Phrygian fire.

His hair and beard were clotted stiff with gore;

The ghastly wounds he for his country bore,

Now stream'd afresh.

I wept to see the visionary man;

And, whilst my trance continued, thus began;

O light of Trojans, and support of Troy, Thy father's champion, and thy country's joy! O, long expected by thy friends! From whence Art thou so late return'd to our defence? Alas! what wounds are these? What new disgrace Deforms the manly honours of thy face?

The spectre groaning from his inmost breast, This warning, in these mournful words express'd.

"Haste, goddess born! Escape by timely flight, The flames and horrours of this fatal night, Thy foes already have possess'd our wall; Troy nods from high, and totters to her fall. Enough is paid to Priam's royal name, Enough to country, and to deathless fame. If by a mortal arm my father's throne Could have been sav'd—this arm the feat had done. Troy now commends to thee her future state, And gives her gods companions of her fate; Under their umbrage hope for happier walls, And follow where thy various fortune calls." He said, and brought from forth the sacred choir, The gods and relics of th' immortal fire.

Now peals of shouts came thund'ring from afar, Cries, threats, and loud lament, and mingled war. The noise approaches, though our palace stood

Aloof from streets, embosom'd close with wood; Louder and louder still I hear th' alarms Of human cries distinct, and clashing arms. Fear broke my slumbers. I mount the terrace.; thence tlte town survey, And listen what the swelling sounds convey. Then Hector's faith was manifestly clear'd; And Grecian fraud in open light appear'd.. The palace of Deipholus ascends In smokey flames, and catches on his friends. Ucalegon burns next; the seas are bright With splendours not their own, and shine with sparkling light. New clamours and new clangours now arise, The trumpets' voice, with agonizing cries. With phrenzy seiz'd, I run to meet th' alarms, Resolv'd on death, resolv'd to die in arms.

But first to gather friends, with whom t' oppose,

If fortune favour'd and repel the foes,

By courage rous'd, by love of country fir'd,

With sense of honour and revenge inspir'd.

Pantheus, Apollo's priest, a sacred name,

Had scap'd the Grecian swords and pass'd the flame:

With relics loaded, to my doors he fled,

And by the hand his tender grandson led.

"What hope, O Pantheus? Whither can we run?

Where make a stand? Or, What can yet be done!

Scarce had I spoke, when Pantheus, with a groan,

"Troy is no more! Her glories now are gone.

The fatal day, th' appointed hour is come,

When wrathful Jove's irrevocable doom Transfers the Trojan state to Grecian hands:

Our city's wrapt in flames; the foe commands.

To several posts their parties they divide;

Some block the narrow slreetsj some scour the wide;

The bold they kill; th' unwary they surprise;

Who fights meets death, and death finds

him who flies."

XIV.—*Moloch the fallen Angel, to the infernal powers, inciting them to renew the War*—Milton.

MY sentence is for open war. Of wiles More unexpert, I boast not; then let those

Contrive who need c or when they need, not now.

For while they sit contriving, shall the rest,

Millions that stand in arms, and longing wait

The signal to ascend, sit ling'ring here,

Heav'ns fugitives, and for their dwelling place

Accept this dark opprobrious den of shame,

The prison of his tyranny, who reigns By our delay? No; let us rather choose,

Arm'd with hell flames and fury, all at once,

O'er heaven's high towers to force resistless way,

Turning our tortures into horrid arms,

Against the tori'rer; when, to meet the noise

Of his almighty engine, he shall hear Infernal thunder; and, for lightning, see

Black fire and horrour shot with equal rage

Among his angels—and his throne itself,

Mix'd with Tartarean sulphur and strange fire,

His own invented torments. But perhaps,

The way seems difficult and steep to scale,

With upright wing, against a higher foe.

Let such bethink them, if the sleepy drench

Of that forgetful lake benumb not still,

That in our proper motion we ascend

Up to our native seat; descent and fall

To us is adverse. Who but felt of late,

When the fierce foe hung on our broken rear

Insulting, and pursued us through the deep,

With what compulsion and laborious flight,

We sunk thus low? Th' ascent is easy

then.

Th' event is fear'd. Should we again provoke

Our stronger, some worse way his wrath may find,

To our destruction; if there be in hell,

Fear to be worse destroy'd: What can be worse

Than to dwell here, driven out from bliss, condemn'd

In this abhorred deep to utter woe;

Where pain of unextinguishable fire,

Must exercise us without hope of end,.

The vassals of his anger, when the scourge

Inexorable, and the tort'ring hour

Calls us to penance? More destroy'd than thus

We should be quite abolish'd and expire.

What fear we then? What doubt we to incense

His utmost ire? Which to the height enrag'd,

Will either quite consume us, and reduce

To nothing this essential, (happier far,

Than miserable, to have eternal being)

Ot if our substance be indeed divine,

And cannot cease to be, we are at worst

On this side nothing; and by proof we feel

Our power sufficient to disturb this heaven,

And with perpetual inroads to alarm,

Though inaccessible, his fatal throne;

Which, if not victory, is yet revenge.

XV—*Speech of Belial, advising Pence.*
—Ir. I SHOULD be much for open war, O peers,

As not behind in hate, if what was urg'd

Main reason to persuade immediate war,

Did not dissuade the most, and seem to cast

Ominous conjecture on the whole success;

When he who most excels in feats of arms,

In what he counsels, and in what excels,

Mistrustful, grounds his courage on despair

And utter dissolution, as the scope

Of all his aim, after some dire revenge.

First, what revenge? The towers of heaven are fiU'd

With armed watch, that render all access

Impregnable; oft on the bordering deep

Incamp their legions; or, with obscure wing,

Scout far and wide, into the realm of night,

Scorning surprise. Or could we break our way

By force, and at our heels all hell should rise

With blackest insurrection, to confound

Heaven's purest light—yet our great enemy,

All incorruptible, would on his throne,

Sit unpolluted; and the etherial mould,'

Incapable of stain, would soon expel

Her mischief, and purge off (he baser fire,

Victorious. Thus repuls'd, our final hope

Is fiat despair. We must exasperate

Th' almighty victor to spend all his rage,

And that must end us; that must be our cure,

Te be no more. Sad fate! For who would lose,

Though full of pain, this intellectual being,

Those thoughts that wander through eternity,

To perish rather, swallow'd up and lost

In the wide womb of uncreated night,

Devoid of sense and motion? And who knows,

Let this be good, whether our angry foe

Can give it, or will ever? How he can,

Is doubtful; that he never will is sure.

Will he, so wise, let loose at once his ire,

Belike through impotence, or unaware,

To give his enemies their wish, and end

Them in his anger, whom his anger saves

To punish endless? Wherefore cease we then?

Say they who counsel war, we are decreed,

Reserv'd and destin'd to eternal woe;

Whatever doing, what can suffer more.,

What can we suffer worse? Is this then worst,

Thus sitting, thus consulting, thus in arms?

What when we fled amain, pursued and struck-With heaven's afflicting thunder, and besought The deep to shelter us? This hell then seem'd A refuge from those wounds; or when we lay Chain'd on the burning lake? That sure was worse. What if the breath that kindled those grim fires, Awak'd should blow them into sevenfold rage, And plunge us in the flames? or from above Should intermitted vengeance arm again His red right hand to plague us? What if all Her stores were open'd and this Armament Of hell should spout her cataracts of fire. Impendent horrours, threat'ning hideous fall One day upon our heads; while we, perhapsDesigning or exhorting glorious war, Caught in a fiery tempest, shall be hurl'd Each on his rock transfix'd, the sport and prey Of wrecking whirlwinds, or forever sunk Under yon boiling ocean, wrapt in chains; There to converse with everlasting groans, Unrespited, unpitied, unspriev'd, Ages of hopeless end! This would be worse, War, therefore, open or conceal'd, alike My voice dissuades.

SECTION V. TIC PIECES.

I. DIALOGUES.

I,—*Belcottr and Stockwell.*—West Indian. *Stockw.* MR. BELCOUR, I am rejoiced to see you; you are welcome to England.

Bel. I thank you heartily, good Mr. Stockwell. You and I have long conversed at a distance; now we are met; and the pleasure this meeting gives me, amply compensates for the perils I have run through in accomplishing it. *Stock.*

What perils, Mr. Belcour? I could not have thought you would have met with a bad passage at this time o'year. *Bel.* Nor did we. Courier like, we came posting to your shores, upon the pinions of the swiftest gales that ever blew. It is upon English ground all my difficulties have arisen; it is the passage from the river side I complain of. *Stock.* Indeed! What obstructions can you have met between this and the river side? *Bel.* Innumerable! Your town's as full of defiles as the island of Corsica; and I believe they are as obstinately defended. So much hurry, bustle and confusion on your quays 5 so many sugar casks, porter butts and common council men in your streets; that unless a man marched with artillery in his front, it is more than the labour of an Hercules can effect, to make any tolerable way through your town. *Stock.* I am sorry you have been so incommoded. *Bel.* Why, truly it was all my own fault. Accustomed to a land ofslaves, and out of patience with the whole tribe of customhouse extortioners, boatmen, tidewaiters and waterbailiffs, that beset me on all sides, worse than a swarm of moschettoes, I proceeded a little too roughly to brush them away with my ratan. The sturdy rogues took this ia dudgeon; and beginning to rebel, the mob chose different sides, and a furious scuffle ensued; in the course of which, my person and apparel suffered so much, that I was obliged to step into the first tavern to refit, before I could make my approaches in any decent trim. *Slock.* Well, Mr. Belcour, it is a rough sample you have had of my countrymen's spirit; but I trust you will not think the worse of them for it. *Bel.* Not at all, not at all: I like them the better.— Were I only a visitor, I might perhaps wish them a little more tractable; but, as a fellow subject, and a sharer in their freedom, I applaud their spirit— though I feel the effects of it in every bone in my skin. Well, Mr. Stockwell, for the first time in my life, here am 1 in England; at the fountain head of pleasure; in the land of beauty, of arts and elegancies. My happy stars have given me a good estate, and the conspiring winds have blown me hither to spend

it. *Slock.* To use it, not to waste it, I should hope; to treat it, Mr. Belcour, not as a vassal over whom you have a wanton despotic power, but as a subject whom you are bound to govern with a temperate and restrained authority. *Bel.* True, Sir, most truly said; mine's a commission, not a right; I am the offspring of distress, and every child of sorrow is my brother. While I have hands to hold, therefore, I will hold them open to mankind. But Sir, my passions are my masters; they take me where they will; and oftentimes they leave to reason and virtue, nothing but my wishes and my sighs. *Stock.* Come, come, the man who can accuse, corrects himself. *Bel.* Ah I That is an office I am weary of. I wish a friend would take it up; I would to heaven you had leisure for the employ. But did you drive a trade to the four corners of the world, you would not find the task so toilsome as to keep me from faults. *Stock.* Well, I am not discouraged. This candour tells me I should not have the fault of selfconceit to combat; that, at least, is not amongst the number. *Bel-*No; if I knew that man on earth who thought more humbly of me than I do of myself, I would take his opinion, and forego my own. *Stock.* And were I to choose a pupil, it should be one of your complexion: so if you will come along with me, we will agree upon your admission, and enter upon a course of lectures directly. *Bel.* With all my heart. II.
—*Lady Tuimly and Lady Grace*—
Provoked Husband. *Lady T.* OH, my dear Lady Grace! How could you leave me so unmercifully alone all this while? *Lady G.* I thought my Lord had been with you. *Lady T.* Why, yes—and therefore I wanted your relief; for he has been in such a fluster here *Lady G.* Biess me! For what? *Lady T.* Only our usual breakfast; we have each of us had our dish of matrimonial comfort this morning—we have been charming company. *Lady G.* I am mighty glad of it; sure it must be a vast happiness, when man and wife can give themselves the same turn of conversation! *Jjidy T.* Oh, the prettiest thing in the world! *Lady G.* Now I should be afraid, that where two people are every day togeth-

er so, they must be often in want of something to talk upon. *Lady T.* Oh, my dear, you are the most mistaken in the world! Married people have things to talk of, child, thatj never enter into the imagination of others. Why, here's my Loid and I, now; we have not been married above two short years, you know, and we have already eight or ten things constantly in hank, that whenever we want company, we can take up any one of them for two hours together, and the subject never the flatter; nay, if we have occasion for it, it will be-as fresh next day too, as it was the first hour it entertained us.' *Lady G.* Certainly that must be vastly pretty. *Lady T.* Oh, there's no life like it! Why, t'other day, for example, when you dined abroad, my Lord and I, after a pretty cheerful *tete a teU* meal, sat us down by the fire side, in an easy, indolent, pick tooth way, for about a quarter of an hour,as if we had not thought of one another's being in the room.—At last, stretching himself and yawning—My dear, says he——aw you came home very late last night. 'Twas but just turned of two, says I. 1 was in bed aw-by eleven says he. So you are every night, says I Well, says he, I am amazed you can sit up so late. How can you be amazed, says J, at a thing that happens so often? Upon which we entered into a conversation—and though this is a point that has entertained us above fifty times already, We always find so many pretty new things to say upon it, that I believe in my soul it will last as long as I liye.
Lady G. But pray, in such sort of family dialogues, (thougli extremely well for passing the time) does'nt there now and then enter some little witty sort of bitterness? *Lady T.* Oh yes! Which does not do amiss at all. A smart repartee, with a zest of recrimination at the head of it, makes the prettiest sherbert. Aye, aye, if we did not mix a little of the acid with it, a matrimonial society would be so Jusc'ous, that nothing but an old liquorish prude would be able to bear it. *Lady G.* Well, certainly you have the most elegant taste *Lady T.* Though to tell you the truth, my dear, 1 rather think we squeezed a little too much lemon into

it this bout; for it grew so sour at last, that I think 1 almost told him he was a fool ami he again talked something oddly of turning me out of doors. *Lady G.* Oh! Have a care of that. *Lady T.* Nay, if he should, I may thank my own wise father for it. *Lady* G. How so-? *Lady* T. Why, when my good Lord-first opened his honorable trenches before me, my unaccountable papa, in whose hands I then was, gave me up at discretion*Lady G.* How do you mean? *Lady T.* He said ilie wives of this age were come to that pass, that Ire would not desire even his own daughter should be trusted with pinmoney; so that my whole train of separate inclinations are left entirely at the mercy of a htigbaad's odd humour. » *Lady G.* Why, tliat indeed is enough to make a woman of spirit look about her. *Lady T-.* Nay, but to be serious, my dear—What would you really have a woman do in my case? *Lady G.* Why if I had a sober husband as you have, I would make myself the happiest wife in the world, by being as sober as he. *Lady T.* Oh, you wicked thing! How can you teaze one at this rate, when you know he is so very sober that (except giving me money) there is not one thidg in the world he can do to please me. And I, at the same lime, partly by nature, and partly, perhaps, by keeping the best company, do with my soul love almost every thing he hates. I dote upon assemblies; my heart bounds at a ball, and at an opera—I expire. Then I love play to distraction; cards enchant me—and Bice—put me out of my little wits. Dear, dear hazard! O what a flow of spirits it gives one! Do you never play at hazard, child? *Lady G.* Oh, never! I dont think it sits well upon women; there's something so masculine, so much the air of a rake in it. You see how it makes the men swear and curse; and when a woman is thrown into the same passion—why— *Lady T.* That's very true; one is a little put to it, sometimes, not to make use of the same words to express it. *Lady G.* Well, and upon ill luck, pray what words are you really forced to make use of? *Lady f.* Why, upon a very hard case, indeed, when a sad wrong word is rising just to one's tongue's

end, I give a great gulph and—swallow it. *Lady G.* Well—and is it not enough to make you forswear play as long as you live? *Lady T.* Oh yes: I have forsworn it. *Lady G.* Seriously? *Lady T.* Solemnly, a thousand times; but then one is constantly forsworn. *Lady G.* And how can you answer that? *Lady T.* My dear, what v.e say when we are losers, we look upon to be no more binding than a lover's oath, or a great man's promise. But I beg pardon, child: I should not lead you so far into the world; you are a prude, and design to live soberly. *Lady G.* Why, I confess my nature and my education do in a good degree confine me that way. *Lady T.* Well, how a woman of spirit (for you don't want that, child,) can dream of living soberly, is to me inconceivable; for you will marry, I suppose. *Lady G.* I can'l tell but I may. *Lady T.* And wont you live in town? *Lady G.* Half the year I should like it very well. *Lady T.* My stars! And you would really live in London half the year, to be sober in it J *Lady G.* Why not? *Lady T.* Why can't you as well go and be sober in the country? *Lady G.* So I would—t'other half year. *Lady T.* And pray, What comfortable scheme of life would you form now for your summer and winter sober entertainments? -*Lady G.* A scheme that I think might very well content us. *Lady T.* Oh, of all things, let's hear it. *Lady G.* Why, in summer I could pass my leisure hours in riding, in reading, walking by a canal, or sitting at the end of it under a great tree; in dressing, dining, chatting with an agreeable friend; perhaps hearing a little music, taking a dish of tea, or a game at cards—soberly; managing my family, looking into its accounts, playing with my children, if I had any; or in a thousand other innocent amusements—soberly; and possibly by these means, I might induce my husband to be as sober as myself. *Lady T.* Well, my dear, thou art an astonishing creature! For such primitive antediluvian notions of life have have not been in any head these thousand years. Under a great tree I ha! ha! ha! But I beg we may have the sober town scheme too—for I am charmed with the country one.

Lady G. You shall, and 1211 try to stick to my sobriety there too. *Lady T.* Well, though I am sure it will give me the vapours, I must hear it. *Lady G.* Wei, then, for fear of your fainting, madam, I will rust so far come into the fashion, that I would never be dressed out of it—but still it should be soberly; for I can't think it any disgrace to a woman of my private fortune not to wear her lace as fine as the wedding suit of a first dutchess; though there is one extravagance I would venture to come up to. *Lady T.* Ay, now for it *Lady G.* I would every day be as clean as a bride. *Lady T.* Wh3', the men say that's a great step to be made one.-Well, now you are drest, pray let's see to what purpose. *Lady G.* I would visit—that is, my real friends;—but as little for form as possible.—I would go to court; sometimes to an assembly, nay, play at quadrille—soberly. I would see all ihe good plays; and because 'tis the fashion, now and then go to an opera; but I would not expire there—for fear I should never go again. And lastly, I can't say, but for curiosity, if I liked my company, Imight be drawn in once to a masquerade; and this, I think, is far as a woman can go—soberly. *Lady T.* Well, if it had not been for that last piece of sobriety, I was just agoing to call for some surfeit water. *Lady G.* Why, don't you think, with the farther aid of breakfasting, dining, taking the air, supping, sleeping, (not to say a word of devotion) the four and twenty hours might roll over in a tolerable manner? *Lady* T. Tolerable? Deplorable! Why, child, all you propose is but to endure life; now, I want—to enjoy it. III.—*Priuli and Jaffier.*—Venice Preserved.

Pri. NO more! I'll hear no more! Begone, and leave me.

Jaff. Not hear me? By my sufferings, but you shall!

My lord, my lord! I'm not that abject wretch

You think me. Patience! Where's the distance throws

Me back so far, but I may boldly speak

In right, though proud oppression will not hear me?

Pri. Have you not wronged me?

-» *Jaff.* Could my nature e'er
Have brook'd injustice, or the doing wrong,
I need not now thus low have bent my-self,
To gain a hearing from a cruel fatber.
Wrong'd you?
Pri. Yes, wrong'd me. In the nicest point,
The honour of my house, you've done me wrong.
When you first came home from travel,
With such hope6 as made you look'd on,
By all men's eyes a youth of expecta-tion,
Pleas'd with your seeming virtue, I re-ceiv'd you;
Courted and sought to raise you to your merits!
My house, my table, nay my fortune too,
My very self was yours; you might have us'd me
To your best service; like an open friend
I treated, trusted you, and thought you mine:
When in requital of my best endeav-ours,
You treacherously practis'd to undo me;
Seduc'd the weakness of my age's dar-ling,
My only child, and stole her from my bosom.
Jaff. 'Tis to me you owe her;
Childless you had been else, and in the grave
Your name extinct; no more Priuli heard of.
You may remember, scarce five years are past,
Since, in 3'our brigantine, you sail'd to see
The Adriatic wedded by our duke;
And I was with you. Your unskilful pi-lot
Dash'd us upon a rock; when to your boat
You made for safety; entered first your-self;
Th' affrighted Belvidera, following next,
As she stood trembling on the vessel's side,
Was by a wave wash'd off into the deep;
When, instantly, I plung'd into the sea,
And, buffeting the billows to her rescue,
Redeem'd her life with half the loss of mine;
Like a rich conquest, in one hand I bore her,
And with the other dash'd the saucy-vaves,
That throng'd and press'd to rob me of my prize.
I brought her; gave her to your despair-ing arms;
Indeed, you thank'd me; but a nobler gratitude
Rose in her soul; for, from that hour she lov'd me,
Till, for her life, she paid me with her-self.
Pri. You stole her from me; like a thief you stole her
At dead of night; that cursed hour you chose
To rifle me of all my heart held dear.
May all your joys in her prove false as mine j
A sterile fortune and a barren bed
Attend you both; continual discord make
Your days and nights bitter and griev-ous still:
May the hard hand of a vexatious need
Oppress and grind you; till, at last, you find
The curse of disobedience all your por-tion.
Jaff. Half of your curse you have be-stow'd in vain:
Heaven has already crown'd our faith-ful loves
With a young boy, sweet as his moth-er's beauty.
May he live to prove more gentle than his grandsire,
And happier than his father.
Fri. Mo more.
Jaff. Yes, all; and then—adieu forever.
There's not a wretch that lives on com-mon charily
But's happier than I; for I have known
The luscious sweets of plenty; every night
Have slept with soft content about my head,
And never wak'd but to a joyful morn-ing;
Yet now must fall; like a full ear of corn,
Whose blossom 'scap'd, yet's wither'd in the ripening.
Pri. Home and be humble, study to re-trench;
Discharge the lazy vermin of thy hall,
Those pageants of thy folly;
Bet ice the glitt'ring trappings of thy wife,
To humble weeds, fit for thy little state:
Then to soane suburb cottage both re-tire:
Drudge to feed a loathsome life.
Home, home, I say.— *Exit.*
Jaff. Yes, if my heart would let me—
This proud, this swelling heart, home would I go,
But that my doors are hateful to my eyes,
Fill'd and damm'd up with gaping cred-itors.
I've now not fifty dwats in the world;
Yet still I am in love, and pleas'd with ruin.
Oh, Belvidera! Oh! She is my wife—
And we will bear our wayward fate to-gether—
But ne'er know comfort more.
IV.—*Boniface and Mmtvelh—EAvx* Stratagem. *Bon.* THIS way, this way, Sir.
Aim. Your'e my landlord, I suppose.
'*Bon.* Ves, Sir, I'm old Will Boniface; pretty well known upon this road, as the saying is. *Aim.* 0, Mr. Boniface, your servant. *Bon.* O, Sir—What will your honour please to drink, as the saying is? *Aim.* I have heard your town of Litch-field much famed for ale; I think I'll taste that. *Bon.* Sir I have now in my cellar ten tun of the best ale in Stafford-shire; 'tis smooth as oil, sweet as milk, clear as amber, and strong as brandy; and will be just fourteen years old on the fifth day of next March, old style. *Aim.* You're very exact, I find, in the age of your ale. *Bon.* As punctual, Sir, as I am in the age of my children:— I'll show you such ale!—Here, tapster, broach number 1706, as the saying is.— Sir, you shall taste my *anno domini.*— I have lived in Litchfield, man and boy, above eight and fifty years, and I be-lieve, have not consumed eight and fifty

ounces of meat. *Aim.* At a meal,.you mean, if one may guess by ylur bulk. *Bon.* Not in my life, Sir: I have fed pure-ly upon ale: I have eat my ale, drank ray ale, and I always sleep upon ale. *Enter tapster, with a tankard.*

Now, Sir, you shall see. Your worship's health: *drinks*

—Ha! Delicious, delicious! Fancy it Burgundy, only fancy it—and 'tis worth ten shillings a quart.

Aim. drinks 'Tis confounded strong. *Bon.* Strong! It must be so, or how should we be strong that drin k it! *Aim.* And have you lived so long upon this ale, landlord? *Bon.* Eight and fifty years upon my credit, Sir; but it killed my wife, poor woman, as the saying is. *Aim.* How came that to pass! *Bon.* I don't know how, Sir—She would not let the ale take its natural course, Sir; she was for qualifying it every now and then with a dram, as the saying is; and an honest gentleman, that came this way from Ireland, made her a present of a dozen bottles of usquebaugh—but the poor woman was never well after—but, however, I was obliged to the gentle-man, you know. *Aim.* Why, Was it the usquebaugh that killed her? *Bon.* My la-dy Bountiful said so—she, good lady, did what could be done 5 she cured her of hree tympanies— but the fourth car-ried her off. But she's happy, and I'm contented, as the saying is. *Aim.* Who is that lady Bountiful you mentioned? *Bon.* Odd's-my life, Sir, we'll drink her health:—*drinks* —My lady Bountiful is one of the best of women. Her last hus-band, Sir Charles Bountiful, left her worth a thousand pounds a year; and I believe she lays out one half on't in charitable uses, for the good of her neighbours. *Aim.* Has the lady been any other way useful in her generation? *Bon.* Yes, Sir, she has had a daughter by Sir Charles— the finest woman in all our country, and the greatest fortune. She has a son too, by her first husband; 'squire Sullen, who married a fine lady from London t'other day; if you please, Sir, we'll drink his health, *drinks' Aim.* What sort of a man is he? *Bon.* Why, Sir, the man's well enough; says little, 'Iiinks less, and does—nothing at all,

faith; but he's a man of great estate, and values nobody. *Aim.* A sportsman, I suppose! *Bon.* Yes, he's a man of plea-sure; he plays at whist, and smokes his pipe eight and forty hours together sometire es. *Aim.* A fine sportsman tru-ly!—and married, you say? *Bon.* Ay; and to a curious woman, Sir—But he's my landlord; and so a man, you know, would not Sir, my humble service to you. *drinks.*—Though I value not a far-thing what he can do to me; I pay him his rent at quarter day: I have a good running trade—I have but one daughter, and I can give her but no matter for that. *Aim.* You're very happy, Mr. Boniface; pray What other company have you in town? *Bon.* A power of fine ladies; and then we have the French Officers. *Aim.* O, that's right, you have a good many of those gentlemen: Pray how do you like their company? *Bon.* So well as the say-ing is, that I could wish we had as many more of them. They're full of money, and pay double for every thing they have. They know, Sir, that we paid good round taxes for the taking of 'em;—and so they are willing to reimburse us a lit-tle; one of 'em lodges in my house. *Bell rings'—I* beg your worship's pardor. I'll wait on you again in half a minute

V.—*Lovegold and Lappet.*—Miser. *Love.* ALL's well hitherto; my dear mon-ey is safe.— Is it you Lappet?

Lap. I should rather ask if it be you, Sir: why, you look so young and vigor-ous *Love.* Do I? Do I? *Lap.* Why, you grow younger and younger every day, Sir; you never looked half so young in your life, Sir, as you do now. Why, Sir, I know fifty young fellows of five and twenty, that are older than you are. *Love.* That may be, that may be, Lappet, considering the lives they lead; and yet I am a good ten years above fifty. *Lap.* Well, and what's ten years above fifty? 'tis the very flower of a man's age. Why, Sir, you are now in the very prime of your life. *Love.* Very true, that's very true, as to understanding; but I am afraid, could I take off twenty years, it would do me no harm with the ladies, Lappet.—How goes on our affair with Marianna? Have you mentioned any thing about what her mother can give

her? For uowadays nobody marries a woman, unless she bring something with her besides a petticoat. *Lap.* Sir, why, Sir, this young lady will be worth to you as good a thousand pounds a year, as ever was told. *Love.* How! A thousand pounds a year? *Lap.* Yes, Sir. There's in the first place, the article of a table; she has a very little stomach:— she does not eat above an ounce in a fortnight; and, then, as to the quality of what she eats, you'll have no need of a French cook upon her account. As for sweetmeats she mortally hates them; so there is the article of desserts wiped off all at once. You'll have no need of a confectioner, who would be eternally bringing iu bills for preserves, con-serves, biscuits, comfits, and jellies, of which half a dozen ladies would swal-low you ten pounds worth at a meal. This, I think, we may very moderately reckon at two hundred pounds a year at least. For clothes, she has been bred up at such a plainness in them, that should we allow but for three birthnight suits in a year, saved, which are the least a town lady would expect, there go a good two hundred pounds a year more.—For jew-els (of which she hatesthe very sight) the yearly interest of what you must lay out in them would amount to one hun-dred pounds.—Lastly, she has an'utter detestation for play, at which I have known several moderate ladies lose a good two thousand pounds a year. No, let us take only the fourth part of that, which amounted to five hundred, to which if we add two hundred pounds on the table account, two hundred pounds in clothes, and one hundred pounds in jewels— there is, Sir, your two thou-sand pounds a year, in hard money. *Love.* Ay, ay, these are pretty things, it must be confessed, very pretty things; but there is nothing real in them. *Lap.* How, Sir! is it not something real to bring you a vast store of sobriety, the inheritance of a love for simplicity of dress, and a vast acquired fund of hatred for play? *Love.* This is downright raillery, Lappet, to make me up a for-tune out of the expenses she won't put me to.— But there is another thing that disturbs me. You know this girl is young, and young people generally love one another's company; it would ill agree with a person of my temper to keep an assembly for all the young rakes, and flaunting girls in town. *Lap.* Ah, Sir, how little do you know of her! This is another particularity that I had to tell you of;—she has a most terrible aversion to young people, and loves none but persons of your years. I would advise you, above all things, to take care not to appear too young. She insists on sixty, at least. She says that fifty six years are not able to content her. *Love.* This humour is a little strange, me-thinks. *Lap.* She carries it further, Sir, than can be imagined. She has in her chamber several pictures; but, what do 3'ou think they are? None of your smoothfaced young fellows, your Adonises, your Parises and your Appollos: No, Sir, you see nothing there, but your handsome figures of Saturn, king Priam, old Nestor, and good father Aiichises upon his son's shoulders. *Love.* Admirable! This is more than I could have hoped; to say the truth, had I been a woman, I should never have loved young fellows. *Lap.* I believe you: pretty sort of stuff, indeed, to be in love with your young fellows! Pretty masters, indeed, with their fine complexions, and their fine feathers! *Love.* And do you really think me pretty tolerable? *Lap.* Tolerable! you are ravishing: If your picture was drawn by a good hand, Sir, it would be invaluable! Turn about a little, if you please—there, what can be more charming? Let me see you walk—there's a person for you; tall, straight, free and degagee; Why, Sir, you have no fault about you. *Love.* Not many—hem—hem—not many, I thank heaven; only a few rheumatic pains now and then, and a small catarrh that seizes me sometimes. *Lap.* Ah, Sir, that's nothing; your catarrh sits very well upon you, and you cough with a very good grace. *Love.* But tell me, What does Marianna say of my person? *Lap.* She has a particular pleasure in talking of it; and I assure you Sir, I have not been backward, on all sucli occasions, to blazon forth your merit, and to make her sensible how advantageous a match you will be to her? *Love.* You did very well and I am obliged to you. *Lap.* But, Sir, I have a small favour to ask of you;—I have a lawsuit depending, which I am on the very brink of losing, for want of a little money; *He looks gravely* and you could easily procure my success, if you had the least friendship for me.—You can't imagine, Sir, the pleasure she takes in talking of you: *He looks pleased* Ah! how you will delight her, how your venerable mien will charm her! She will never be able to withstand you.———But, indeed, Sir, this lawsuit will be a terrible consequence to me; *lie laoks grave again* I am ruined if I loose it; which a very small matter might prevent—ah! Sir, had you but seen the raptures with which she heard me talk of you. *He resumes his gaiety* How pleasure sparkled in her eyes at'the recital of your good qualities! In short, to discover a secret to yoa, which I promised to conceal, I have worked up her imagination till she is downright impatient of having the match concluded. *Love.* Lappet, you have acted a very friendly part; and I own that I have all the obligations in the world to you. *Lap.* 1 beg you would give me this little assistance, Sir; He *looks* serious It will set me on my feet, and I sliall be eternally obliged to you. *Love.* Farewell; I'll go and finish my dispatches. *Lap.* I assure you, Sir, you could never assist me in a greater necessity. *Love.* 1 must give some orders about a particular affair. *Lap.* I would not importune you, Sir, if I was not forced by the last extremity. *Lave.* I expect the tailor, about turning my coat;— don't you thiok this coat will look well enough turned, and with new buttons, for a wedding suit? *Lap.* For pita's sake, Sir, don't refuse me this small favor: I shall be undone, indeed, Sir. If it were but so small a matter as ten pounds, Sir *Love.* I think I hear the tailor's voice. *Lap.* If it were but five pounds, Sir; but three pounds, Sir; nay, Sir, a single guinea would be of service for a day or two. *As he offers to go out on cither side, she intercepts him.* *Love.* 1 must go, I can't stay hark, there! Somebody calls me—1 am very much obliged to you, indeed; J am very much obliged to you. *Lap.* Go to the devil, like a covetous good for nothing villain as you are. Ramile is in the right; however, I shall not quit the affair; for though I get nothing out of him, I am sure of my reward from the other side. VI.—*Cardinal Wolsey and Cromwell.*—Henry VIII. *Wol.* FAREWELL, a long farewell to all my greatness! This is the state of man; to day he puts forth The tender leaves of hope; tomorrow blossoms, And bears his blushing honours thick upon him; The third day comes a frost, a killing frost, And when he thinks, good easy man, full surely His greatness is a ripening, nips his shoot—— And then he falls, as I do. I have ventur'd, Like little wanton boys that swim on bladders, These many summers in a sea of glory; But far beyond my depth; my high blown pride At length broke under me-; and now has left me,

Weary and old with service, to the mercy

Of a rude stream that must forever hide me.

Vain pomp and glory of the world, 1 hate ye!

I feel my heart new open'd. Oh, how wretched

Is that poor man that hangs on princes' favours!

There is, betwixt that smile he would aspire to,

That sweet regard of princes, and his ruin,

More pangs and fears than war or women have;

And when he falls, he falls like Lucifer,

Never to hope again. *Enter* Cromwell.

Why, how now, Cromwell?

Crom. I have no power to speak, Sir. *Wol.* What, amaz'd

At my misfortunes? Can thy spirit wonder

A great man should decline? Nay if you weep,

I'm fallen indeed

Crom. How does your grace? *Wol.* Why, well;

Never so truly happy, my good Cromwell.

I know myself now, and 1 feel within

me
A peace above all earthly dignities;
A still and quiet conscience. The king has cur'd me,
I humbly thank his Grace j and from these shoulders,
These ruined pillars, but of pity taken
A load would sink a navy, too much honour.
Oh, 'tis a burden, Cromwell, 'tis a burden
Too heavy for a man that hopes for heaven!
Crom. I'm glad your grace has made that right use of iU *Wol.* I hope I have:
I'm able, now, naethinks,
Out of a fortitude of soul 1 feel,
T' endure more miseries, and greater far,
Than my weak heai ted enemies dare offer.
What news abroad?
Crom. The heaviest and the worst
Is vour displeasure with the king.
Wol. God bless him! *Crom.* The next is, that Sir Thomas Moore is chosen Lord Chancellor in your place. *Wol,* That's somewhat sudden
But he's a learned man. May he continue
　　Long in his highness' favour, and do justice,
　　For truth's sake and his conscience; that his bones,
　　When he has run his course, and sleeps in blessings,
May have a tomb of orphan's tears wept on him!
What more?
Crom. That Cranmer is return'd with welcome;
Installed Lord Archbishop of Canterbury.
Wol. That's news indeed!
Crom. Last, that the Lady Anne,
Whom the king hath in secrecy long married,
This day was view'd in open as his queen,
Going to chapel! and the voice is now
Only about her coronation.
Wol. There was the weight that pull'd me down: 0
Cromwell!
The king has gone beyond me; all my

glories
In that one woman I have lost forever.
No sun shall ever usher forth my honours,
Or gild again the noble troops that waited
Upon my smiles. Go, get thee from me, Cromwell;
I am a poor fall'n man, unworthy now
To be thy lord and master, seek the king—
(That sun, I pray, may never set;) I've told him
What and how true thou art; he will advance thee;
Some little memory of me will stir him,
(I know his noble nature) not to let
Thy hopeful service perish too. Good Cromwell;
Neglect him not; make use now and provide
For thine own future safety.
Crom. Oh, my lord!
Must I then leave you? Must I needs forego
So good, so noble, and so true a master?
Bear witness, all that have not hearts of iron,
With what a sorrow Cromwell leaves his lord!
The king shall have my service; but my prayers,
Forever and forever shall be yours.
Wol. Cromwell—I did not think to shed a tear
In all my miseries—but thou hast forc'd me,
Out of thy honest truth, to play the woman
　　Let's dry our tears; and thus far hear me, Cromwell;
And when I am forgotten as I shall be,
And sleep in dull cold marble, where no mention
Of me must more be heard—say then, I taught thee:
Say, Wolsey, that once rode the waves of glory,
　　And sounded all the depths and shoals of honour,
　　Found thee a way, out of his wreck, to rise in;
　　A sure and safe one, though thy master raiss'd it.
　　Mark but my fall, and that which ru-

ined me.
　　Cromwell, I charge thee, fling away ambition:
　　By that sin fell the angels; how can man, then, (though the image of his maker) hope-to win by't?
　　Love thyself last; cherish those hearts that wait thee:
　　Corruption wins not more than honesty.
　　Still in thy right had carry gentle peace,
　　To silence envious tongues. Be just and fear not.
　　Let all the ends thou aim'st at be thy country's,
　　Thy God's and truth's; then, if thou fall'st, O Cromwell,
　　Thou fall's! a blessed martyr. Serve the king
　　And pri'thee lead me in
　　There take an inventory of all I have;
　　To the last penny, 'tis the king's. My robe,
　　And mine integrity to heaven is all 1 dare now call my own. Oh, Cromwell, Cromwell!
　　Had I but serv'd my God with half the zeal
　　I serv'd my king—he would not in mine age
　　Have left me naked to mine enemies.
Crom. Good Sir, have patience. *Wol.* So I'have. Farewell
The hopes of court! My hopes in heaven do dwell.

V1I.—*Sir Charles and Lady Racket.*—
　　Three Weeks After Marriage. *Lady R.* O LA! I'm quite fatigued—I can hardly move Why don't you help me you barbarous man?
Sir C. There—take my arrri *Lady R.* But I wont be laughed at 1 don't love you.
Sir C. Dont you? *Lady R.* No. Dear me!
This glove! Why don't you help me off with my glove? Pshaw! You awkard thing; let it alone; you an't fit to be about me. Reach me a chair—you have no compassion for me-"-I am so glad to sit down—Why do you drag me to routs?—You know I hate e'm. *Sir C.* Oh! There's no existing, no breathing, unless one does as other people of fashion do. *Lady R.* But I'm out of humour—I lost all my money. *Sir* CL How

much? *Lady R.* Three hundred. *Sir C.* Never fret for that—I don't value three hundred pounds, to contribute to your happiness. *Lady R.* Don't you? Not value three hundred pounds to please me? *Sir C.* You know I don't. *Lady R.* Ah! You fond fool!—But I hate gaming—It almost metamorphoses a woman into a fury.—Do you kuow that I was frighted at myself several times tonight? I had a huge oath at the very lip of my tongue. *Sir C.* Had you? *Lady R.* I caught myself at it—and so I bit my lips. And then 1 was crammed up in a corner of the room, with such a strange party, at a whist table, looking at black and red spots—Did you mind 'em? *Sir C.* You know I was busy elsewhere. *Lady R.* There was that strange unaccountable woman, Mrs. Nightshade. She behaved so strangely to her husband—a poor, inoffensive, goodnatured, good sort of a good for nothing kind of a man.— But she so teazed him— "How could you' play that card? Ah, youv'e a head, and so has a pin.—You're a numskull, you know you are— Ma'am he's the poorest head in the world;—he does not know what he is about; you know you don't— Ah, fie! I'm asham'd of you!" iSt'r C. She has served to divert you, I see. *Lady R.* And then to crown all there was my lady Clackit, who luns on with an eternal volubility of nothing, out of all season, time and place. In the very midst of the game, she begins—" Lard, Ma'am, I was apprehensive 1 should not be able to wait on your ladyship my poor little dog, Pompey—the sweetest thing in the w orld!--A spade led! There's the knave.—1 was fetching a walk, Me'em, the other morning in the Park—a fine frosty morning it was-1 love frosty weather of all things— let me look at the last trick and so Me'em little Pompey—and if your ladyship was to seethe dear creature pinched with the frost, mincing his steps along the Mall— with his pretty little innocent face—1 vow i don't kuow what to play—And so, Me'em, while I was talking to Captain Flimsey—your ladyship knows Captain Fliinsey. —Nothing but rubbish in my hand!—I can't help it.— And so,

Me'era, five odious frights of dogs beset my poor little Pompey—the dear creature has the heart of a lion; but who can resist five at once?—And so Pompey barked for assistance—the hurt he received was upon his chest— the doctor would not advise him to venture out till the wound is healed, for fear of an inflamation. Pray what's trumps? *Sir C.* My dear, you'd make a most excellent actress. *Lady R.* Well, trow, lets go to rest—but, Sir Charles, how shockingly you play'd that last rubber, when I stood looking over you! -*Sir C.* My love, I play'd the truth of the game. *Lady R.* No, indeed my dear, you played it wrong. *Sir C,* Po! Nonsense! You don't understand it. *Lady R.* I beg your pardon, I'm allowed to play better than you. *Sir C.* All conceit, my dear! I was perfectly right. *Lady R.* No such thing, Sir Charles; the diamond was the play- . *Sir C.* Po! Po! Ridiculous! The club was the card, against the world. *Lady R.* Oh! No, no, no—I say it was the diamond. *Sir C.* Madam, I say it was the club. *Lady R.* What do you fly into such a passion for? *Sir G.* Death and fury, Do you think I don't know what I'm about? I tell you once more, the club was the judgment of it. *Lady R.* May be so'—have it your own way. *Sir C.* Vexation! You're the strangest woman that ever lived; there's no conversing with you.—Look ye here, my Lady Racket-—'tis the clearest case in the world— I'll make it plain in a moment. *Lady R-*Well, Sir; ha, ha, ha f -*Sir C.* 1 had four cards left—a trump had led—-they were six no, no, no—they were seven, and we nine ——-then, you know——-the beauty of the play was to *Lady R.* Well, now, 'lis amazing to me that you can't see it. Give me leave, Sir Charles—your left hand adversary had led his last trump— and he had before finessed the club, and roughed the diamond—now if you had put on your diamond—— *Sir C.* But, Madam, we played for the odd trick. *Lady R.* And sure the play for the odd trick *Sir C.* Death and fury! Can't you hear me? *Lady R.* Go on, Sir. *Sir C.* Here me, I say. Will you hear me? *Lady R.* I never heard the like in my life. *Sir*

C. Why then you are enough to provoke the patience of a Stoic. Very well, madam! You know no more of the game than your father's leaden Hercules on the top of the house. You know no more of whist than he does of gardening. *Lady R.* Ha, ha, ha! *Sir C.* You're a vile woman, and I'll Dot sleep another night under one roof with you. *Lady R.* As you please, Sir. *Sir C.* Madam, it shall be as I please—I'll order ray chariot this moment. Going. 1 know how the cards should be played as well as any man in England, that let me tell you—*Going* And when your family were standing behind counters, measuring out tape, and bartering for Whitechapel needless, my ancestors, my ancestors, Madam, were squandering away whole estates, at cards; whole estates, my lady Racket— *She hums a tune.'* Why, then, by all that's dear to me, I'll never exchange another word with you, good, bad, or indifferent. Look ye, my lady Racket— thus it stood——the trump being led, it was then my business *Lady R.* To play the diamond, to be sure. *Sir C.* I have done with you forever; and so you may tell your father. *Lady R.* What a passion the gentleman is in! Ha! ha! I promise him I'll not give up my judgment. *Reenter* Sir Charles. *Sir C.* My lady Racket—look'ye, Ma'am, once more out of pure good nature *Lady R.* Sir, I am convinced of your good nature. *Sir C.* That, and that only, prevails with me to tell you, the club was the play. *Lady R.* Well, be it so—I have no objection. *Sir C.* 'Tis the clearest point in the word-- we were nine, and—— *Lady R.* And for that very reason, you know the club was the best in the house., *Sir C.* There's no such thing as talking to you.. You're a base woman—I'll part with you forever, you may live here with your father, and admire his fantastical evergreens, till you grow as fantastical yourself— I'll set out Tor London this instant.—— *Stops at the door* The club was not the best in the house. *Lady R.* How calm you are! Well, I'll go to bed. Will you come? you had better-Poor Sir Charles. *Looks and laughs, then exit.* *Sir C.* That case is provoking—Crosses *to the opposite door where she utent out.* I tell you the diamond was not the play; and here I take my final leave of you— *Walks back as fast as he can* I am resolved upon it; and i know the club was not the best in the house. V11 *I. Brutus and Cassius.*—Sh «.Kes»e A Ee.

Cas. THAT you have wrong'd me, doth appear in this?

You have condemn'd and noted Lucius Pella

For taking bribes here of the SarcHans; Wherein my letter (praying on his side, Because I knew the man) was slighted of.

Bru. You wrong'd yourself to write in such a case.-

Cas. At such a time as this, is it not meet Tiliat every nice offence should bear its comment?

Bru. Yet let me tell you, Cassius, you yourself

Av much condemn'd to have an itching palm,

To sell and mart your offices for gold, To undeservers.

Cas. I an itching palm?

You know that you, are Brutus that speak this,.

Or, by the gods, this speech were else your last.

Bru. The name of Cassius honours this corruption,

And chastisement doth therefore hide its head.

Cas. Chastisement?

Bru. Remember March, the Ides of March remember-

Did not great Julius bleed for justice sake?

What! shall one of us,

That struck the foremost man of all this world,

But for supporting robbers; Shall we now

Contaminate our fingers with base bribes?

And sell the mighty space of our large honours,

For so much trash as may be grasped thus?

I had rather be a dog and bay the moon, Than such a Roman.

Cas. Brutus, bay not me:

I'll not endure it. You forget yourself To hedge me in: I am a soldier,

Older in practice, abler than yourself, To make conditions.

Bru. Go to! You are not, Cassius.

Cas. I am. *Bru.* I say you are *not. Cas.* Urge me no more: 1 shall forget myself? Have mind upon your health: tempt me no farther. *Bru.* Away, slight man! *Cas.* Is't possible! *Bru.* Hear me, for I will speak.

Must T give way and Toom to your rash choler?

Shall I be frighted when a madman stares?

Cas. Must I endure all this! *Bru.* All this! Ay, more. Fret till your proud heart breaks Go, show your slaves how choleric you are, And make your bondmen tremble. Must 1 budge? Must I observe you? Must *I* stand and crouch Under your testy humour-J You shall digest the venom of your spleen, Though it do split you; for, from this day forth, I'll use you for my mirth, yea, for my laughter, When you are waspish. *Cas.* Is it to come to this? *Bru.* You say you are a better soldier;

Let it appear so; make your vaunting true;

And it shall please me well. For my own part

1 shall be glad to learn of noblemen.

Cas. You wrong me every way; you wrong me Brutus;

I said an elder soldier, not a better.

Did I say better?

Bru. If you did I care not. *Cas.* When Cesar liv'd he durst not thus have mov'd me. *Bru.* Peace, peace; you durst not so have tempted biro. *Cos.* I durst not f *Bru.* No. *Can.* What! durst no tempt him? *Bru.* For your life you durst not.

. *Cas.* Do not presume too much upon my love.

I may do that I shall be sorry for.

Bru. You have done that you should be sorry for

There is no terrour, Cassius, in your threats j..

For 1 am arm'd so strong in honesty, That they pass by me as the idle wind, Which I respect n#t. I did send to you For certain sums of gold, which you denied me;

I-had father coin my heart,

And drop my blood for drachmas, than to wring,

From the hard hands of peasants, their vile trash,

By any indirection. I did send To you for gold to pay my legions j Which you denied me. Was that done like Cassius?-

Should I have answered Cains Cassius so? u

When Marcus Brutus grows so covetous,

To lock such rascal counters from his friends,

Be ready, Gods, with all your thunderbolts

Dash him in pieces.

Cas. I denied you not. *Bru.* You did. *Cas.* I did not; he was but a foot That brought my answer back, Brutus hath riv'd ray heart. A friend should bear a friend's infirmities; But Brutus makes mine greater than they are. *Bru.* I do not. Still you practice them on me. *Cas.* You love me not. *Bru.* I do not like your faults. *Cas.* A friendly eye could never see such faults. *Bru.* A flatterer's would not, though they dd appear As huge as high Olympus.

Cas. Come Anthony! And young Octavius, Come! Revenge yourselves alone on Cassius:

For Cassius is a weary of the world

Hated by one he loves; brav'd by his brother;

Check'd like a bondman; all his faults observ'd,

Set in a note book, learn'd and conn'd by rote——

To cast into my teeth. There is my dagger,

And here my naked breast within, a heart

Dearer than Plutus' mine, richer than gold;

If that thou need st a Roman's, take it forth: 1 that denied thee gold will give my heart.

Strike as thou did'sl at Cesar; for I know,

When thou did's't hate him worst, thou lovs't him better

Than eter thou lovs't Cassius.

Bru. Sheath your dagger,

Be angry when you will, it shall have

scope,

Do what you will, dishonour shall hs humour.

O Cassius! you are yoked with a lamb,

That carries anger as the flint bears fire;

Who much enforced, shows a hasty spark,

And straight is cold again.

Cas. Hath Cassius lived

To be but mirth and laughter to his Brutus,

When grief and blood ill temper'd vexeth him!

Bru. When I spoke that, 1 was ill tempered too. *Cas.* Do you confess so much? Give me your hand. *Bru.* And my heart too. *Embracing Cas.* O Brutus! *Bru.* What's the matter? *Cas.* Have you not love enough to bear with me, When the rash humour which my mother gave me, Makes me forgetful? *Bru.* Yes, Cassius; and from henceforth, When you are over earnest with your Brutus,

He'il think your mother chides, and leave you so.

II.—SPEECHES AND SOLILOQUIES.

1.—*Hamlet's Advice to the Players.*—

Tragedy Of Hamlet. SPEAK the speech, I pray you, as I pronounced it to you; trippingly on the tongue. But if you mouth it, as many of our players do, I had as. lief the town crier had spoken my lines. 'And do not saw the air too much with your Lands; but use all gently: For in the very torrent, tempest, and, as I may say, whirlwind of your passion, you must acquire and beget a temperance that may give it smoothness. Oh! it offends me to the soul, to "hear a robusleous. perriwig pated fellow tear a passion to tatters, to very rags, to split the,ears of the groundlings; who (foi the most part) are capable of nothing bat inexplicable dumb shows and noise. Pray you avoid it.

Be not too tame, neither; but iet your own discretion be your tutor. Suit the action to the word the word to the action! with this special observance, that you *o'er step not the modesty of nature;* for any thing so overdone is from the purpose of playing; whose end is—to hold as'twere, the mirror up to nature; to show virtue her own feature, scorn

her own image, and the very age and body of the time, his form and pressure- Now, this overdone, or come tardy of, though it make the unskilful laugh, cannot but make the judicious grieve; the censure of one of which must, inyotw allowance o'er weigh a whole theatre of others. Oh f There be players that I have seen play, and heard others praise, and that highly, that, neither having the accent of Christian, nor the gait of Christian, pagan nor man, have so strutted and bellowed, that 9 have thought some of Nature's journeymen had mademen and not made them-well, they imitated humanity so 'abominably.

II.—*Douglas- Account of himself;'*— Tragedy Of Doogla3.

My name is Norval. On the Grampian hills

My father feeds his flocks; a frugal swain,

Whose constant cares were to increase his store,

And keep his only son,-myself at home.

For I had heard of battles, and I long'd

To follow to the field some warlike lord;

And Heaven soon granted what my sire denied.

This moon, which rose last night, round asmy shield-

Had not yet fill'd her horns, when, by her light,

A band of fierce barbarians, from the hills,

Rush'd like a torrent down-upon the vale,

Sweeping our flocks and herds. The shepherds fled

For safety and foe succour. 1 alone,

With bended bow and qiiiiver full of arrows,

Hover'd about the enemy, and mark'd

The road he took; then hasted to my friends,.

Whom, with a troop of fifty chosen men,.

I met advancing. The pursuit I led,.

Till we o'ertook the spoil encumber'd & &.

We fought—and conquer'd. Ere a sword was drawn,

An arrow from my bow had pierc'd their chief,

Who wore that day the arms which now I wear.

Returning home in triumph, I disdain'd

Thesherpherds slothful life; and having heard

That our good king had suinmon'd his bold peers,

To lead their warriours to the Carron side,

I left my father's house, and took with me

A chosen servant to conduct my steps—

Yon trembling coward, who forsook his master.

Journeying with this intent, I pass'd these towers,

And heaven directed, came this day to do.

The happy deed, that giids my humble name.

III.—*Douglas' Account of the Hermit.* —1b. BENEATH a mountain's brow, the most remote And inaccessible, by shepherd's trod, In a deep cave, dug by no mortal hand, A hermit liv'd; a melancholy man, Who was the wonder of our wand'ring swains. Austere and lonely, cruel to himself, Did they report him; the cold earth his bed, Water his drink, his food the shepherd's aims. I went to see him; and my heart was touch'd With rev'rence and with pity. Mild he spake; And, entering on discourse, such stories told, As made me oft revisit his sad cell. For he had been a soldier iti his youth; And fought in famous battles, when the peers Of Europe, by the bold Godfredo led, Against th' usurping infidel display'd The blessed cross, and won the Holy Land. Pleas'd with my admiration, and the fire His speech struck from me, the old man would shake His years away, and act his young encounters: Then, having show'd his wounds, he'd sit him down, And all the live long day discourse of war. To help my fancy, in the smooth green turf He cut the figures of the marshall'd hosts; Dscrib'd the motions, and explain'd the use Of the deep column and the lengthen'd line, The square, the crescent, and the phalanx firm;

For, all that Saracen or Christian knew

Of war's vast art, was to this hermit known.

IV.—*Sempronius' Speech for War.*—Tbag. *or* Cato. MY voice is still for war. Gods! Can a Roman senate long debate, Which of the two to choose, slavery or death! No—let us rise at once, gird on our swords, And at the head of our remaining troops, Attack the foe, break through the thick array Of his throng'd legions, and charge home upon him. Perhaps some arm more lucky than the rest, May reach his heart, and free the world from bondage Rise, Falliers, rise; 'tis Rome demands your help: Rise and revenge her slaughter'd citizens, Or share their fate. The corps of half her senate Manure the fields of Thessaly, while we Sit here deliberating in cold debates, If we should sacrifice our lives to honour, Or wear them out in servitude and chains. Rouse up, for shame! Our brothers of Pharsalia Point at their wounds, and cry aloud, To battle: Great Pompey's shade complains that we are slow, And Scipio's ghost walks unreveng'd amongst us.

V.—Lucius' *Speech for Peace.*—Ib. MY thoughts, I must confess, are turn'd on peace; Already have our quarrels fill'd the wotld With widows and with orphans: Scythia mourns Our guilty wars, and earth's remotest regions Lie half unpeopled by the feuds of Rome: 'Tis time to sheath the sword, and spare mankind. 'Tis not Cesar, but the gods, my Fathers I The gods declare against us, and repel Our vain attempts. To urge the foe to battle (Prompted by blind revenge and wild despair) Were to refute th' awards of Providence, And not to rest in heaven's determination. Already have we shown our love to Rome; Now let us show submission to the gods. We took up arms, not to revenge ourselves, But free the commouwealth. VVlica this euduilSj

Arms have no further use. Our country's cause,
That drew our swords, now wrests them from our hands.
And bids us not delight in Roman blood Unprofitably shed What men could do, Is done already-Heaven and earth will witness,

If Rome must tall that we are innocent.

VI—*Hotspur's Account of the Fop.*—Henry IV MY liege I did deny no prisoners.
But I remember when the fight was done,
When I was dry with rage and extreme toil,
Breathless and faint, leaning upon my sword,
Came there a certain lord; neat; trimly dress'd;
Fresh as a bridegroom; and his chin new reap'd,
Show'd like a stubble land, at harvest home.
He was perfum'd like a milliner;
And 'twixt his finger and his thumb, he held
A pouncet box, which, ever and anon,
He gave his nose.
And still he smil'd and talk'd:
And as the soldiers bare dead bodies by,
He call'd them untaught knaves, unmannerly,
To bring a slovenly unhandsome corse
Betwixt the wind and his nobility.
With many holiday and lady terms
He question'd me;. amongst the rest, demanded
My prisoners, in your majesty's behalf;
I then, all smarting with my wounds, being gall'd
To be so pester'd with a popinjay,.
Out of my grief and my impatience,
Answer'd—negligently—I know not what—
He should or should not; for he made me mad,
To see him shine so brisk, and smell so sweet,
And talk so like a waiting gentlewoman,
Of guns, and drums, and wounds, (heaven save the mark!)
And telling me, the sovereign'st thing on earth
Was spermaceti for an inward bruise;
And that it was great pity, (so it was)
This villanous saltpetre should be digg'd
Out of the bowels cf the harmless earth,
Wlrch many a good tall fellow had destroyed
So cowardly; and but for these vile guns,'
He would himself have been a soldier.
This bald, unjointed chat of his, ray. lord/
I answer'd indirectly, as I said;
And I beseech you, let not this report Come current for an accusation,
Betwixt my love, and your high Majesty.

VII.—*Hotspur's Soliloquy on the Contents of a Latter.*—Ib. "BUT, for mine own part my lord, I could be well contented to be there, in respect of ihie love I bear yeur house.": He could be contented to be there! Why is he not then?—In respect of the love he bears our house? He shows in this he loves his own barn better than he loves our house. Let me see some more. ''The purpose you undertake is dangerous." Why, that's certain? 'tis dangerous to take a cold, to sleep, to drink; but I tell you, my lord, Fool, out of this nettle danger, we pluck this flower safely. The purpose you undertake is dangerous; the friends you have named uncertain; the time itself unsorted; and your whole p«t too light for the counterpoise of so great an opposition."—Say you so, say you so? I say unto you again, you are a shallow, cowardly hind, and you lie. What a lackbrain is this! Our plot is a good plot as ever was laid; our friends true and constant; a good plot; good friends, and full of expectation; an excellent plot, very good friends. What a frosty spirited rogue is this! Why, my lord of York commands the plot, and the general course of the action. By this hand, if 1 were now by this rascal, I could brain him with his lady's fan. Is there not my father, my uncle and myself? Lord Edmund Mortimer, my lord of York, and Owen Glendower? Is there not besides, the Douglas'? Havel not all their letters to meet me inarms by the ninth of the next month? And are not some of them set forward already? What a Pagan rascal is this! An infidel —Ha! You shall see now, in very sincerity of fear and cold heart, will he to the king, and lay opeu all our proceedings. O! I could divide myself, and go to buffets, for moving such a dish of skimmed milk with so honourable an action. Hang him! Let him tell the king. We are prepared. I will set forward to night.

VIII.—*Othello's apology for his Marriage.*—

Tragedy Of Othello. Most potent, grave and reverend seignors:

My very noble and approv'd good masters:

That I have la'en away this old man's daughter,

It is most true; true, I have married her;

The very head and front of my offending

Hath this extent; no more. Rude am 1 in speech,

And little bless'd with the set phrase of peace:

For since these arms of mine had seven years pith,

Till now, some nine moons wasted, they haveus'd

Their dearest action, in the tented field;

And little of this great world can I speak,

More than pertains to feats of broils and battle;

And therefore, little shall I grace my cause,

In speaking of myself. Yet by your patience,

I will a round unvarnish'd tale deliver,

Of my whole course of love; what drugs, what charms,

What conjuration, and what mighty magic,-

(For such proceedings I am charg'd withal)

I won his daughter with.

Her father lov'd me; oft invited me;

Still question'd me the story of my life

From year to year; the battles, seiges, fortunes,

That I had past.

I ran it through, e'en from my boyish days

To the very moment that he bade me tell it.

Wherein I spake of most disastrous chances:

Of moving acidents by flood and field;

Of hair breadth 'scapes in th' imminent deadly breaclt;

Or being taken by the insolent foe,

And sold to slavery; of my redemption thence,

And with it all my travel's history.

All these to hear

Would Desdemona seriously incline;

But still the house affairs would draw her thence:

Which ever as she could with baste dispatch,

Sh'd come again, and with a greedy ear

Devour up my discourse. Which I observing,

Took once a pliant hour, and found good means

To draw from her a prayer of earnest heart,.

That I would all my pilgrimage dilate j

Whereof by parcels she had something heard,

But not distinctly. I did consent;

And often did beguile her of her tears,

When I did speak of some distressful ttroke

That my youth suffer'd. My story being done,

She gave me for my pains a world of sighs.

Sh swore in faith, 'twas strange, 'twas passing strange;

'Twas pitiful; 'twas wond'rous pitiful;

She wish'd she had not heard it; yet she wish'd

That heaven had made her such a man. She thank'd

And bade me, if I had a friend that lov'd her, me,

I should but teach him how to tell my story,

And that would woo her. On this hint I spake; -She lov'd me for the-dangers I had pass'd;

And I lov'd her, that she did pity them.

This only is the witchcraft which I've us'd.

IX.—*Henry* IV's *Soliloquy on Sleep.*—

Shakespeare. How many thousands of my poorest subjects

Are at this hour asleep! O gentle sleep!

Nature's soft nurse! how have I frighted thee,

That thou no more wilt weigh my eyelids down,

And steep my senses in forgelfulness?

Why rather, sleep, liest thou in smoaky cribs,

Upon uneasy pallets stretching thee,

And hush'd with buzzing night flies to thy slumber.

Than in the perfum'd chambers of the great,

Under the canopies of costly stale,

And lull'd with sounds of sweetest melody?

O thou dull god! Why liest ihou with the vile, in loathsome beds, and leav'st a kingly couch,

A watchcase to a common larum bell?

Wilt thou upon the high and giddy mast,

Seal up the shipboy's eyes and rock his brains..

In cradle of the rude imperious surge,

And in the visitation of the winds,

Who take the ruffian billiows by the tops,

Curling their monstrous heads, and hanging them

With deaPuing clamours in the slipp'ry shrouds,

That with the hurly death itself awakes;

Canst thou, O partial sleep, give thy repose

To the wet sea boy in an hour so rude,

And in the calmest and the stillest night,

With all appliances and means to boot,

Deny it to a king? Then happy, lowly clown!

Uneasy lies the head that wears a ciown.

X.—*Capt. BobadiVs Method of defeating an Army.* Every Man In His Humobr. I WILL tell you, Sir, by the way ofprivate and under seal, 1 am a gentleman; and live here obscure, and to myself; but were *1* known to his Majesty and the Lords, observe me, I would undertake, upon this poor head and live, for the public benefit of the state, not only to spare the entire lives of his subjects in general, but to save the one half, nay three fourths of his yearly charge in holding war, and against what enemy soever. And how would 1 do it, think you? Why thus, Sir.—-I would select nineteen more to myself, throughout the land; gentlemen they should be; of good spirit, strong and able constitution.-1 would choose them by an instinct that I have. And I would teach these nineteen the special rules-; as your Punto, your Reverso, your Stoecata, your Imbroccata, your Passada, your Montonto; till they could all play very near, or altogether, as well as myself. This done: say the enemy were forty thousand strong. We twenty would come into thefield, the tenth of March, or thereabouts,at'd we would challenge twenty of the enemy; they could not, in their honour, refuse us. Well—we would kill them; challenge twenty more—kill them; twenty more—kill them; twenty more—kill them too. And thus, would we kill every man, his ten a day—that's ten score: Ten score—that's two hundred; two hundred a day—five days, a thousand: Forty thousand—forty times five—five times forty—two hundred days kill them all up by computation. And this 1 will venture my poor gentlemanlike carcase to perform (provided there be no trea'son practised upon us) by fair and discreet manhood; that is civilly—by the sword.

XI.—*Soliloquy of Hamlet's Vnch, on the Murder of his Brother.*—Tragedy Op Hamlet-

OH! my offence is rank; it smells to heaven *f*
It hath the primal, eldest curse upon it 1
A brother's murder! Pray I cannot,
Though inclination be as sharp as 'twill—
My stronger guilt defeats my strong intent)
And like a man to double business bound,
I stand in pause where 1 shall first begin—
And both neglect. What if this cursed hand
Were thicker than itself with brother's blood—
Is there not rain enough in the sweet heavens
To wash it white as snow? Whereto serves mercy,
But to confront the visage of offence?
And what's in prayer, but this twofold force?
To be forestalled ere we come to fall—
Or pardon'd being down? Then I'll look up.
My fault is past. But Oh! What form of prayer
Can serve my turn? Forgive me my foul murder,
That cannot be, since I am still possess'd
Of those effects for which I did the murder—
My crown, my own ambition, and my queen.
May one be pardoned, and retain th' offence?
In the corrupted currents of this world,
Offence's gilded hand may shove by justice:
And oft 'tis seen, the wicked prize itself
Buys out the laws. But 'tis not so above.
There is no shuffling—there the action lies
In its true nature, and we ourselves compell'd,
E'en to the (eeth and forehead of our faults,
To give in evidence. What then? What rests?
Try what repentance can. What can it not?
Yet what can it, when one cannot repent?
Oh, wretched state! Oh, bosom black as death!
Oh, limed soul, that struggling to be free,
Art more engag'd! Help, angels! Make assay!
Bow, stubborn knees—and, heart, with strings of steel,
Be soft, as sinews of the new born babe!
All may be well.

XII.—*Soliloquy of Hamlet on Death*—
Tr. TO be—or not to be that is the question,
Whether 'tis nobler in the mind to suffer
The flings and arrows of outrageous fortune—
Or to take aims against a sea of trouble;
And, by opposing end them? To die—to sleep—
f
No more? And, by a sleep, to say we end
The heartache, and the thousand natural shocks
That flesh is heir to. 'Tis a consummation
Devoutly to be wish'd. To die—to sleep
To sleep, perchance to dream—ay, there's the rub—
For, in that sleep of death, what dreams may come,
When we have shuffled off this mortal coil,
Must give us pause. There's the respect,
That makes calamity of so long life;
For, who would bear the whips and scorns of time,.
Th' oppressor's wrong, the proud man's contumely
The pangs of despis'd love—the law's delay—
The insolence of office, and the spurns
That patient merit of the unworthy takes—
When he himself might his quietus make
With a bare bodkin? Who would fardels bear,
To groan and sweat under a weary life,
But that the dread of something after death,
(That undiscover'd country, from whose bourn
No traveller returns) puzzles the will,
And makes us rather bear those ills we have,
Than fly to others that we know not of?
Thus conscience does make cowards of us al!;
And thus the native hue of resolution
Is sicklied o'er with the pale cast of thought;
And enterprizes of great pith and moment;
With this regard, their current's turn away,
And lose the name of action.

XIII.—*Falstaff's Encomium on Sack.*— Henry IV. A GOOD sherris sack hath a twofold operation in it It ascends me into the brain; dries me there, all the foolish, dull and crudy vapours which environ it; makes it apprehensive, quick, inventive; full of nimble, fiery *atii* delectable shapes; which delivered over to the voice, Uk tongue, which is the birth, becomes excellent wit. Tl second property of your excellent sherris, is the warminj of the blood *j* which, before,cold and settled, left the liver white and pale,, which is the badge of pusillanimityand cowardice. But the sherris warms it, and makes it course from the inwards to the parts extreme. It illuminate the face5 which, as a beacon, gives warning to all the res' this little kingdom, man, to arm; and then, the vital commoners, and inland petty spirits, muster me all to their captain, the heart; who great and puffed up with this retinue, doth any deed of courage—and this valour comes of sherris. So that skill in the weapon is nothing without sack, for that sets it awork; and learning, a mere hoard of gotd kept by a devil till sack commences it, and sets it in act and use. Hereof comes it that Prince Harry is valiant; for the cold blood he did naturally inherit of his father, he hath, like lean, sterile and bare land, manured husbanded and tilled, with drinking good, and a good store of fertile sherris. If I had a thousand sons, the first human principle I would teach them, should be—to for swear thin potations, and to adict themselves to sack.

XIV.—*Prologue to the Tragedy of Cata.* —Pope. To wake the soul by tender strokes of art,
To raise the genius and to mand the heart,
To make mankind in conscious virtue bold,
Live o'er each scene, and he what they behold;
For this the tragic muse first trod the stage,
Commanding tears to stream through every age;
Tyrants no more their savage nature kept,
And foes to virtue wondered how they wept.
Our author shuns by vulgar springs to move
The hero's glory or the virgin's love:-
In pitying love we but our weakness show,
And wild ambition well deserves its woe.
Here tears shall flow from a more gen'rous cause j
Such tears as patriots shed for dying laws:
He bids your breast with ancient ardours rise,
And calls forth Roman drops from British eyes;
Virtue confess'd in human shape he draws,
What Plato thought, and godlike Cato was:
No common object to your sight displays,
But what, with pleasure, heaven itself surveys:
A brave man struggling in the stormsotfate, i
And greatly falling with a falling state!
While Cato gives his little senate laws,
What bosom beats not in his country's cause l
Who sees him act, but envies every deed?
Who hears him groan, and does not wish to bleed?
E'en when proud Cesar, 'midst triumphal cars,
The spoils of nations and the pomp of wars,
Igiiobly vaiu, and impotenily great,
Show'd Rome her Cato's figure drawn in state;
As her dead father's rev'rend image pass'd,
The pomp was darken'd aDd the day o'ercast,
The triumph ceas'd—tears gush'd from every eye;
The world's great victor pass'd unheeded by;
Her last good man, dejected Rome ador'd,
And honor'd Cesar's less than Cato's sword.
Britons attend. Be worth like this approv'd;
And show you have the virtue to be mov'd.
With honest scorn the first fam'd Cato view'd
Rome learning arts from Greece, whom she subdu'd.
Our scene precariously subsists too long
On French translation and Italian song.
Dare to have sense yourselves; assert the stage;
Be justly warm'd with your own native rage.
Such plays alone should please a British ear,
As Cato's self had not disdain'd to hear.

XV.— *Cato's Soliloqiiy on the Immortality of the Sovl*
Tragedy Of Cato. IT must be so—Plato thou reasonest well! Else, Whence this pleasing hope, this fond desire, This longing after immortality? Or, Whence this secret dread, and inward horrour, Of failing into nought? Why shrinks the soul' Back on herself, and startles at destruction? 'Tis the divinity that stirs within us: 'Tis heaven itself that points out an hereafter, And intimates Eternity to man. Eternity!—thou pleasing, dreadful thought! Through what variety of untried being, Through what new scenes and changes must we pass The wide, th' unbounded prospect lies before me; But shadows, clouds and darkness rest upon it. Here will I hold. If there's a Power above us, (And that there is, all nature cries aloud Through all her works) he must delight in virtue; And that which he delights in must be happy. But when? Or where? This world was made for Cesar. I'm weary of conjectures this must end them.
Laying his hand on his sword.
Thus I am doubly arm'd. My death and life,
I My bane and antidote are both before me.
This in a moment brings me to an end;
But this informs me I shall never die.
The soul, secur'd in her existence, smiles
At the drawn dagger, and defies its point.
The stars shall fade away, the sun himself
Grow dim with age, and nature sink in

years;
But thou shalt flourish in immortal youth;
Unhurt amidst the war of elements,
The wreck of matter, and the crush of worlds.

XVI.—*Speech of Henry V. to his Soldiers at the Siege of Harfleur.*—Shakespeare's Henry V.

ONCE more unto the breach, dear friends oncemore.
Or close the wall up with the English dead.
In peace there's nothing so becomes a man
As modest stillness and humility;
But when the blast of war-blows in our ears.
Then imitate the action of the tyger;
Stiffen the sinews, summon up the blood,
Disguise fair nature with hard favour'd rage j-
Then lend the eye a terrible aspect s
Let it pry o'er the portage of the head
Like the brass cannon; let the brow o'erwhelm it,
And fearfully as doth a galled rock
O'erhang and jutty his confounded base,
Swili'd with the wild and wasteful ocean.
Now set the teeth, and stretch the nostril wide;.
Hold hard the breath, and bend up every spirit
To its full height. Now on, you noblest English-;
Whose blood is fetch'd from fathers of war proof;
Fathers, that, like so many Alexanders,
Have in these parts from morn till even fought,
And sheath'd their swords for lack of argument.
Dishonour not your mother; now attest
That those whom you call'd fathers did beget you.
Be copy now to men of grosser blood,
And teach them how to war. And you, good yeomen..
Whose limbs were made in England, show us here
aa
The metal of your pasture; let us swear

That you are worth your breeding; which I doubt not;
For there is none of you so mean and base,
That hath not noble lustre in your eyes.
I see you stand like greyhounds in the slips,
Straining upon the start. The game's afoot:
Follow your spirit; and. upon this charge,
Cry, God for Harry, England and St. George!

XVIT—*Speech of Henry V, before the Battle of Aginmrt, on the Earl of Westmoreland's wishing for more mm from England*—1b. WHAT'S he that wishes more men from England? My cousin Westmoreland? No, my fair cousin; If we are mark'd to die, we are enow To do our country loss; and, if to live, The fewer men, the greater share of honour. No, no, my Lord; wish not a man from England. Rather proclaim it, Westmoreland, throughout my host, That he who hath no stomach to this fight, May straight depart; his passport shall be made; And crowns, for convoy, put into his purse. We would not die in that man's company. This day is called the feast of Crispian. He that outlives this day, and comes safe home, Will stand a tiptoe, when this day is nam'd, And rouse him at the name of Crispian. He that outlives this day, and sees old age, Will yearly, on the vigil, feast his neighbours, And say, Tomorrow is St. Crispian; Then will he strip his sleeve, and show his scarsOld men forget, yet shall not ail forget, Biii they'll remember, with advantages, What feats they did that day. Then shall our names, Familiar in their mouths as household words, Harry the king, Bedford and Exeter, Warwick and Talbot, Salisbury and Glo'ster, Be in their flowing cups, freshly remembered. This story shall the good man teach his son: And Crispian's day shall ne'er go by, From this time to the ending of the world, But we and it shall be remembered;

We few, we happy few, we band of brothers;
For he today that sheds his blood with me,

Shall be my brother; be he e'er so vile,
This day shall gentle his condition.
And gentlemen in England, now abed,
Shall think themselves accurs'd they were not here;
And hold their manhood cheap, while any speaks
That fought with us upon St. Crispian's day.

XVIII.—*Soliloquy of Dick the Apprentice.*—,

Farce, The Apprentice. THUS far we run before the wind. An apothecary!

Make an apothecary of me! What, cramp my genius over a pestle and mortar; or mew me up in a shop, with an alligator stuffed, and a beggarly account of empty boxes! To be culling simples, and constantly adding to the bills of mortality! No! no! It will be much better to be pasted up in capitals, The Part Op Romeo By A Young GENTLEMAN WHO NEVER APPEARED ON ANY STAGE BEFORE!

My ambition fires at the thought. But hold; mayn't

I run some chance of failing in my attempt? Hissed— pelted—laughed at— not admitted into the green room; —— that will never do—down, busy devil, down, down; try it again—loved by the women—envied by the men— applauded by the pit, clapped by the gallery, admired by the boxes. "Dear colonel, is'nt he a charming creature? My lord, don't you like him of all things?—Makes love like an angel!-What an eye he has! rFine legs!

1 shall certainly go to his benefit." Celestial sounds! And then I'll get in with all the painters, and have myself put up in every print shop—in the character of Macbeth! "This is a sorry sight." *(Stands an altitude.)* In the character of Richard, "Give me another horse! Bind up my wounds!" This will do rarely.—
—And then I have a chance of getting well married——O glorious thought; I will enjoy it, though but in fancy. But what's o'clock? It must be almost nine. I'll away at once; this is club night—the spouters are all met—little think they I'm in town—they'll be surprised to see me off I go; and then for my assignation with my master Gargle's daughter.

XIX.— *Caseins instigating Brutus to join the Compaq against Cesar.*—Tbag. Op Julius Cesab.

HONOUR is the subject of my story.
I cannot tell what you and other men
Think of this life; but for my single self,
I had as lief not be, as live to be
In awe of Such a thing as myself.
I was born free as Cesar; so were you:
We both have fed as well; and we can both
Endure the winter's cold as well as he.
For once upon a raw and gusty day,
The troubled Tiber chafing with his shores,
Cesar says to me, " Dar'st thou, Cassius, now
Leap in with me into this angry flood,
And swim to yonder point?" Upon the word,
Accoutred as I was, I plunged in,
And bade him follow: so indeed he did.
The torrent roar'd and we did buffet it
With lusty sinews; throwing it aside,
And stemming it with hearts of controversy.
But ere we could arrive the point propos'd,
Cesar cry'd, "Help me Cassius, or I sink."
I, as.(Eneas, our great ancestor,
Did from the flames of Troy, upon his shoulder
The old Anchises bear; so, from the waves of Titer.
Did I the tired Cesar; and this man
Is now become a god; and Cassius is
A wretched creature, and must bend his body,
If Cesar carelessly but nod on him.
He had a fever when he was in Spain,
And when the fit was on him, I did mark
How he did shake; 'tis true; this god did shake;
His coward lips did from their colour fly;
And that same eye, whose bend doth awe the world,
Did lose its lustre; I did hear him groan:
Ay, and that tongue of his that bada the Romans
Mark him and write his speeches in their books,
"Alas!" it cry'd: "Give me some drink Titimus;

As a sick girl. Ye gods it doth amaze me,
A man of such a feeble temper, should
So get the start of the majestic world)
And bear the palm alone.—-
Brutus and Cesar! What should be in that Cesar?
Why should that name be sounded more than yours?
Write thein together; yours is as fair a name;
Sound them; it doth become the mouth as well:
Weigh them; it is as heavy: conjure with 'em;
Brutus will start a spirit as soon as Cesar.
Now in the name of all the gods at once,
Upon what meats doth this our Cesar feed,
That he has grown so great? Age, thou art sham'd;
Rome thou hast lost the breed of noble bloods.
When went there by an age, since the great flood,
But it was fam'd with more than with one man?
When could they say, till now, that talk'd of Rome,
That her wide walls encompass'd but one man?
Oh! You and 1 have heard our fathers say,
There was a Brutus once, that would have brook'd
Th' infernal devil, to keep his state in Rome,
As easily as a king.

XX.—*Brutus' Harrangue on the Death of Cesar.*—Ib. ROIV1ANS, Countrymen and Lovers!—Hear me for my cause; and be silent that you may hear. Believe me for mine honour; and have respect to mine honour, that you may believe. Censure me in your wisdom; and awake your senses, that you may the better judge.—If there be any in this assembly, any dear friend of Cesar's, to him, I say, that Brutus'love to Cesar was no less than his. If, then, that friend demand why Brutus rose against Cesar, this is my answer: Not that I loved Cesar less, but that I loved Rome more. Had you rather Cesar were living, and

die all slaves; than that Cesar were dead, to live all freemen? As Csar loved me, I weep for him; as he was fortunate, I rejoice at it; as he was valiant, I honour him,; but, as he was ambitious, I slew him. There are tears for his love, joy for his fortune, honour for his valour, and death for his ambition.—Who's here so base, that would be a bondman? If any, speak; for him I have offended. Who's here so rude that would not be a Roman? If any, speak; for him I have offended. Who's here so vile, that will not love his country? If any, speak; for him I have offended. I pause for a reply

None! Then none have I offended. I have done no more to Cesar than you shall do to Brutus. The question of his death is enrolled in the Capitol; his glory not extenuated, wherein he was worthy j nor his offences enforced for which he suffered death.

Here comes his body, mourn'd by Mark Antony; who, though he had no band in his death, shall receive the benefit of his dying, a place in the commonwealth; as which of you shall not? With this T depart—that as I slew my best lover for the good of Rome, I have the same dagger for myself, when it shall please my country to need my death.

XXI.—*Antony's Oration over Cesar's Body.*—ItFRIENDS, Romans, Countrymen! Lend me your ears.
I come to bury Cesar, not to praise him.
   The evil that men do, lives after 4hem;
   The good is oft interred with their bones:
   So let it be with Cesar! Noble Brutus
   Hath told you, G»esar was ambitious.
   If it were so, it was a grievous fault;
   And grievously hath Cesar answer'd it.
   Here under leave of Brutus, and the rest, (For Brutus is an honourable man,
   So are they all, all honourable men)
   Come I to speak in Cesar's funeral.
   He was my friend, faithful and just to me:
   But Brutus says, he was ambitiousj
   And Brutus is an honourable man.
   He hath brought many captives home to Rome,
   Whose ransoms did the general cof-

fers fill:

Did this in Cesar seem ambitious?

When that the poor have cried, Cesar hath wept!

Ambition should be made of sterner stuff.

Yet Brutus says he was ambitious;

And Brutus is an honourable man.

You all did see, that, on the Lupercal,
1 thrice presented him a kingly crown;

Which he did thrice refuse: Was this ambition?

Yet Brutus says he was ambitious;

And sure, he is an honourable man.

I-«peak not to disprove what Brutus spoke;

But here I am to speak what I do know.

You all did love him once; not without cause;

What cause withholds you theu to mourn for him?

O judgment! Thou art fled to brutish beasts,

And men have lost their reason. Bear with me:

My heart is in the coffin there with Cesar;

And I must pause till it come back to me.

But yesterday the word of Cesar might

Have stood against the world! now lies he there,

And none so poor to do him reverence,

0 Masters! If I were dispos'd to stir

Your hearts and minds to mutiny and rage,

1 should do Brutus wrong, and Cassius wrong;

Who, you all know, are honourable men.

I will not do them wrong—I rather choose

To wrong the dead, to wrong myself and you,

Than I will wrong such honourable men.

But here's a parchment with the seal of Cesar;

I found it in his closet: 'tis his will.

Let but the commons hear this testament, (Which, pardon me, I do not mean to read)

And they would go and kiss dead Cesar's wounds,

And dip their napkins in his sacred blood—

Yea, beg a hair of him for memory,

And, dying, mention it within their wills,

Bequeathing it, as a rich legacy,

Unto their issue.

If you have tears, prepare to shed them now.

You all do know this mantle: I remember

The first time ever Cesar put it on;

'Twas on a summer's evening in his tent,

That day he overcome the Nervii

Look! in this place ran Cassius' dagger through-

See what a rent the envious Casca made

Through this the well beloved Brutus stabb'd;

And, as'he pluck'd his cursed steel away,

Mark how the blood of Cesar follow'd it!

This, this was the unkindesl cut of all!

For when the noble Cesar saw him stab,

Ingratitude, more strong than traitors' arms,

Quite vanquish'd him! Then burst his mighty heart,

And in his mantle muffling up 1ms face,

E'en at the base of Pompey's statue,

(Which all the while ran blood) great Cesar fell.

0 what a fall was there, my countrymen!

Then I, an4 you, and all o/us fell down;

Whilst bloody treason flourished over us.

O, now you weep: and I perceive you feel

The dint of pity! These are gracious drops.

Kind souls! What, weep you when you behold

Our Cesar's vesture wounded? Look you here!—

Here is himself—marr'd, as you see, by traitors.

Good friends! Sweet friends! Let me not stir you up

To such a sudden flood of mutiny!

They that have done this deed are honourable!

What private griefs they have, alas, I know not,

That made them do it! They are wise and honourable.

And will, no doubt, with reason answer you.

1 come not, friends, to steal away your hearts? 'I am no orator, as Brutus is-;

But, as you know me all, a plain, blunt man,

That love my friend—and that they know full well,

That gave me public leave to speak of him!

For I have neither wit,-nor words, nor worth,

Action, nor utterance, nor power of speech,

To stir men's blood—I only speak right on, I

I tell you that which you yourselves do know—

Show you sweet Cesar's wounds, poor, poor, dumb

mouths,

And bid them speak for ire. But, were T Brutus,

And Brutus Antony, there were an Antony

Would ruffle up your spirits, and put a tongue

In every wound of.Cesar, that should move

The stones of Rome to rise and mutiny.

XXII.—*Fahtaff's Soliloquy on Honour.*
—Henry iv. OWE heaven a death! 'Tis not due yet; and I would be loth to pay him before his day. What need I be so forward with him that calls not on me? Well, 'tis no matter—honour pricks me on.—But how, if honour prick me off when I come on? How then? Can honour set to a leg? No; an arm? No; or take away the grief of a wound? No. Honour hath no skill in surgery, then? No. What is honour? A word. Viiat is that word honour?.. Air j a trim reckoning. Who bath it? He that died a Wednesda)'. Doth he fee! it? No. Doth he hear it? No. Is it insensible, then? Yea, to the dead. But will it not live with the living? No. Why? Detraction will not suffer it. Therefore, I'll none of it. Honour is a mere 'scutcheon— and so ends my catechism.

XXIII—*Pari of Richard* Ill's *Soliloquy the night preceding the Battle of Bos-*

worth.—Tragedy Of Richard III.

'TIS now the dead of night, and half the world

Is with a lonely solemn darkness hung;

Yet I (so coy a dame is sleep to me)

With all the weary courtship of

My care tir'd thoughts, can?t win her to my bed,

Though e'en the stars do wink, as'twere, with over watching.

I'll forth, and walk a while. The air's refreshing,

And the ripe-harvest of the new mown hay

Gives it a sweet and wholesome odour.

How awful is this gloom! And hark! From camp to camp

The hum of either army stilly sounds,

That the fix'd sentinels almost receive

The secret whisper of each other's watch!

Steed threatens steed in high and boasting neighings,

Piercmg the night's dull ear. Hark! From the tents.

The armourers, accomplishing the knights,

With clmk of hammars closing rivets up,

Give dreadful note of preparation: while some,

Like sacrifices, by their fires of watch,

With patience sit, and inly ruminate

The morning's danger. By yon heaven, my stern

Impatience chides this tardy gaited night,

Who, like a foul and ugly witch, does limp

So tediously away. I'll to my couch,

And once more try to sleep her into morning.

XXI Yir-r/ie *World compared to a Stage*—As You Like It.

ALL the world is a stage;

And all the men and women, merely players.

They have their exits and their entrances;

And one man, in his time, plays many parts,

His acts being seven ages. At first, the Infant;

Mewling and puking in the nurse's arms.

And then the whining Schoolboy; with his satchel,

And shining morning face, creeping like a snail,

Unwillingly to school. And, then the Lover,

Sighing like furnace; with a woeful ballad

Made to his Mistress' eyebrow. Then, a Soldier;

Full of strange oaths, and bearded like the pard;

Jealous in honour; sudden and quick in quarrel;

Seeking the bubble reputation,

Even in the cannon's mouth. And then, the Justice;

In fair round belly, with good capon lin'd;

With eyes severe, and beard of formal cut;

Full of wise saws and modern instances:

And so he plays his part. The sixth age shifts

Into the lean and slipper'd pantaloon;

With spectacles on nose, and pouch on side;

His youthful hose well sav'd, a world too wide

For his shrunk shank; and his big manly voice,

Turning again towards childish treble, pipes

And whistles in his sound. Last scene of all,

That ends this strange eventful history,

Is second Childishness, and mere Oblivion;

'Sans teeth, sans eyes, sans taste, sans every thing.

Concise Passages, Exemplifying Certain Particulars, On The Proper Expression Op Which, The ModulationAnd Management Op The Voice In Reading And Spell? Ing Principally Depend.

I'.—*Examples of* Antithesis; *or, the Opposition of Words or Sentiments.* 1. THE manner of speaking is as important as the matter. *Chesterfield.* 2. Cowards die many times; the valiant never taste of death but once. *Shakespeare.* 3. Temperance, by fortifying the mind and body, leadsto happiness; intemperance, by enervating the mind andbody, ends generally in misery. *-Art of Thinking.* 4. Title and ancestry render a good man more illustrious; but an ill one more contemptible. Vice is infamous,though in a prince; and virtue honourable, though in a peasant. *Spectator.* 5. Almost every object that attracts our notice, has its. bright and its dark side. He who habituates himself to look at the displeasing side, will sour his disposition, and, consequently, impair his happiness; while he who constantly beholds it on the bright side, insensibly ameliorates his temper, and, in consequence of it, improves his own happiness, and the happiness of all around him *World.* 6 A wise man endeavours to shine in himself; a fool to outshine others. The former is humbled by the sense of his own infirmities; the latter is lifted up by the discovery of those which he observes in others. The wise man considers what he wants; and the fool what he abounds in. The wise man is happy when he gains his own approbation; and the fool, when he recommends himself to the applause of those about him. *Spectator.* 7. Where opportunities of exercise are wanting, temperance may in a great measure supply its place. If exercise throws oil ail superfluities, temperance prevents them; if exercise clears the vessels, temperance neither satiates nor overstrains them;—exercise raises proper ferments in the humours, and promotes the circulation of the blood, temperance gives nature her full play, and enables her to. exert herself in ail her force and vigouE; if exercise dissipates a growing.distemper, temperance starves it. *Spectator.* 8. 1 have always preferred cheerfulness to mirth. The latter 1 consider as an act, the former as a habit of the mind. Mirth is short and transient, cheerfulness fixed and permanent. Those are often raised into the greatest transports of mirth, who are subject to the greatest depressions of melancholy. On the contrary, cheerfulness, though *t* does not give the mind

such an exquisite gladness, prevents us from falling into any depths of sorrow; Mirth is like a flash of lightning, that breaks through a gloom of clouds, and glitters for a moment; cheerfulness keeps up a kind of day light in the mind, and fills it with a steady and'perpetual serenity. *Spectator.* 9. At the same time that 1 think discretion the most useful talent a man can be master of, I look upon cunning to be the accomplishment of little, mean, ungenerous minds. Discretion points out the noblest ends to us, and pursues the most proper and laudable methods of attaining them; cunning has only private, selfish aims, and sticks at nothing which may make them succeed; discretion has large and extended views, and like a well formed eye, commands a whole horizon; cunning is a kind of shortsightedness, that discovers the minutest objects, which are near at hand, but is not able to discern things at a distance, *Spectator.* 10. Nothing is more amiable than true modesty, and nothing more contemptible than the false. The one guards virtue; the other betrays it. True modesty is ashamed to do any thing that is repugnant to the rules of right reason; false modesty is ashamed to do any thing that is opposite to the humour of the Company. True modesty avoids every thing that is criminal; false modesty, every thing that *h* unfashionable. The latter is only a general undetermined instinct; the former is that instinct, limited and circumscribed by the rules of prudence and religion. *Spectator.* 11. How different is the view of past life, in the man-who i3 grown old in knowledge and wisdom, from that of him who is grown old in ignorance and folly! The latter is like the owner of a barren country, that fills his eye witli the prospect of naked hills and plains, which produces nothing either profitable or ornamental; the former beholds a beautiful and spacious landskip, divided into delightful gardens, green meadows, fruitful fields; and can scarce cast his eye on a single spot of his possessions, that is not covered with some beautiful plant or flower.—
—*Spectator.* 12. As there is a worldly happiness, which God perceives to be

no other than disguised misery; as there are worldly honours, which, in his estimation, are reproach; so there is a worldly wisdom, which in his sight, is foolishness. Of this worldly wisdom, the characters are given in the scriptures, and placed in contrast with those of the wisdom which is from above. The one is the wisdom of the crafty; the other, that of the upright: The one terminates in selfishness; the other in charity: The one, full of strife, and bitter envying; the other, of mercy and good fruits *Blair.* 13. True honour, though it be a different principle from religion, is that which produces the same effects. The lines ofaction though drawn from different parts, terminate in the same point. Religion embraces virtue as it is enjoined by the law of God; honour, as it is graceful and ornamental to human nature. The religions man fears, the man of honour scorns, to uo,an ill action. The latter considers vice as something that is beneath him; the former, as something that is offensive to the Divine Being; the one, as what is unbecoming, theother, as what is forbid d en. *Gua rdian.* 14: Where is the man that possesses, or indeed can be required to possess, greater abilities in war, than Pompcy? One who lias-fought more pitched battles, than others have maintained personal disputes! Carried on more wars than others have acquired-knowledge of by reading! Reduced more provinces than others have aspired to, even in Uioiig.il! Whose youth was trained ty the professional. arms, not by precepts derived from others, but by the highest offices of command! Not by personal mistakes in war, but by a train of important victories; not by a series of campaigns, but by a succession of triumphs. *Cictro* 15. Two principles in human nature reign,
Selflove to urge, and reason to restrain;
Nor this a good, nor that a bad we call,
Each works its end—to move or govern all—Pope 16. In point of sermons, 'tis confess'd Our English clergy make the best; *Bat* this appears, we must confess,
Not from the pulpit, but the press.
They manage, with disjointed skill,

The matter well, the manner ill;
And, what seems paradox at first,
They make the best, and preach the worst.—*Byram.* 17. Know, Nature's children all divide her care; The fur that warms a monarch warm'd a bear. While man exclaims, " See all things for ray use?" "See man for mine!" replies-the pamper'd goose: And just as short of reason he must fall,
Who thinks all made for one, not one for all.—*Pop"* 18. O thou goddess,
Thou divine Nature! How thyself thou blazon's!
In these two princely boys! They are as gentle
As zephyrs blowing below the violet,
Not wagging his sweet head; and yet as rough
(Their royal blood enchaf'd) as the rud'st wind
That by the top doth take the mountain pine,
And make them stoop to the vale *Shakespeare.* 19. Te ease in writing comes from art, not chance, As those move easiest who have learn'd to dance. 'Tis not enough no harshness gives offence; The sound must seem an echo to the sense. Soft is the strain when zephyr gently blows, And the smooth stream in smoother numbers flows; But when loud surges lash the sounding shore, The hoarse rough verse should like the torrent roar. When Ajax strives some reek's vast weight-to thro) The line, too, labours, and the words move slow: Not so when swift Camilla scours the plain,
Flies o'er the unbending corn, and skims along the main. *Pope.* 20. Good name in man and woman
Is the immediate jewel of their souls.
Who steals my purse, steals trash; 'tis something, nothing;
'Twas mme, 'tis his, and has been slave to thousands.
But he that filches from me my good name,
Robs me of that which not enriches him,
And makes me poor indeed. *Shakespeare.* II.—*Examples of* Enumeration; *or the mentioning of particulars.* 1. I CONSIDER a human soul, without education, like marble in the quarry; which

shows none of its inherent beauties, till the skill of the polisher fetches out the colours, makes the surface shine, and discovers every ornamental cloud, spot and vein, that runs through the body of it. *Spectator.* 2. The subject of a discourse being opened, explained and confirmed; that is to say, the speaker having gained the attention and judgment of his audience, he must proceed to complete his conquest over the passions; such as imagination, admiration, surprize, hope, joy, love, fear, grief, anger. Now he must begin to exert himself; here it is that a fine genius may display itself, in the use of amplification, enumeration, interrogation, metaphor, and ev«ry ornament that can render a discourse entertaining, winning, striking and enforcing. *Baillie.* 3. I am persuaded, that neither death nor life; nor angels, nor principalities, nor powers; nor things present, nor things to come; nor height, nor depth; nor any other creature; shall be able to separate us from the love of God, which is in Christ Jesus our Lord *St. Paul. 4.* Sincerity is, to speak as we think, to do as we pretend and profess, to perform and make good what we promiseand really to be what we would seem and appear to be *Tillotson.* 5. No blessing of life is any way comparable to the enjoyment of a discreet and viituous friend; it eases and unloads the mind, clears and improves the understanding, engenders thought and knowledge, animates virtue and good resolutions, sooths and allays the passions, and finds employment for most of the vacant hours of life. *Spectator.* 6. The brightness of the sky, the lenghthening of the days, the increasing verdure of the spring, the arrival of any little piece of good news, or whatever carries with it the most distant glimpse of joy, is frequently the parent of a social and happy conversation. *World. 7.* In fair weather, when my heart is cheered, and I feel that exultation of spirits, which results from light and warmth, joined with a beautiful prospect of nature, 1 regard myself as one placed by the hand of God, in the midst of an ample theatre, in which the sun, moon and stars, the fruits also,

and vegetables of the earth, perpetually changing their positions or their aspects, exhibit aa elegant entertainment to the understanding as well as te the eye. Thunder and lightning, rain and hail, the painted bow and the glaring comets, are decorations of this mighty theatre; and the sable hemisphere, studded with spangles, the blue vault at noon, the glorious gildings and rich colourings in the horizon, I look on as so many successive scenes. *Spectator.* 8.' Complaisance renders a superiour amiable, an equal agreeable, and an inferiour acceptable. It smooths distinction, sweetens conversation, and makes every one in the company pleased with himself; It produces good nature and mutual benevolence, encourages the timorous, sooths the turbulent, humanizes the fierce, and distinguishes a society of civilized persons from a confusion of savages. In a word, complaisance is a virtue that blends all orders of men together, in a friendly intercourse of words and actions, and is suited to that equality in human nature, which every man ought to consider, so far as is consistent with the Older and economy of the world. *Guardian.* 9. It is owing toour having early imbibed false notions of virtue, that the word *Christian* does not carry with it at first view, all that is great, worthy, friendly, generous and heroic. The man who suspends his hopes of the rewards of worthy actions till after death; who can bestow, unseen j who can overlook hatred; do good-to his slanderer; who can never be angry stf his friend; severlevenaFul to his enemy—is certainly formed for the benefit of society. *Spectator.* 10. Though we seem grieved at the shortness of life, in genera!, we are wishing every period of it at an end. The minor longs to be of age—then to be a man of business— then to make up an estate—then to arrive at honours— then to retire. The usurer would be very well satisfied, to have all the time annihilated that lies between the present 'moment and the next quarter day—the politician would be contented to lose three years in his life, could lie place things in the posture which he fancies they will stand in, after

such a revolution of Urne-and the lover would be glad to strike out of his existence, all the moments that are to pass away before the happy meeting. 11. Should the greater part of people sit down and draw up a particular account of their time, what a shameful bill would it be! So much in-eating, drinking and sleeping beyond what nature requires;" so much in revelling and wantonness; so much for the recovery of last night's intemperance; so much in gaming, plays and masquerades; so much in paying and receiving formal and impertinent visits; so much in idle and foolish prating, in censuring and reviling our neighbours; so much for dressing out our bodies, and in talking of fashions; and so much wasted and lost in doing nothing at all. *Sherlock.* 12. If we would have the kindness of others, we must endure their follies. He who cannot persuade himself to withdraw from society, must be content to pay a tribute of his time to a multitude of tyrants; to the loiterer who wakes appointments he never keeps—to the consulter, "who asks advice which he never takes—to the boaster, who blusters only to be praised—to the complainer, who whines only to be pitied—to the projector, whose happiness is to entertain his friends with expectations, which all but himself know to be vain—to the economist, who tells of bargains and settlements—to the politician, who predicts the consequences of deaths, battles and alliances —to the usurer, who compares the state of the different funds—and to the talker, who talks only because he loves to be talking *Johnson.* 13. Charity suffereth long, and is kind; charity en vieth not; charity vaunteth not itself; is not puffed up; doth not behave itself unseemly; seeketh not her own; is not easily provoked; thinketh no evil; rejoiceth not in iniquity, but rejoiceth in the truth; beareth all things, believeth all things, hopeth all things, endurelh.all things. *St. Paul.* 14. Delightful task to rear the tender thought,

To teach the young idea how to shoot,

To pour the fresh instruction o'er the mind,

To breathe th' enliv'ning spirit, and to

fix
The generous purpose in the glowing breast-
Thomson. 15. Dread o'er the scene the Ghost of Hamlet stalks—
Othello rages—poor Monimia mourns—
And Belvidera pours her soul in love.
Terrour alarms the breast—(he comely tear
Steals o'er the cheek. Or else the comic muse
Holds to the world a picture of itself,
And raises, sly, the fair impartial laugh,
Sometimes she lifts her strain, and paints scenes
Of beauteous life; whute'er can deck mankind,
Or charm the heart, the generous Bevil show'd.
Thomson. 16. Then *Commerce* brought into the public walk The busy merchant; the big warehouse built; Rais'd the strong crane; choak'd up the loaded street With foreign plenty; and thy stream, O *Thames,* Large, gentle, deep, majestic, king of floods!

Chose for his grand resort. On either hand, Lke a long wintry forest, groves of masts Shoot up their spires; the bellying sheet between, Possess'd the breezy void; the sooty hulk Steer'd sluggish on; the splendid barge along Rowed regular, to harmony; around, The boat, light skimming, stretch'd its oary wings; While, deep, the various voice of fervent toil, From bank to bank increas'd; whence ribb'd with oak, To bear the British thunder, black and bold,-The roaring vessel rush'd into the main.——
Thomson. 17. 'Tis from high life high characters are drawn; A saint in crape is twice a saint in lawn.

A judge is just; a chancellor juster still;

A gownman learn'd; a bishop—what you will:
Wise, if a minister; but, if a king,
Mor# wise, more leara'd, more just, more every thing.
Pope. 18. 'Tis education forms the common mind;
Just as the twig is bent, the tree's inclinM.
Boastful and rough, your first son is a

square;
The next a tradesman, meek, and much a liar;
Tom struts a soldier, open, bald and brave;
Will sneaks a scriv'ner, an exceeding knave.
Is he a churchman? Then he's fond of power;
A quaker? Sly; a presbyterian? Sour;
A smart freethinker? All things in an hour. *Pope.* 19. See what a grace was seated on his brow;
Hyperion's curls; the front of Jove himself:
An eye like Mars, to threaten and command;
A station like the herald Mercury.
New lighted, on a heaven kissing hill;
A combination, and a form indeed,
Where every god did seem to set his seal,
To give the world assurance of a man. *Shakespeare.* 20. The cloud capt towers, the gorgeous palaces, The solemn temples, the great globe itself,
Yea, all which it inherit, shall dissolve;
And, like the baseless fabric of a vision, Leave not a wreck behind. *Shakespeare.*
III.—*Examples of* Suspension; *or a delaying of the Sense.* 1. AS beauty of person, with an agreeable carriage, pleases the eye, and that pleasure consists in observing that all the parts have a certain elegance, and are proportioned to each other; so does decency of behaviour obtain the approbation of all with whom we converse, from the order, consistency and moderation of our words and actions. *Spectator.* 2. If Pericles, as historians report, could shake the firmest resolutions of his hearers, and set the passions of all Greece in a ferment, when the public welfare of his country, or the fear of hostile invasions, was the subject; What may we not expect from that orator, who with a becoming energy, warns his auditors against those evils which have no remedy, when once undergone, either from prudence or time. *Spectator..* 3. Though there is a great deal of pleasure in contemplating (he material world, by which I mean that great system of bodies into which nature

has so curiously wrought the mass of dead matter, with the several relations which those bodies bear to one another; there is still something more wonderful and surprising in contemplating the world of life, or those various animals with which every part of the universe is furnished.—*Spectator.* 4. Since it is certain that our hearts cannot deceive us in the love of the world, and that we cannot command ourselves enough to resign it, though we every day wish ourselves disengaged from its aluremenls-; let us not stand upon a formal taking of leave, but wean ourselves from them while we are in the midst of them.
Spectator. 5. When a man has got such a great and exalted soul, as that he can look upon life and death, riches and poverty, with indifference, and closely adheres to honesty, in whatever shape she presents herself; then it is that virtue appears with such a brightness, as that all the world must admire her beauties. *Cicero.* 6. To hear a judicious and elegant discourse from the pulpit, which would in print make a noble figure, murdered by him who had learning and taste to compose it, but having been neglected as to one important part of his education, knowing not how to deliver it, otherwise than with a tone between singing and saying, or with a nod of bis head, to enforce, as with a hammer, every emphatical word, or with the same unanimated monotony in which be was used to repeat *Qute genus* at Westminister school; What can be imagined more lamentable? Yet what more common. *Burgh.* 7. Having already shown how the fancy is affected by the works of nature, and afterwards considered, in general, both the works of nature and 'art, how they mutually assist and complete each other, in forming such scenes and prospects, as are most apt to delight the mind of the beholder; I shall, in this paper, throw together some reflections on that particular art, which has a more immediate tendency than any other, to produce those primary pleasures of the imagination, which have hitherto been the subject of this discourse *Spectator.* 8. The causes of good and evil are so various and un-

certain, so often entangled with each other, so diversified by various relations, and so much subject to accidents which cannot be foreseen; that he, who would fix his condition upon incontestible reasons of preference, must live and die inquiring and deliberating. *Johnson.* 9 He, who through the vast immensity can pierce,

Sees worlds on worlds compose one universe,

Observe how system into system runs,

What other planets circle other suns;

What varied being people every star,

May tell, why heaven has made us as we are.

Pope. 10. In that soft season when descending showers Call forth the greens, and wake the rising flowers $ When opening buds salute the welcome day,

And earth, relenting, feels the genial ray;

As balmy sleep had charm'd my cares to rest,

And love itself was banish'd from my breast;

A train of phantoms in wild order rose,

Andjoin'd, this intellectual scene compose.-*Pope*

11. Nor fame I slight, nor for her favours call:

ihe comes unlook'd for, if she comes at all.

But, if the purchase cost so dear a price,

As soothing folly, or exalting vice;

And if the muse must natter lawless sway,

And follow still where fortune leads the way

Or, if no basis bear my rising name'

But the fall'n ruins of another's fame;

Then teach me, heaven, to scorn the guilty bays c

Drive from my breast that wretched lust of praise.

Unblemish'd let me live, or die unknown;

O, grant me honest fame, or grant me none.

12. As one who long in populous city pent,

Where houses thick and sewers annoy the air

Forth issuing on a summers morn, to breathe!

Among the pleasant villages and farms

Adjoin'd from each thing met conceives delights i he smell of grain, or tedded grass, or kine,

Or dairy, each rural sight, each rural sound;

If 'chance, with nymph like step, fair virgin pass,

What pleasing eeni'd for her now pleases more,

She most, and in her look sums all delight:

Such pleasure took the serpent to behold

This flowery plat, the sweet recess of Eve,

Thus early, thus alone.——*Milton.*

IV.—*Examples of* Parenthesis; *or words interposed in*

Sentences.

1. THOUGH good sense is not in the number, nor always, it must be owned, in the company of the sciences; yet it is (as the most sensible of the poets has justly observed) fairly worth the seven. ' *Melmoth.* 2. An elevated genius, employed in little things, appears (to use the simile of Longinus) like the sun in his evening declination: he remits his splendour, but retains his magnitude; and pleases more though he dazzles less.——*Johnson.* 3. The horrour with which we entertain the thoughts of death (or indeed of any future-evil) and the uncertainty of its approach, All a melancholy mind with innumerable -apprehensions and suspicions.——*Spectator.* 4. If envious people were to ask themselves, whether they would exchange their entire situations with the persons envied, (1 mean their minds, passions, notions, as well as their persons, fortunes, dignities, &c.) I presume the self love, common to all human nature, would generally make tbem prefer their own condition.-*Skentstone.* 5. Notwithstanding all the care of Cicero, history informs us that Marcus proved a mere blockhead; and that nature (who it seems, was even with the son for her prodigality to the father) rendered him incapable of improving, *fay* all the rules of eloquence, the precepts of philosophy, his own endeavours, and the most

refined conversation in Athens *Spectator.* 6. The opera (iu which action is joined with music, in order to entertain the eye at the same time with the ear) - 1 must beg leave (with all due submission to the taste of the great) to consider as a forced conjunction" of two thiogs, which nature does not allow to go together. *Burgh.* __I, As to my own abilities in speaking (for I shall admit this charge although experience has convinced me tliat what is called the power of eloquence depends, for the most part, upon the hearers, and that the characters of public speakers are determined by that degree of favour, which you vouchsafe to each) if long practice, T say, hath given me any proficiency in speaking, you have ever found it devoted to my country.——*Demosthenes.* 8, When Socrates' fetters were knocked off, (as was usual to be done on the day that the condemned personwas to be executed) being seated in the midst of his disciples, and laying one of his legs over the other, in a very unconcerned posture, he began to rub it, where it had been galled by the iron; and (whether it was to show the indifference with which he entertained the thoughts of his approaching death, or (after his usual manner) to takeev-.ery occasion of philosophising upon some useful subject) he observed the pleasure of that sensation, which now arose in those very parts of his leg, thnt just bafore had been so much pained by fetters. Upon this he reflected on the nature of pleasure and pain in general, and how constantly they succeeded one another. *Spectator.* 9. Let us (since life can. little more supply. Than just to look about us and to die) Expatiate free, o'er all this scene of man;

A mighty maze! But not without a plan. *Pope..* 10. His years are young, but his experience oldj.

His head unmellow'd, but his judgment ripe;

And, in a word (for far behind his worth

Come all the praises that 1 now bestow)

He is complete in feature and in mind,

With all good grace to grace a gentleman

Shakespeare's Two Gentlemen of

Verona. 11. That man i' the world, who shall report, he has A better wife, let him in nought be trusted,

For speaking false in that. Thou art alone (If thy rare qualities, sweet gentleness,

Thy meekness, saintlike wifelike government,

Obeying in commanding, and thy parts

Sovereign and pious, could but speak thee out)

The queen of earthly queens.— *Shakespeare's Henry .&'* 12. Forthwith, (behold the excellence, the power, Which God hath in his mighty angels plac'd) Their arms away they threw, and to the hillk (For earth hath this variety from heaven,

Of pleasure situate in hill and dale)

Light as the lightning's glimpse, they ran, they flewf

From their foundations loos'ning to and fro,

They pluck'd the seated hills, with all tlieir load,

Rocks, waters, woods; and, by the sliaggy tops

Uplifted, bore them in their hands *Paradise Lost.*

V.—*Examples of* Interrogation, *or Questioning.* 1. ONE day, when the Moon was under an eclipse, she complained thus to the Sun of the discontinuance of his favours. My dearest friend, said she, Why do you not shine upon me as you used to do? Do 1 not shine upon thee? said the Sun: lam very sure that 1 intended it.

0 no! replies the Moon; but I now perceive the reason. 1 see that dirty planet the Earth is got between us. *Dodsleifs Fables.* 2. Searching every kingdom for a man who has the least comfort in life, Where is he to be found? In the royal palace. What, his Majesty? Yes; especially if he be a despot. *Art of Thinking.* 8. You have obliged a man j very well! What would you have more? Is not the consciousness of doing good a sufficient reward? *Art of Thinking.* 4. A certain passenger at sea had the curiosity to ask the pilot of the vessel, what death his father died of. What death? said the pilot. Why he perished at sea, as my

grandfather did before him. And are you not afraid of trusting yourself to an element that has proved thus fatal to your family? Afraid! By no means; Is not your father dead? Yes, but he died in his bed. And why then, returned the pilot, are you not afraid of trusting yourself in your bed? *'Art of Thinking.* 5. Is it credible, is it possible, that the mighty soul of a Newton should share exactly the same fate with the vilest insect that crawls upon the ground? that, after having laid open the mysteries of nature, and pushed its discoveries almost to the very boundaries of the universe, it should, on a sudden, have all its lights at once extinguished, and sink into everlasting darkness and insensibility?— *Spectator.* 6. Suppose a youth to have no prospect either in sitting in Parliament, of pleading at the bar, of appearing upon the stage, or in the pulpitj Does it follow that he need bestow no pains in learning to speak properly his native language? Will he never have occasion to read, in a company of his friends, a copy of verses, a passage of a book or newspaper? Must he never read a discourse of Tillotson, or a chapter of the Whole Duty of Man, for the instruction of his children and servants? Cicero justly observes, that address in speaking is highly ornamental, as well as useful, even in private life. The limbs are parts of the body much less noble than the tongue; yet no gentleman grudges a considerable expense, of time and money, to have his son taught to use them properly; which is very commendable. And is there no attention to be paid to the use of the tongue, the glory of man? *Burgh.* 7. Does greatness secure persons of rank from infirmities, either of body or mind? Will the headach, the gout or fever, spare a prince any more than a subject? Wiien old age comes to lie-heavy upon him, will his engineers relieve him of the load? Can his guards and sentinels, by doubling and trebling their numbers, and their watchfulness, prevent the approach of death? Nay, if jealousy, or even ill humour, disturb his happiness, will the cringes of his fawning attendants restore his tranquility? What comfort has he in reflecting (if

he can make the reflection) while the cholic, like Prometheus' vulture, tears his bowels, that he is under a canopy of crimson velvet, fringed with gold? When the pangs of the gout or stone, extort from him screams of agony, do the titles of Highness or Majesty come sweetly into his ear? If he is agitated with rage, does the sound of Serene, or Most Christian, prevent his staring, reddening and gnashing his teeth like a madman? Would not a twinge of the toothach, or an affront from an inferiour, make the mighty Cesar forget that he was emperour of the world?—— *Montaigne.* 8. When will you, my countrymen, when will you rouse from your indolence, and bethink ypurselves of what is to be done?—When you are forced to it by some fatal disaster? When irresistible necessity.drives you? wJiat think you of the disgraces which are already come upon yon? 1s not the past sufficient to stimulate your activity? Or,. do you wait for somewhat more forcible and urgent? How lone will you amuse vourselves with inquiring of one a-i notlier after news, as you ramble idly about the streets?

What news so strange ever came to Athens, as that a

Macedonian should subdue this state, and lord it over

Greece?—*Demosthenes.*

9. What is the blooming tincture of the skin,

To peace of mind and harmony within? What the bright sparkling of the finest eye,

To the soft soothing of a calm reply? Can comeliness of form, or shape, or air,

With comeliness of word or deeds compare?

No:—Those at first th' unwary heart ma' gain;

But these, these only, can the heart retain *Gay.*

10. Wrong'd in my love, all proffers I disdain:

Deceiv'd for once I trust not kings again.

Ye have my answer—What remains to do,

Your king, Ulysses, may consult with

you.

What needs he the defence, this arm cau make?

Has he not walls no human force can shaker

Has he not fenc'd his guarded navy round

With piles, with ramparts, and a trench profound?

And will not these, the wonders he has done,

Repel the rage of Priam's single son?—*Pope's Homer.* VI.—*Examples of* Climax, *or a gradual increase of Sense or Passion.*

I. CONSULT your whole nature. Consider yourselves, not only as sensitive, but as rational beings; not only as rational, but social; not only as social, but immortal;—*Blair.* 3. Whom he did foreknow, he also did predestinate; and whom he did predestinate, them he also called; and whom he called, them he also justified; and whom he justified, them he also glorified.—*St. Paul.* 3. What hope is there remaining of liberty, if whatever is their pleasure, it is lawful for them to do; if what is lawful for them to do, they are able to do; if what they are able to do, they dare do; if what they dare do, they really execute; and if what they execute is no way offensive to you.—*Cicero.* 4. Nothing is more pleasant to the fancy, than to enlarge itself by degreesin its contemplation of the various proportions which its several objects bear to each other.j when it compares the body of a man to the bulk of the whole earth; the earth to the circle it describes round the sun; that circle to the sphere of the fixed stars; the sphere of the fixed stars to the circuit of the whole creation; the whole creation itself, to the infinite space that is every where diffused around it, *Spectator.* 5. After we have practised good actions awhile, they become easy; and when they are easy, we begin to take pleasure in them; and when they please us we do them frequently; and by frequency of acts, a thing grows into a habit; and a confined habit is a second kind of nature; and so far as any thing is natural, so far it is necessary, and we can hardly do otherwise; nay, we do it

many times when we do not think of it. *Tillotson.* 6. It is pleasant to be virtuous and good, because that is to excel many others; it is pleasant to grow better, because that is to excel ourselves; it is pleasant to mortify and subdue our lusts, because that is victory; it is pleasant to command our appetites and passions, and to keep them in due order, withm the bounds of reason and religion, because that is empire. *Tillotson.* 7. Tully has a very beautiful gradation of thoughts to show how amiable virtue is. We love a righteous man, says he, who lives in the remotest parts of the earth, though we are altogether out of the reach of his virtue, and can receive from it no manner of benefit; nay, one who died several ages ago, raises a secret fondness and benevolence for him in our minds, when we read his story; nay, what is still more, one who has been the enemy of our country, provided his wars were regulated by justice and humanity.——*Spectator.* 8. As trees and plants necessarily arise from seeds, so are you, Antony, the seed of this most calamitous war. You mourn, O Romans, that three of your armies have been slaughtered—they were slaughtered by Antony; you lament the loss of your most illustrious citizens—they were torn from you by Antony; the authority of this order is deeply wounded—it is wounded by Antony; in short, all the calamities we have ever since beheld (and what calamities have we not beheld?) have been entirely owing to Antony. As Helen was of Troy, so the bane, the misery, the destruction of this state is—Antony.—*Cicero.*

-Give me the cup,

And let the kettle to the trumpets speak,

The trumpets to the cannoneers within,

The cannons to the heavens, the heavens to earth,

Now the king drinks to Hamlet *Trag. of Hamlet.* 10. At thirty, man suspects himself a fool;

Knows it at forty, and reforms his plan;

At fifty, chides his infamous delay,

Pushes his prudent purpose to resolve,

In all the magnanimity of thought,

Resolves and reresolves—then dies the

same.— *Young.*

VII.—*Examples of the principal Emotions and Passsions.*— Admiration, Contempt, Jot, Grief, Courage, Fear, Love, Hatred, Pitv, Anger, Revenge," *and* Jealousy. 1. WHAT a piece of work is man! How noble in reason! How infinite in faculties 1 In form and moving how express and admirable! In action how like an angel! In apprehension how like a god! *Hamlet.* 2. Away! No woman could descend so low.

A skipping, dancing, worthless tribe you are.

Fit only for yourselves, you herd together;

And when the circling glass warms your vain hearts,

You talk of beauties which you never saw,

And fancy raptures that you never knew.—

Fair Penitent.

2. Let mirth go on; let pleasure know no pause,

But fill up every minute of this day.

'Tis yours my children sacred to your loves.

The glorious sun himself for you looks gay;

He shines for ALtamont, and for Calista.

Take care my gates be open. Bid all welcome j

All who rejoice with me to day are friends.

Let each indulge his genius; each be glad,

Jocund and free, and swell the feast with mirth.

The sprightly bowl shall cheerfully go round j

None shall be grave, nor too severely wise:

Losses and disappointments, care and poverty,

The rich man's. insolence, the great man's scorn,.

In wine shall be forgotten all. *Fair Penitent.* A, All dark and comfortless.

Where all those various objects, that butnaw

Employ'd my busy eyes? Where those eyes?

These groping hands are now my only guides,

And feeling all my sight.

0 misery! What words can sound my grief!

Shut from the living whilst among the living;

Dark as the grave, amidst the bustling world;

At once from business, and from pleasure barr'd;

No more to-view the beauty of the spring,.

Or see the face of kindred or of friend!

Tragedy of Lear. 6. Thou speak'st a woman's; hear a warror's wish. Right from their native land, the stormy north, May the wind blow, till every keel is fix'd Immoveable in Caledonia's strand.'

Then shall:w foes repent their bold invasion,

And roving armies shun the fatal shore *Tregedy of Douglas.* 6. Ah! Mercy on my soul! What's thai? My old friend's ghost! They say, none but wicked folks walk. I wish I were at the bottom of a coalpit! La! how pale, and how long his face is grown since his death! He never was handsome; and death has improved very much the-wrong way.—Pray, do pot come near me! I wished you very well when you were alive.—But I could never abide a dead man cheek by jowl with me.—Ah! Ah! mercy on me! No nearer, pray! If it be only to. take your leave of me, that you are come back, I could have excused you. the ceremony with all my heart.—Or if you—mercy-on us!—No nearer, pray—or if you have wrong'd any body, as you always loved money a little, I give you the word of a frighted Christian, 1 will pray, as long as you please, for the deliverance and repose of your departed soul. My good, worthy, noble friend, do, pray,-disappear, as ever you would wish your old friend, Anselm, to come to his senses again.——*Moliere's Blunderer.* 7. Who can behold such beauty and be silent!

O! I could talk to thee forever;

Forever fix and gaze on those dear eyes;

For every glance they send darts through my soul!

Orphan. 8. How like a fawning publican he looks!

1 hate him for he is a Christian:

But more, for that in low simplicity

He lends out money gratis, and brings down

The rate of usance with ns here in Venice.

If I can catch him once upon the hip, 1 will feed fat that ancient grudge I bear him.

He hates our sacred nation; and he rails,

E'en there where the merchants most do congregate,.

On me, my bargains, and my well won thrift,

Which he calls usury. Cursed be my tribe

If I forgive him. *Merchant of Venice.* 9. As, in a theatre, the eyes of men, After a well graced actot leaves the stage,

Are idly bent on him that enters next, Thinking his prattle to be tedious;

Even so, or with much more contempt, men's eyes

Did scowl on Richard. No man cri'd, God savehim!

No joyful tongue gave him his welcome home:

But dust was thrown upon his sacred head:

Which, with such gentle sorrow, he shook off,

(His face still combating with tears and smiles,

The badges of his grief and patience:) That had not God, for some strong purpose, steel'd

The hearts of men, they must perforce have melted;

And barbarism itself have pitied him *Richard lid.* 10. Hear me, rash man, on thy allegiance hear me. Since thou hast striven to make us break our vow, (Which nor our nature nor our place can bear) We banish thee forever from our sight And kingdom. If, when three days are expir'd, Thy hated trunk be found in our dominions, That moment is thy death. Away!

By Jupiter this shall not be revok'd. *Tragedy of Lear.* 11. If it will feed nothing else, it will feed my revenge. He

hath disgraced me, and hindered me of" half a million, laughed at my losses, mocked at my gains, scorned my nation, thwarted my bargains, 'Cooled my friends, heated mine enemies. And what's his reason? I am a Jew. Hath not a Jew eyes? Hath not a Jew hands, organs, dimensions, senses, affections, passions? Is he not fed with the same food, hurt with the same weapons, subject to the same diseases, healed by the same means, warmed and cooled by the same summer and winter, as a Christian is? If you prick us, do we not bleed? If you tickle us, do we not laugh? If you poison us, do we not die? And if you wrong us, shall we not revenge? If we are like you in the rest, we will resemble you in that. If a Jew wrong a Christian, what is his hrmility? Revenge. If a Christian wrong a Jew, what would his sufferance be, by Christian example? Why, revenge." The villany you teach me I will execute; and it shall go hard, but I will better the instruction. *Merchant of Venice.* 12. Ye Amaranths! Ye roses, like the morn!

Sweet myrtles, and ye golden orange groves!

Joy giving, love inspirirg, holy bower! Know, in thy fragrant bosom, thou receiv'st

A murd'rer? Oh, 1 shall stain thy lilies, And horrour will usurp the seat of bliss! Ha! She sleeps

The day's uncommon heat has overcome her.

Then take, my longing eyes, your last full gaze—

Oh, what a sight is here! How dreadful fair!

Who would not think that being innocent!

Where shall I strike? Who strikes h«r, strikes himself—

My own life's blood will issue at her wound—

But see she smiles! I never shall smile more—

It strongly tempts me to a parting kiss— Ha, smile again! She dreams of him she loves.—

Curse on her charms! I'll stab her thro' them all.

Revenge.

CPSIA information can be obtained at www.ICGtesting.com
Printed in the USA
BVOW09s2036080915

417119BV00013B/261/P

9 781230 231839